FOUNDATIONS OF CRIMINAL JUSTICE

PROFESSIONAL THIEVES AND THE DETECTIVE

BY

ALLAN PINKERTON

with a new introduction by

Vern L. Folley

AMS PRESS INC.
NEW YORK
LONDON   TORONTO
1973

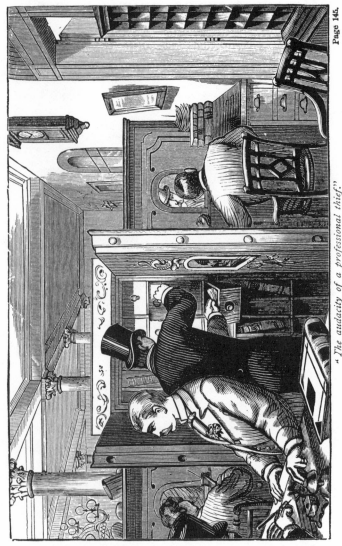

"The audacity of a professional thief."

Page 145.

THE EDGEWOOD MYSTERY AND THE DETECTIVE.

—————◆◆◆—————

¹LIGHTNING STEALERS AND THE DETECTIVE.

CONTENTS.

LIST OF ILLUSTRATIONS.

[ix]

FOUNDATIONS OF CRIMINAL JUSTICE

always becoming available. Interesting, too, of course, is the ingenuity of Allan Pinkerton in rising to the investigative challenges presented by criminals and their ever-new ventures. This tends to show how the police and law enforcement agencies have always risen to meet the task at hand.

Interesting also is the description given by Pinkerton of the criminal. He obviously had little or no sympathy for criminals and believed in fast apprehension and adjudication. His in depth understanding of criminals, however, were very sophisticated for the times and should be of considerable interest to today's criminologist, sociologist, and correctional administrators. Although he had no compromise for crime, he did possess a keen understanding of crime causation and the criminal.

I believe this book, written in 1880, is one of the best available means for the law enforcement student to fully understand and appreciate the climate of law enforcement during the mid-nineteenth century. It also facilitates one's understanding of law enforcement as we know it today. I recommend that all law enforcement officers, aspiring police officials, and the general public read this book. It is an outstanding contribution to law enforcement literature and certainly leads one to a fuller understanding of the development of law enforcement in the United States.

Dr. Vern L. Folley
Harrisburg Area Community College
Harrisburg, Penna.

obvious that many communities and business agencies relied upon private detective agencies rather than on the public police departments. This reliance can be attributed to two things: first, only a few communities had a publicly supported law enforcement agency to provide such services; and second, existing agencies did not have the manpower or expertise necessary to handle criminal investigations effectively. Their approach to the apprehension of criminals was likely to be rudimentary and more often than not, the so-called detectives would be unsuccessful.

The geographical problem encountered by Pinkerton's detectives demonstrates the emerging need for state and federal police agencies whose officers could work across jurisdictional boundaries. For example, the Edgewood murder described by Pinkerton required his detectives to pursue the murderer across state lines, from New York to New Jersey. Another case in his book, "Crimes Dealing with Telegraphy," describes a case where Pinkerton detectives had to travel to distant western locations in order to build the necessary case which led to the apprehension of the perpetrator.

This book also very adequately describes to what degree crime is an act of opportunity. For example, Pinkerton sketches many crimes dealing with banks that were possible because of the unstable currency then in existence. Because of the lack of stable and uniform money, criminals were able to devise several methods of robbing or defrauding banks. When currency became stable, such crimes were harder to commit and, consequently, the opportunity no longer existed.

Another interesting revelation from his book is the lack of security then existing in the banks. It is obvious that their problems with the various kinds of robberies and burglaries led to the rather sophisticated security of today. It would be virtually impossible now to commit the kinds of crimes described by Pinkerton. Of interest, too, is the ingenuity of the criminals in discovering the weaknesses of bank security and capitalizing upon it.

Another fascinating aspect of the book is the way it demonstrates how technological advances provided new frontiers for criminality. For example, the advent of the telegraph provided new opportunities for fraud and other criminal acts. *Professional Thieves and the Detective* traces the step-by-step investigations of several crimes related to the telegraph which are fascinating, exciting, and, at the same time, illustrate how new opportunities for crime are were written for the general public rather than for academic purposes. Concurrently, the public of that time read his books for enjoyment much as we presently read books from the bestseller list. Allan Pinkerton had a highly simplified style of writing which was enjoyable to read and conducive to easy understanding. This volume, *Professional Thieves and the Detective*, was originally published in 1880 by the G. W. Carleton & Company. The book, like all of his writings, is based on authentic detective sketches collected from Pinkerton's confidential files.

Professional Thieves and the Detective was very appropriate to the times. It was a time of high migration, urban development, industrialization, and an increasing crime rate. People in general were becoming acutely aware of the crime problem and, thus, eager to broaden their knowledge of crime detection. Of course, many of the readers were people fascinated with the suspense and intrigue presented in his stories. It was during these years that law enforcement agencies were just beginning to develop and citizens were obviously more keenly aware of the need for law enforcement than ever before. Their curiosity was at a high peak and they purchased Pinkerton's books and read them as novels.

In addition, crime detection by local police forces, where they existed, was rather rudimentary in nature and readers were particularly captivated by the sophisticated and professional methods utilized by Pinkerton and his detectives. His style of writing was also quite fluent and stretched the imagination of the readers. In addition, Pinkerton already had a national reputation which unquestionable encouraged the purchase and wide distribution of his books.

It is quite certain that many law enforcement officials learned from his writings and adopted his methods within their agencies. In fact, his techniques of surveillance are still widely used by police agencies throughout the United States. It would seem that some of our federal and state law enforcement agencies are still using similar approaches to criminal apprehension as those described in this book by Pinkerton. Certainly, Allan Pinkerton can be considered one of the first, if not the first, professional detective in the United States.

Professional Thieves and the Detective is certainly relevant to the study of law enforcement in the United States as it very dramatically describes crime detection in that time. It illustrates the methods that were then successful, as well as inherent problems related to the times. As one reads the book, for example, it becomes formed a partnership with a lawyer, E. G. Rucker, and established a private detective agency. Within a year, he resigned his city position and assumed full control of the agency which is now known as the most famous private detective agency of all time. Many books, articles, and movies include exploits of "Pinkerton men." In all instances, these stories depict the Pinkerton detective as a "master sleuth."

The solution of many crimes and capture of numerous criminals earned the agency the reputation that took on national proportions. Finally, at the invitation of General George B. McClellan, Pinkerton agreed to organize and administer a secret service operation for the Ohio Department which McClellan commanded. Pinkerton organized and administered a highly efficient secret service agency for the Ohio Department. When McClellan became Commander-in-Chief, Pinkerton moved his headquarters to Washington, D. C., where he subsequently became involved in the direction of counter-espionage during the Civil War. During his stay in Washington, Pinkerton went under the name of Major E. J. Allan. So successful was his masquerade that even his fellow officers were unaware of his real identity. He resigned his post when General McClellan was removed in 1869, but continued to serve as investigator of numerous claims against the government.

At the conclusion of the Civil War, Pinkerton again devoted full attention to his detective agency and it continued to expand. Eventually, he established regional offices in Philadelphia and New York.

In 1869, Pinkerton suffered a slight paralytic stroke and had to give up his actual field investigation activities. Due to his paralytic condition, he left the field work entirely to his employees and sons, devoting his full attention to administrative duties and those investigative techniques that could be handled in the office. He did, however, direct most investigations from his office and can be considered a master-mind behind most apprehensions. Following his death in 1884, the business was continued by his sons, who have continued to uphold the prestigious name of Pinkerton.

Allan Pinkerton wrote many books which were primarily based on cases handled by him or the agency. He has a total of eighteen volumes to his credit, but the most notable are: *Criminal Reminiscences and Detective Sketches* (1879); *The Spy of the Rebellion* (1883); *Thirty Years a Detective* (1884); and of course, *Professional Thieves and the Detectives* (1880). All of Pinkerton's books

The author of this book, Allan Pinkerton, was born in Glasgow, Scotland, on August 25, 1819. Perhaps his understanding and interest in criminal investigation can be attributed to the fact that his father, William Pinkerton, was a sergeant on the local police force. When Allan was ten his father was seriously injured while on duty during the Chartist riots and never walked again. He died four years later and, due to the family's poor financial situation, Allan was apprenticed as a cooper at the age of twelve.

As a young man, Allan Pinkerton was quite active in the Chartist movement, a widespread attempt to improve the conditions of the laboring classes and bring about political reforms. His active role and leadership in this movement led him to fear political reprisal and he therefore migrated to the United States in 1842. He initially established residence in Chicago, but within a year moved to the Scotch settlement of Dundee, where he established a cooper's shop. His shop eventually grew into a successful business employing eight people.

The primary event that destined Allan Pinkerton to become a detective was his role in the capture of a counterfeiting ring. While cutting hoop poles on an isolated island, he came upon an obvious meeting place of counterfeiters. Pinkerton subsequently led a party of men who captured the entire ring. This experience earned him a reputation as a crime fighter and detective among the townspeople and businessmen. Therefore, when any illegal activities were apparent or suspected, the townspeople would call upon Pinkerton to solve the case and apprehend the criminal. In 1846, he became a deputy sheriff for Cane County and his subsequent activities expanded his reputation yet further. His work in this capacity led him to be appointed as deputy sheriff in Cook County, Illinois. In 1850, Pinkerton was attached to Chicago's newly organized police force as its first and only detective.

As history tells us, these were the years when the railroads were on the financial throne. There were many beneficial ramifications stemming from the rise of the railroad empire, but at the same time their existence provided new opportunities for the criminal. There are many tales of famous (or rather infamous) train robberies during this era of American history.

Troubled with the ever-increasing number of train robberies and crimes directed against the railroads, several railroad presidents requested Pinkerton's help. In response to their urging, Pinkerton

Early Investigation Methods

A Preface to the New Edition of

PROFESSIONAL THIEVES AND THE DETECTIVE

brilliant exploits—their daring and recklessness in the pursuit of their nefarious callings, are attempted to be fully shown and intelligently depicted.

The wonderful achievements of these men who live beyond the law and without the pale of civilized and honorable society, are detailed from actual experiences and from an intimate knowledge of the participants in the events which are now made public; and should the sad results which invariably follow a life of sin and crime—the surety of punishment, and oftentimes a violent death—exercise an elevating influence upon those before whom these pages may come, and by the influence of terrible examples inculcate the lesson of obedience to law and the pursuit of an honorable calling, I shall be rewarded by the consciousness of having performed my duty to humanity, and in upholding the supremacy of the Ordinances of Society.

ALLAN PINKERTON.

CHICAGO, *November*, 1880.

mysteries which surround the Criminal, but which **must** eventually present themselves to the intelligent eye of the Detective.

In the narrative of "The Lightning Stealers" will be related the adventures of two bold men who endeavored, by their knowledge of the science of Telegraphy, to impose upon commercial communities a variety of spurious intelligence; through which, by the aid of moneyed co-conspirators, the innocent and the unsuspecting would be duped, and the unprincipled would largely profit by their duplicity.

The "Edgewood Mystery" presents an entirely different phase of humanity, and deals with the impecunious and improvident mechanic, who murders his friend and the playmate of his earlier days for the paltry gain of a few dollars, or perhaps from a weak yielding to the promptings of the demon of jealousy.

"Booming Logs" treats of a subject as novel in its conception as it is interesting in its development, and the Lumber interests, which suffered largely from the operations of dishonest men, were protected through the vigilance and daring of the attaches of my Agency.

In the numerous sketches which are here presented, almost every degree of Crime, and every variety of Criminals are depicted. Their multifarious schemes for possessing themselves of the wealth of others--their

Defendant in a Court of Quarter Sessions. He appears quite as frequently as the well-dressed, polished, and educated gentleman, as the distinguished foreigner and as the profound scientist, as he does in the guise of the ignorant ; the open defier of the law or the midnight robber.

Through all grades of society the evil influences of a desire to enrich oneself at the expense of others is manifested ; through all classes of humanity, the greed of gain, the ambition to be rich without labor, or the disposition to yield to passions—which in weak natures are uncontrollable—are lamentably apparent ; and the Detective is required to mingle with the dissimilar, and often desperate, natures, which compose this great army of Law Breakers which now infest the community.

In my extended experience, I have frequently been an actor in episodes which have partaken of the elements of both Tragedy and Comedy, some of them startling in their nature, and with a deep infusion of the pure romance of life ; while others have often caused the eyes to twinkle with merriment and the lips to curl with a smile at the humorous side of the various scenes that would from time to time be presented to my view.

In the succeeding pages will be found a series of incidents which will fully justify my previous expressions, and will throw a ray of light upon some of the hidden

PREFACE.

In again submitting to the public a volume of my Detective Experiences, a few words of introduction may not be out of place.

The life of a Detective is naturally a varied and excitable one. At one time he is engaged in the pursuit of the hardened Criminal, whose hands are crimson with the blood of his victim—at another, the Burglar, whose manipulations of the protecting appliances which have been invented to secure the wealth of others from his rapacious grasp, engrosses his attention—and anon he is found working his silent way through the intricate mazes of science, where the Counterfeiter and the Forger, with their miraculous chemicals and deft handiwork, require not only a familiarity with their mode of procedure, but an astute knowledge of human nature and their various characteristics.

The Criminal is not always the rough and uncouth

14193

Library of Congress Cataloging in Publication Data

Pinkerton, Allan, 1819-1884.
   Professional thieves and the detective.

   Reprint of the 1881 ed.
   1. Detectives. I. Title.
HV7914.P66 1973   364.12   73-156031
ISBN 0-404-09133-4

Original size of this volume was 5 1/8 X 7 11/16
AMS edition is 5 1/2 X 8 1/2

Foundations of Criminal Justice Series. General
Editors: Richard H. Ward and Austin Fowler, John Jay
College of Criminal Justice

Reprinted from an original copy in the collections of
the Columbia University Library

Manufactured in the United States of America

PROFESSIONAL
THIEVES <small>AND THE</small> DETECTIVE

CONTAINING NUMEROUS

DETECTIVE SKETCHES

COLLECTED FROM PRIVATE RECORDS.

BY

ALLAN PINKERTON,

AUTHOR OF

"Mississippi Outlaws and Detectives," "Expressman and the Detectives,"
"Mollie Maguires and Detectives," "Spiritualists and Detectives,"
"Criminal Reminiscences," Etc., Etc.

WITH A

SKETCH OF THE AUTHOR

HOW HE BECAME A DETECTIVE, &c.

ILLUSTRATED.

NEW YORK:

G. W. Carleton & Co., Publishers.

CINCINNATI

W. E. DIBBLE.

(SOLD ONLY BY SUBSCRIPTION)

BOOMING LOGS AND THE DETECTIVE.

CRIMINAL REMINISCENCES.

HOW I BECAME
A DETECTIVE.

O N the romantic Fox River—called the Pish-ta-ka in the original Potawatamie language—and about thirty-eight miles northwest of the city of Chicago, is located the beautiful village of Dundee. It has probably at this writing a population of three thousand inhabitants, and is one of the brightest and most prosperous towns of Illinois.

The town was originally settled by a few sturdy people, the hardy Scotch, as its name would indicate—as also that of the splendid little city of Elgin, but five miles distant—and who occupied to some extent the outlying farms; so that the place and community, while never accomplishing anything remarkable in a business way, has had a steady, quiet growth, has lived its life uninterruptedly and peacefully, and possesses the pleasantest evidences of steady prosperity and constant, quiet happiness. If this would be easily observed by the visitor, its beautiful location would attract still greater attention.

Before you, looking up-stream, you would see at your feet the rapid river which has just leaped the great dam from which the mills and manufactories are fed, and, above this, stretching and winding away into the distance like a ribbon of burnished silver, it would still be seen, gliding along peacefully with a fair, smooth bosom, wimpling fretfully over stony shallows, or playing at hide-and-seek among the verdure-cov ered islands, until the last thread-like trail of it is lost in the gorges beyond. To the right, just beyond the little basin which holds its part of the village, rise huge hills from which here and there issue forth beautiful springs, while now and then a fine roadway, hewn out between, leads to the Indian Mounds and the splendid farms beyond. To the left, over the opposite portion of the village, the eye ranges over a succession of elevations dotted with handsome residences and embowered by gardens, with the hills and the uplands beyond, as well as the highway, or "river road," threading along in and out of sight among the tree-covered bluffs; while, facing about, you will see the river moving peacefully along, until lost in the valleys and their forests below.

The town rests there on the banks of this beautiful stream, and between the guardian hills upon either side, like twin nests where there is always song and gladness.

In the time of which I write, however, all this was different; that is, the town was different. The river ran down like a silvery ribbon from among the islands just the same; the splendid hills were all there, crowned with fine forests as they are now; but the town itself did not contain probably over three hundred inhabitants all told, the business portion only consisting of a few country stores, a post-office, a blacksmith-shop or two, a mill, and two small taverns able to accommodate a few travel- ers at a time, but chiefly depending for their support upon the custom of the farmers who straggled into the village on rainy

days, "election time," or any other of the hundred-and-one occasions which mark out events in the lives of back-country
people.

There was then one rough bridge across the river, built of
oaken beams and rude planks, in a cheap, common fashion;
and at either end of this were clustered, each side of the street,
all the stores and shops of the place, save one.

That shop was my own; for there I both lived and labored,
the "Only and Original Cooper of Dundee."

This shop was the farthest of any from the business center
of the village, and stood just back of, and facing, the main
highway, upon the crest of a fine hill, about three hundred
yards distant from the bridge.   It was my home and my shop.

I had straggled out here a few years before, and by industry
and saving had gradually worked into a comfortable business
at my cooper's trade, and now employed eight men.   I felt
proud of my success because I owed no man, had a cheery little
home, and, for the early days, when it was pretty hard to get
along at all, I was making a comfortable living.

My cooper-shop and house were one building—a long, one-
story frame building with a pleasant garden about, some fine
old trees near, and always stacks of staves and hoop-poles quite
handy.   At one end we lived, in a frugal, but always cheery
way, and at the other end was the shop, where, as nearly all
my hands were German, could be heard the livelong day the
whistled waltz, or the lightly-sung ballad, now in solo, now in
chorus, but always in true time with the hammering of the adz
and the echoing thuds of the "driver" upon the hoops as they
were driven to their places.

This was my quiet, but altogether happy mode of life in

the beautiful village of Dundee, in the summer of 1847, at which time my story really begins, but, to give the reader a better understanding of it, I will have to further explain the existing condition of things at that time.

There was but little money in the West, which was then sparsely settled. There being really no markets, and the communication with eastern cities very limited, the producer could get but little for his crops or wares. I have known farmers in these times "hauling," as it was called, wheat into Chicago for a distance of nearly one hundred miles, from two to five streams having to be forded, and the wheat having to be carried across, every bag of it, upon the farmer's back, and he not then able to get but three shillings per bushel for his grain, being compelled to take half payment for it in "truck," as store goods were then called.

There was plenty of dickering, but no money. Necessity compelled an interchange of products. My barrels would be sold to the farmers or merchants for produce, and this I would be compelled to send in to Chicago, to in turn secure as best I could a few dollars, perhaps, and anything and everything I could use, or again trade away.

Not only did this great drawback on business exist, but what money we had was of a very inferior character. If one sold a load of produce and was fortunate enough to secure the entire pay for it in money, before he got home the bank might have failed, and the paper he held have become utterly worthless. All of these things in time brought about a most imperative need for good money and plenty of it, which had been met some years before where my story begins, by several capitalists of Aberdeen, Scotland, placing in the hands of George

Smith, Esq., also an Aberdonian, sufficient funds to found a bank in the Great West.

Milwaukee, then a city of equal importance with Chicago, was chosen as the point, and the Wisconsin Legislature, in 1839, granted a charter to the institution, which was known as The Wisconsin Marine and Fire Insurance Company, which, in its charter, also secured banking privileges.

But a few years had elapsed before the bills of this institution gained a very wide circulation throughout the Northwest. Branch agencies were established at Chicago and various points in the West, as also an agency for the redemption of the bills at Buffalo; and at the time of which I write, Chicago, having taken rapid strides to the front, had in reality become the central office, although the Wisconsin organization and Milwaukee headquarters were still retained.

Many reasons obtained to cause these bills—which were of the denominations of one, two, three, five, and ten—to be eagerly sought for. The company were known to have large and always available capital at command; its bills were always redeemable in specie; and with the personal character of George Smith, who stood at the head of the concern, there was created an almost unequaled public confidence in it and its management. In fact, the bills soon became known far and wide as "George Smith's money," and "as good as the wheat," the farmers would say.

Smith himself was a Scotchman of very decided and even erratic character; and the old settlers of Chicago and the West have many an interesting incident to relate of his financial career. One, serving for many, to give an idea of the peculiarities of the man, and showing how he gained a great reputation in those times and in that section, is as follows :

The almost immediate popularity of "George Smith's money" caused considerable envious feeling; and the officers of several other western banking institutions sought, as far as possible, by various means to prevent the encroachment upon their business.

At one time a small bank near the central part of Illinois, in order to assist in the depreciation of this particular money, began the policy of refusing to receive the Wisconsin Marine and Fire Insurance Company's bills at par, which for a time caused in certain sections considerable uneasiness among the holders of those bills.

The quiet Scotchman in Chicago said never a word to this for some time, but at once began gathering together every bill of this bank he could secure. This was continued for several weeks, when he suddenly set out alone and unattended for central Illinois, being roughly dressed and very unpretentious in appearance.

Reaching the place and staggering into the bank, he awkwardly presented one hundred dollars in the Fire and Marine bills, requesting exchange on Buffalo for a like sum.

The cashier eyed him a moment, and then remarked sneeringly :

" We don't take that stuff at par."

" Ah ! ye dinna tak it, then ?"

" No," replied the cashier; " 'George Smith's money' is depreciating rapidly."

" Then it's gaun down fast, is it ?" responded Smith, reflectively.

"Oh, yes; won't be worth fifty cents on a dollar in six months!"

"It'll be worth nae mair than fifty cents? An' may yours be worth a huner' cents on a dollar, *noo ?*"

"Certainly, sir, always. If you should happen to have ten thousand dollars' worth about you at the present time," replied the cashier, as he gave the stranger another supercilious look, "you could get the gold for it in less than ten seconds."

"Then," said the travel-stained banker, with a very ugly look in his face, as he crashed down a great package upon the counter, containing twenty-five thousand dollars in the bills of the opposition bank, "Mister George Smith presents his best respects tae ye, and would be obleeged tae ye if ye wad gie him the specie for *this !*"

This shrewd stroke of business policy had its legitimate effect. The bank in question could not instantly redeem so large a sum, and opposition of an unfair character in that and other directions, through the notoriety given this practical humiliation, was effectually ended.

In countless other ways this early western financier established credit and compelled respect, until, as I have said, "George Smith's money" was as good as the gold throughout the entire western country, and this fact, in time, caused it to be taken in hand by eastern counterfeiters.

This brings me again to the main part of my story.

Just after noon of a hot July day in the year mentioned, a gentleman named H. E. Hunt, then keeping a small general store in, and now a wealthy merchant at, Dundee, sent word to my shop that he wished to see me immediately at his place.

I was busy at my work, bareheaded, barefooted, and having

no other clothing on my body than a pair of blue denim over-
alls and a coarse hickory shirt, my then almost invariable costume; but I started down the street at once, and had hardly
reached Hunt's store before the proprietor and myself were
joined by a Mr. I. C. Bosworth, then another storekeeper of
the village, and now a retired capitalist of Elgin, Illinois, the
place previously referred to.

"Come in here, Allan," said Mr. Hunt, in a rather mysterious manner, leading the way to the rear of the store, while
Bosworth and myself followed; "we want you to do a little job
in the detective line."

"Detective line?" I replied, laughing; "why, my line is the
cooper business. What do I know about that sort of thing?"

"Never mind now," said Mr. Bosworth, seriously, "we
know you can do what you want done. You helped break up
the 'coney men' and horse-thieves on 'Bogus Island,' and we
are sure you can do work of this sort if you only will do it."

Now the reference to breaking up the gang of "coney"
men and horse-thieves on "Bogus Island," calls for an explanation.

I was actually too poor to purchase outright a wheel-barrow load of hoop-poles, or staves, and was consequently compelled to cut my own hoop-poles and split my own staves. In
the pursuit of this work I had found a little island in the Fox
River, a few miles above Dundee, and but a few rods above the
little post-town of Algonquin, where poles were both plentiful
and of the best quality; and one day while busy there I had
stumbled upon some smoldering embers and other traces indicating that the little island had been made quite common use
of. There was no picnicking in those days—people had more

serious matters to attend to—and it required no great keenness
to conclude that no honest men were in the habit of occupying
the place. As the country was then infested with coin-coun-
terfeiters and desperate horse-thieves, from the information I
give, the sheriff of that county (Kane) was able to trace the
outlaws to this island, where subsequently I led the officers who
captured the entire gang, consisting of men and women, securing their implements and a large amount of bogus coin ; while,
in honor of the event, the island ever since has been known as
" Bogus Island."

Upon this faint record Messrs. Hunt and Bosworth based
my claim to detective skill, and insisted on my winning new
laurels, or, at least, attempting to do so.

"But what is it you wish done ?" I asked, very much preferring to return to the shop, where my men and their work
needed my attention.

Mr. Hunt then explained that they were certain that there
was then a counterfeiter in the village. They both felt sure
he was one, although they had no other evidence save that the
party in question had been making inquiries as to the where
abouts of " Old man Crane."

Old man Crane was a person who from general reputation
I knew well. He lived at Libertyville, in the adjoining county
of Lake, not more than thirty-five miles distant, bore a hard
character generally, and it was suspected that he was engaged
in distributing for eastern counterfeiters their worthless money.
Nearly every blackleg that came into the community invariably
inquired for " Old man Crane," and this fact alone caused the
villagers to give him a wide berth. Besides this fact, but recently counterfeits on the ten-dollar bill of the Wisconsin Ma-

2

rine and Fire Insurance Company's Bank had made their ap
pearance, and were so well executed as to cause serious trouble
to farmers and country dealers. Pretty positive proof had
come to light that Crane had had a hand in the business; and
the fact that a respectable appearing man, a stranger, well
mounted and altogether mysterious, and also well supplied with
money, had suddenly shown himself in the village, to begin
quietly but searchingly making inquiries for " Old man Crane,"
seemed to the minds of my friends to be the best of evidence
that the stranger was none other than the veritable counterfeiter who was supplying such old reprobates as Crane with the
spurious ten-dollar bills on George Smith's bank.

But this was curious business for me, I thought, as, protesting against leaving my work for a will-o'-the-wisp piece of business, which, even should it happen to prove successful, would
pay me nothing, I said : " Now, see here, what do *I* know about
counterfeiting ?"

"Oh, we *know* you know enough about it !" they both
urged, anxiously.

"Why," said I, laughing at the absurdity of the idea of
turning detective, " I never saw a ten-dollar bill in my life!"

And neither had I. There I stood, a young, strong, agile,
hard-working cooper not exactly green, perhaps,—for I consider no man verdant who does well whatever he may have in
hand,—barefooted, bareheaded, dressed, or rather, almost undressed, in my hickory and denims, daring enough and ready
for any reckless emergency which might transpire in the living
of an honest life, but decidedly averse to doing something entirely out of my line, and which in all human probability I
would make an utter failure of. I had not been but four years

in America altogether. I had had a hard time of it for the time I had been here. I had *heard* of all these things I have mentioned concerning banks and money, but I had positively never seen a ten-dollar bill!

A great detective I would make under such circumstances, I thought.

"Come now, Allan," urged Mr. Hunt, "no time is to be wasted. The man is down there now at Eaton Walker's har ness-shop, getting something done about his saddle."

"But what am I to do?" I asked.

"Do?—Well!—*do* the best you can!"

I suddenly resolved to do just that and no less; although I must confess that, at that time, I had not the remotest idea how to set about the matter.

So I began by strolling leisurely about the street for a few minutes, and then, villager-like, sauntered into the saddlery shop.

Eaton Walker, a jolly, whole-souled, good-hearted fellow, was perched upon his bench, sewing away, and when I entered merely looked up from his waxed-end and nodded, but made no remark, as my being in his place was a very common occur- rence.

There was the usual quota of town stragglers loafing about the shop, and looking with sleepy eyes and open-mouthed at the little which was going on about the place.

I passed, as I entered the shop, a splendid horse hitched outside. It was a fine, large roan, well built for traveling; and in my then frame of mind I imagined from a casual glance that it was a horse especially selected for its lasting qualities, should an emergency require them to be put to a test.

The owner of the animal, the person who had caused so much nervousness on the part of Messrs. Hunt and Bosworth, was a man nearly six feet in height, weighed fully two hundred pounds, was at least sixty-five years of age, and was very erect and commanding in his appearance. I noticed all this at a careless glance, as also that his hair was dark, though slightly tinged with gray, and his features very prominent. His nose was very large, his mouth unusually so, and he had a pair of the keenest, coldest small gray eyes I have ever seen, while he wore a large, plain gold ring on one of the fingers of his left hand.

I made no remark to him or to any person about the place, and merely assumed for the time being to be a village loafer myself. But I noticed, without showing the fact, that the man occasionally gave me a keen and searching glance. When the work had been completed by Walker, I stepped outside and made a pretense of being interested, as any country gawky might, in the preparations for the man's departure; and was patting the horse's neck and withers as the stranger came out with the saddle and began adjusting it, when I carelessly assisted him in a free-and-easy country way.

There were, of course, a number of people standing about, and a good deal of senseless chatting going on, which the stranger wholly refrained from joining in; but while we were both at work at the saddle, he said, without addressing me, but in a way which I knew was meant for my ears: " Stranger, do you know where Old man Crane lives ?"

I took my cue from the manner in which this was said, and followed it to the best of my ability. I was now as certain as either of my friends that the man was a blackleg of a danger

ous order, whatever his special line of roguery might be. **We** were both busy at the saddle on the side of the horse **where** there were the fewer loungers, and being close together, I replied in the same tone of voice:

"Cross the river to the east, take the main road up through the woods until you come to Jesse Miller's farmhouse. Then *he* will tell you; but if you don't want to ask"—and I put considerable meaning into this—"hold the road to the northeast and inquire the direction to Libertyville. When you get there you will easily find the old man, and he is as good **as** cheese!"

He then said, in the same cautious voice as before:

"Young man, I like your style, and I want to know **you** better. Join me over the river in some ravine. I want **to** talk to you."

"All right," I rejoined, "but you better let me go ahead. I'll have to go up to the shop first and put on my boots and hat. I'll be as quick as I can, and will start on first. Then you follow on, but not too closely. I'll be up in some of **the** gorges, so we can talk entirely by ourselves. But I'll tell **you** the truth, stranger," said I, rather indifferently, "upon **my** word, I don't care very much about going, because I've **already** lost too much time at the shop to-day."

He had by this time finished saddling his horse, but he continued adjusting and readjusting things so as to gain time **to** say what he wished; and to my intimation that I cared **very** little about leaving my work, he responded:

"Don't fail to join me. *I'll make it worth something to you!*" He then added flatteringly: "You're as good a **man** as I've met lately."

I then moved forward to fasten the reins, and he edged along toward me, asking carelessly: " Do you know John Smith, of Elgin ?"

" I know all the Elgin John Smiths," I replied. " Do you mean the gunsmith ?"

" Yes," he answered tersely.

" Well, I know John," I continued; " that is, he has repaired my rifle and shotgun several times ; but he might not remember me. I never had much talk with him."

" He's a square man," replied the stranger. " *I'm* his uncle. I came up from Elgin this morning. Smith didn't know just where Crane lived. He told me that he traded here, and that the boys were over here a good deal, so that I would be likely to find somebody here who could readily direct me to his place."

" Well," J said rather curtly, " we've talked too much already. It won't do. I'll join you over the river soon."

With this I carelessly walked away towards my shop, and at some little distance turned to see the stranger now engaging Eaton Walker in conversation with an evident purpose of gaining time.

" Well," I thought, as I hastened on, " there's no doubt now. This man is certainly a counterfeiter. John Smith is always loaded down with it. He gets it from old Crane; and this man at Walker's is the chief of the gang traveling through the West to supply these precious rascals. But then," it suddenly occurred to me, " what business of mine is all this? Good gracious! I've got a lot of barrels to make, my men need attention, and everything is going to the Old Harry while I am playing detective!"

But having got thus far my will had been touched, and I resolved to carry the matter through, whatever might be the result. While putting on my hat and boots hastily, Hunt and Bosworth came in, and I quickly related what I had learned.

Looking down the hill, we could see the stranger slowly moving across the bridge, and as I was starting in the same direction my friends both urged:

"Now, Pinkerton, capture him sure!"

"Oh, yes," I replied, "but how am I to get at all this?"

"Why, just get his stock, or some of it, and then we'll have him arrested."

"Oh, yes," said I, "but, by thunder! it takes money to buy money! I've got none!"

"Well, well, that's so," remarked Mr. Hunt; "we'll go right down to the store. You drop in there after us, and we'll give you fifty dollars."

All this was speedily done, and I soon found myself over the bridge, past the horsemen, and well up the hill upon the highway.

It was a well-traveled thoroughfare, in fact, the road leading from all that section of the country into Chicago; but it was in the midst of harvest-time, and everybody was busy upon the farms. Not a soul was to be seen upon the road, save the stranger and myself, and almost a Sabbath silence seemed to rest over the entire locality. The voices of the birds, which filled the woods in every direction, were hushed into a noon-day chirping, and hardly a sound was to be heard save the murmuring of the rills issuing from the sides of the hills and from every nook in the gorges and glens.

I confess that a sense of insignificance stole over me, originating doubtless from the reflection causes by this silence and almost painful quiet ; and I could not but realize my unfitness for the work before me.   There I was, hardly more than a plodding country cooper, having had but little experience save that given me by a life of toil in Scotland and my trip to this country, and no experience of things in this country save that secured through a few years of the hardest kind of hard work. For a moment I felt wholly unable to cope with this keen man of the world, but as I was gaining the top of the hill I glanced back over my shoulder, and noticing that the horseman was following my instructions to the letter, I reasoned that, from *some* cause, I had gained an influence over this stranger, or *he* thought he had secured such a one over me, as would enable me, by being cautious and discreet, to obtain a sufficiently close intimacy with him to cause the disclosure of his plans, and possibly ultimately result in his capture.

I had now reached the top of the hill, and taking a position which would permit of my being seen by no person save the horseman, I waited until he had approached near enough for me to do so, when I signaled him to follow, and then struck into the woods over a narrow trail about two hundred yards, to a beautiful little opening on the banks of a purling brook, leaping down the descent towards the river from a limpid spring a few feet above the spot I had chosen for the interview.

But a few moments elapsed before the stranger, dashing in over the trail in fine style, leaped from his horse with a good deal of dexterity for a man of his age, and carelessly flinging the bridle-rein over the limb of a small sapling, passed me with a smile of recognition, proceeded to the spring, where he took a long, deep draught, and then, returning to where I was seated upon the velvety greensward, threw himself carelessly down upon the ground beside me.

There we two lay—the stranger, with his keen, sharp eyes, and his altogether careless, but always attentive manner, closely regarding me, and looking me over from toe to tip; while I assumed an equal carelessness, but was all intent on his every movement. I saw the handles of two finely-mounted pistols protruding from inner coat-pockets, and I did not know what might happen. I was wholly unarmed, but I was young, wiry, powerful, and though I had nothing for self-protection save my two big fists and my two stout arms, I was daring enough to tackle a man or beast in self-defense at a moment's warning.

After a moment's silence, he said:

"Well, stranger, I'm a man of business from the word 'go.' What's your name and how long have you been about here?"

"My name's Pinkerton. I've been here three or four years, coopering some, and harvesting some; but coopering's my trade. You'd have seen my shop if you had come up the hill. I manage to keep seven or eight men going all the time. But times are fearfully hard. There's no money to be had; and the fact is," said I, looking at him knowingly, "I would like to get hold of something better adapted to getting more ready cash out of—especially if it was a good scheme—so good that there was no danger in it. But what's *your* name and where did you come from?" I asked abruptly.

He scarcely heeded this, and, Yankee-like, replied by asking where *I* came from before locating in Illinois.

"From Scotland," I replied, "from Glasgow. I worked my way through Canada and finally found myself here with

2*

just a quarter in my pocket. What little I've got has been through hard work since. But, my friend," said I, smiling, "the talk is all on one side. I asked *you* something about yourself."

"Well," he said, still looking at me as though he would read me through and through, "they call me 'Old man Craig.' My name is Craig—John Craig—and I live down in Vermont, near Fairfield; got a fine farm there. Smith, down here at Elgin, is a nephew of mine; and old Crane, over at Liberty- ville, and myself, have done a good deal of *business* together."

"Oh, yes," said I, nodding, "I understand."

"But you see," resumed the counterfeiter, "this part of the country is all new to me. I've been to Crane's house before, but that was when I came up the lakes to Little Fort,* and when I got through with my visit there I always went into Chicago on the 'lake road.'"

"And of course you both stopped at the Sauganash," I said, meaningly.

"Certainly we stopped there," replied Craig, musingly.

"I *know* that Foster's a man that can be depended on," I remarked, with considerable meaning upon the word "know."

"He's a square man, Foster is," rejoined the counterfeiter; "and, Pinkerton, I believe you're the right sort of a man too. I sold Foster a big pile the last time I was in Chicago." And then, quick as thought, he said, looking me in the eyes: "Did you ever 'deal' any?"

"Yes, Mr. Craig," I replied, "but only when I could get a first-class article. I frequently 'work off' the stuff in paying

* The city of Waukegan, in Lake County, Illinois, was called "Little Fort" by the early settlers.

my men Saturday nights, when traveling through the country and on the merchants here in Dundee, who have all confidence in me. But I wouldn't touch anything like it for the State of Illinois, unless it was as good in appearance as the genuine article. Have you something really good, now?" I concluded, indifferently.

" I've got a ' bang up' article," said the stranger, quietly.

"But I don't know *what* you've got," I persisted. " I thought you were going over to old Crane's?"

" Well, so I was, Pinkerton; but I believe you're a good, square man, and I don't know but I had as soon sell to you as him."

" I think you had better see Crane,'" said I, indifferently. " He's probably expecting you, and, as it's afternoon now, it would be a good idea for you to make the best time you can there."

" How far is it ?" he asked.

" Oh, thirty-five miles or thereabouts, and as you've got a good horse, you can make it by dark or before."

He rose as if undecided what to do, and without making any further remark at the time, took his horse to the spring and watered it.

He then returned, and again throwing himself down beside me, remarked carelessly :

"But I haven't yet showed you what I've got. Here are the 'beauties;'" and he whipped out two ten-dollar bills, counterfeits on the Wisconsin Marine and Fire Insurance Company's money.

I looked at them very, very wisely. As I have already said, I had never seen a ten-dollar bill in my life; but I exam ined them as critically as though I had assisted in making the genuine bills, and after a little expressed myself as very much pleased with them.

They were indeed "beauties," as the old rascal had said, and in all my subsequent detective experience I have hardly seen their equal in point of execution and general appearance. There was not a flaw in them. To show how nearly perfect they had been made, it is only necessary to state that it was subsequently learned that several thousand dollars in these spurious bills had been received unhesitatingly at the bank and its different agencies, and actually paid out and received the second time, without detection.

"Come, now, Pinkerton, I'll tell you what I'll do," continued Craig, earnestly; "if you'll take enough of this, I'll give you the entire field out here. The fact is, Crane's getting old; he isn't as active as he used to be; he's careless also, and, besides all this, he's too well known."

"Well," said I thoughtfully, "how much would I have to take?"

"Only five hundred or a thousand," he replied, airily.

"On what terms?" I asked.

"Twenty-five per cent. cash."

"I cannot possibly do it now," I replied, as though there was no use of any further conference. "I haven't anywhere near the amount necessary with me. I *want* to do it like thunder, but when a man can't do a thing he can't, and that's all there is about it."

"Not so fast, my man; not so fast," answered the old rogue reassuringly. "Now, you say these lubberheads of merchants down at the village trust you?"

" Yes, for anything."

" Then can't you make a raise from them somehow ? You'll never get such another chance to do business with a square man in your life ; and you can make more money with this in one year than any one of them can in ten. Now, what can you do, Pinkerton ?"

I assumed to be studying the matter over very deeply, but, in reality, I had already decided to do as the man wished ; for I knew that Messrs. Hunt and Bosworth would be only too glad to have the matter followed up so closely. Finally I said : " I'll do it, Craig ; but it won't answer for you to be seen hanging about here. Where shall we meet, and when ?"

" Easy enough," said he, grasping my hand warmly. " I won't go over to old Crane's at all. If he wants any of the stuff after this, he'll have to come to you. I only let Smith have about one hundred dollars in the bills, and that out of mere friendship, you know. When he wants more, I'll make him come to you too. Now, I'll go right back down there, and you can meet me at Smith's this evening."

" Oh, no ; no you don't, Craig !" I answered, with an appearance of deep cunning. " I'm willing to take the whole business into my hands, but I don't propose to have every Tom, Dick and Harry understand all about the business from the beginning. I'll find my own customers," I concluded, with a protesting shake of my head.

" Well, that *is* best. You're right and I'm wrong. Where'll we meet ?" he asked.

" I've a capital place," I replied. " Do you know where the unfinished Baptist Church and University are, down at Elgin ?"

" Let me see," he said, smiling. " I ought to know. I'm

a splendid Baptist when I'm in Vermont—one of the deacons, as sure as you live! Are they up on the hill?"

"Yes, the same," I answered. "It's a lonesome enough place to not be likely to meet anybody there; and we can arrange everything in the basement."

"All right," he acceded, laughing heartily, "and the next time I write my wife, damn me if I don't tell her that I dedicated the new Baptist Church at Elgin, Illinois!"

I joined in this little merriment at the expense of the Elgin Baptist Church; and then Craig, who had begun to feel very cheerful and friendly, went into quite a lengthy account of himself and his mode of operations.

As before stated, he said that he was located in Fairfield, Vermont. This location was chosen from the ready facility it offered for getting into Canada, should danger at any time present itself. He owned a large and fine place, and was legitimately engaged in farming, was wealthy, and had been a counterfeiter for many years, keeping two first-class engravers constantly employed, and he warmly invited me to visit him, should I ever happen that way—although it was morally certain at that time, to him as well as myself, that it would be a very long time before I began traveling for pleasure—and I received all this for what it was worth, but fervently promised him a call, while mentally observing: "Ah! my man, if everything works right, maybe that the call will come sooner than you are expecting it!"

What chiefly interested me, however, was what he told me concerning his mode of operations.

He said that he never carried any quantity of counterfeit money upon his person. This twenty dollars which he had shown me was the largest sum he ever had about him. This was simply and only a sample for use, as it had been with me. Should be arrested, not one piece of paper which would not bear the most rigid inspection, although he had always upon his person about two thousand dollars in genuine money, chiefly in eastern bank bills. No person, understanding the condition of things at that time, could be persuaded to condemn a stranger in a new country, and unfamiliar with its money, for having twenty dollars of spurious money in so large a sum as two thousand dollars.

I asked him why he did not pad his saddle with the bills and carry them with him, in this manner, for convenience. I made this inquiry, more than anything else, to draw from Craig his manner of supplying parties, and I was successful, for he immediately replied:

"No, that wouldn't do. To begin with, the horse would sweat the pad and badly discolor the bills, and, in the next place, somebody might be as curious as yourself and rip open the saddle. Oh, no, no; I've got a better scheme than that. I've got a fellow, named Yelverson, as true as steel and as shrewd as a man can be made. He follows me like a shadow, but *you* will never see him. He is never seen by any living person with whom I have business. I simply show my samples and make the trade. I receive the money agreed upon from the buyer, and then tell him that I *think* he will find the specified sum in my money in a certain place at a designated time.

"He goes there, and never fails to find the bills. But Yelverson is not seen in the transaction, and in the meantime, I have hidden my samples, as well as the money received by me, which *might* be marked, so that if there should be any treachery, nothing could be proven against me. I have a good deal of Canada trade, and it is all effected in this manner. Old John Craig is never caught napping, young man!"

The last remark was evidently made by the counterfeiter to give me to understand that though he had given me, or pretended to give me, very freely, his valuable confidence, that he was not a man to be trifled with in any particular, and I fully believed this of the man already.

I was satisfied that he had a good deal of the honor which is so frequently referred to as existing between thieves. There is no doubt but that this man always kept his word. In that sense he was honorable. This kind of honor was a necessity to his nefarious business, however, and I fail to perceive, as many sentimentalists do, where the criminal deserves the credit for being honorable when that peculiar quality is only used for the worst purposes, and is as much required by the criminal as the bread he eats.

It was now fully half-past one o'clock, and I suggested to the counterfeiter that we conclude our interview, as some stragglers might happen that way.

"You will be on hand, Pinkerton ?" asked Craig, as he rose from the grass.

"There's my hand on it," said I, quietly.

"And you'll bring enough money to take five hundred ?"

"I'm certain I can raise that much," I replied. "But see here. Don't you come down through the village again. It will cause talk, and couple you with myself in the village gossip in a way that won't do for me at all."

He agreed with me in this, and I then directed him to take

what was called the "upper road " past General McClure's old place, and having got this well fixed in his mind, agreed to meet him at the designated place in Elgin, at about four o'clock, bade him good-by and took my departure.

I hastened towards the village, and saw on my way, just as I was descending the brow of the hill, my counterfeiter friend well along the upper road, halting his horse to wave me a good-luck, or good-by, as it might be taken, to which I merely nodded a reply, and then made all possible speed to Mr. Hunt's store, where I quickly reported the result of my interview to Messrs. Hunt and Bosworth.

They were very gleeful over my success in working into the confidence of the counterfeiter, but both were rather apprehensive that the money *was* in the man's saddle, that Yelverson was a myth, and that possibly we had lost an opportunity of securing either. But I felt pretty certain that Craig would be on hand at Elgin according to appointment, and, securing the required amount of money, one hundred and twenty-five dollars, and a bite of lunch, I set out on foot for Elgin. The place was only about five miles from Dundee, and five miles for me then was as nothing; so that, a few minutes before four, I was within the deserted structure.

I looked into every conceivable corner and cranny, but could discover the counterfeiter nowhere.

I passed outside and looked in every direction, but still he was not to be seen. Tired and worried about the whole matter, I retired within the basement, and had been sitting upon one of the loose timbers there but a few minutes, brooding over the loss of my day's work, and disgusted with the whole business, when Craig suddenly entered and smilingly greeted me.

"Why, helloa, Pinkerton, you're ahead of time."

"I told you I would be here," I replied.

"Well, did you bring the money with you?"

"Certainly I did. Here it is," said I, counting out one hundred and twenty-five dollars as carelessly as though accustomed to handling comfortable sums of money.

He looked it over more carefully than suited me exactly. The act seemed to hold a faint trace of suspicion, but he found it to be in eastern bills and correct in every particular.

"Coopering must be pretty profitable work?" he remarked with a light laugh.

"Oh, fair, fair," I answered, indifferently. "Does pretty well when one can do some other quiet business along with it."

"Oh, I see," he said pleasantly. "Now, Pinkerton, you go outside for a few minutes, and keep a sharp lookout, lest somebody may be watching. Remain outside four or five minutes, and if you see no one by that time, come back."

I went out as directed, but I could not but feel that I had placed myself in the man's power completely, as far as giving him a fair opportunity to abscond with my friends' money was concerned, and, though a new hand at this kind of bellows, I determined to be as keen as he was shrewd. So, instead of leaving the building altogether, for the time mentioned, I started off for a little distance, and, quickly returning up through a small ravine, took a position near an open window, just in time to observe my Baptist friend from Vermont placing something beneath a wide, flat building-stone in one corner of that portion of the basement where we had been together.

This much seen, I got away from the place as speedily as I could, and at once sought a small eminence near the building, and made a great pretense of keeping a close watch on the locality.

While thus occupied, I observed, out of the corner of my eye, that Craig had appeared at one of the entrances, and was closely watching my movements. Apparently satisfied at last, he gave a low whistle, attracting my attention, of course, when he then motioned me to join him.

As I entered I told him that I had looked everywhere, but was unable to see any person about.

"That's all right," he replied pleasantly, and then, looking at me in a quizzical sort of a way, asked:

"Pinkerton, what would you think if I told you that Yelverson had been here during your absence outside, and left the five hundred in my bills?"

"Well, I don't know," I answered; "I'd *almost* think you'd got Old Nick working along with you!"

"Perhaps I have, perhaps I have," he returned quietly. "Look under that stone over yonder."

I went to the place indicated, and, lifting the stone which from the outside I had seen him busied with, I picked up a neatly-made package.

"I *think* you will find what you bought inside it," remarked Craig.

I opened the package, and found that it contained fifty ten-dollar bills. They were the counterfeits, but, as I have already stated, were most handsomely executed.

I make this open confession to my readers:

For a moment the greatest temptation of my life swept over

me. A thousand thoughts of sudden wealth and a life free from the grinding labor which I had always known, came rushing into my mind. Here in my hands were five hundred dollars, or what professed to be, every one of them as good as gold, if I only chose to use it. The purchasing power of five hundred dollars then, the use which could be made of it, the large gain which would accrue from its judicious investment, were one and all ten times what they are now. What would it not purchase? Why, to my mind then it was a great fortune!

All this and more pressed upon me with such weight—the first and last time in my whole life—that with this struggle in my memory, while I have always been unshaken in my determination to never lose sight of a criminal when it once becomes my duty to pursue him, I can never think of one undergoing the first great temptation to crime, whether he has resisted or fallen, without a touch of genuine human sympathy.

I am satisfied that this showed in my face somewhat, but was taken by him to indicate cupidity and eagerness at the prospect of large profits as his " wholesale agent " in that section, and soon after probably stood me in good service.

We sat down upon one of the timbers and chatted pleasantly for a time, during which he informed me that Yelverson had at once returned to Smith's, where his horse was stabled, and ere then was on his road toward Chicago, where he, Craig, should rejoin him on the next day, after passing the night at his nephew's.

My thought was to get the two together and nab them both, if it were in my power. I saw that I had no possible opportunity to do this in Elgin, for, according to Craig's statement, Yelverson was well on the road to Chicago, out of all danger

of pursuit; and even should I cause Craig's arrest, from what
I already knew of his character and habits, his conviction on
my unsupported evidence would prove difficult.

Accordingly, while sitting there and chatting away with
Craig, all these things were playing back and forth like a swift
shuttle through my mind, with the following result.

"Look here, Craig," said I, "if you wouldn't be in too big
a hurry about getting back home, I'll tell you what I'll do. I
believe I could make arrangements to buy you out altogether."

"Well, now, that's a good idea, Pinkerton," returned the
counterfeiter thoughtfully, but evidently pleased at the proposition.

"How much have you got?" I asked.

"I haven't any," he answered, with a sly look. "Yelverson
has about four thousand dollars in the stuff, I believe."

"All right," I replied. "Craig or Yelverson, it's all the
same so I get it. Now I've been thinking that I could take a
trip out to Naperville, in Du Page County, and St. Charles,
Geneva, Batavia, Aurora, and Oswego, in this county, and work
off the greater part of what I've got, and while at Oswego, see
Lawyer Boyd, who, I am certain, will take a share with me."

"How long will this take you?" inquired Craig.

"I can't tell," said I; "not more than three or four days at
the outside, I think."

"Well, try, and see what you can do. I would like to sell
my horse and my entire outfit too, and go back by the lakes, if
I can."

"All right, Craig," said I. "I'm pretty sure that I can buy
everything. I'll try hard, and think that if I can see Bill Boyd,

at Oswego, there'll be no doubt about our being able together
to take everything you have."

"Good-by, then," said the counterfeiter, shaking my hand
warmly. "I'll spend the night with Smith, go into Chicago
to-morrow, and wait there at the 'Sauganash' for you four or
five days. But, mind you, be discreet!"

With this we parted, Craig going over the hills into the
woods behind the town, to make some slight detour before re-
joining the gunsmith, and I, with my five hundred dollars in
counterfeit bills on the Wisconsin Marine and Fire Insurance
Company's Bank, starting on foot for home, where I arrived
just as the sun was setting behind the grand hills of Dundee,
upon what I then felt was the most exciting and eventful day
of my life.

Messrs. Hunt and Bosworth were on the *qui vive* of expectation, and listened to my recital with the greatest interest; but
they both seemed apprehensive that the counterfeiter would not
keep faith with me, and had probably set out from Elgin for
some distant point as soon as I had started for home, and would
leave us all in the lurch with five hundred dollars in counterfeit money on our hands for all our trouble and officiousness.

I confess that, being new to the business, I had something
of a like fear, or distrust; but still, in revolving the matter in
my mind, I could not but always come back to the first impression I had gained of my Vermont friend, to the effect that,
criminal though he was, he was a man who, when he had
passed his word, would be certain to keep it.

With a view of allaying the anxiety of my friends, and also
satisfying my own curiosity concerning the matter, I promised
that early the next morning I would take some measures to

learn definitely the whereabouts of the counterfeiter. And so, tired, partly discouraged, and fully satisfied in my own mind that I was not born to become a detective, I went home, and sought my bed with a feeling that the little cooper-shop, my good wife, and our plain, homely ways, were, after all, the best things on earth, and, altogether, better than any other sort of life or attainments possible for man to secure.

Prompt to my promise, I was up betimes the next morning; and, after a hasty breakfast, secured a horse, and was soon rapidly cantering off in the direction of Elgin, where I arrived by the time the villagers of the little town were stirring about their several avocations. I proceeded directly to the house of John Smith, the gunsmith.

Before I had reached the same, my spirits were measurably raised to observe, sitting there upon the rough porch, shaded with roses and honeysuckles, the veritable gentleman from Vermont who had given us all so much uneasiness.

He was smoking his pipe and enjoying the morning as composedly as any man well could, and, as I approached, looked up with a pleasant smile of greeting.

He advanced quickly to the gate, and grasped my hand heartily, saying quietly:

"Helloa, Pinkerton, what's up?"

"Only myself," I answered jokingly.

"Have you got started out on your trip this early?" he inquired.

"Yes; I believe if anything's worth doing, it's worth doing quickly and thoroughly. I'm on my way down the river to take in the towns I mentioned yesterday. I'll see Boyd to-morrow, get back as quick as I can, and meet you as agreed at the 'Sauganash,' in Chicago."

"You'll do, you'll do," said Craig encouragingly.

"I just thought I'd call on my way, shake hands with you, and show you I was at work carrying out my part of the agreement."

"Glad you stopped; glad you stopped. Make as good time as possible, for I want to get through here and get back East. The church interests always languish while I am away," he added, laughing.

And so, with a cheery good-by, we again parted.

I rode away ostensibly for St. Charles, but, after getting some little distance frem Elgin, took a detour, and, riding through the little post-town of Udina, reached Dundee some time before noon.

The information secured through this little ruse satisfied both myself and my Dundee friends that dependence could be placed upon meeting Craig in Chicago. This was what I most desired; for, alone in the country, and not knowing what secret companions he might have near him, ready to spring to his aid at the lifting of his finger, made an attempt at his capture, with my then inexperience, simply foolish, and something not to be thought of.

Three intervening days were passed in frequent consultations with Messrs. Hunt and Bosworth, very little attention to my casks and barrels, and a good deal of nervous plotting and planning on my own part; and before daybreak on the fourth morning I had caught the last glimpse of the little village of Dundee, nestling like a bird by the gleaming river, and was speeding my horse at a brisk pace over the winding highway toward Chicago.

I arrived in that then thriving, but little city, during the early forenoon, and my first move was to procure warrants for the arrest of both Craig and Yelverson, as I had high hopes of now being able, by a little good management, to get the two men together; and I easily secured the services of two officers, one of whom I directed to follow and watch the movements of Craig, which would undoubtedly, if there was any such person as Yelverson, bring the two men together. My idea was to then wait until they had separated and were so situated that immediate communication would be impossible, and thus capture Yelverson; while, after this had been effected, myself and the second officer would attend to Craig. But, as fine as all this looked in a plan, it was doomed, as the reader will observe, to prove *merely* a plan.

After all these arrangements were perfected, I went to the Sauganash Hotel. The officers were merely constables, and one was stationed outside the house, to follow Craig wherever he might go, or whoever might come in contact with him, should he be observed to meet any person with whom he might appear to have confidential relations; while the other officer was located inside the hotel, to cause Craig's arrest whenever the proper time arrived.

I wanted to bring things about so that I could capture the men with the money upon them, or in the very act of passing it; but circumstances and my own youth and inexperience were against me.

I had been seated in the office of the hotel but a few minutes when Craig entered, smoking a cigar. He saw me

3

I then moved forward to fasten the reins, and he edged along toward me, asking carelessly: "Do you know John Smith, of Elgin?"

"I know all the Elgin John Smiths," I replied. "Do you mean the gunsmith?"

"Yes," he answered tersely.

"Well, I know John," I continued; "that is, he has repaired my rifle and shotgun several times; but he might not remember me. I never had much talk with him."

"He's a square man," replied the stranger. "*I'm* his uncle. I came up from Elgin this morning. Smith didn't know just where Crane lived. He told me that he traded here, and that the boys were over here a good deal, so that I would be likely to find somebody here who could readily direct me to his place."

"Well," I said rather curtly, "we've talked too much already. It won't do. I'll join you over the river soon."

With this I carelessly walked away towards my shop, and at some little distance turned to see the stranger now engaging Eaton Walker in conversation with an evident purpose of gaining time.

"Well," I thought, as I hastened on, "there's no doubt now. This man is certainly a counterfeiter. John Smith is always loaded down with it. He gets it from old Crane; and this man at Walker's is the chief of the gang traveling through the West to supply these precious rascals. But then," it suddenly occurred to me, "what business of mine is all this? Good gracious! I've got a lot of barrels to make, my men need attention, and everything is going to the Old Harry while I am playing detective!"

"Have you got the money."

Page 50.

drinks; but I observed, without showing that I did so, that Craig was very careful in this respect. We soon parted, and I must confess that I began to have a presentiment that matters were beginning to look a little misty. I could not imagine what the outcome would be; but that Craig had become suspicious of something, was certain.

I could not of course then know, without exposing myself, what was done, or how Craig acted, but I afterward learned that he seemed perplexed and doubtful about what he should do. He started out rapidly in the direction of the lake, suddenly halted, returned, started again, halted again, and then walked aimlessly in various directions, occasionally giving a quick look back over his shoulder as if to determine whether he was being followed.

Whatever he might have thought about this, at last he returned to the hotel with the air of a man who had determined upon something, and entered the office.

Not making any move as though he desired to see me, I soon moved toward him, and finally said:

"Well, Craig, are you going to let me have the money?"

He looked at me a moment with a puzzled air of surprise, the assurance of which I have never since seen equaled, and replied quietly:

"What money?"

I looked at him in blank amazement, and finally said:

"The money you promised me."

With a stolidity that would have made a Grant or a Wellington, he rejoined:

"I haven't the honor of your acquaintance, sir, and therefore cannot imagine to what you allude."

If the Sauganash Hotel had fallen upon me, I could not have been more surprised, or, for the moment, overwhelmed.

But this lasted but for a moment. I saw that my fine plan had fallen to the ground like a house of straw. Yelverson had not been located; probably no counterfeit money could be found upon Craig; and there was only my own almost unsupported evidence as to the entire transaction, as the reader has been given it; but I also saw that there was only one thing to do, and that was to make Mr. Craig my prisoner. I therefore said:

"All right, John Craig; you have played your game well, but there are always at least two at a really interesting game, and I shall have to take you into custody on the charge of counterfeiting."

I gave the signal to the officer, and Craig was at once arrested; but he fairly turned the tables upon me then by his assumed dignity and gentlemanly bearing. Quite a crowd gathered about, and considerable sympathy was expressed for the stately, gray-haired man who was being borne into captivity by the green-looking countryman cooper from Dundee.

Not a dollar in counterfeit money was found upon Craig, as I had feared. He was taken to Geneva, in Kane County, lodged in jail, and, after the preliminary examination, admitted to bail in a large sum. While awaiting the arrival of friends to furnish the required bonds, he was remanded; and it was soon noticed by the frequenters of the place that Craig and the sheriff, whose apartments were in the jail building, had become very intimate. He was shown every courtesy and favor possible under the circumstances, and the result was that the community was suddenly startled to learn that the now famous counterfeiter had mysteriously escaped—leaving, it was said, the sheriff of Kane County considerably richer in this world's goods from the unfortunate occurrence.

This was the outcome of the matter; but though this great criminal, through the perfidy of an official, had escaped punishment, the affair was worth everything to the Wisconsin Fire and Marine Insurance Company in particular, and the entire West in general—it having the effect for a number of years to drive counterfeiters entirely from our midst.

But I cannot resist relating, in connection with the termination of the case, another incident characteristic of George Smith.

With all his business success, like Dickens' "Barkis," he became considerably "mean," and finally obtained the *sobriquet*, among his friends and acquaintances, of old "Na!" on account of the abruptness and even ugliness with which he would snap out his Scotch "na!" or no, to certain applicants for banking or other favors.

As soon as I had got Craig safely in jail, Messrs. Hunt and Bosworth, who had expended nearly one hundred and fifty dollars in the matter, saw that they had nothing left for their pains save the counterfeit five hundred dollars, and that even was deposited in the hands of the Kane County court clerk; so it devolved upon me to go into Chicago, see George Smith, and get from him, if possible, so much money as had been expended, and a few dollars for my own services.

So I took my trip, after a vexatious delay was admitted to the presence of the mighty banker, and tersely stated my errand.

He heard me all through, and then remarked, savagely:

" Have ye nae mair to say ?"

" Not anything," I replied, civilly.

" Then I've just this tae speak; ye was not authorized **tae do** the wark, and ye have nae right t' a cent.   I'll pay this, I'll pay this; but mind ye, noo," and he shook his finger at me in no pleasant way, " if ye ever do wark for me agin that ye have nae authorization for, ye'll get ne'er a penny, ne'er a penny!"

In fact, it was hard work for the close-fisted Scotchman to be decently just in the matter, and I am certain the incident has been of service to me during these later years in causing prudence in all such undertakings.

The country being new, and great sensations scarce, the affair was in everybody's mouth, and I suddenly found myself called upon, from every quarter, to undertake matters requiring detective skill, until I was soon actually *forced* to relinquish the honorable, though not over-profitable, occupation of a cooper, for that of a professional detective, with the result and a career of which the public are fully acquainted; all of which I owe to " Old John Craig" and this my first detective case.

CRIMINAL SKETCHES.

CHAPTER I.

A Remarkable Criminal.

DURING the month of August, 1879, there died, in the city of Toronto, in Canada, a noted thief and pickpocket, whose varied career of crime would form an interesting addition to the calendar of criminal romance.

This man was James Kern, or, as he was more generally and familiarly known, Jimmy Papes.

But little is known of his early history, except that during his minority he was apprenticed to a prominent printer, for the purpose of learning "the art preservative of all arts." Possessed of a restless, roaming disposition, the restraints of business soon became irksome and onerous, and he sought relief in the company of profligate companions, whose influence soon manifested itself.

He became loose in his habits, frequenting gambling-saloons, and in a short time he had sufficiently progressed upon the downward track, and, becoming a pickpocket, attained quite a celebrity for the dexterity with which he could relieve the un-suspecting of their valuables.

Once started upon the dangerous plane of criminality, the pace he traveled was a fast one, and the incidents of his life were a rapid succession of daring adventures, successful operations, alternate wealth and poverty, and continuous excitement.

He was a spendthrift by nature and disposition. Having no idea of the value of money, it slipped through his fingers like sand. He lived upon the best fare that could be obtained, and displayed a lavishness in his expenditures that bespoke a liberal heart and a generous mind.

He was an inveterate gambler, reckless in his wagers, and facing the tiger of fortune with a courage that would have been worthy of a better cause. Frequently, when his "luck," as he called it, was upon him, he would win large sums of money, which he would afterwards squander with the liberality and abandon of a prince.

During the years of the war he became quite noted as a pickpocket, confining his operations principally to the cities of Philadelphia, New York and Washington, and it was during this time that, in company with a "pal" of his, he entered the service of the Provost Guard, then on duty in the capital. Acting in this capacity, and dressed in the uniform of United States soldiers, they would be detailed for duty at the theaters and various places of amusement in the city. Washington being very much crowded during this important period of the country's existence, the theaters were largely patronized, and during the opening hours, when the vast crowds were pushing and jostling each other in their eager efforts to gain admission,

these soldier pickpockets reaped a plentiful harvest and invariably escaped detection.

Tiring of the confinements of a soldier life, he left the service by deserting from his regiment and came to Philadelphia
While in that city he became an actor in a very peculiar episode.
Watching for the arrival of the trains at the Baltimore Depot,
and selecting an individual from the number of disembarking
passengers, as a victim, he soon relieved him of a rather por-
tentous-looking wallet, which he congratulated himself would
prove a very valuable addition to his income.

Upon reaching a place of safety, he examined his booty and
found that, instead of being filled with money, as he had confidently expected, the pocket-book contained voluminous papers,
which proved conclusively that the gentleman whom he had
relieved was an accredited agent of the Southern Confederacy.
He also found that many of the documents, while compromising the individual himself, would prove of incalculable
value to the United States. As for money, all that he found
was a trifling sum scarcely worth mentioning.

Determining, however, to turn this pocket-book to advantage, he traced the gentleman whom he had relieved, to the La
Pierre House, where he had engaged quarters.

Procuring a badge and assuming an air of dignity and stern-
ness, he was ushered into the presence of the scion of rebellion.
Representing himself as a detective in the Secret Service of the
Government, he informed the astonished Southerner that he
must consider himself under arrest, at the same time giving
him to understand that his mission was known, and his papers
confiscated.

The dismay and confusion of the poor victim was painful

3*

to behold, and finally Papes, in his governmental character. agreed to settle the matter and allow his prisoner to escape, upon the payment of five thousand dollars, because, as he stated, "*he was opposed to locking anybody up.*"

The offer was eagerly accepted and the money paid over, after which Papes turned to the much-relieved gentleman, and said :

"You have bargained for your own safety, sir; not for the return of the papers found upon you. They must be turned over to the Government, and you must leave the city at once."

This the chivalric Confederate promised to do, and Papes redeemed his word by anonymously forwarding the contents of the wallet to the War Department, where they were afterwards found to be of valuable service in some very important operations.

Thus his life passed on until he reached the age of thirty years, when he was smitten with the charms of a daughter of a well-known thief then residing in Cleveland, Ohio, John Connolly, familiarly known as "Old Jack Connolly." For a time their married life was a happy one, three children being born to them, of which the father appeared to be very fond. He seemed to take a great interest in his household, providing liberally for his family, and furnishing his wife with many costly articles of jewelry and wearing apparel.

He did not, however, discontinue his operations in the " crooked" line, and as his ventures frequently compelled him to be absent from home for lengthy periods, and numerous temptations being offered to the pretty and somewhat lonely and susceptible wife, Papes soon discovered evidences of infidelity upon her part, which caused a separation. After this dis covery his disposition underwent a change, and, instead of desiring and enjoying the comforts of home, he became a sort of wandering Arab, and soon was identified with operations of a varied character, and with the criminals of almost every section of the country.

He no longer confined himself to the manipulations of the pickpocket, but tried his skill in almost every department of criminal science. At one time he would be associated with a gang of "bank bursters" in one section, and soon after he would be heard from working in an entirely different locality in silk robberies, or, in criminal parlance, among "swag-getters." Again he would appear as a "bank sneak," and anon he would return to his old love for picking pockets.

It was during the war that, while riding in a crowded street car with a companion, he stood before a gentleman who was sitting down, and who wore in his immaculate shirt front a diamond stud of large dimensions and of great value. This gentleman was Joab Allen, the great Western trader and contractor. At that time large diamonds were not often seen, and this particular one was fastened on each side by a small gold chain, which ran back to and was fastened upon the suspenders.

The bait was too tempting for the ambitious pickpocket, and he resolved to possess himself of the glittering gem. Giving a peculiar cough to his companion, who was seated beside the gentleman, he commenced operations. Drawing a newspaper from his pocket, he opened its folds and began reading. Soon the movement of the car, or some other cause, brought him nearer to the unsuspecting Mr. Allen, and the newspaper, now wide open, was held out nearly under his chin. Of course,

with this screen between his face and the remainder of his person, the shirt front with its sparkling ornament was completely
hidden from view. Under the cover of this paper Papes succeeded in cutting the gold chain upon either side, and in a few
minutes the diamond stud was dexterously removed from its
snow-white resting-place to the pocket of the daring thief. So
rapidly and quietly was this done that even his companion was
unaware of its success, until Papes, hastily looking out of the
window of the car, and folding up his paper, hurriedly left,
escaping unsuspected with his valuable booty.

As a matter of course, the loss was soon discovered, and
the indignart Joab Allen immediately secured the services of
detectives to ferret out the thief and to effect the restoration of
his property. All to no avail, however. No clue could be obtained of the guilty individual, and as Papes kept very quiet
after this event he was not even suspected.

Finding the efforts of the detectives to be futile, Mr. Allen
inserted an advertisement in the newspaper, offering a reward
of two thousand dollars for the return of the diamond and
" no questions asked."

This announcement met the eyes of the watchful Papes,
and after instituting inquiries which satisfied him of the truthfulness of the offer and of the safety of negotiating with the
loser, he visited Mr. Allen and arranged for the return of the
stud for the sum named, which return was effected, Papes receiving four new crisp five-hundred-dollar bills for his labor.

During the interview which took place at this time, Mr.
Allen became quite inquisitive as to the manner in which the
theft had been accomplished, and, replacing the stud in his
bosom, requested Papes to give him an example of his skill.

To this, however, Papes demurred, saying that it was impossible to do anything of the kind while the person before him was suspicious and upon his guard. Their conversation lasted some little time, during which several amusing anecdotes were related, to the infinite amusement of Mr. Allen, who, being a genial gentleman, enjoyed a joke immensely. At last Papes arose to retire, and with a graceful bow he handed to the surprised gentleman the identical stud, which had been removed from his shirt under his very eyes.

With a laughing good-by he disappeared, leaving the gentleman transfixed with wonder and astonishment at the audacious success of his light-fingered visitor.

Shortly after this he got into difficulty, being caught in the act of robbing ex-Sheriff Church, of Chicago, of his watch, and was arrested and bound over to await his trial. Not fancying the imminent possibility of a sojourn in prison, Papes forfeited his bail bond, and getting together a gang of thieves, he effected his escape and made a tour through Canada.

In the course of their journey they reached Montreal, and entering a broker's office in that city, Papes engaged the clerk in an argument upon a difficult problem relating to the exchange of some money which he desired to effect. While Papes was thus " stalling " his victim, a confederate slyly sneaked behind the desk, and snatching a package of five thousand dollars, succeeded in getting away, after which Papes concluded his business and left.

He had not departed many minutes when a cripple entered the office upon an errand of the same nature, having some money to exchange. This cripple, being of a petulant disposition, exhibited a wonderful degree of pertinacity in claiming every cent that could be demanded, and spent a goodiy time in disputing for what he asserted to be his rights. Immediately after the departure of the irritable cripple the money was missed, and he was instantly suspected of the theft. He had not gone many steps from the door when he was arrested and searched, but nothing of suspicious character being found upon him, and giving a very creditable account of himself, he was discharged, his amiability by no means increased by his communication with the police.

The authorities then began to suspect that Papes knew something of the affair, and this coming to the ears of that gentleman he determined to leave the town. Dividing the money between his confederates, he and a companion, Johnny Cook by name, arranged with "Old Jack Connolly," the father of his wife, and whose hands were entirely clear of this transaction, that they two would go to a small station about twelve miles up the road, while Connolly was to leave Montreal by the train and look out for the officers, and should any of them be upon the train to signal to the two others, who, being thus warned, would not take passage thereon. Unfortunately for the success of this enterprise, the watcher yielded to a prevailing weakness of his and drank himself stupidly drunk, and when the train arrived at the appointed place failed to put in an appearance. Papes and Cook therefore, seeing no warning signal from the approaching train, and imagining that everything was perfectly safe, fearlessly entered the cars and were immediately pounced upon by the detectives. They were returned to Montreal, and after due trial were condemned to five years' imprisonment at Kingston.

The hitherto-successful thief found that existence at King-

"Oh, yes, take this and bury four more of them for me."

ston was anything else but pleasant, particularly so at this place, where American prisoners were treated with unusual harshness. He therefore determined to escape, and succeeded in bribing one of the guards, but unfortunately this guard was discovered, and Papes was severely punished for his attempt.

Finding it impossible to evade the watchfulness of the prison officials, he settled down to good behavior and was soon thereafter appointed a book-keeper in the prison.

By his attention to his duties and his exemplary deportment he shortened his term of imprisonment considerably, and ingratiating himself with the authorities he succeeded in obtaining good positions for such American convicts as he believed he could afterwards depend upon, all of whom profited by his example, and reduced their time of service. He also, by fictitious entries in the books, at the time of their commitment, shortened the terms of imprisonment of such Americans as he desired to favor.

He left the prison, however, very much broken in health, and after obtaining his liberty began drinking very hard.

During all his life he evinced a genial, happy disposition, which won him many friends, even among the officers of the law. He was most excellent company, possessing an inexhaustible fund of anecdote, and a resource of witticism, as spontaneous as it was enjoyable. He was a great favorite among his companions, and, when he was known to be in town, he was immediately surrounded by a score of admirers, all ready to do him a service or to laugh at his jokes.

Entering a saloon one day, in which were assembled a number of pickpockets and thieves, he noticed that something unusual was taking place. Upon inquiring he ascertained that a very deserving and energetic police-officer had died, and that, his family being in destitute circumstances, these law-defying gentlemen—some of whom had passed through the hands of the deceased officer—with a generous irony, often manifested by this class of people, were taking up a collection to defray the expenses of the funeral, each one subscribing a dollar for that benevolent purpose. Upon requesting a subscription from Papes, he placed his hand in his pocket, and handing a five-dollar note to the solicitor, with a peculiar twinkle in his eye, said:

"What! a dollar to bury a policeman? oh, yes—take this, and bury four more along with him!"

Papes used to relate with a great deal of unction an anecdote of a noted police-officer in one of the eastern cities, who had the reputation of not being as sincere in the performance of police duty as he was expected to be.

This officer was stationed at one of the railroad depots in the city, and Papes, desirous of working upon the crowds there with as much freedom as possible, and knowing the character of the officer in question, approached him from behind. Placing a twenty-dollar gold piece in each hand, he laid them gently over the eyes of the guardian of the law, and asked:

"Can you see anything now?"

The officer, somewhat surprised, but realizing the situation at once, replied:

"Not a thing!" and raising his hands the gold pieces dropped into them, and were immediately transferred to his pocket.

Papes walked off laughing, but had not proceeded far when he felt a gentle tap upon his shoulder, and turning around

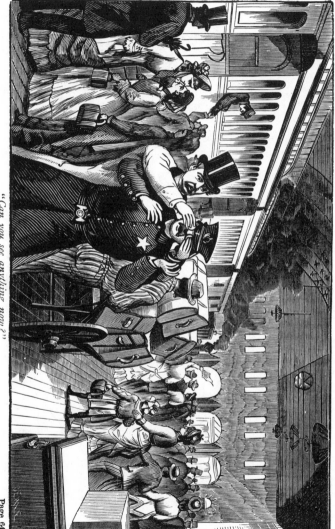

"Can you see anything now?"

beheld the officer whose optics he had just succeeded in closing so metallically.

With a serious, inexpressive countenance, and in a solemn voice, the officer addressed him :

"If you will put another one into my mouth, I cannot even speak."

Finding it useless to argue with such a rapacious individual, the coin was forthcoming, and the indefatigable Papes plied his calling successfully, without let or hindrance from the doughty officer, who had been rendered blind and speechless by the influence of the "Mighty Dollar."

In July, 1878, a man stepped into the office of the Receiver General in Toronto, Canada, desiring to purchase a draft. Behind him came another man, deeply intent in reading a newspaper. While the first gentleman was being attended to— the second spreading his paper in such a manner that the view of the surroundings were obscured—a sneak thief entered, and crawling upon his hands and knees behind the desk, quietly abstracted a package containing twenty-five thousand dollars, which lay immediately alongside of the absorbed and unsuspecting accountant.

A few days afterward a jewelry store in the same city was entered, and in almost the identical manner was robbed of thirty-six valuable watches.

In both of these exploits Papes was the inventor, the prime mover, and active participant.

After these events he returned to the States, where, being quite flush from his recent successes, he traveled extensively over the country, visiting his numerous friends, living high, spending his money freely, and having a good time generally.

When I first knew him he was a tall, stoutly-built, fine-looking man with hair once dark, but now prematurely gray. His features were rather heavy, and nis upper lip was covered with a mustache. His eyes were gray, but bright and piero ing—while the whole expression of his face, although exhibiting great shrewdness, was at once pleasing and good-natured. He was invariably well-dressed, and to one who possessed no knowledge of his calling, he would have appeared as a well-to-do, jolly-looking gentleman.

He was not strong, however, constitutionally—his lungs being affected for a long time—and after this junketing tour he began to evince unmistakable evidences of the consumption which had now taken firm hold upon him.

It was at this time, and while quite thin and scarcely able to speak, he visited Pittsburg, Pa., with a party of skillful thieves. Driving up to the entrance of the bank, his apparent sickness and inability to leave the carriage afforded sufficient excuse for requesting the cashier to come out to him upon the sidewalk, for the purpose of transacting some business. While thus engaging the officer of the bank, his confederates entered and robbed it of about six thousand nine hundred dollars, which lay within easy reach.

One of his latest adventures was the robbery of the State Treasurer's office at Springfield, Illinois. Papes, in company with Ross Salisbury, another noted sneak thief, and two unknown companions, visited the department, and calling the attention of Mr. Beveridge, the assistant treasurer, Papes desired to procure a one-thousand-dollar bill for small bills which he offered. Beveridge being a man advanced in years, his movements were necessarily slow—and a shortage of two or three dollars being discovered, another counting of the money was required.

While thus engaging the attention of the assistant treasurer, his confederates succeeded in abstracting fifteen thousand dollars from a counter along side of the gentleman in charge.

The exchange was finally made, and Papes, pocketing the bill thus obtained, immediately left the office.

The loss was soon discovered, and suspicion attaching to Papes, he was arrested. He had, however, changed his fine dress for the garb of a laboring man, and when presented before the despoiled official he failed to identify him, and he was accordingly dismissed.

Finding it too warm for him, however, Papes determined to leave, and taking a southward bound train, was soon on his way out of the city. The detectives had not ceased to be suspicious, and Papes had not been long upon the train before his watchful eyes discovered that he was being "shadowed." He was perfectly cognizant of the running time of the various trains, and he knew that at a certain point upon the road, the train in which he was traveling would be passed by another train going northward. Instantly his mind was made up, and as they neared the point at which the trains would pass, he arose carelessly from his seat and entered the water-closet— quietly followed by the shadow, who stationed himself at the door.

Quick as a flash, however, he leaped through the car window and reached the ground in safety, and in a few minutes boarded the other train that came flying along, and was soon upon his way to Chicago, while the patient shadow was demurely guarding the door of the water-closet into which his man had entered. His discomfiture at finding the bird flown beggars description.

Arriving in Chicago he divided the money and returned to Toronto. Here the ravages of disease began to tell perceptibly upon him and he grew gradually worse, and finally died in August, 1879. At his decease he was found to be almost penniless and was buried by his friends.

Thus passed away one of the most successful criminals of the day. During his career he had certainly obtained many thousands of dollars, but at his death was found to be almost a pauper.

Large-hearted, liberal to a fault, no appeal was ever made to him in vain. Numerous charitable actions can be traced to him, and his heart was ever open to the cry of distress or the appeals of the necessitous.

What he might have been had he chosen to tread the straight path of life we cannot tell, but certain it is that many of the qualities which he possessed would have adorned the character of any man, even in the higher walks of honor and respectability.

While we can have no sympathy with his nefarious calling, we cannot but regard with feelings of pity and charity the uses which were made of talents that would have enabled him to walk among his fellows admired and respected, had he devoted them to honorable pursuits and to laudable aims.

CHAPTER II.

A Bank-Sneak's Costly Railway Ride.

CRIMINALS, among each other, have standing and tone, precisely as do members of society. The most shrewd and cunning members of the different "professions" have just as high a regard for their reputations as have the most *au fait* gentlemen in society, or the most fascinating belles of the lead ing circles of fashion.

A brilliant raid upon a bank, an extraordinary swindle in Wall street, a splendid haul by a faro bank, or three-card-monte crowd, a neatly executed burglary, a fine piece of check-raising, or a handsomely-made counterfeit bond, Government note or bank-bill, are each accomplishments, in their line, to be as proud of, and to cause as much praise and envy as the most laudable success can compel in commercial, social or literary circles.

On the same principle, a failure, or any foolish error, causes the same proportion of derision; and the "professional" who permits himself to fail in any undertaking he may have in hand immediately loses caste, which he can only recover by some bolder stroke and more brilliant victory. These people have also a keen relish for anything savoring of a huge joke upon one of their number; and the satisfaction in its enjoyment is increased in just the proportion that the subject of derision has won celebrity in his particular calling; and the cause for the merriment has been the result of his lapse from his usual caution and cunning.

The following incident, which caused much enjoyment among the more able class of criminals throughout the country at the time of its occurrence, illustrates how the shrewdest among them occasionally become so careless as to deserve the severest censure from the fraternity, as well as to at least subject them to an unsought and sudden deliverance into the hands of justice.

The hands of justice did not happen to be groping around on this particular occasion, however. If they had been, two shrewd criminals would not have escaped with merely a costly railway ride and the subsequent raillery of their companions.

A "bank-sneak" is one who, with confederates, makes an excuse of transacting some sort of business at a bank during a time when few of the employees are within. The attention of the cashier or paying teller, and whoever else may be on duty, is wholly absorbed by the principal "sneak" and his accomplices, by various devices, when some dexterous little fellow, one of the gang trained for this work, "sneaks" in behind the partitions and secures whatever may be captured. It is daring work, but, like most other grades of thievery, principally requires coolness, keenness and presumption. Very large sums have thus been secured, indeed, almost equaling in amount that captured in the most successful operations upon bank vaults. James Griffin, Frank Knapp, Dan Noble and Jack Tierney once got over a quarter of a million in government

bonds from the office of the Royal Insurance Company in **New York**, in this very manner.

Charlie King was, and is, a professional bank-sneak. He was shrewd, cautious, jolly, and full of pleasant tricks and jokes with his friends. In fact, he was a handsome, round-faced, happy-hearted fellow, who considered his method of getting on in the world very funny and agreeable, and was never more happy than when pursuing his vocation in the manner of a practical joke, which was made to hit his friends right and left, so that when he made a little slip on the New York and New Haven railroad one night in the early part of November, 187–, which might have resulted in depriving him of his liberty for the greater portion of the rest of his life, he became the subject of ridicule and jest which has never ceased, and which still follows him among the friends of his ilk.

He and a confederate named Mathews had only a week before " sneaked " the bank of a provincial manufacturing town of Connecticut, and had secured thirteen thousand dollars— thirteen one-thousand dollar bills. They had been down to New York and paid the regular percentage to certain disreputable detectives, who make a business of watching for the games of such men and compelling " fair divide " in order to insure, at least, *their* protection, and were then preparing for a raid upon a bank at Springfield, in the same State, making their headquarters at the United States Hotel in Hartford, and accounting for there presence there in a neat and business-like manner.

To get matters into shape for the Springfield raid, frequent **trips** were made by King and Mathews from Hartford to the former city, the night, or the "owl" train, as it was called, always being chosen, to lessen the chances of being observed.

On the night in question, King and Mathews had purchased tickets for Springfield, and started for that city on conductor McMillen's train. They very modestly occupied a seat together, and King, drawing his hat over his eyes, doubled himself up in the end next the window for a nap, while Mathews, taking good care to attract no notice, fell in with the fashion of the tired passengers about, and leaned forward, resting his head on the back of the seat in front.

Travelers over the New York and New Haven road will remember that this particular train is usually very crowded, and as it stops frequently, the conductor is compelled to use the greatest expedition in the collection of tickets and fares. Coming hurriedly through the car in which the professionals were meekly ensconced, Mathews gave him his ticket, receiving a check, and King, who had fallen into a heavy drowse, put his hand in his vest-pocket and took something from it, which he handed to conductor McMillen, who, with the remark, "I'll attend to you shortly," passed rapidly on.

A passenger leaving the seat next behind the "bank-sneaks," Mathews at once occupied it, and seated himself comfortably for a nap, like his accomplice, but was shortly disturbed by some loud talk near him.

"Let me see, you gave me your fare, didn't you?" asked the conductor, tapping the drowsy Mr. King on the shoulder.

"Eh!" replied the latter, slightly startled by the salutation, which was too much like that of an officer to be pleasant to a criminal.

"You gave me your fare, didn't you?"

"You gave me your fare, didn't you?" the conductor persisted.

"Yes," was the gruff reply, as King saw it was only tho conductor, and then settled himself for another nap.

The conductor hesitated a moment, and again looked keenly at the drowsy passenger, while nervously fumbling with a largo roll of bills. He then tapped him on the shoulder more energetically than before, and said:

"If you paid your fare, where's your check?"

"Dunno; give ye a ticket to Springfield; d—n it! can't ye give a man a little peace?"

McMillen hesitated again, and seemed perplexed. Then he said, with considerable meaning, "You didn't give me a thousand-dollar bill, or anything of that sort, did you? Where's the man that sat with you?"

By this time the other passengers in the immediate vicinity of the conductor and the bank robbers had begun to awaken and become interested. The peculiar action of the conductor, his puzzled look, his hesitancy, his perplexity, and yet his persistent effort to find a somebody whom he was certain he had not yet concluded his business with, attracted attention. A close observer would also have noticed that at the mention of the thousand-dollar bill Mr. Mathews, who had also settled himself snugly for as good a rest as could be got under such circumstances, suddenly straightened himself up, as if to get a more clear idea of what was going on, and as if, also, there might appear an opportunity for him to say something needful.

Conductor McMillen still stood there, irresolute. King had got fairly awake, and was becoming both scared and ugly, as

4

he noticed a score of faces turned upon him, while the glare of the conductor's lantern fell full upon his own.

"What in —— *do* you want, anyhow?" King blurted out savagely.

"Somebody along here, and I'm pretty sure it was you," replied the conductor, "gave me a large bill, and I want to give him his change and a check."

"Well, it wasn't me. I gave you a ticket—bought it in Hartford—and then turned over and went to sleep, and if I can't be let alone, I'll find out why."

"Yes, that's so!" interrupted Mathews, alarmed at the turn things had taken. "I saw him give you a ticket, but you did not give him any check."

"Where's the other man that was sitting with him?" said McMillen, incredulously.

"He got off at the last station, or went into another car," coolly replied Mathews.

McMillen eyed the two men for a moment, and then, bundling his money into his pocket, remarking with pretty strong terms that he'd be dashed if the whole thing did not beat him, passed on.

Both of the sharpers knew something was wrong, but they were too keen and bright in their particular calling to appear to know each other, or pay any further attention to what either one of them would have given a hundred-dollar bill to understand. King could imagine no *reason* for any disturbance, but while quietly lying in his seat, racked his brain to call to mind the slightest cause; while Mathews felt the greatest alarm, recollecting the conductor's remark concerning the thousand-dollar bill, which brought to his memory the last job the gang had done, and the possibility of arrest, which, from the circum-stances, appeared to him to be imminent.

On the arrival of the couple at Springfield, they started in different directions, and, after various turns and doublings, in order to deceive any one who might be following them, as to their course, finally reached their headquarters at the Massasoit House.

King got into his room first, and, turning on the gas, his first hurried act was to unbutton his vest and rip open the waistband of his pantaloons. Then he got a needle and thread from a small case in the bureau, and seated himself as if for work. Laying down the needle a moment, he carelessly put his thumb and forefinger into his vest pocket, when suddenly a look of horror spread over his face; for, instead of pulling out a neatly-folded thousand-dollar bill, which it was his inten-tion to sew into his waist-band, his astonished search only secured a clean, new ticket from Hartford to Springfield!

At this moment Mathews knocked and was admitted to the room.

The whole thing was very quickly made clear, and King cursed his own foolishness and carelessness, which had permitted him to so far forget himself as to give a railroad conductor a thousand-dollar bill for a railway ticket.

The two worthies immediately left Springfield and went into cover, awaiting the result of any newspaper publicity which might be given to the singular incident, for such a mis-take was very likely to lead to their arrest.

In the meantime conductor McMillen reported the matter at headquarters and turned in the money. The reporters got hold of the affair, so far as the conductor could understand it, and the company advertised for a claimant for the money.

Upon this advertisement being seen by King and Mathews, they immediately proceeded to New York, and made arrangements to "coach" a party so he could identify the bill and give the conductor certain reasons to believe that he had taken it from him; but so fearful were they that this was only some keen ruse by detectives to get a clue to the robbers of the bank from which the thirteen thousand-dollar bills were taken, that the scheme fell through at the last moment, and but one claimant for the money has ever, under any circumstances, appeared.

This was conductor McMillen himself. He left the employ of the company a few years subsequent to the incident here related, when he began suit against the company for the amount of the thousand-dollar bill, less the price of the fare from Hartford to Springfield. So far as I can learn, the case is in litigation yet, and will cost both the company and ex-conductor McMillen more than the entire amount being fought over; while it is ever recollected and referred to by the more elegant classes of criminals, or by all those making it a business to keep posted in criminal matters, as "Charlie King's Extravagance," or the most expensive railway ride on record.

CHAPTER III.

Disobeying Orders, or, the Missing Cash Box.

TO disobey orders is one thing—to be a thief is quite an-other. If, however, the young man will carefully obey the orders of his superior, he may very frequently save himself a vast amount of worriment and annoyance, which would not come to him except through inattention to or disobedience to the proper directions given by others, who know what is to be done, and how and when it is to be accomplished.

How many characters have been blasted by a thoughtless action or a careless performance of duty! and to those who have no resources in the world to rely upon but character and ability, how important it is that the first should be preserved in its purity in order that the second may have full scope and opportunity for the display of its powers legitimately employed and properly directed.

But it is too true that the best of characters may sometimes prove inadequate to the task of saving a man from dishonor. How many men have been discharged from places of trust, at a time when their services seemed to be the most needed, and without any sufficient cause given for the action! Many times, in the hurry and rush attendant upon the transaction of a large business, goods and money have been missed, and rather than

devote the time and attention necessary to the discovery of the
real criminals, employers have disposed of the existing perplexity by the premature discharge of the person against whom
the most plausible theory of dishonesty can be justified by a
hurried overlooking of the premises.

In many such cases, a young man thus disposed of, even
with a recommendation and with numerous friends, has had
his prospects blighted forever, and finds himself condemned
without a hearing, punished without proof, and stigmatized as
dishonest without just cause or proper investigation.

It is true that in a majority of such cases it will be found
that the person upon whom the weight of punishment falls is
one who has been careless or inattentive to his duties—has
been in the habit of disregarding orders, or of forgetting their
observance at a time when observance was a virtue. But I
have always thought that a proper investigation should always
precede an action which operates to the detriment of a man's
character for honesty, as well as that a careful attention to instructions is absolutely necessary to make a valuable employee,
or a trusted servant.

These reflections are called to mind by an event which
occurred in the city of Pittsburg, in the year 1864, and which
for a time resulted in obscuring the character of two trusted
employees of a mammoth railroad enterprise.

The event was the robbery of the Pittsburg, Fort Wayne
and Chicago R. R. Co., under the most mysterious circumstances. The facts of the case were as follows: The paymaster of the road, a man whose integrity had hitherto been
regarded as above question or reproach, and his brother, who
was acting as his assistant, had been busily engaged during the

day, in counting out and making up packages of money, for the payment of the employees along the road, in accordance with the pay-roll of the company.

It appeared that the company had recently procured a new safe, with all the modern appliances for security and safety, which was to be used for the reception of money and valuable papers, and that the old one was designed thereafter to be used only for ordinary purposes. Early upon the afternoon in question, the cashier, who was about to go home, explicitly cautioned the paymaster against putting his money into the old safe, as it had been found to be insecure. This instruction was heard by all the clerks in the office, who were already aware of the fact that the old safe was not used for the reception of money. The cashier departed, and the paymaster and his assistant proceeded with their labors, and when their task was completed, and the money all arranged in the iron box ready for distribution upon the morrow, the paymaster, in a moment of forgetfulness, or from pure carelessness, did the very thing he had been cautioned against—he deposited his cash box in the condemned safe, and locked it.

After doing this, entirely unconscious of the results that were to follow his action, in company with his assistant he repaired to a hotel close by for tea, after which they were to start out on the evening train. During all the time of his absence, the thought never occurred to him that he had either forgotten or willfully disobeyed the warning given by the cashier.

After partaking of their repast, the two men returned to the office and prepared for their journey. The paymaster opened the safe, and to his wonderment and dismay, discovered that the cash box, which he had but a few minutes before safely locked therein, was missing. He stood for a moment as if thunderstruck, and then the memory of the emphatic warning of the cashier recurred to him with the full force of an accusation. He had deliberately disobeyed orders, and the robbery of the safe was the consequence.

Unable to credit his senses, he made a closer examination of the interior of the safe, but all to no purpose; the money was gone, and with its departure there came a full realization of the position which he would occupy upon the morrow.

It was too late to do anything that night. The cashier resided out of town; and in a sort of despairing stupor, the unfortunate man spent the night in a state of mental unrest bordering upon frensy.

The next day ugly rumors were afloat. The public became aware that the paymaster and his assistant had been suspended from duty. Further particulars could not be learned, but the wagging tongue of gossip was soon busy with the reputation of the disgraced officer. Vague charges of previous misdeeds were put in circulation; his neat little home, which was the result of economy and hard labor, was soon alleged to have been purchased with the proceeds of dishonesty.

Everybody seemed to have grown suddenly wise about the antecedents of the poor man, who sat at his fireside with distressed face and aching heart, as, surrounded by his once happy family, he contemplated the dreadful effect of this one act of disobedience. They were paying the fearful penalty. They fell under the social ban. Friends, who had been loud in their professions of regard, grew cold and dropped away while the jealous and the envious were busy in their damaging remarks and damning insinuations.

At the office of the company the matter was not spoken of. The order had been issued, and no one was allowed to mention the subject. It seemed that with the discharge of the officers the matter was to be dropped and no further proceedings were to be had in the matter.

After awhile the affair passed away, and, except for the manly defense that was made by one of the newspapers of Pittsburg, which had investigated the antecedents of the paymaster, public criticism had consigned him to the pillory, and society had ostracized him entirely.

This paper, however, declared its belief in his innocence. They declared that he was a man of most economical habits; he did not drink, he did not smoke, he did not gamble; and with this defense, manly and upright as it was, comment ceased, and the subject was seemingly dropped.

Not so, however. Immediately upon the perpetration of the robbery I had been informed of the circumstances. Upon my advice, the company had outwardly refrained from an extended examination. Under my instructions the impression was created that no investigation was to be made into the matter, and that with the discharge of the derelict paymaster all proceedings in the case were at an end.

For myself, I was fully convinced at the outset of the innocence of the two men who suffered under the disgrace thus brought about. The record of their previous good and unimpeachable character weighed very heavily in my judgment. Dark as was the cloud that seemed to hang over these two men, they never betrayed the slightest embarrassment peculiar to

4*

persons guilty of a crime; though they were downcast and sorrowful, they maintained an upright and fearless demeanor, and I determined to effect their complete vindication as well as to discover the real criminal, and, if possible, secure the return of the stolen money.

The habits of every clerk in the office were closely, but unobservedly, watched, and very soon I discovered one individual among the number who I thought would not escape the toils that I would weave around him, and who, I had no doubt, was the successful thief. He soon grew uneasy under the restraints of office duty, and soon after resigned his situation and left the office, with an unsullied character and a stainless reputation.

He was of a respectable family, and the new habits which he was now forming created sorrow and alarm in the household in which he had been tenderly reared and carefully nurtured. But, if he was the guilty man, he must be punished. The reputation of two innocent men demanded this, and the purity of the outraged law required it.

Among the new acquaintances which he formed was one who suited his peculiar disposition to a nicety, and they soon became inseparable companions.

Wherever the young man, whom we will call Henry Marvin, desired to go, he found a willing party in George Andrews. Several months had now elapsed, and the new year of 1865 had been duly ushered in. Shortly after this time the Legislature of Pennsylvania met at Harrisburg, and, yielding to Marvin's solicitations, George Andrews accompanied him to that city, for the purpose of discovering what excitement there was to be found at the capital.

They had a glorious time, and seemed to fare well wherever they went—the late clerk being particularly hospitable to the Pittsburghers whom he met in Harrisburg. Their "good time" lasted pretty well, until one morning, upon awakening after a particularly jolly night, they were confronted with the alarming fact that their exchequer was empty, or at least nearly so. This was a bad state of affairs where there was so much fun to be had, and Pittsburg was no longer sufficiently attractive for them to return.

They had projected a trip to New York when they left home, but how was the journey to be accomplished without money? The two young men therefore resolved themselves into a self-constituted committee on ways and means. The young ex-clerk was equal to the emergency, however, and volunteered to supply the necessary funds, provided his chum would consent to remain at the capital for a day or two, so that he could go to Pittsburg and return.

To this George Andrews demurred, and suggested the possibility of his companion forgetting to come back, and thus leaving the other in the lurch.

"If you go back to Pittsburg, you won't return here, and then I'll be in a fine scrape, without money or friends, in a strange city."

"Don't you be alarmed about that," replied the ex-clerk. "You'll see me back again quick enough, and with plenty of money to see us through."

"What guarantee have I that you will return? and if you don't, how am I likely to get back myself without help?"

Under the excitement of this little debate, the tongue of the ex-clerk became considerably unloosed, and he made a revelation to his companion that fully convinced him that Henry Marvin knew exactly what he was about.

The ex-clerk did know exactly where he could put his hands upon the funds which he wanted, but they must be obtained from a source that neither his friends, his mother or any other person living could dream of—and then, of course, with replenished pockets, he would return to Harrisburg immediately.

The arguments were too conclusive, the information was too satisfactory, and Henry Marvin started upon his return to Pittsburg, while George Andrews was to await his coming back to the capital.

The train had no sooner left the depot, bearing the ex-clerk upon his journey westward, than his chum, entering a telegraph office, dispatched the following message to his principal in cipher :

"*Henry Marvin started for Pittsburg, and will be due at — o'clock. He returns for money. Says he stole the cash box, and that it is buried in his mother's garden near the tree. He expects to return here immediately.*"

The detective had evidently triumphed this time, and justice would soon be done.

Long before Henry Marvin arrived at Pittsburg, I was in possession of the paymaster's long-lost box, and another trusty detective, with one of the Mayor's police, awaited the arrival of the train, which carried the financier upon his return for his buried treasure.

The train arrived, and as Henry Marvin alighted, he was welcomed back by these two new acquaintances, who insisted upon enjoying his society and bearing him company.   He

"*Upon the table stood the resurrected Cash Box.*"

desired to go home, but he was induced to proceed to the Mayor's Office, as he was suspected of some complicity with the almost forgotten robbery of the paymaster's cash box.

His surprise at such a reception and such a request, must, of course, be imagined, and his semblance of perfect astonishment at being even suspected of such a thing was a very excellent piece of acting indeed.

He explained that he had resigned from his position of his own accord, and that no one had even hinted a breath of suspicion against him, and that his character was above reproach. His air of injured innocence was very nicely assumed, and was maintained all the way from the depot to the office of the Mayor.

Arrived at the office of that functionary, however, he found an interesting party awaiting him, while upon the table in the center of the room stood the resurrected cash box—a dumb, but convincing witness of his duplicity and his crime. Here, too, were gathered the cashier of the railroad company, the paymaster and his assistant, myself and two operatives; and before this array the courage of the young man gave way completely, and he broke into tears.

The end had been accomplished. One reputation had been destroyed, but two others had been completely vindicated. The innocence of the paymaster was proven, and the crime of the guilty thief was fully shown.

The money was nearly all recovered, and the young man made a full confession of his actions.

In one home there reigns a profound sorrow for a degenerate child, who has brought ruin upon his own family, and disgrace upon the fair fame of two innocent men.

In another home the joyful face of a fond wife looks **into** the beaming eyes of a vindicated husband, while **happy** children, with merry voices, sound the gladsome tidings.

The lesson to the paymaster was an enduring one, and **to** this day there is no more exact man in the employ of the company, or a stricter disciplinarian in the management of the affairs of his office.

Henry Marvin was tried and convicted—and the thoughtless young thief expiated his crime by a term of imprisonment.

CHAPTER IV.

A Deluded Banker-Detective.

NOT a great many months ago, it is said, although I cannot vouch for the truth of the story, a carriage drove up before one of the most palatial of Chicago's hotels, and out of it got a certain gentleman, whom I will call Mr. Barker, the junior partner of a local banking firm. He was also a well known man of the world, and was warmly received by the clerks of the hotel, and, as it was dinner-time, was ushered into the dining-room.

Mr. Barker appeared to be in an especially good humor, and chatted a while with the clerk. In the course of the conversation he asked whether a gentleman named Viscount Fleury, from Paris, had not arrived the previous day, and in order to aid the clerk in recognizing him, he added that he had a very military air. The question was immediately answered in the affirmative. The banker said that he would like very much to make the acquaintance of the gentleman, and the clerk ordered the head waiter to reserve a place for Mr. Barker at the Frenchman's table.

The banker had hardly taken his seat, when the gentleman for whom he was inquiring, a tall, finely-formed person, stepped into the room.

[87]

Without paying any attention to the banker, he sat down at the table near him. After soup was through with, Mr. Barker made some incidental remarks. The Frenchman, who was alone, showed no disinclination to respond, and the two were soon engaged in conversation, in which Mr. Barker found opportunity to introduce himself as a member of the banking firm of Barker Brothers, we will say. The banker was, as has been stated, a man of the world. The viscount was a Frenchman, and the conversation, naturally turned on the gayer things of interest in Chicago, a subject better calculated than any other to bring young men, as they both were, closer together.

After dinner the two had a bottle of " Mumm " and a cigar. The Viscount then said, inadvertently :

" By the way, my dear Mr. Barker, do you know where I can get the cash on drafts on the Bank of California for about one hundred and twenty thousand ? I am going to leave to-morrow for France, and I should prefer to take my money with me in United States bonds."

Mr. Barker said that he would be very glad to accommodate him. " My carriage," said he, " is now in front of the door, and, if you choose, we will go right over to the bank. In half an hour you can have your bonds, and then I will be at your service to show you the sights of Chicago."

Fifteen minutes after the carriage stopped before the bank, and the banker led his French friend through the front office— in which, besides the numerous clerks, there were several other persons, apparently customers—back into his private office. There he invited his guest to sit down, and he took a seat opposite him. The Viscount drew a large pocket-book from

"These securities have been stolen!"

his vest-pocket and was about to open it, when Mr. Barker snatched it from his hand.

"What does this mean?" said the Frenchman, springing to his feet.

The banker stood up before him, eyed him from head to foot, and said to him quietly: "It means, my dear Viscount, that I know perfectly well who you are. You are Laffitt, cashier of the firm of L., T. & Co., bankers, of San Francisco, and these securities which you have here in your pocket-book represent money stolen from your firm."

"You must be out of your senses," said the Frenchman. "Either give me back those papers which you have taken from me like a robber, or I will give an alarm."

"Just as you choose," said the banker; "only I want to say that there are officers in citizen's clothing in that office, and that I am something of a detective myself. Mr. T., of the firm you have robbed, is an old school friend of mine. Since he knew that you would, of course, keep out of the way of every one with whom you had business relations, he applied to me, sent me a full and complete description of you, and told me all that it was necessary for me to know. In fact, it is not to the credit of your shrewdness that you permitted yourself to be bagged so easily. Your arrival here was discovered this morning, and it would not have taken half a detective to have picked you up anywhere; and now, my dear Laffitt, or Viscount Fleury, if you prefer that title, you are caught."

The false Viscount had hardly cast a glance at the letter, before he sank back upon his seat apparently overcome with consternation.

In the meantime Mr. Barker looked over the contents of

the pocket-book and found them all right. Then his eyes
rested upon the unhappy Frenchman. The sight touched him,
and he said, with more warmth than the scamp deserved:

"You see what crime leads to, but you must not be entirely discouraged. My friend T. says that you invested ten
thousand dollars of your money in the business. In view of
the good services which you had previously rendered, and out
of consideration for your family, he gives it to you. I am
authorized to pay you ten thousand dollars. Here is the money
in bills. Take it and try to earn your living honestly. I give
you, in my own name, and that of my old friend, your former
employer, the assurance that nobody shall ever know anything
concerning your misconduct."

Tears flowed down the cheeks of the unmasked swindler.
He pressed Mr. Barker's hand warmly, and, since he had apparently lost his desire to see the gayer side of life as it is to
be seen in Chicago, he hurried from the bank.

The banker Barker was delighted at having performed his
mission so well, and could not resist inviting all the officers and
clerks of the bank about him, to explain how very shrewd and
keen he had been, and how very brilliant a detective he would
make. He wrote at once to San Francisco about the good success which had attended his efforts, and placed the securities
which he had received at the disposition of L., T. & Co.; when
that house informed him by return mail that they knew nothing about Laffitt or Viscount Fleury, and that the securities
which Barker had forwarded were worthless forgeries.

The shrewd swindler, the alleged Viscount Fleury, had
never even seen a member of the San Francisco banking firm,
but in some mysterious manner had learned of the intimacy

existing between the bankers, and then forging the securities, which were even worthless as forged ones, had also forged and forwarded to the Chicago banker the letter in which was a splendid description of himself, as he was gotten up for that particular scheme, in which he flattered him on his natural detective ability, and pointed out a way for the capture of the securities, also very urgently showing why he did not want the man arrested, and why he did want him paid ten thousand dol· lars in bills. It was a beautiful scheme on the part of the handsome Frenchman, and probably something of a lesson to the banker.

CHAPTER V.

A Life of Crime.

THE inexorable scythe of death is unremitting in its opera tion, and the ranks of men are continually being depleted by its agency. To-day a nation mourns a fallen hero ; to-morrow a philosopher has laid down the burden and joined "the innumerable caravan." High and low, rich and poor, the good and great, the moralist and the criminal, must all sooner or later "pass under the rod" and yield to the inevitable.

As our eyes fall upon the lines that announce the final departure of some great luminary in the toiling mass of humanity, we experience a sense of regretfulness akin to sorrow. We remember the glorious deeds that have made his name famous ; we recall with pride the noble aspirations which prompted the heroic action, and in our hearts we render the meed of praise to the great soul that slumbers in the grave.

Not only in the high places, where " death loves a shining mark," but in the humble walks of life, the dread visitor comes and a family circle is saddened. A quiet, honorable life is ended, and there is sorrow upon friendly faces and grief in friendly hearts.

But there is another place, strongly built and iron-barred,

whose huge walls of stone stand frowning and grim to resist attack from within and without ; whose vaulted passages and iron doors defy the entrance of any except he bear the badge of authority; within whose gloomy chambers dark-browed criminals count the weary hours that drag along, and murmur at the fate that has overtaken them.

Death knocks at the portals of the prison, and the gates fly open at his magic touch. Silently and solemnly he stalks along the dimly-lighted corridors, and, pausing before the narrow door, demands the life of him who dwells within. The demand is irrevocable, and the rigid form upon the narrow bed, the sightless eyes from which the light has gone forever, the cold hands folded over a heart as cold, proclaim that the dreadful summons has not been in vain, and that a wicked heart is dumb and a plotting brain has ended its functions.

From the turretted walls of the Eastern Penitentiary in Philadelphia, a short time ago, the black herald of death demanded a criminal's life, and Lewis C. Clermont, after a career of sin and crime as romantic and startling as it was consistent and successful, yielded to the call and rendered up his account with time.

The career of this man almost from his infancy was a continuous episode of criminal operations, many of which border upon the realms of romance.

When in the prime of his manhood he was a singularly handsome man. Firm and erect, of medium height, his shoulders were broad and firmly set, while his waist was tapering and graceful as a woman's.

His features were finely cut and handsome, and his eyes were wonderful in their beauty and expression—large and dark blue in co.or, they would light up with sudden passion or melt into the softness of affection that would startle the victim of his anger or thrill the object of his tenderness.

His black hair, slightly curling, was worn long and pushed back from his high white forehead, falling nearly to the collar of his coat; and his upper lip was ornamented with a long, gracefully-drooping black mustache, which became him well, and gave an added charm to his handsome face.

Faultlessly neat in his tastes, his clothing was of the most fashionable cut and of the best material, while his linen was of the finest quality, and immaculate in its purity and whiteness.

No one to have seen him in the drawing-room or upon the promenade, would have imagined that this brilliant, captivating exterior was but the mask under which lurked the demon of crime—the shining diadem that adorned the death-dealing basilisk.

He was possessed of a liberal education, was an extensive linguist, and by varied reading had attained a degree of culture far beyond the average.

His parents were of eminent respectability and of undoubted honor—his father at one time occupying an honorable public office of prominence—and they have painfully felt the disgrace and shame which this degenerate son has brought upon them.

The first criminal action in which he was known to have been engaged was the robbery of a safe in Illinois, when he acted in collusion with one " Billy " Wray—an old-time safe burglar of notorious character.

After this he started a banking institution in a small town in Minnesota, where, by his pleasing manners, he succeeded in gaining the confidence of a number of the prominent business men of the place, who became depositors and intrusted their funds to his keeping. Having received a large amount of money in this way, he endeavored to make arrangements with "Bob" Scott and "Jim" Dunlap—who were afterwards con· cerned in the Northampton Bank robbery—to rob the bank. These worthies being pretty well acquainted with the character of the gentleman with whom they were dealing, demanded the payment of ten thousand dollars in advance, before undertaking the work. As this amount was not forthcoming, the matter fell through, and a short time afterwards Clermont committed the robbery himself, and fled to San Francisco.

He was then quite a young man, and soon, by high living and gambling, his funds rapidly disappeared, and he was forced to the disagreeable necessity of laboring for his subsistence.

He obtained a position upon one of the street car roads in that city, and while thus engaged his fine appearance and pleasing address attracted the attention of Walter Patterson and Ira Garside, two well-known "check raisers" and forgers, who have lured many young men into their toils who afterward became criminals.

Resigning his position in San Francisco, he accompanied these two men upon a tour through the country and made considerable money. Their system of operation was to present at the desk of a bank in some country town forged letters of introduction from the cashiers of prominent banks to their correspondents, and a forged certified check upon the same institution. This check would be deposited in the bank, and they would then draw upon it for a lesser amount, and, receiving the money, would suddenly decamp before the duped officials would receive the disappointing intelligence that both check and letters were forgeries, and that they were the victims of the gentlemanly scamps now beyond their reach.

In all these operations they were very successful and amassed a great deal of money, but, suspicion attaching to them, Clermont, with his ill-gotten gains, departed for Europe. He traveled extensively upon the Continent, visited the Holy Land and finally returned to Germany.

Here he was traced by my operatives to all the watering places, and the German police, being informed of his doings, watched him so closely that he deemed it inadvisable to ply his calling there, and he returned to the United States in 1874.

While abroad he visited Stuttgart, and was for a time the guest of Baron Shindle—who is none other than the famous Max Shinburne—who is particularly desired by various parties in New Hampshire and Pennsylvania, and of whose remarkable adventures I have previously written.

Clermont was married before this to a charming little lady in Chicago, whose devoted attachment to him induced many acts of self-sacrifice upon her part, which, I am afraid, were inadequately appreciated by her dashing, handsome and unprincipled husband.

Having linked her fortunes with his, and discovering the precarious nature of his calling, she never faltered in her love for him, but clung to him with all the fondness and devotion that the heart of woman is capable of, remaining true and steadfast to the end.

Returning from Europe during the summer season, and while the various sea-side resorts were populated by the wealth and beauty and fashion of the social magnates, Clermont went to Long Branch, and, establishing himself at the West End Hotel, under the name of Louis La Desma, the son of a rich merchant in Cuba, soon ingratiated himself into the society of the highest circles.

His handsome face, graceful figure, his faultless attire and his charming conversational powers soon made him quite an admired favorite, and many little episodes of tender romance and stolen meetings with the fair daughters of our modern aristocracy fell to his lot, while dwelling by the sea-washed shores of this delightful city.

Among the numerous belles of the gay and enjoyable season, whose hearts throbbed more quickly in his presence, whose cheeks flushed with pleasure at his coming, and whose modest eyelids drooped in rapturous confusion beneath the ardent glances of his own wondrous orbs, was Josephine Dumel. She was a beautiful, blonde lady, with the features of a Venus, the form of a Juno, and was the widow of one of the scions of Philadelphia aristocracy.

Being quite wealthy and remarkably attractive, she had numerous admirers, and her suitors were legion, but until the arrival of the interesting and handsome Cuban, she had remained proof against their blandishments, and continued to mourn the memory of her departed husband.

Like the ancient hero, however, La Desma came and saw and conquered, and in a short time the beautiful widow succumbed to the fascinations of the romantic-looking stranger, and they were married. The ceremony took place in New York, after which the happy couple returned to Philadelphia.

Their short but apparently delightful honeymoon was spent at the palatial residence of the bride, and Clermont, pretending

5

to be a prominent actor in the Cuban rebellion, stated that it was necessary for him to remain closely at home, as he might be pounced upon by the spies of the government, who infested all the eastern cities. He was always armed *cap-a-pie*. His richly-jeweled pistol lay upon the table when he sat down to write a letter or converse with his wife, and he never retired for the night without a small armory beneath his pillow.

His grand and gloomy airs and the peculiarities of his disposition seemed to exercise a strange fascination upon the lady of his choice, and his slightest wish was absolute law in the household.

After a few weeks dalliance in quiet and happy seclusion he suggested a short trip to Europe, and this instantly meeting the views of his wife, preparations were at once commenced for their departure. Madame La Desma converted all her portable property into ready money, and, packing up her diamonds, worth nearly twelve thousand dollars, they were prepared to leave.

Suddenly Clermont, with an exhibition of annoyance, remembered that he had forgotten something of importance in the city, and requested his wife to deliver a note which would arrange everything satisfactorily. This the lady cheerfully consented to do, and taking a carriage proceeded to carry out the wishes of her husband. When she returned, to her chagrin and mortification, her beloved had decamped, taking with him about twenty thousand dollars in money and her diamonds and other valuable jewels.

"Hell hath no fury like a woman scorned," says the poet, and the bereaved lady, drying her tears, at once commenced operations with the view of recovering her property and punishing her false lover. My Agency was employed, and

"*Clermont requested his wife to deliver a note that would arrange everything satisfactorily.*" **Page 93.**

upon looking over some of the wearing apparel which the gentleman had left behind him, the name of Lewis C. Clermont was found printed upon one of the inside pockets. Of course, his identity at once became known, and the deserted wife was informed that her gallant husband had taken unto himself a wife before he had yielded to the seductive charms of her beautiful self. At the receipt of this information the lady became exceedingly enraged, and determined to have him arrested if he could be found.

My son, William A. Pinkerton, interested himself in the case, and he soon traced the gentleman to San Francisco. Upon acquainting the police authorities of that city with a description of the man and his antecedents, they were at once enabled to account for the appearance of a successful forger there who had swindled several of their prominent men of various amounts, which aggregated to nearly thirty-five thousand dollars.

His plan there was to offer raised securities to the moneyed men of the city, also to the various banking institutions, as collateral security for loans which he desired to effect, and, being affable in his manner and welcomed by the first families of the city socially, he had no difficulty in being accommodated. Of course detection did not follow until the loans matured, when the valueless collaterals were presented for payment. In San Francisco he operated as Lewis Raymond, and had disappeared before discovery overtook him. As he had mingled quite extensively in the social circles of the Golden City, the swindled gentlemen declined to pursue him for fear that some scandal would result therefrom.

From California he went to Peru, where he remained for

some time under the name of Colonel Ralph Forrest, and but little is known of his career while there.

Early in 1876, a messenger from the office of C. & H, Borie, a prominent banking firm in Philadelphia, entered my Agency there, and informed us of the suspicious actions of a lady who had attempted to purchase a small amount of Reading railroad stock. She had desired the certificates to be made out in those of one share each, and seemed to be doubtful about the name in which they were to be issued, and altogether acted in such a manner as to convince the bankers that something was wrong.

A "shadow" was placed upon the lady, and she was traced to the Bingham House, where she was joined by a man; they then took a carriage and drove out to the West Philadelphia depot, took the train for New York, where they arrived in due time, the detective following in the same train.

From the description given of this man, I had no doubt that he was Lewis C. Clermont—Colonel Ralph Forrest—Lewis Raymond, and lastly Louis La Desma.

A requisition was obtained, and both the gentleman and lady were escorted back to Philadelphia, under the care of attaches of my office, and an investigation of his effects at this time resulted in finding a full assortment of forgers' implements in his possession.

He was tried in Philadelphia at the instance of Mrs. Dumel —upon the double charge of bigamy and larceny—and here the first wife gave another evidence of self-sacrifice and devotion, as rare as it was heroic.

She appeared at the trial, and denied most emphatically the **existence of** a marriage between herself and Clermont, which of course, caused the charge of bigamy to fall; and, with it also fell all hope of convicting the man for stealing from the only legitimate wife he was proven to possess. The wife was enabled to swear thus successfully, because the great fire in Chicago—the city in which his marriage had been performed—had destroyed the Court-House, and all the records which might have disproved her testimony, could they have been procured.

Clermont was therefore discharged from custody, and frequently, during his travels thereafter, my General Superintendent, George H. Bangs, received letters from the bold and dashing forger, informing him of his whereabouts; and a day or two before the last operation that he attempted, he wrote to Mr. Bangs, stating that he would "no doubt hear of something important from him in a day or two."

How *important* it was to one of the actors, the following will show.

In the month of July, 1875, there appeared at Chambersburg, in Pennsylvania, a gentleman, accompanied by his wife and an invalid young man, who was introduced as the brother of the lady.

The gentleman represented himself as Colonel Ralph Rolland, who had commanded the Louisiana Tigers, and had been finally promoted to a Brigadier-Generalship in the rebel army. He was exceedingly affable in his manners, kind and gentle in his deportment, faultless in his dress, and was possessed of a thorough education.

His wife was a beautiful, modest little woman, who appeared to be devoted to her husband and her invalid brother,

and who won many hearts by her gentle and delicate attentionf
to the two gentlemen.

They selected rooms at the prominent hotel in the place,
and settled down to the enjoyment of the comforts and luxuries
of life w'th all the grace and dignity of thorough aristocrats.
Their object in coming to this place was stated to be the health
of the young man, but he, finding no improvement, left for a
more salubrious climate, and the colonel and his wife, who had
formed a decided attachment for the place, concluded to remain,
with the view of eventually settling there definitely.

Of course such a family did not remain long unacknowl-
edged. Sympathy for the sick boy first attracted their attention, and soon the winning manners and cultured minds of the
husband and wife made for them many warm friends among
the wealthy citizens and their families.

Among the number was George R. Messersmith, Esq., a
gentleman of thorough education and refinement, and who occupied the responsible position of cashier of the National Bank
in that place. Their intimacy ripened into a warm friendship,
and Colonel Rolland and his wife became frequent visitors at
the residence of Mr. Messersmith, who occupied the remaining portions of the building used by the bank.

Mr. Messersmith being of an advanced literary turn of
mind, possessed a fine library of rare and valuable works, and
Colonel Rolland professing similar tastes, the two gentleman
would indrlge in cultured criticisms of their favorite authors,
and in friendly converse upon congenial literary topics, both of
them evidently finding reciprocal enjoyment in the expressed
views of the other.

By these means they became generally acquainted, and the colonel having occasion to be absent from the town upon several occasions, the wife was usually invited to the residences of some of her friends, in order that she might not experience the loneliness attendant upon the absence of her husband.

Their residence in Chambersburg continued until March, 1876, when the arrival of another gentleman from the South, who gave his name as D. Johnson, made an addition to the party.

This gentleman, upon his arrival, deposited with the bank two large packages which he represented as containing valuables, and by that means at once established for himself a reputation for wealth.

On the evening of the 24th day of March, Colonel Rolland and Mr. Johnson, lighting their cigars, started from the hotel, apparently for a short stroll. Reaching the residence of Mr. Messersmith they rang the bell, and inquired for that gentleman. Being informed that he was not at home, but would return in a few minutes, they went away, stating that they would call again.

Returning in about fifteen minutes, they were shown into the cashier's room by a Mr. Kindline—a brother-in-law of the cashier, and who also resided with him—and here they found Mr. Messersmith engaged in writing.

For some time the gentlemen conversed in a friendly business manner, Rolland desiring the opinion of the cashier upon the merits of a farm in the vicinity, which he expressed himself as desirous of purchasing.

During the conversation Mr. Johnson presented a package, which he alleged was very valuable, and requested the gentlemanly cashier to place it in the vault of the bank, as he was to leave for New York early the following morning. **Mr.** Messersmith declined to open the vault that evening, stating that he would deposit the package in a safe place, and when the messenger arrived in the morning, it would then be placed in the vault.

To this the other readily consented, and requested the cashier to forward the package to them in New York by express, should they not return for them in the morning. Mr. Messersmith was about noting down the address given him, when suddenly his head was enveloped with a hood or sack, and he felt strong hands clutching at his throat. A handkerchief was thrust into his mouth, and angry voices threatened to shoot him if he attempted to resist or to give an alarm.

Undismayed by these threats, however, the courageous cashier resisted them manfully, and being quite muscular, in his random hitting he knocked one of his assailants to the floor. Realizing the situation fully by this time, he determined to foil the robbers if possible, and immediately called loudly for help.

His cries alarmed his assailants, and they fled precipitately, but before they could reach the front door, they were confronted by Mr. Kindline, who barred their passage. They threatened to shoot, but Mr. Kindline remaining firm, they turned about and ran toward the back of the house, intending to escape through the kitchen.

The alarm had been sounded, and frightened citizens came running toward the bank. Rolland jumped from the porch, but was immediately captured by Mr. Kindline, who had followed them, and by two other gentlemen who had been

"Suddenly his head was enveloped in a hood."

Page 104

attracted by the noise. Rolland was immediately disarmed of an elegant revolver and a jewel-hilted dirk knife, which he carried in either hand, and was placed in custody. Johnson succeeded in making his escape by reaching the rear of the house and scaling the fence.

Upon searching the quondam rebel colonel a package containing thirty thousand dollars, which had been received by the bank that evening by express, was discovered, and which he had evidently seized during the first attack upon Mr. Messersmith.

Johnson was pursued and captured upon a railroad train at Mercersburg, Va., and was brought back to Chambersburg to join the society of his accomplice within the jail at that place.

A search of the rooms occupied by these men at the hotel, revealed the presence of a dark lantern and several burglarious implements, while in the yard of the bank was found a sack containing a full set of cracksman's tools. Several gags, and two bottles of chloroform, thus showing the evident intention of the robbers to make a thorough job of the matter in hand.

At the trial which followed, upon the testimony of some of my operatives and others, the late Colonel of the Louisiana Tigers was fully recognized as the handsome outlaw, who had been previously known as Lewis C. Clermont, with the several aliases already mentioned.

After due trial the daring robbers were convicted and sentenced to a term of ten years in the Eastern Penitentiary, to which they were soon after conveyed. An appeal was taken in their behalf to the Supreme Court, and upon some legal technicality—-it being shown that they were tried for

5*

robbery, and convicted of burglary—a new trial was granted, and they were remanded back to Chambersburg.

While in the Eastern Penitentiary my son, William A. Pinkerton, in company with Charles Thompson Jones of Philadelphia, visited the two men, who were confined together, with the view of identifying the companion of Clermont, who had thus far escaped recognition.

Upon entering the cell, William at once recognized the man as Adney C. Weeks, a resident of Chicago, who had been a carpenter there, and who was married to the sister of Mrs. Clermont. The romantic stories told him by his dashing and unprincipled brother-in-law had no doubt been too much for him, and, yielding to his seductive influences, he became a ready tool in his hands.

As William entered the cell the man known as Johnson immediately covered his face with his hands, as though desiring to evade the gaze of his visitor, and William, having satisfied himself as to the identity of the man, turned to leave the cell. As he did so Clermont requested him to return, and, ascertaining that his companion was recognized, urgently requested him not to divulge his identity to his friends in Chicago, where he had hitherto been regarded as an honest man and an industrious mechanic.

While in the Chambersburg jail, awaiting their second trial, their conduct was most exemplary, and their observance of the prison discipline gained for them the favor of the officials in charge.

Upon their new trial they were again convicted, and this time they were sentenced to a term of servitude of twelve years.

On the morning following their conviction the officer of the prison went his usual rounds, and on stopping before the cell of Clermont discovered to his dismay that the bird had flown. Consternation and alarm followed, the prison was thoroughly searched and pursuit was at once begun; but the wily burglar had succeeded in making good his escape.

He was traced to Chicago and finally arrested and conveyed to the Central Station in that city, awaiting a demand from the Pennsylvania authorities for his conveyance to that State.

While at this station his wife gave another evidence of her faithfulness and devotion, which, while being directed in an improper channel, was none the less the courageous act of a loving and undaunted wife.

Disguising herself in male attire she was admitted to the Central Station, and reaching the hall above the cell where her graceless husband was confined she attempted to drop into his apartment some saws and a pistol, with which he would be enabled to effect his escape. This plan would undoubtedly have succeeded save for the fact that, seeking a confidant in the transaction, the wife was unfortunate enough to select a stool-pigeon of the authorities, who immediately informed them of what was going on, and the effort was frustrated.

He was therefore conducted back to Philadelphia and safely secured in the Eastern Penitentiary. During his incarceration he made frequent attempts to escape, but in all of which he failed of success. He attempted to bribe the keepers, feigned insanity, and secreted tools about his person. At one time he complained of a pain in his back, and a porous adhesive plaster was applied as a remedy. Shortly afterwards, upon taking his bath, he evinced so much care for the medicinal application that suspicion was aroused, and between the plaster and his skin several fine saws were discovered, which had evidently been furnished him by friends from without. At another time excessive anxiety in regard to a pair of new shoes resulted in their examination, and articles of the same nature were found concealed between the soles.

During the entire time of his imprisonment his wife was assiduous in her attentions; never faltering in her love for him or in her efforts to relieve his wants or minister to his necessities. No sacrifice was considered too great, no duty too onerous, no task too laborious for this faithful woman to perform.

Long confinement and the restraints of prison life soon began to have their effect upon him, however, and on the 7th day of August last, after a brief illness, he died in his cell, still attended by the faithful woman who had loved him and cared for him to the last.

This is but another evidence of noble talents wasted, another story of a weak yielding to the tempting voice of the siren of temptation. This man fell a victim to the dazzling allurements of wealth dishonestly obtained, and the punishment, sure and dreadful, has overtaken him.

Immediately upon his decease, his effects were examined, and several large stones were discovered in the hollow handle of his shaving brush. These stones were supposed to be diamonds and of immense value.

Mrs. Dumel, who, it will be remembered, was deceived into a marriage with him, and who is now in straitened circumstances, having lost nearly all she possessed through the machinations of the dishonest man she was induced to marry, upon learning of this fact immediately wrote to me in regard to the matter, believing that the diamonds thus found were none other than those which she had been despoiled of.

A visit was accordingly paid to the widow of the dead criminal, and from her it was learned that the stones—according to her statement—were simply paste imitations of no value, and designed to be used as bribes to the jailers, in order to effect his release from confinement, if possible.

What occasioned much surprise was the seeming forbearance displayed by both of these ladies toward each other. Each married to the same man, each, it is supposed, loved him truly. No word of complaint is breathed, and each one sympathizes with the other in the wrecking of their two lives by the dishonorable actions of their law-defying husband.

What the further result of this investigation will be I cannot as yet determine. Whether the stones will be eventually proven to be genuine and valuable, and thus relieve the distresses of the despoiled Mrs. Dumel, or whether they will be found to be mere imitations, and thus furnish another evidence of the cupidity of the scoundrel who has passed away, the future will develop.

The man is dead, and his story is told.

CHAPTER VI.

A Bold Barber.

BARBERS and tailors have for a long period of time been popularly considered as not possessing an over-supply of those qualities which have made men famous for bravery and daring deeds. It has been said, and even transferred to immortal song, that it required fully nine tailors to make a man; and as to the barber, the only fame he has been in the habit of acquiring has been chiefly through the dexterous use of the razor, not only upon the face, but, as in the case of colored tonsorial artists, of various practical arguments, were the keenest razor and the quickest hand always get the best of the dispute.

But a certain barber in New Milford, Connecticut, on the night of Sunday, March 20, 1871, proved himself brave enough to point a gun, steady enough to pull a trigger, and enough the man for the occasion to deserve, and secure, the thanks of the community.

New Milford is situated on the Housatonic River, and is one of the prettiest towns in that "land of steady habits." The people of the place attend church three times on each succeeding Sunday, and bar-rooms are at a discount in the community. But occasionally lawless men from the city of New

"A Bold Barber"

York visit the peaceful and pious town for the purpose of replenishing their depleted pockets.

On the night in question a daring attempt was made to rob the First National Bank of New Milford, and but for the gallantry and presence of the bold barber already referred to a grand haul would have been made, as nearly all the farmers in the vicinity were in the habit of depositing their spare cash in the bank.

The bank was a one-story building, situated on the main street, near the railroad depot. Contiguous to the bank, and only separated from it by a narrow alleyway, was a two-story frame house, having a barber's shop on the first floor. On the second floor was the residence of the barber, where he slept and took his meals; and his windows overlooked the windows of the bank.

About midnight of the day mentioned the barber, fatigued with the toils of the day, was about retiring, when he heard strange noises proceeding from the bank. He went to the window and saw several rascals at work with their tools with great zeal, in forcing open locks and drawing bolts. Seizing his gun, which was hanging upon the wall, he awaited until he got a good opportunity to get as large a crowd as possible together, when he discharged its contents through the window squarely into the party.

A howl of pain from several voices was the result of this, and the robbers beat a precipitous retreat. Some citizens were awakened and alarmed by the report of the gun, and in their rushing to the bank, everything was found in confusion. The outside door had been completely shattered and the second door had been made ready for opening. A full set of burglars'

tools was found in the bank. Three pieces of string led in
different directions—north, east and west—while a man had
been posted at each end of these, opposite the bank, and to the
right and left of the bank, to signal a warning of the approach
of individuals, or of any other danger necessary to be made
aware of; but the prompt action of the bold barber made all
their work of no avail, all their precautions futile, and prevented the burglars securing over fifty thousand dollars in bills and
government bonds, which were snugly stowed away within the
vaults.

CHAPTER VII.

Making Settlements.

I HAVE been all my life irrevocably and unalterably opposed to compounding crimes with criminals. I have held as an unchangeable principle, that with the proper encouragement the honest detective could not only bring professional thieves to justice, but also secure for their patrons the larger portion of what plunder may have been taken. But it is much easier for certain classes of detectives, who care less for personal integrity and the honor of their profession than for quick gains, to fraternize with thieves and become the agent between them and the parties robbed, than with unceasing labor and unimpeachable integrity to follow the outlaw class to the bitter end and compel the return of their plunder, and their punishment for the crimes they have been guilty of.

So it has come about that in every city there may be found numbers of these detectives, who seek every opportunity of securing newspaper notoriety for trifling achievements, so that they may secure public confidence, while all their mind and energies are bent upon secretly increasing their acquaintance and intimacy with known and unknown burglars and forgers, to whom they unblushingly offer their services to arrange settlements and secure immunity from punishment.

As old Fagan, the great thief-trainer, in Dickens' *Oliver Twist*, was immeasurably worse than the young thieves he trained, so are these skulking scamps more dangerous and despicable than those for whom they operate, and are morally responsible, if not legally, for much of the nefarious work done, for the simple reason that, were not these opportunities offered for making settlements with plundered banks and business men, and in such a manner that prosecution is always avoided, the danger of deception and consequent punishment would be so great that the vast army of aristocratic thieves of the present time would soon dwindle away to straggling parties of hunted and desperate guerrillas.

If these agents or "go-betweens" are responsible for the daring and increase of thieves, certain business men are responsible for the existence of these "go-betweens." Their bank or business-house is entered and robbed, and during the hullaballoo and excitement an irresponsible and slinking agent, called a detective, presents himself, and vaguely hints that he has "certain information" which will lead to the recovery of the funds, or a partial recovery. After a deal of dickering and negotiating, during which time the agent is drawing heavily on the parties already robbed, the proceeds of the robbery are returned if they are in stocks and securities, upon the payment of a handsome percentage, and if they were in cash and government bonds, after a still handsomer deduction from the amount taken, when the "agent" receives a large bonus from the thieves for his trouble, and the parties who have recovered the portion of their property are compelled to agree not to prosecute.

For one such robbery and settlement, half a dozen more

follow, and in the interests of business safety, I cannot too strongly urge that, whenever a robbery of funds occurs, that those meeting with the misfortune should never, under any circumstances, employ officers who work for rewards, or who hint at compromising with thieves. All this sort of thing increases business insecurity, and elevates impudent professional burglars to almost a business standing.

In order to give my reader an idea of how these "settlements" are made by these bogus private detectives, as well as by official detectives, to a certain extent, I will relate a *bona fide* instance coming under my notice several years since.

On July 23, 1875, the National and Savings Bank of Winthrop, Maine, was entered, and the safe blown open, and robbed of about ninety thousand dollars, mostly in government, railway and municipal bonds, the principal portion of the loss falling upon the Savings Bank, and the National Bank only suffering a loss of about ten thousand dollars. It was a bold and skillfully executed bank robbery, and though a reward of ten thousand dollars was promptly offered, there appeared but little prospect that the local officers in whose hands the matter was placed, would accomplish anything.

A few days subsequent to the robbery, a certain New York "detective," of the sort I have described, happened in town. He had been in Boston, he said, working up some very important case, of course, and being so near Winthrop, thought he would take a run up to the place and satisfy his curiosity concerning the bank robbery. He had an inkling, he stated, of who the robbers were, and he truly believed that he could, by careful work, after a short time lay his hands upon the men, or at least, if that could not be done, could "work back"

the bonds, o1 a greater portion of them, to the rightfu‌
owners.

The safe which had been blown open had been sent to
Bostcn, and replaced by a stronger one; but the detective.
whom for convenience I will call Mr. Crooker, learned all the
particulars of the robbery, and all the little minutiæ concerning
the appearance of the safe, and though not getting much encouragement from the bank officers, after promising to communicate with them, took his departure.

A few days after he had gone, the bank officers received
a letter from Crooker asking for a full description of the supposed robbers. This information was promptly sent. At a
still later day another letter was received from Crooker, to the
effect that in his opinion the robbers or property might be
reached, but in a few days more he was in hopes to fully satisfy himself whether or not his opinion was well founded.
When this time had expired, another letter was received by
the bank officers, from Crooker, requesting them to send one
of their number to New York without delay, with authority
to act for them.

When this last letter was received, the bank trustees had a
meeting immediately, and decided to comply with Crooker's
request. The result was, one of the bank trustees was unanimously selected to proceed to New York and see Crooker.

On September 6, the bank officer started for New York,
reaching that city the next forenoon. He found Crooker at
his "office," which, for prudential reasons, as Crooker said,
was in the hallway of French's Hotel. Here the bogus detective informed the trustee that he had been approached by a
middleman in the interest of the robbers, who offered to make

a restitution of the property on certain conditions. Any man of ordinary judgment could hardly understand why the middleman had not made personal application to the bank officers. Why could not this mysterious middleman have dealt directly with the bank ?

The truth of the matter was simply that Mr. Crooker was all the middleman there was in the business, and the party who had "approached" him was merely one of the robbers. The bogus detective was merely a blind ; a willing tool for the burglars ; simply the something to be used to protect the thieves, effect the settlement, pocket his share of the proceeds and secure immunity, and, if the whole truth were known, it would not be a strange thing to have learned that Mr. Crooker was, himself, engaged either in the planning of, or in actual participation with the robbers.

As the result of the bank trustee's interview with Crooker, an arrangement was made for a meeting with this middleman two days later. At about noon of that day the meeting occurred at a secluded place in the city, and not in a desirable locality. It was held in a room over a bar-room frequented by the lower and perhaps more dangerous class of society.

Prompt to the hour of appointment the middleman put in an appearance. He was a sharp, off-hand fellow, who evidently knew his business. The first question which the bank officer put to him was whether he was the person authorized to act for the parties holding the stolen property. His reply was :

"I have been requested to, and have consented to."

"Do you know," continued the officer, "of the whereabouts of the parties ?"

"I do not."

" Should any arrangement be made at this meeting, how long
a time on your part do you need to carry it out ?'

" Probably ten days—a week at least."

" Should any arrangement be made to-day, am I to understand," remarked the officer, "that such arrangement embraces
the Government bonds stolen ?"

" It cannot embrace Government bonds, nor the currency
taken, but all the other securities taken."

The trustee eyed the man for a moment, and then remarked :
" Am I to regard your answer as a final one in relation to Government bonds ?"

" Yes," replied the man firmly, "the Government bonds
cannot be restored."

Turning to Mr. Crooker, who had all the time sat there
with the air of one performing a great public duty, when he
was in reality only playing his part in the grand scheme of
robbery, the officer said : " If this be the fact, I don't know
as I have any further business with this man."

At this point in the conversation there ensued a painful
silence, during which the so-called " middleman " maintained
an air of absolute indifference, as he smoked a cigar and twirled
a cane which he carried.

The silence was finally broken by Crooker, who remarked,
according to pre-arrangement, " Cannot some portion of the
bonds be reached in some way ?"

" No, they cannot," replied the man firmly.

Colonel Wing then observed : " Inasmuch as I am here,
we may as well see upon what terms the proposed securities
can be returned."

" My directions are for twenty per cent.," said the robber.

Colonel Wing then raised the question whether the twenty per cent. had reference to the face of the bonds or their market value, at the same time stating that a portion of the bonds had become greatly depreciated since their purchase by the bank.

To this the man replied coolly, " As a business man, I should say that the twenty per cent. should apply to the market value of the bonds."

" Is this proposition your ultimatum?" asked Colonel Wing.

"Yes, these are my instructions."

At this stage of the proceedings, the accommodating Mr. Crooker suggested an adjournment of the interview to a time three hours later, which proposition was approved. Another place was also agreed upon for the next interview.

Now, this little maneuver was simply for the purpose of delaying matters and causing the representative of the bank to get, as it were, a glimpse of the property, and thus become the more anxious to secure it at any sacrifice. The change of place of meeting was to give an air of importance and mystery to the entire transaction.

The real object, however, was to permit the wily Mr. Crooker to consult with the robbers and get their very best terms.

When the second meeting did take place, the alleged middleman was not present; but Mr. Crooker, quite naturally, acted as his mouth-piece. The latter then told Colonel Wing that the best and only terms on which the property would be restored was on payment of ten thousand dollars, and that, even then, none of the property returned would include **either** the money or Government bonds taken from the bank.

Crooker also reported that he was satisfied that the **thieves** had disposed of the money and Government bonds, and that both were now beyond their reach.

Colonel Wing then asked time of Crooker to report the result of his negotiations to the trustees of the bank, and ascertain whether they would accede to, or decline, the proposition.

Crooker pretended to approve of this course, but at the same time intimated that any unnecessary delay would certainly prove dangerous; as such men as these great bank-robbers were very reckless fellows—cared no more for ten thousand dollars than ordinary men would for a dollar—and after they had condescended to take upon themselves the risk of any manner of negotiation, anything looking like trifling, or which might be construed by them as indicating treachery, might result in their immediate disappearance and the utter destruction of the securities.

Colonel Wing then returned to Maine and reported the result of his mission to the bank officers, who were unanimously of the opinion—as they then saw no other means of securing the property, and the bank had been placed in the hands of a Receiver for the purpose of winding up its affairs—that the terms proposed should be accepted.

Colonel Wing then obtained an order from the court, authorizing him to offer a reward not exceeding ten thousand dollars, for the recovery of the securities, and he was furnished the necessary funds for his mission.

Mr. Crooker, who had, of course, been kept well informed of how matters had been going in Maine, made a pretense **of** being in Baltimore, engaged on a very "heavy case" for the Government, all of which was simply for the purpose of keepi ig up his appearance of respectability; and to that city the bank officer now went, prepared to close the negotiation.

On the two meeting in the monumental city, Crooker communicated by telegraph with the bank-robbers' agent in New York city, and received a response from him to the effect that he would meet the two on a designated evening, at the St. Nicholas Hotel, in New York.

Arriving at that city, Crooker first met the agent alone, claiming it was necessary to be certain that the former arrangement would be strictly adhered to. This meeting between Crooker and the agent was alleged to have been held at the St. Nicholas, agreeable to the dispatch received at Baltimore; and Colonel Wing was also informed that another place of meeting for the same evening had been arranged for, when the stolen property should be delivered into the hands of Crooker, and by him placed in the possession of Colonel Wing, who, in return, should hand over the ten thousand dollars, in payment therefor, to Crooker, who should give the same to the agent.

The place of meeting agreed upon was up town, in a small back room, up two flights of stairs, in a building occupied by a saloon, and, altogether, a villainous room in a villainous location.

At the hour designated, Colonel Wing and Crooker were promptly on the spot, where, after waiting a few minutes, a knock at the door of the apartment in which they were seated was heard, and, on being told to "come in," the robbers' "agent" appeared, his presence there being in accordance with the previous arrangement.

6

In his hand he held a package, and Colonel Wing at once noticed that it was not the same person who had played his part so coolly and nonchalantly at the meeting held in Duane street, the week previous.

He entered the room with a sidewise movement, leaving the door partially open. It was evident that he did not wish to be recognized. He had on a thick, heavy overcoat, with the collar drawn up around his neck, and wore a soft hat drawn well down over his head. Besides this, he held a white handkerchief to his face, which completely concealed his features, with the exception of his eyes, which he never, in a single instance, fixed on Colonel Wing, but kept looking downward throughout his entire stay.

There is no question, in my mind, that this man, like the person who had officiated at the previous interview, was simply one of the enterprising Mr. Crooker's men, who was palmed off upon Colonel Wing in this mysterious and awe-inspiring manner, to impress upon him, as he was entirely ignorant of these "bogus detective" tricks, the wonderful act of official kindness he, Mr. Crooker, was executing.

Advancing to Crooker the mysterious stranger asked, in a very hoarse, and apparently altered voice, if he held the money?

Crooker then turned to Colonel Wing, and requested him to pass it over, which he did

The package handed to Crooker contained the ten thousand dollars, all of the denomination of one-hundred-dollar bills, which Colonel Wing had drawn through the banking-house of C. M. Bailey, in exchange for a draft on Boston, drawn by the

"*Making Settlements.*"

National Bank of Winthrop, which he had brought from that city.

When Crooker received the package, Colonel Wing requested him to count it, and at the same time to hold it until the package which the robber's agent had brought with him had been examined.

After Crooker had solemnly counted the money and found it to be entirely correct, the thief's agent instantly left the room without so much as a word of farewell. He had played his part neatly and made his exit in a manner best suited to keep up the air of mystery.

Colonel Wing then began looking over the package, which occupied nearly two hours, as he was particular to have the bonds which it was found to contain correspond with the schedule of the stolen property he had with him. Everything was found to be all right, everything being returned as it had been agreed upon, and he was unexpectedly and pleasantly disappointed to find that none of the papers had been injured by the explosion of the safe.

After Colonel Wing had expressed himself satisfied with the condition of the papers, Crooker stepped out, and, as he informed the colonel, found the agent and paid him. The probabilities are that he merely stepped into the hallway and distributed the money about his person, when the bank officer, everything being concluded, returned to the St. Nicholas, where he was sojourning, and deposited the securities in the safe.

This ended the transaction, with the following result:

The banks lost originally ninety thousand dollars in currency, Government bonds and negotiable securities. Of this amount forty thousand dollars was in currency and Government bonds, which were immediately converted into currency.   Fifty thousand dollars in securities was taken, foɪ which the thieves, through their agent, the " bogus detective," secured ten thousand dollars in cash; so that, altogether, the bank-robbers secured fifty thousand dollars in money and complete immunity from punishment; all of which would never have resulted had not this system of " go-between bogus detectives " been in existence.

There are many other modes of accomplishing the " making of settlements" or " working back " stolen property, as it is called ; but they all contain the villainous go-between principle shown in this account, and they invariably disclose the earmarks of the fraudulent detective, who is worse than a thief, because, under the cloak of a respectable calling, which is more than any other a necessity to business men, he *makes* thieves by rendering their calling safe and profitable.   There never existed a more pestilential set of rogues, and they would disappear from necessity, should all reputable business men join in their extermination by utterly ignoring them.

CHAPTER VIII.

A Gentlemanly Thief, or, the Robber on the Seas.

IN 1875, there appeared upon the criminal horizon an in
dividual who for a long time baffled the efforts of the
detectives to fasten his crimes upon him, and to escape the
just punishment of the laws which he violated with such im-
punity.

Jean Sprungli—or, as he was wont to style himself, Springly
—was a very gentlemanly appearing man, of fine personal ap
pearance and possessed of considerable education. A Swiss by
birth, he had traveled so extensively and spoke several languages
so fluently, that it was almost impossible to determine of what
nationality he had sprung.

His first appearance in the United States was made in 1875,
when he came under my notice as being suspected of robbing
some of the passengers upon the American steamship *Illinois,*
then and now commanded by that excellent seaman and admirable gentleman, Captain Shackford.

At an interview which was had with Sprungli at this time,
it was learned that he had at one time been an extensive merchant in Africa, and that, failing upon that continent, he had
engaged in mercantile pursuits in Peru. This venture also appeared to have been unsuccessful, and, finding legitimate busi·

ness unprofitable, he had voluntarily commenced the practice of criminality which, until his final arrest and imprisonment, he continued with various degrees of profit, but always with sufficient good fortune to gratify his tastes and provide for his needs.

The business which he thus chose for himself and which he seemed to prefer to the more honorable positions of legitimate trade, was the novel one of crossing and recrossing the ocean, upon the various first-class steamers, in the character of an opulent and very agreeable cabin passenger.

During the daytime he would engage the passengers in conversation, in which his learning and his extensive travels served his purpose to a wonderful degree, and made him a very entertaining companion upon a monotonous ocean voyage. By this means he would be enabled to inform himself of the habits, and in many cases of the possessions of his fellow-passengers, and then, by watching his opportunity, he would slip into their state-rooms while their occupants were absent or asleep, and help himself to all the valuables that came within his reach.

For two years passengers upon the steamers of the Pacific Line from Liverpool to Lisbon made frequent and dire complaints of being robbed, but all resulting in the discovery of no information that would lead to the apprehension of the thief or the recovery of the articles stolen.

In 1874 a very extensive and seemingly mysterious robbery was committed on board the steamer *Potosi*. A general feeling of suspicion was manifested, and both passengers and cabin servants were carefully examined, and their trunks searched, with the view of fastening the robbery upon some one of them. So skillfully had the robbery been performed, however, that the real criminal successfully eluded not only detection but suspicion, while many innocent persons were not only compelled to suffer the actual loss of articles stolen, but to endure the mortification of being suspected of the thefts. A young French officer on board the *Potosi* was so impressed with a sense of shame upon being suspected, that he blew his brains out in the Lisbon lazaretto, preferring, as he stated, voluntary death to the stigma of being suspected as a thief.

On the list of passengers appeared the name of Jean Sprungli. He was well and favorably known by the officers of the ship—and, indeed, by many of the passengers. He had been a frequent sojourner at Lisbon, where he made his headquarters at the Hotel Central, and where he was regarded with great favor by every one—by the guests, for his universal courtesy and charming conversational powers; by the proprietors, for his pecuniary punctuality; and by the attendants, for his affable treatment and liberality.

Certainly, a gentleman so much admired could not be associated with the robbery of his fellow-passengers, and not a breath of suspicion was uttered against him, while others, entirely innocent, were compelled to submit to the humiliating formula of a search.

Although succeeding so admirably in evading actual suspicion in the *Potosi* affair, Sprungli deemed it expedient to transfer the sphere of his operations to some other steamship line, and in 1875, he engaged a stateroom on the American steamship *Illinois*.

Nothing occurred upon the journey from Liverpool to Philadelphia to mar the pleasure of the voyage—the wealthy and urbane Jean Sprungli had made himself universally popular, and was the recipient of urgent invitations to visit his fellow-voyagers should his stay in Philadelphia warrant such a proceeding.

As the vessel neared the entrance to Delaware Bay, and just as the Cape May lighthouse could be plainly discerned, and when the necessity for getting one's effects together occurred, some one discovered to his dismay that he had been robbed. Upon this fact becoming known a general overlooking of baggage was instituted, and soon one after another of the passengers, with rueful faces, would make the unpleasant announcement that they, too, had suffered in a similar manner, and that many of their valuables — watches, jewelry, and clothing—were no longer in their possession.

When the vessel reached the dock I was immediately notified of the occurrence, and the Superintendent of my Philadelphia Agency was directed to undertake the examination. Of course no one was permitted to leave the vessel, and a thorough search was instituted of the baggage of every passenger, yet, strange to say, without discovering a single clew to the robbery or of finding a single article of the stolen property.

Sprungli's trunks were examined among the rest, and the means by which his plunder was successfully hidden from the minute investigation of the detectives will be shown hereafter.

Sprungli did **not,** however, seem to fancy the American police, and soon returned to his old game of steamship robbing.

In July he took passage on one of the Pacific Line of steamers again. This time the *Liguria.* It would have been better for him had he waited a little longer. No sooner

had the vessel sailed than the Liverpool police, who had become alarmed at the frequency of robberies on these vessels,
and had determined to make a general investigation of every
steamer that sailed, telegraphed to the authorities of Bordeaux
to watch for certain suspicious characters who had been on
board the Pacific steamers when the other robberies occurred.

Acting upon these instructions, an able French detective
went on board the vessel at Bordeaux; but fortune seemed to
favor her admirer, and Neptune assisting in the work, the
officer became so sea-sick that he was unable to leave his berth
during the entire voyage. Up to this time no event had occurred upon the journey to disturb the good-nature and
thorough enjoyment of the passengers. Sprungli, as usual,
had performed his part of the entertainment with great success, and was hailed by one and all as a genial gentleman,
whose society was enjoyable and whose conversation was both
edifying and instructive.

On the first night, however, after leaving Bordeaux, a
series of robberies took place, many of the passengers losing
sums of money, watches, rings and other valuables. The excitement became intense. Everybody suspected everybody
else and were suspected in turn; that is, everybody except Mr.
Sprungli, who bore his own alleged losses with marked serenity, sympathized so acutely with those of others, and whose
voice was raised the loudest in indignation at the unknown
perpetrators of the crime.

Despite his cheerfulness, however, he became at last an object of quiet suspicion. He had overplayed his part, and some
of his previous admirers had been enabled to see through the
gloss and tinsel of his pretensions. When the vessel reached

6*

Vigo, a telegram was quietly sent to the Lisbon agent of the steamship company, asking him to confer with the police.

This conference was had, and when the vessel arrived at her destination, the authorities were upon the lookout for Sprungli, and special agents were detailed to watch the passengers as they disembarked.

Among the first to leave the ship was Sprungli. With a jaunty, self-satisfied air he bade farewell to his fellow-passengers, and, stepping lightly upon the gangway, he landed upon the sacred soil of Portugal.

Behind him, however, followed the "shadow," and after walking aimlessly about the streets of the city for some time, he took a street car and proceeded to the Custom House, apparently with the object of overseeing the inspection of his baggage.

Without notifying him of their intention, the police added their vigilance to his own, but their scrutiny met with no reward. No indications appeared to exist of an attempt at smuggling, and everything in his possession seemed to be honestly his own.

This ordeal over, the newly-landed passenger was about to leave the Custom House, when one of the detectives politely introduced himself, and stated that he was under instructions to escort Mr. Sprungli and his belongings to the office of the Civil Governor.

Mr. Sprungli at once became indignant, and protested that such action was a gross insult upon the honor and dignity of a gentleman, and that, should this course be insisted upon, he would be forced to regard the functionary who had given the order as a very *uncivil* governor indeed. Despite his bluster

The discovery of the stolen valuables.

Page 181

and his threat to invoke the protecting aid of the Swiss lion, the police proved inexorable, and he was compelled, very much against his will, to pay his respects to the Governor, and his trunks were again subjected to a thorough search.

Again nothing suspicious was discovered, and Mr. Sprungl., with the air of injured and outraged dignity, was about to withdraw, when Casterno Bianco, chief of the detectives, noticed that the iron-work of the trunks, instead of being riveted, were fastened with screws, several of which appeared to be loose and unsettled. The iron bands about the trunks were directed to be unscrewed, and then, between the outside and the lining, there were exposed to view sixteen secret compartments, each filled with quite a jeweler's stock of watches, chains, studs, pearls, diamonds, and other valuables, together with rather a goodly stock of shining sovereigns.

Thus brought face to face with his crimes, the dignity and bravado of Sprungli at once gave way, and he made a full confession of his transactions, but by some means entirely inscrutable he succeeded in evading the authorities at Lisbon and left for Cadiz, where, however, he was again arrested.

An attempt was then made to have him sent back to England, but through some informality, and the efforts of a keen lawyer, he for the second time succeeded in evading the law.

He again took passage for America, but his fame had preceded him. To the affair of the *Illinois* was now added that of the *Liguria*, and when he landed in November, 1877, at Philadelphia, he found my men upon the lookout to receive him, and to watch his movements.

He came to America apparently for the purpose of visiting

his wife, a beautiful woman, devotedly attached to him, but who was now living at service with a family residing in Camden, New Jersey. My men watched him very closely. He went first to the Girard House, where he registered his name and announced himself as from New York city. He remained here but a day or two, and one day, while he was temporarily absent, a lady called at the hotel, representing herself as his wife, and requesting permission to await his return.

Sprungli at this time appeared to be in straitened circumstances. The "haul" that had been made by the authorities at Lisbon had evidently been a serious loss to him.

Shortly after the arrival of his wife he was discovered pawning a seal-skin sacque and some valuable dresses, for a comparatively small sum of money, after which he liquidated his bill at the hotel and removed to one of more humble pretensions.

At this time a warrant was sued out against him by one of his unfortunate fellow-passengers of the *Illinois*, and just as he was about to indulge in an afternoon ride, one of my men stepped up and arrested him upon the charge.

He appeared to be very much discomfitted by this proceeding, but knowing that resistance would be useless, he at once submitted, and was conducted quietly away to the office of a magistrate, who held him in default of bail to await his trial. Here again the technicalities of the law were successfully invoked in his favor, and owing to some flaw in the indictment, ingeniously urged by an able attorney, he was discharged.

During his imprisonment, frequent conversations were had with this remarkable man. His fine appearance to a casual observer would at once have disarmed suspicion. His scholarly attainments won general admiration, and his bearing under all the trying circumstances through which he passed proved unmistakably that his early days must have been spent amid the refining influences of wealth and education.

His wife was devotion itself; she never left him during his trial, and seemed as proud of the questionable discharge which secured his freedom, as though it had been an absolute acquittal and an honorable justification.

During one conversation, impressed by his address and attainments, and being charitably disposed toward the unfortunate, it was suggested to him the wisdom of becoming an honest man, and earning a livelihood by honorable means.

" What can I do ?" he asked.

" Why, sir, with your knowledge, you could become an admirable teacher, and one whose talents would prove of incalculable benefit in improving the minds of the young."

With the spirit of a Charley Bates or an Artful Dodger, Sprungli declined the proposition with the utmost disdain.

" Why," said he, " as a teacher I could not make more than a hundred dollars a month ;" and then he added—" when I was a boy I had that much for pocket-money alone."

Finding this man incorrigible, I determined to allow him to pursue his own course, knowing full well that sooner or later his sins would find him out, and his punishment be accorded.

Once at liberty, Sprungli left the United States, and for a long time was not heard of. It was evident, however, that he had not adopted the kindly advice that had been given him, or if he had done so, he had not found its operation to his liking.

During the early part of 1879, happening incidentally to notice, in a paper which was picked up carelessly, an account of some mysterious robberies on the steamers plying between Liverpool and Quebec, I immediately recognized Sprungli's handiwork, and wrote to that effect to the Canadian police authorities, and in a few days the bold corsair was again a prisoner, and this time his punishment was to overtake him.

The particular charges upon which he was arrested were of robbing one individual of twenty-one gold sovereigns, another of some diamond studs, and of the theft of a £100 Bank of England note from another. The strangest part of the proceedings are that, notwithstanding the proofs of his guilt and notorious as was the evidence against him, the jury did not agree upon their verdict against him until they had been locked up for several days.

After a long and serious deliberation they pronounced him guilty, and it is quite probable that the rest of his days will be passed in jail—his sentence being for twenty years.

This was a very remarkable case of criminal life. A man reared in luxury, embarking in business, failing to succeed, and then taking up the profession of a thief. During the whole of his criminal career, however, he was not known to have associated with criminals of any description whatever; always moving in honorable society and conducting himself in every other respect as a gentleman of wealth and education.

Possessed of talents which, properly conducted, would have entitled him to the renown of his fellow-men, he chose the paths of crime, and now, instead of being honored and respected, he is an inmate of a prison and an outcast from society.

CHAPTER IX.

An Exceptionally Successful Amateur Detective.

IT is not very frequent that private citizens engage in the detective business, and it is quite as infrequent for them to make successes in their endeavors when they do make such attempts ; but there are exceptions to all rules, and the following instance is a very bright illustration of a gentleman, never accustomed to the wiles of criminals, exhibiting particularly good sense, while a professional "shover of the queer," as those who dispose of counterfeit money are called, with all his shrewdness and keenness, was completely outgeneraled, and himself and his confederates finally captured and made to suffer the penalty for their crimes.

In June, 1869, a descent by the Government authorities was made upon a counterfeiters' den at Mott Haven, a small village in Westchester county, about eight miles from New York, and it was then thought that the fountain-head, from whence there flowed vast sums of spurious scrip, had been completely annihilated. But this manufactory was only a side-show. The boundless West was then, and is now, better suited for this nefarious business, and it is there that most of this class of work was done.

But the evil-doer is safe nowhere, and although he may for

a time thrive and prosper, yet his time is sure to come, soonei or later.

A pleasant and agreeable traveling companion is a treasure·trove in any part of the world. Many lasting friendships have first originated in casual meetings on steamboat or railway car, hundreds and thousands of miles from home. Now a Mr. Merritt, an old and wealthy citizen of Elmira, New York, about two months after the capture of the counterfeiters referred to, was coming East to Omaha from Cheyenne over the Union Pacific railroad. He was occupying a seat alone, and in a very pleasant and self-satisfied frame of mind was studying the faces of the passengers about him, when his gaze happened to alight upon the countenance of a very neatly-dressed and intelligent appearing young man whom Mr. Merritt imagined he had seen before. The eyes of the two meeting, a sort of half-defined recognition took place, without either of the two then making any further demonstration towards following up a previous acquaintance, if one had ever before existed.

In a short time, however, the young gentleman sauntered back and forth through the cars as if to stretch his limbs, and finally terminated the walk by taking a seat beside Mr. Merritt and engaging that gentleman in conversation. If either had at any time previously met or seen the other, no reference whatever was made to the fact, each gentleman evidently being a quiet, self-possessed man of the world, with too much good breeding and native politeness to introduce a recollection which might prove incorrect and lead to embarrassing explanations; but, in the course of an hour, the young man's winning manners had evidently completely gained Mr. Merritt's

good will. Their chatting was at first of a most commonplace character, but, by and by the young man, who introduced
himself as Mr. Wilson, of Wisconsin, began a narration of his
history. It was romantic, decidedly. He had sprung from
nothing to wealth, riches, and opulence. His domains were
vast and his greenbacks—countless! He did not mention
worthless, however.

"By the way, Mr. Merritt," remarked Mr. Wilson, with an
air of familiarity of the country through which they were
traveling, "we are just coming to our dinner station, and I
have no less change than a fifty-dollar bill, and you know
there's always a rush at such places. Can you accommodate
me? I shall thank you ever so much," said Mr. Wilson,
earnestly.

"Certainly, sir, with pleasure," answered Mr. Merritt, producing his well-filled purse and counting out fifty dollars in
genuine legal-tender notes of Uncle Sam. He then handed the
money to Mr. Wilson, who in turn gave him a bright, crisp
fifty-dollar bill, which Mr. Merritt put in his pocket. He
knew it was counterfeit; but he said nothing.

They dined at Mr. Wilson's expense. A princely dinner it
was, too; for Mr. Wilson was none of your niggardly fellows
who begrudge a few dimes, or even a few dollars; but after
dinner, while the wealthy young gentleman from Wisconsin
was enjoying his Havana in the smoking-car, Mr. Merritt was
buried in deep thought. He taxed his brain to guess whether
he had ever seen that face before. He was a retired merchant,
and while in business he had come in contact with all classes of
people. The voice, the manner, everything about his new acquaintance, seemed familiar to him.

He kept on thinking, and after straining his memory as much as he could, a ray of sunshine shone on him. He was certain now that he remembered the gentleman. Yes, it was he. Ten years before he had passed a one-hundred-dollar bill upon him; and four weeks previous he had been shown the picture of this very man as one who was wanted by the authorities for complicity with the counterfeiters captured at Mott Haven, New York.

Mr. Merritt, being a man of means, had plenty of leisure on his hands, and he at once determined to use it, if possible, towards furthering the ends of justice. He was certain that the counterfeiting business required manufacturers, and, as there was much risk, a large amount of capital, and he was inclined to cultivate his young friend to, if possible, secure his confidence, a knowledge of how his business was conducted, the location of its headquarters, and the men who were engaged with him.

Pursuant to this plan, he gradually evinced a great liking for Mr. Wilson, flattered him, won his real regard and confidence, and, at Wilson's suggestion, became his traveling companion. They traveled together from Omaha to St. Louis, thence to St. Joseph and Kansas City, then up to Davenport, Dubuque, St. Paul, and down to Janesville, a flourishing city on the Rock river in Wisconsin, during which present trip Mr. Wilson revealed his secret to Mr. Merritt, and proposed that he, having large means, should engage in it; to all of which the latter, after some apparent hesitation, finally consented.

Wilson lauded the business to the skies, and displayed fully ten thousand dollars' worth of the stuff. He said that they

"Quite a carousal was inaugurated."

must stop at Janesville, because his " business friends and the house " were located near that city.

Mr. Merritt had no objection to this arrangement; on the contrary, he was rejoiced to know Mr. Wilson's friends and become engaged in so lucrative a business.

Arriving at Janesville, they took a short ride into the country, and finally reached a fine mansion. They walked in, and after Mr. Merritt had been kept waiting in a very pleasant par lor for some little time, he was conducted up-stairs and given a most friendly introduction to some half-dozen intelligent-appearing designers, engravers and printers. Dies, plates, engravings, engraving tools, hand presses, proof-paper and, in fact, every thing necessary for the counterfeiters to carry on their business, were scattered about in the wildest profusion.

Mr. Merritt passed the night with his new-made companions, and quite a carousal was inaugurated in honor of this substantial addition to their number, and prospective large acquisition to their capital, and, on the whole, a jolly and sociable crew they were.

It was arranged that young Wilson should return to Elmira with Mr. Merritt, who was to arrange his business affairs in that city, so as to permit him to return to the West with ten thousand dollars—the amount which had been agreed upon; and the two, before starting, were to visit Madison, the capital of Wisconsin, in company with two others of the gang who were just on the point of leaving for Northwest Wisconsin and Minnesota, with a large supply of the " queer " to work off in that section of the country; and on the next morning, according to this arrangement, the four set out from the house to Janesville, where they were to take the train.

Arriving there, Mr. Merritt, on same pretext or **other,** found opportunity to telegraph the authorities at Madison **a** brief cutline of matters, and a request that officers should be detailed to meet the party on their arrival in that city.

On reaching Madison, Mr. Merritt pointed out the counterfeiters to the officers, and they were immediately taken into custody.

"What under Heaven is this for?" gasped Mr. Wilson, the wealthy Wisconsin gentleman.

"On this gentleman's charge, sir, on the charge of counterfeiting!" replied the officer quietly.

"My God! My God! have you betrayed us?" exclaimed Wilson, addressing Mr. Merritt.

"This is not the first time we have met," said Mr. Merritt. "We saw each other, first, several years ago at Elmira. You passed a counterfeit one-hundred-dollar bill upon me then, and I presume we are pretty nearly even now."

The wretch bowed his head, and he and his companions were conducted to jail. Fifty thousand dollars in spurious money were found on their persons. Officers at once returned to Janesville and captured the entire gang; upwards of five hundred thousand dollars in counterfeit money, and a most magnificent counterfeiting outfit being captured, and the entire party were eventually convicted and sentenced to various terms of imprisonment in the Wisconsin State penitentiary at Waupun.

CHAPTER X.

Audacity of Professional Thieves.

THE supreme assurance of many professional thieves is startling in the extreme. The same grade of talent, bravery,
and brilliancy of execution in the life of an honest man would
make him a great financier, or a great general of armies or
commander of multitudes.

Probably as striking an example of this kind of a person as
there ever was noticed among American criminals was found
in the case of Chauncey Johnson, a notorious New York
"sneak." This term will be found explained elsewhere, and
is applicable, in a criminal sense, only to that class whose profession is to secure packages of money or valuables from banks
or business houses while those engaged within are too busied to
notice their presence.

It will not be necessary to relate the man's history, although
nearly every criminal, the world over, has lived a life of
romance and interesting adventure, and I will only give a few
instances in this man's career which will illustrate the characteristics mentioned in the subject as being not only peculiar to
him, but common with many of the higher grade of criminals.

He was capable of filling any position in the banking or
mercantile business, or in social life, and this peculiar pro-

ficiency fitted him for operating in such schemes as would yield him large returns for his information when so applied. He almost invariably worked alone, and relied entirely upon his own ingenuity and cunning for success, or to extricate himself from trouble should the same overtake him.

His first noted exploit was the robbery of the Bank of the State of New York, in December, 1853. This robbery was committed in broad daylight, and in the presence of the officers and employees of the institution. Johnson entered the bank by the front door, about noon, took off his hat and overcoat, put on a linen duster which he found hanging on the wall, stuck a pen behind his ear and coolly walked around behind the counter, and began busying himself like an old hand.

Soon his eye fell upon a carpet-bag lying under the counter. He took this, not seeing anything else at hand, and left the bank. Going directly to a beer saloon which he frequented, he tossed it over to the bar-keeper, asking him to keep it for a few days. Here the valise was kicked about for some time, it being supposed that it merely contained old clothing, but, in reality, it contained nearly forty thousand dollars in five-dollar bills—nearly the entire circulation of the bank of that denomination. Finally taking it to his mother's house, Johnson hid the valise, only removing one thousand dollars, with which he immediately repaired to a gambling house, and began betting heavily. Information was given that Johnson was unusually flush with five-dollar bills, and, on leaving the place, he was arrested, the balance of the money recovered, and the shrewd thief was given three years and six months in the State penitentiary.

In 1858 he was again captured while in the act of robbing a large New York silk-house, after he had been fired upon by a policeman several times, and had been wounded in the head by a spent ball, which cut the scalp slightly, and then fell into his pocket. For this offense he was given four years, but was pardoned out after he had served two.

Shortly after his release, one day he leisurely strolled down to the Adams' Express office, and seeing a clerk there who looked like himself, he conceived a plan of robbing the place. The manner in which he accomplished the job showed the resources of his genius and the sublime audacity of his nature. He loitered outside the office until the clerk went to dinner, then entered it, put on the clerk's linen duster, put a pen over his ear, and went to work as lazily as though he was an old employee. No one in the office even suspected that he was any other person than the genuine clerk, who had a moment before gone to dinner. But Johnson had no time to lose, and he began looking about for something to lay his hands upon. Finally he got hold of a package of money, which he quietly slipped into his pocket, and when a favorable opportunity occurred he left the place as unceremoniously as he had entered it. Only a few thousand dollars were taken, but what a wonderful assurance and nerve such an act must have required!

Among his boldest operations was the robbery of the Bank of North America at Philadelphia in the summer of 1861.

In this he had a confederate, and the trick done in this instance, although it is quite similar to the regular bank sneak game, is called "weeding" a bank.

Johnson's confederate engaged the teller in conversation,

when the former, with a piece of wire bent up at one end like a hook, which he ran through the iron railing in front of the desk, pulled out a package of bills from under the teller's hands and pocketed it.

The money was immediately counted in a near resort, and, to the chagrin of the thieves, was found to be a package of one-dollar bills, only containing sixty dollars all told.

"Let's go back and make it an even hundred or get caught," said Johnson.

"Agreed;" replied his companion, and the two re-entered the bank, and began fishing for another pile.

But they were not so fortunate this time.

The package now chosen happened to contain new bills, and, as it was disappearing, crackled and rattled so as to attract the attention of the teller, who, with the help of the cashier, succeeded in catching Johnson, although his confederate escaped, and he was given five years at the Eastern Penitentiary of Pennsylvania, but was in some mysterious manner liberated at the expiration of about half the term of sentence.

Many additional instances of the man's daring could be given, but with the following, occurring at the Fifth Avenue Hotel, New York, in 1870, those already related will suffice to illustrate the traits of assurance and audacity in criminals.

At six o'clock in the evening of the year mentioned, a well-dressed and respectable-appearing stranger, with an overcoat thrown carelessly over his arm, entered the hallway of the hotel from the Broadway entrance, and deliberately entered the office as though he belonged there, or had pressing business with the proprietor. The office was simply an inclosure, situated on the south side, near the center of the grand hall.

The safe occupied the center of this inclosure, and on each side and back of it were desks at which clerks were busily engaged with their backs toward the safe. Another clerk was at the counter in front, attending to the incoming guests. Two of the proprietors and another gentleman were standing near the safe when the stranger entered, but without noticing him, retired into the private office.

The strange gentleman, who was Johnson, of course, followed them, and after looking for a moment at the pictures which adorned the walls, made his exit into the outer office and approached the safe, the door of which was standing open. The clerks heard some one come from the private office, but, supposing that it was one of the proprietors, paid no attention to his movements. This was a part of Johnson's plan to disarm suspicion; but one of the house-porters, who sat opposite on the north side of the hall, watched his actions suspiciously. He saw him approach the safe, open the door, abstract a portion of the contents, and then walk quietly out of the office, down the grand hall toward the Broadway entrance.

The porter instantly crossed over to the office, and asked the clerk if that gentleman (pointing to Johnson) was stopping at the hotel.

The clerk did not know. He had not noticed him before.

"Well," said the porter, "he has just been taking something from the safe."

"He has?" exclaimed the clerk; "go at once and stop him!"

The porter, in another moment, was at Johnson's side, and,

7

just as he was entering the door to the reading-room, took him by the arm and said: "Here, I want you!"

Johnson turned partly around, exhibiting a face not at all startled, but full of innocent surprise.

"I'll be back in one moment," he said blandly, as he con tinued his walk at a slightly increased rate of speed; when the porter, taking him roughly by the arm, replied: "But I want you *now!*" and then forcibly conducted him into the private office.

Here he was searched, when a package of money was found upon his person, which was identified as one previously deposited in the safe, while subsequently four packages of papers, of no value to anybody save the proprietors of the hotel, were found upon the floor where they had been dexterously deposited by the cunning thief previous to being searched.

New York breathed freer when the identity of the prisoner became known, but, through some trick of his friends and debauchery of justice, he was privately sentenced to but one year at Sing Sing, which he served, and was again turned loose upon the public, which he has ever since been afflicting in his brilliant and audacious manner.

CHAPTER XI.

A Cruel Destiny.

I MUST admit that among the thousands of hardened criminals with whom my detective experience has brought me in contact, there have arisen many instances where I have in my own mind felt a deep commiseration with, and sympathy for, numbers of this outlaw class. I have no manner of apology for their guilt, and there is no man on earth who would be more relentless than myself in running them to the ground, and assisting in placing them where they must pay the full penalty of their misdoing. Of this everybody is well aware; but, I repeat, there are instances, many of them, where these people have become reckless, desperate criminals, not from choice, or any natural depravity or bent in that direction, but from what have seemed the most luckless of all possible circumstances, forcing and driving them on to the first crime, which, perhaps to cover, another crime seems imperative, and before the desperation of the condition is realized, what was recently an honest citizen has now become hedged in by fear of exposure, by moral cowardice and by reckless companions, that the abandonment of the criminal life so unfortunately begun, is rarely a possibility.

An instance illustrating this class of misfortune came to

[147]

light in 1867, and though neither myself nor any members of
my force were engaged in bringing the facts to light, they have
always interested me, and I think will prove entertaining to
many of my readers.

During the month of October of the year mentioned, a
notorious character, named Jefferson Knight, was arrested at
New Haven, Connecticut, on the charge of horse-stealing,
whose record proved exceedingly romantic.   In the hope of escaping punishment he made a confession implicating several of
his confederates, resulting in the discovery of silverware and
other property worth over fifteen thousand dollars, which had
been concealed in the loft of a small church at Little Neck,
Long Island, where the robbery occurred.

These disclosures, however, failed to secure clemency for
Knight, and he was sentenced for a term of years at Sing Sing,
from which prison he subsequently escaped.   While in Sing
Sing, his deportment was remarkable for unusual excellence,
and, though habitually quiet and reserved, he performed with
alacrity and cheerfulness any task imposed upon him.   Holding himself aloof from his fellow-criminals, he became a
marked convict ;   and when strange-looking men, whose
bronzed features betokened a tropical life, and whose numerous
scars proclaimed them wielders of the sword, began to call at
the prison for the purpose of seeing Knight, the latter was regarded by those around him as possessing a secret of no
inconsiderable importance.   The mysterious pressure brought
to bear upon Knight by his visitors, at last brought on brain
fever, and while convalescing in the prison hospital, he penned
a confession of his past crimes, and presented it as a true
statement to Dr. Collins, the then prison physician, in reward,

as he said, for the sympathy and kindness extended to him by the latter.

In this confession, it appeared that Knight was the only survivor of a small party of guerrillas, who had concealed over a million of dollars in coin, which had been captured from the troops of Maximilian, during the effort made by that ill-fated emperor to perpetuate his rule in Mexico.

This confession, for many corroborative reasons, was implicitly believed by the prison people as well as the officers at Sing Sing. Knight stated that he was born and brought up in Queens county, Long Island, where his father died when he was about nine years old, leaving his mother and three young children without adequate means of support. When able to do for himself, he worked for different people in Queens county, where he bore a good character, after which he went to learn a trade at Little Neck, Long Island. Here he formed the acquaintance of some reckless, dissipated men, and soon acquired habits of intoxication, until one night, while under the influence of liquor, he was persuaded by two of his companions to participate in a robbery. He was detected soon after, but received warning in time to avoid arrest by leaving the neighborhood.

A reward was offered for his apprehension, but he made his way in safety to Philadelphia. It was winter; he had but little money, and he sought in vain for honest employment. Standing one day leaning against a lamp-post in a rather desperate mood, he felt a hand laid on his shoulder, and, turning, found himself face to face with a well-known desperado of Queen's county.

The latter had heard of his misfortune at Little Neck, and

appeared overjoyed at meeting him. Seeing no other means open to him of making a living then, he consented to become a pal of his desperate companion; but after participating in a series of burglaries in Philadelphia and vicinity, he became tired of the nefarious business, and engaged as one of the crew of a whaling vessel bound for the Pacific Ocean.

Not long afterwards he found himself shipwrecked on the coast of Chili, where he was the recipient of extreme kindness on the part of the natives. Having formed a desire to remain there until he could so retrieve his fortunes as to be able to return home and again resume the position of a respectable man in society, he secured a berth upon a coasting vessel. Meantime the owner had become very much attached to him, and insisted that Knight should make a home at his house whenever the vessel was in port. His employer had one child, a most beautiful and amiable girl, one possessing all the grace and beauty of those ravishingly handsome women of the far South, who have descended from the old Spanish grandees who formerly reigned like rich princes in that fruitful, sensual land, and a strong attachment at once sprang up between the two, resulting in a marriage engagement, which had the full sanction of young Knight's employer.

Notwithstanding his troubles in the States, which Knight hoped soon to be able to settle, he considered himself a fortunate man, and seemed on the high road to prosperity and the resumption of an honorable life. But the harsh destiny to which I have referred ruled otherwise.

While making a voyage from Valparaiso to Caledra, his vessel, which he then commanded, was hailed by a large square-rigged schooner, ordering him to "lay to." Not liking the appearance of the rakish-looking craft, he paid no attention to the command, but made all haste to escape the vessel, which, in a moment more, threw open a portion of her bulwarks, from which the muzzle of a gun immediately projected, and a heavy charge of grape-shot came tearing over the deck, killing all of his crew except two.

The pirates, for such they were, then boarded him, and he was taken a prisoner to their vessel, his hands and feet pinioned, and he confined between decks, after which his own vessel was stripped of everything of value and then sunk.

Next day he was brought on deck, when the pirate captain informed him that he could either hold himself in readiness to obey his orders or else "walk the plank." The ship finally entered the Gulf of Mexico, where Knight made an unsuccessful attempt to escape. The captain then required that he should take an oath not to leave the vessel, which he refused to do, when he was again confined between decks, and in that situation he remained for three months, during which time the most terrible of crimes were committed by the pirates. He ultimately consented to take the oath dictated by the captain, and was again allowed to go on deck. Shortly after his liberation he discovered that there was a great deal of dissatisfaction existing among the crew, and, in an evil moment, he succeeded in inciting a mutiny.

The men were about equally divided, and a bloody fight followed; but when those who were on the side of the officers saw that their leaders had fallen, they surrendered, and he found himself in command of the pirate schooner. Not liking this dangerous position, he subsequently resolved to destroy the vessel, which object he accomplished soon afterwards.

He then made his way into Mexico and crossed the Isthmus of Panama, but on arriving at Tonala he could find no means of getting back into Chili, which he made a desperate struggle to reach, so that he might account to his employer, the owner of the vessel which the pirates had captured and sunk, for his long and mysterious absence. At the former place he fell in with a band of men who had just joined the Mexican army, who forced him to accompany them, but who offered to share generously with him any plunder which might fall into their hands. This command was headed by an ambitious captain, who thought that he could do better by detaching his men from the main body of the Mexican army, to pursue a guerrilla style of warfare. This he did, taking with him altogether about two hundred men; and for nearly a year they were shifting from place, wherever the largest amount of plunder could be secured.

At last their numbers became greatly reduced, and the French army, having grown tired of their repeated raids, began to use vigorous efforts for their capture. About this time the captain, who had conceived a great liking for Knight, informed him that he was soon to make an incursion which would probably be his last, as he intended disbanding his men.

The contemplated raid was for the purpose of capturing a large amount of treasure which was soon to be conveyed under a strong guard, from Vera Cruz to the City of Mexico. This capture was subsequently successfully effected; but the French troops pursued them so closely, that the captain, fearing they would be overtaken, and perhaps lose the booty in a fight, determined to conceal the treasure in the mountains.

Not wishing his men to know where the gold was hidden,

one night, the captain selected him and a few other followers, by whose united assistance the treasure was finally securely buried. They were still being pursued by the enemy in superior numbers, and after several days, were finally surrounded. Although his captain had a commission from the Mexican Government, they knew that if taken they would be treated as bandits, and they therefore determined to cut their way through the French lines, or perish in the attempt.

While carrying out this last resolve, nearly the whole band, including the captain, were killed, a few of them escaping only to be recaptured in a short time. Knight, who was among the number, was placed in a small tent, his hands and feet tied, and a guard placed over him. About midnight he was visited by an officer, who, having first sent away the guard lest they should be overheard, begged him to disclose the hiding-place of the coin, but he refused to talk upon the subject unless his hands and feet were first loosened.

No sooner had the officer complied with his preliminary terms, than Knight grasped the officer by the throat and choked him until he was almost lifeless. Then stripping him of his uniform and securing his arms, he bound and gagged the half-unconscious man. Hastily donning the officer's clothes he then passed out of the enemy's line unmolested.

Knight then made his way into Texas, and thence worked his passage back to New York as best he could, arriving in the latter city some time in the winter of 1866. Being in a destitute condition he was ashamed to call upon his friends after an absence of so many years, and shortly met a companion with whom he again began a career of crime, his chief object being the acquisition of sufficient means to carry him back to Chili,

7*

so that he might secure the woman he loved, as well as to show the kind man who had befriended him that he had not been ungrateful for it all.

Some uncontrollable influence seemed to force him into the depths of crime, and once he had plunged into it, it appeared as though Satan himself were helping him, as in a few weeks he found himself the possessor of several thousand dollars. Having conceived the idea of purchasing a small vessel in which to sail for Chili, he exercised all his criminal ingenuity for some months, and had succeeded in securing funds almost sufficient for that purpose, when a treacherous friend, in whom he had placed confidence, concocted a plan to rob and murder him. This man, though failing to take his life, succeeded in robbing him of every dollar he had.

Knight then determined to get money at all hazards and return to Chili; but was arrested while attempting to perpetrate his next crime, with the results as already stated.

As if this were not enough to crush him, the French officer from whom he had made his escape had tracked him to the United States, and to the door of his cell in Sing Sing, and, with the connivance of some of the prison officials, for months tormented his very life out of him, to ascertain where the treasure had been hidden in Mexico. This ex-officer coaxed, threatened, bullied and made liberal promises by turns; but Knight knew that the captain under whom he had fought in Mexico had a commission from the Mexican Government, and he considered the money a lawful prize, that he would give up under no circumstances. But finally his persecutors attacked him on a tender point. They had in some manner ascertained the residence of his old employer and his daughter, the woman he loved, and now began such ceaseless and cruel threats to the effect that his disgrace should be revealed to her, unless the location of the treasure was divulged, that under all the terror of such a result, and the burden of his prison shame and blasted hopes, the convict finally succumbed to a terrible attack of brain fever, during the convalescence from which, as already related, Knight made the confession to Dr. Collins, the substance of which has here been given.

But the fate of Knight was as sad as his career had been disastrous. For a year or two after his recovery he plodded along, an exemplary prisoner, at Sing Sing; when suddenly he made his escape from that stronghold, by digging a hole through its roof. Then, for a year or more, all his genius was set towards securing money by whatever means were first presented, and enough was thus gained to enable him to purchase a small ship, with which he set sail for Chili, but while his vessel was off the coast of Cuba, it was run into by a Spanish man-of-war, and instantly sunk with all on board; so that the little Chilian girl still waits for her absent lover; the kind old ship-owner still waits in vain for his missing vessel; and the vast sum of gold taken from the luckless French still lies buried from the eyes of greedy fortune-hunters, in the rugged mountain fastnesses of far-off Mexico.

CHAPTER XII.

Criminal Ingenuity.

THE real talent frequently displayed by criminals, not only in concocting schemes for plunder, but in various attempts to secure liberty after they have been grasped in the clutches of the law, is simply remarkable.

In noticing these matters, as I have been compelled to repeatedly, I could not but reflect that had this genuine genius been devoted to honorable pursuits, how greatly would society have gained thereby. Not half the assiduity and patience thus exhibited, would make any man respectable, many men rich, and some men great.

I have already noted in other sketches the talent and ingenuity developed by great or noted criminals like Max Shinburne, Jack Canter or E. S. Piper, and cannot pass another instance illustrative of this feature of crime, coming under my notice, which occurred in the Providence jail, in the summer of 1869, although the prisoner was one occupying a very obscure corner in the great criminal society of the country.

The name of the prisoner was Charles Williams. He was awaiting trial for burglary, and from the very moment he was incarcerated, he exercised the most wonderful thrift and perseverance in attempts to escape. No one knew where he was

"*Criminal Ingenuity.*" — *Attempted Escape.*

from, or who he was. He had simply been apprehended by the local officers for an adroit burglary, and, with others, was awaiting his turn for a card of transfer to the State penitentiary—one of the homeless, houseless, nameless, characterless wretches which infect humanity with their presence, and impose great burdens upon society, in order to protect itself from their lawlessness. That was all: and no interest would have attached to him, had he not developed an inordinate propensity to regain his liberty.

He had hardly been in his cell twenty-four hours when he was discovered in the act of disappearing through the roof. Being captured and locked up, he took the matter philosophically and turned his attention to the science of invention.

After the first attempted escape it was thought judicious to lock Williams up, and he was, therefore, constantly confined in his cell, except when bathing or taking exercise in the yard.

On one of these occasions he had obtained a piece of rusty old saw-file, which he used in constructing, out of some of the furniture in his cell, a machine for opening his door.

First, he made a saw of a piece of the iron of which his bed-frame was made, with which he was able to cut whatever pieces of wood he needed. Then, taking a board forming a shelf, he split it in pieces and made a square after the style of a carpenter's steel square, only this was of common pine, by tying the ends of two pieces at right angles.

Holding one end of this in his right hand, he could thrust the square through between the bars of his cell-door, which was placed pretty deep in the recess of the wall, and, turning the contrivance down, he could bring the other angle of the square down on a line with the keyhole on the outside, and about eighteen inches from the inside of the door.

Next, the patient, plodding fellow began the construction of a key from a portion of heavy metal taken from his ration-dish.

When new, these ration-dishes had two handles, but as they got old, and were banged about with no gentle handling by the keepers and prisoners, they often lost a handle and were used with one; no particular attention being paid to the loss.

Williams had shrewdly observed this, and had taken a handle with a wire in it, the fact not being noticed when the dish was removed from his cell, though a very careful system of surveillance had been instituted over the prisoner.

Days and weeks were consumed in the manufacture of this key. Think of the long, tireless hours used in the work! how the man, panting for liberty—though a single honest motive may never have stirred his outlaw-nature, and he may never have had a higher instinct for freedom than would have entered the dim consciousness of a caged beast, but every energy of his life and being bent upon the completion of the task. The same application, the same sacrifice, the same supreme patience, outside of a prison, and working upon some invention for the benefit of his fellow-men, would have made this imprisoned man famous!

The key, which, after so long a time, he had completed in a way which would have done credit to a locksmith with the pride in his work which cheery old Nicholas Varden in Dickens' *Barnaby Rudge* was shown to have had, had a wooden pulley attached to the shank. Then this patient worker had taken a portion of his shirt, and unraveled from it hundreds of cotton threads. Slowly and carefully he had taken these threads, and spun them into string, nearly two yards in length, which was found to have been made as strong and as perfect as the best of small-sized fishing line.

This string was neatly wound in the groove of the pulley wheel, and passed to an angle of the rudely-constructed square, around a pivot and along the side of the square he held in his hand.

The whole being completed, he put his apparatus through the grating and carefully felt for the keyhole by delicately moving his machine from point to point until the key entered. But the poor fellow had miscalculated somewhat, and the key, though it entered the socket readily, did not pass some of the obstructions of the lock, and when he pulled on the string, which he expected by the aid of the pulley and square would have the effect of turning back the bar, the strain from the leverage on the shank of the key was so severe that it broke the key, leaving a portion of the key in the lock.

An officer observed this, and also heard the disappointed man exclaim : " Damnation ! I'm up in a balloon this time ! It's all over. The damned thing's gone."

At this moment a prisoner passed his cell, to whom Williams whispered : " For God's sake, pull out that key !"

His cell, however, was then examined. The ball and chain had been removed from his leg in a truly ingenious manner A piece of hard wood from his stool was fitted to the hole in the leg-iron and a hole was made in this piece of wood a little smaller than the screw, the end being sewed with a black linen thread. When inserted and turned, the thread cut strong enough to turn the spring and unlock the irons.

These are merely instances of his inventive genius. Probably not persevering or talented enough to accomplish a single
honorable and good thing outside of prison, his creative faculty,
when he was himself caged, was simply boundless.

Remarkably observing, he readily adapted means to ends,
and seemed to make everything subserve his purpose. Having
nothing in his possession in the shape of tools but the rusty
piece of old file, everything else needed was made from articles in his cell. Although sixty-eight prisoners used similar
articles in their respective cells, yet this man, in his persistent
efforts to escape, gave the officers more trouble than all the
other prisoners. His intention on this occasion, as he confessed, was to secrete himself outside of his cell and attack the
officer on duty at night, and with a view to deceiving the
officer on his rounds, Williams had arranged a stuffed figure on
his bed, using for the purpose his drawers and some straw from
his mattress, putting his boots on the legs of the figure, and
attaching to it the ball and chain from which he had so suc
cessfully cleared his own leg.

But notwithstanding all his brilliant attempts at escape,
Williams was finally securely landed in the penitentiary, where
he served his term, and then, like a dirty pebble fallen in a
great sea, dropped back into his unknown place in the dark
ocean of criminals.

CHAPTER XIII.

A Clever Bank Robbery.

NEARLY every manner of bank robbery will be found explained under different subjects given in this book of sketches and reminiscences, but I doubt whether it is possible to find elsewhere throughout the records of crime so cool and audacious, and yet so shrewd and well-planned a robbery as that of the Kensington Bank, in the city of Philadelphia, in January, 1871.

This bank is located in the old district of Kensington, which was one of the districts of Philadelphia previous to consolidation in 1854. The neighborhood surrounding the bank is principally composed of shipbuilding and manufacturing establishments, and is not, by any means, considered one of the most attractive localities of Philadelphia. The isolated position of the bank from the other banking-houses of the city necessarily caused its surveillance by the police to be much less The building occupied had been remodeled from a substantial dwelling-house, but, although it contained excellent vaults and safes, was hardly the sort of a structure necessary to such a purpose, and would, without outside vigilance and care, naturally seem to be just the spot to be chosen for the operations of daring and skillful bank burglars.

In such a condition of things, the enforcement of constant precautions would seem to have been only evidences of ordinary care and judgment, as the building had so many weak points about it.

All the fear that the officers seemed to entertain, however, was that the building might tempt some of the ordinary riffraff of the locality to break into it for what slight plunder might be secured about the offices, and, at first, only one watchman was employed; but, finally, as he probably got lonesome, the employment of a second watchman was urged upon the officers, and reluctantly secured. These were provided with huge revolvers for close work, if it ever should come to that, and shot-guns for winging any game that might be necessary to attack at longer range. This much provided for, everybody felt happy and safe in the condition of the bank and its treasure.

But these precautions, such as they were, were of no avail Trickery, and that of the most adroit and skillful kind, accomplished, as it always does in criminal matters, what no force or ruffianism could hope to attain.

At about five o'clock in the afternoon of the 29th of January, 1871, two men called at the bank. There were present only watchman Holmes and the cashier, a gentleman named McConnell. One of the strangers was dressed in a full police uniform, carrying a club and wearing a shield.

"Is this Mr. McConnell?" asked the policeman.

"Yes sir," he replied; "what's wanted?"

"Perhaps your valuables," replied the policeman, smiling.

"All right," said McConnell; "anybody that's got a big

enough draft can draw all we've got!" and then he added more seriously: "what's up, anyhow?"

"Well, it's just this," said the policeman, in a brusque, business way; "the lieutenant"—meaning, of course, the lieutenant of the district—"sent me over to caution you folks to use a little more vigilance for a time. Several suspicious characters have been seen slouching about the neighborhood."

"Thank you; thank you," said McConnell, really gratified at this exhibition of kindness on the part of the lieutenant. "We will have everything ready to give people of that kind a warm reception."

McConnell, after giving instructions to the watchman, and promising to have word sent to his companion to be on hand at the bank an hour earlier than usual, took his departure.

The policeman and his companion loitered about the place for a little time, chatting pleasantly with the watchman, and finally started away, remarking:

"I may be back and see you during the evening."

"All right—I wish you would," said Holmes; "but do you know, I think it's all fudge!"

"Well, whether it is or not, *I* tell you—*shoot the first man who attempts to enter the building to-night!*"

"I'll do it, sure," rejoined Holmes, with a nod and a wink. "Have no fears, though; we are fully prepared for anybody."

Watchman Murphy had not yet arrived, but when he did come, Holmes told him of what had occurred, and the two set about putting things in order. The revolvers were cleaned, reloaded, and placed conveniently upon a table; and the loaded guns in a neighboring closet were examined, while the two men cracked all sorts of jokes about a possible attack, and how they

would distinguish themselves heroically should one be attempted.

Between seven and eight o'clock a tap was heard at the
door, and Holmes, remembering what the policeman—as he
supposed him to be—had told him, concluded his friend had
returned, and without the slightest suspicion of wrong, opened
the door.

"I told you to shoot the *first* man you saw trying to come
in," said the policeman, laughing.

"Some of you fellows ought to be shot, the papers say," replied Holmes, shaking his hand heartily. "Who's this with
you?"

"Oh, only a neighbor up in Spring Garden street, that s
trying to sell me a little place up there. Come in, Bob," he
concluded, addressing the alleged neighbor.

Bob did go in with the rest.

"We thought we better come around and see how you are
getting on," resumed the policeman; "the lieutenant thinks
there will be an attack made to-night. He wouldn't give me
any particulars. You know these d——d police officers like to
appear wise."

Holmes was a good, honest soul, nearly sixty years of age,
altogether unsuspecting of evil, and Murphy was not much
younger, while being altogether as simple. The policeman and
his friend were asked to sit down, which they did. Then a
regular story-telling time was entered into. The weather was
discussed; city politics were talked over; all sorts of subjects were
introduced, and, finally, that of burglars and bank-robberies
came up. This was a fruitful theme, and the policeman and
his friend wonderfully entertained the watchmen with stories

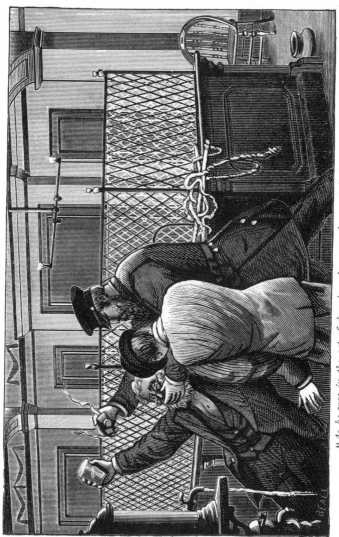

"As he was in the act of drawing the water he was seized from behind."

of this description, gradually drawing from them the resources of the Kensington Bank, what its entire protection consisted of how the vaults were constructed, what locks were in use, and, in fact, the minutest particulars within the watchmen's knowledge of the bank, and everything it contained.

Nearly an hour was pleasantly passed in this manner, when Bob, the neighbor, of Spring Garden street, proposed to Murphy to take a walk as far as the corners, in either direction, in order to see if any suspicious characters were lurking about, as he and his friend had noticed, he said, two hard-looking customers near the bank as they came in.

Murphy caught at this suggestion and went out, Holmes and the two men being left behind. In a few minutes one of the men said he was terribly thirsty, and Holmes volunteered to get him some water. As the hydrant was situated at the rear of the building, he walked back in that direction, being followed by the strangers. As he was in the act of drawing the water, he was seized from behind, his arms held, and a rope gag thrust in his mouth.

In vain he tried to free himself. He was tripped down, tied, handcuffed, and rendered entirely helpless. He was then carried into the cashier's room, and laid upon the floor, and one of the rascals placed, pistol in hand, as a guard upon him.

He had not been long in this disagreeable situation, before he heard the door open and men enter. Then there was a struggle and a faint cry, and a heavy fall upon the floor. His companion, Murphy, was then brought back, tied, gagged and handcuffed, like himself, and laid down beside him.

For a considerable time after all was quiet. Then there was a deal of hammering and noise kept up for a couple of hours or more. By and by the guard retired; then the noises ceased, and by considerable effort Holmes succeeded in freeing his feet, doing it with his hands, which were "ruffled" or tied behind him. The neighbors were soon aroused and the police notified, but before the handcuffs could be removed, the services of a blacksmith were found necessary.

Now here was a piece of business that deserves high rank among the most brilliant of bank robberies. The whole job, which was planned and its execution led by Frank McCoy or "Big Frank," something about whom will be subsequently given, was one which showed, in its entirety, the most careful calculation of time and conditions, the ablest judgment of character, and the most consummate daring and personal bravery; and is only another illustration of what I am continually urging upon bankers and business men, which is simply to *personally* know that their safes and vaults are constantly and completely guarded, and that far greater precautions should be used.

Now, in this instance, it was developed that Murphy was a shoemaker, and was in the habit of taking his "kit" of tools to the bank, and, through the night, of doing various pieces of "cobbling" for himself and friends. This fact alone prevented a discovery of what was going on in the bank in time to frustrate the robbery; for the neighbors were accustomed to hearing the shoemaker's hammering, and the genuine police were also accustomed to it. The hammering within the bank on this night was repeatedly heard by both the police and those living in adjacent houses; but was not given any particular attention from this fact. The robbers had shrewdly calculated on all this, and this weakness of the bank management in permitting anything besides constant watchfulness within the building, proved the robbers' strength.

Too much blame cannot be attached to such negligence on the part of bank officers. The cashier's first duty on being apprised of the threatened danger was not merely to take the matter so airily, but to have doubled the force within the bank, and then provided watchmen on the outside to keep an eye not only upon any persons skulking about the building, but close guard upon the inside guard themselves.

I have found in my almost unlimited experience in these matters that it is often a good thing to have watchmen watching watchmen.

But the negligence of the Kensington Bank officers was not at all exceptional. Bankers, from a policy of false economy, will only provide one or two old fellows as watchmen, whom a school-boy might easily overcome; take no precautions to see that even these men are responsible, or at least ever vigilant, and then, after a few years of this sort of "economy," have the pleasure of coming down town of a morning to find their banking-palace in a hubbub, and treasure enough taken to have protected their places absolutely for a quarter of a century!

The robbers of the Kensington Bank secured upwards of seventy-five thousand dollars in cash and Government bonds, not a penny of which was ever recovered, nor were any of the perpetrators ever apprehended, at least, on that distinct charge.

Frank McCoy, the leader of the Kensington Bank robbery, with "Jimmy" Hope, "Jimmy" Brady, and Joe Howard, another combination of notorious bank-bursters, were, in the fall of 1873, arrested for participation in the robbery of the First National Bank of Wilmington, Delaware. They were all convicted and sentenced to receive forty lashes at the pillory, as well as ten years' imprisonment.

About eight months subsequent to their incarceration they escaped from prison at New Castle, where a steam-tug had been provided by friends, and thus were for a time placed beyond the clutches of justice.

They were, after a time, re-captured, but managed to escape, and immediately set about consummating a plan for the robbery of a bank at Suffolk, Virginia. In this they were peculiarly unfortunate, being arrested in the very act. McCoy made a strong fight for his liberty, having large means at his command, and consequently plenty of friends and the ability to secure able counsel. But he was finally convicted on the strength of the testimony of my son, William A. Pinkerton, whom, as a mere matter of justice to a suffering commercial community, I authorized to proceed from Chicago and complete the robber's unmistakable identification.

But the same parties, at different times, again managed, through consummate skill and lavish bribery, to effect prison escapes before the expiration of their terms of sentence, continuing their career of crime. Their present whereabouts are as follows :

" Big Frank " is still at large, making his headquarters among the criminal gentry of New York city.

" Jimmy " Brady was arrested for a brilliant piece of shoplifting in New York city, after a running fight on the street with the officer (this sort of procedure being called in the slang of criminals " running a muck "). He was recognized as an escaped convict from Sing Sing, and on all the indictments found against him was finally given fifteen years' imprisonment and sent to Auburn for that term, the prison of that place being his present place of residence.

"Jimmy" Hope was apprehended at Deep River, Connecticut, for participation in the robbery of the First National Bank at that place, and, while awaiting trial for *this* crime, was taken on a requisition to Dexter, Maine, for the robbery, in company of "Sam" Perris, *alias* "Wooster Sam," of the Dexter National Bank, and is now awaiting the disposition of his case at that city; while Joe Howard, the last member of this particular gang of most dangerous men, was captured for complicity with George Mills, *alias* Bliss *alias* White, and "Pete" Curly, in the robbery of the First National Bank of Barre, Vermont, and, also being recognized as an escaped Sing Sing convict, was returned to Auburn, to serve his unexpired term, and is now within its safe walls, in company with his old friend "Jimmy" Brady.

8

CHAPTER XIV.

A Burglar's Death.

ABOUT midnight, on the twenty-ninth day of May, 1879, a wagon, to which was attached an antiquated sorrel horse, whose four white feet shone through the gloom, was driven on board the boat at Astoria Ferry, Brooklyn, New York. The floor of the wagon was covered with some loose straw, and upon this was laid a peculiar-looking object, covered with two stable blankets and a piece of oil-cloth. Upon the driver's seat sat two men, rough-looking customers, who might be readily mistaken for street hucksters or tramps. Silently the boat crossed the river, and upon landing, the wagon was driven away as rapidly as the labored movements of the stiff-jointed animal would permit.

Over Harlem Bridge they rattled, and by a circuitous route, as though their intention was to evade a pursuit, they reached a lonely place called Tramps' Rock, near Yonkers. Driving up to the edge of the woods, the two men alighted, and going to the rear end of the wagon, caught roughly hold of the burden they had carried so far, and drew it towards them Then taking hold of either end of the mysteriously enveloped bundle, which appeared to be very heavy, they entered the woods.

[170]

"They caught roughly hold of the burden they had carried so far."

After walking, or rather staggering a short distance, they laid it down and proceeded to remove the covering which enveloped it. Soon the face and form of a man was exposed to view, rigid and dead. Taking from his pocket a pistol, one of the men leaned over the corpse, and placing the muzzle close to the white forehead, deliberately discharged it. Then laying the weapon down within reach of the stiffened fingers of the dead man, they silently left the spot, and entering their wagon, drove away in the direction in which they came.

A few days after this, some farmers in the neighborhood, passing through the wood, discovered the lifeless remains which had been so secretly and mysteriously deposited there. The authorities were at once notified, and an investigation commenced. Inquiries soon developed the fact that the dead man was none other than George Leslie—alias George L. Howard—a noted burglar, who was well known in criminal circles, for his daring and boldness in the precarious occupation he had followed, and whose skill and success had excited the wonder and admiration of his companions in crime, as well as both police authorities and detectives.

It was at first supposed that the man had committed suicide, but from the discovery of two pistol wounds, and both from a different weapon, the belief was forced upon all that he had been foully murdered, and then conveyed to the place where he was found.

The body was claimed by friends and decently interred in a cemetery in New York, and, after an unprofitable investigation, the matter passed out of public notice.

A brief history of this remarkable man may not prove un-interesting.

George Leonidas Leslie—or as he was more widely known, George L. Howard—was born of English parents in a little village in the State of New York. His father being quite wealthy, and idolizing his son, gave him an excellent education. He graduated at a western university before he was eighteen, with high honors. He was bright, intellectual, and developed much mechanical ingenuity, and high hopes were entertained by his father that a brilliant career was before him. Prior to the completion of his studies, however, his father died, and after a time his mother remarried. The step-father was not, as might be expected, a great favorite with George and his sister, and serious family difficulties were engendered in consequence.

Mr. Leslie, at his death, left a large sum of money for his children, but placed the control of it in the hands of his widow, and very soon after her second marriage the custody of this money was transferred to the step-father and was eventually swallowed up in his business.

Of course this action created much trouble and dissatisfaction in the family, and George, being of an impulsive disposition, accused his step-father of robbing them. The result of this was, that after the impetuous boy had bitterly upbraided both his mother and his step-father, he was driven from home.

Thus cast upon his own resources, he led a wandering, vicarious life. He engaged in business in Milwaukee; was proprietor of a hotel in San Francisco, and, later, had established himself in St. Louis.

He soon, however, fell into bad company, and the war breaking out about this time, he, in company with one Mike Stafford, became quite notorious as a bounty-jumper—making a great deal of money in that way, and being always successful in escaping detection.

He soon made the acquaintance of James Dunlap, Robert Scott, and others of that ilk, and quickly developed into one of the most reckless and scientific burglars and "safe-crackers" in the fraternity.

He was in Chicago at this time, and, being hard pressed for money, he proposed to some of his "pals" to attempt the robbery of a safe in a prominent banking-house in that city, by overpowering the watchman and "bucking and gagging" him— a process that is known as the "stick up" game.

"Why," said one of the company, "Pinkerton's men watch that place, and his man is around there almost all of the time."

"Well," replied he, "we can tie him up."

"Yes," urged the other, "but the sergeant goes around every half hour, and the man will soon be missed."

"It wouldn't be much extra trouble to dispose of the sergeant, would it?" said the reckless man.

"Well, even then," persisted his more timorous companion, "the regular police officer will make his round, and he will discover the absence of the private watchman outside."

"There's no help for it, then," at last said Howard, "the policeman will have to be tied up too."

His companions, however, did not possess the reckless courage for an undertaking that involved an attack upon four watchful men, and, much to the disgust of Howard, the "job" was abandoned.

In 1869, he came to Philadelphia and engaged board with a widow lady, in one of the most aristocratic localities in the Quaker City. Howard was a very handsome man, pol-

ished and well educated, speaking the French, German and
Spanish languages, and being respectful and assiduous in his
attentions to the ladies, and off-hand and good-natured in his
intercourse with the gentlemen, he soon became a general favorite.   He had introduced himself as George L. Howard, and
represented that he was engaged as a revenue detective under
the Government.

About this time the "Beneficial Savings Fund Society"
in that city was entered and robbed, the safes broken open, and
one million three hundred thousand dollars, in bonds, securities
and money were carried off, and soon after the revenue detective disappeared.

The lady with whom he boarded had a very beautiful and
accomplished daughter, with whom Howard soon became intimately acquainted—a mutual affection being the result.   Two
or three years after his disappearance from Philadelphia, he
accidentally met this young lady in Baltimore.   Their acquaintance was thus renewed, his long absence satisfactorily accounted
for, and they were eventually married.

In May, 1870, in company with two other burglars, Howard attempted to rob a jewelry store in Norristown, in Pennsylvania.   They were discovered in the act and were surprised
by a stern command to surrender.   This command his two
companions at once obeyed, and throwing up their hands, were
secured, but Howard, springing behind an awning post, drew
his pistol and defied the officers to arrest him.   Eleven shots
were fired at him, but, strange to say, not one of them took
effect.   He sprang away, but was tripped up after he had succeeded in wounding one of the officers.   The three men were
then locked up, but Leslie, offering bail, was set at liberty, and

forfeiting this, he never appeared for trial. His companions, however, were each sentenced to long terms of imprisonment.

It was after this event that he met the young lady whom he afterwards married. Howard and his bride returned to Philadelphia, and lived in luxurious apartments with his mother-in-law. He was devoted to his beautiful wife, and lavished upon her many costly gifts. He entered the highest circles of society, and by the brilliancy of his conversation, and the wide knowledge which he evinced, he at once obtained an entrée into the inner-sanctuary of Philadelphia aristocracy.

In 1871, Howard, in collusion with some companions, was concerned in the successful robbery of the Kensington Bank, an account of which is given elsewhere, and by which they secured $100,000. He was not discovered, however, and engaged in several very daring robberies in that city shortly afterwards.

He remained in Philadelphia until 1873, making frequent visits to other cities—assigning to his wife his duties as an officer of the Government, as a reason therefor. To follow his numerous burglarious undertakings would be both tedious and laborious, but a careful estimate which has since been made, discloses the fact that during his career he must have received as his share for the various ventures he engaged in over half a million of dollars.

Finding that Philadelphia was getting a trifle too warm for him, he removed with his wife to Brooklyn, and established himself at the Clinton House, in that " City of Churches." Here he became identified with some of the most noted burglars of his day—and his keen perceptions, matchless audacity, skillful mechanical power, and suave manner soon marked him as a virtual chief.

He was an ardent lover of good music, and was familiar with science and literature. He frequented the opera, and seemed to take more delight in the sweet strains of Verdi and Donizetti, than in the vulgar amusements in which his com panions indulged. He was also a great favorite with the ladies, but, in his intercourse with them, was always gentlemanly and refined.

He made a specialty of the " safe combination locks," an invention that, it was claimed, would defy the operations of the most skillful burglar. Whenever anything new was invented he made it his business to discover the secret of its manipulation. He would purchase a safe or a lock, and would not relinquish his task until he had become thorough master of all its intricate machinery. For this talent he was much sought after by the burglars from all sections of the country, and he was at one time interested or had knowledge of most of the successful robberies that took place in the United States. It has been confidently stated by his associates that there was not a combination lock in existence that he could not open.

After Howard removed to Brooklyn, he became intimately acquainted with Shang Draper and " Billy " Porter, two bold and daring burglars who had amassed quite a fortune. Both of these men were married, and to beautiful women, and the rumor soon became current that Howard's attentions to the two ladies were a source of annoyance and jealousy to their husbands. Whether these rumors were founded upon fact or were the idle inventions of enemies, I am unable to say, but Howard continued assiduous in his attentions to his own wife, who loved him too devotedly to indulge in a momentary suspicion of his faithfulness.

About this time he was connected with an unsuccessful attempt to rob "The Manhattan Savings Bank" in New York. By deft management one of their number was admitted as a menial in the service of the bank, and on a Sunday morning the burglars were admitted. The safe was secured with a combination dial lock, with the mechanism of which Howard was perfectly conversant. A hole was bored in the door of the vault, under the dial, and a stiff iron wire was inserted. Three of the four tumblers were in use at the time. Two of them were thrown into an unlocking position, but the third could not be moved; nor could the burglars determine where their calculations were at fault.

After various unsuccessful attempts to force the resisting lock, they were compelled to abandon their labors. They puttied up the hole, painted the putty, and then cleanly swept up the steel filings and unobservedly departed. In the morning the vault door could not be opened, and the maker of the lock was sent for. That gentleman succeeded in opening the door, but was surprised to find some difficulty in working the combination, and he removed the lock for the purpose of ascertaining the difficulty. When the plate was removed, the puttied hole was discovered, and the proofs of an attempted burglary presented themselves to view. To their consternation it was found that if the hole had been bored an eighth of an inch lower, the tumblers would have been aligned and the door opened.

In December of this same year Howard discovered that an actor at the Park Theater was paying attentions to his wife,

8*

and he afterwards surprised her in the act of writing a letter to him.

His jealousy was at once aroused and he treated her very harshly, and immediately sent her home to her mother in Philadelphia. He then sold out his luxurious furniture and his extensive library, and became reckless and dissipated in his habits, frequenting houses of ill-fame and consorting with abandoned characters.

In February, 1877, however, he again became reconciled with his wife; but his jealousy was not stifled and he insisted that she should remain with her mother, while he returned to New York and continued his wild manner of living.

The wife followed him and soon obtained her old control of him, and in April he rented a neat little cottage on Staten Island, and bringing the mother of his wife to this place they again commenced housekeeping.

He soon grew tired of this, and his wife and her mother again returned to Philadelphia, while Howard went back to his old companions.

On the 22d of February, 1878, the Dexter Savings Bank of Maine was closed at its usual hour. James W. Barron, the cashier, was in the habit of working after office hours, and he remained in the bank that afternoon. As he did not return home to tea his family became uneasy about him, and some of them went to the bank to ascertain the cause of his absence.

On entering the building they were confronted with evidences of a struggle in the outer office, and a further search resulted in the discovery of the body of the cashier jammed in

"Meeting her upon the street shortly afterwards, he attempted to draw his pistol and threatened to shoot her."

Page 170.

between the outer and the inner doors of the vault. The man had been gagged and bound, there were several severe wounds upon the head, and a slip noose had been drawn so tightly about his neck that it had cut through the skin. He was alive when found, but died within an hour after his removal.

All that the thieves succeeded in getting was one hundred dollars from the bank and five hundred dollars which they took from the pockets of the murdered man.

In this affair, Howard, although not concerned in the murder, was connected with the attempted robbery, and he became considerably alarmed at the closeness of the pursuit that was at once commenced. He fled to Baltimore, and while there he learned that his wife was visiting in the same city.

He called at the residence where she was stopping, but failed to find her at home, and upon inquiring of some of the neighbors, he was informed that the house did not bear a very good name.

Meeting her upon the street shortly afterwards, he attempted to draw his pistol and threatened to kill her. The lady, however, stoutly asserted her innocence, and Howard, becoming mollified by her explanations, repaired with her to the house, when he discovered that she was simply visiting an aunt, who was a very respectable lady.

Howard soon began to evince a decided melancholy, and seemed to be in constant fear of assassination. He told his wife, at one time, that he had done something that would yet result in his death.

What that something was, remains a mystery to this day

—and no one has yet succeeded in discovering the causes which led to his being murdered.

He returned to Philadelphia with his wife, and one evening, while in the Continental Hotel, he indulged in a violent quarrel with some noted thieves, several of whom were suspected of having been concerned in the murder of Mr. Barron, but against whom no definite proofs could be adduced. In this altercation he was openly accused of an attempt to betray his friends, which so incensed him that he struck his accuser in the face.

The quarrel grew furious, and finally one of the men departed suddenly, and it was alleged in quest of a pistol to shoot Howard. The matter was finally settled, and the party became apparent friends once more.

His old companions began to display in a very decided manner their suspicions with regard to him, and frequent mutterings foretold the coming of the storm. Among those who evinced the most unmistakable antipathy towards him was Shang Draper, with whom Howard had always been upon terms of the closest intimacy, and whose friendship heretofore had seemed to be undoubted.

It was alleged, that while Howard and his wife were living in Brooklyn, they were frequently visited by Mrs. Draper. She was quite a handsome woman, with a fair complexion and a very neat and attractive person. Her eyes, which were light blue, were large and expressive, and, it was stated, dwelt more fondly upon the handsome Howard than was befitting the wife of another.

Howard's pleasing manners had made quite an impression upon that lady, and they became more or less intimate, but not to the extent of arousing the suspicions of his wife, who was perfectly cognizant of the intimacy existing between them. Draper, however, is known to have been exceedingly jealous of Howard's attentions to his wife, and those who knew him anticipated trouble in consequence.

Howard was also unfortunate enough to have excited the jealousy of " Billy " Porter, by the polite attentions which he paid to Mrs. Porter ; and one time when Porter was visiting Canada he got into trouble, and sent for his wife to come to him.

She came, accompanied by Howard, who actively interested himself in behalf of his friend. Upon their arrival Porter upbraided his wife severely, and gave vent to his suspicions of her intercourse with Howard. This matter soon blew over, and frequently thereafter both Porter and Draper availed themselves of Howard's skill in various operations in which they engaged.

Howard had, previous to these events, been regarded as one of the most faithful friends in the " crooked " fraternity, and on one occasion, after robbing a safe near the coal regions, in Pennsylvania, of fifty thousand dollars, Howard and his two friends fled to Washington. They were overtaken by telegraph and arrested. They compromised the matter with the parties, and agreed to surrender up their booty, which had been hidden near the scene of the robbery.

The two friends of Howard were locked up, and Howard giving his word of honor that he would surrender the money, was allowed to depart upon his mission. This he did, and returned faithfully to his friends, making the promised restitution, after which the prisoners were released.

At one time, in Chicago, Howard was suspected of dealing in counterfeit money, and the notorious Felkers, of Chicago, attempted to fasten upon him some evidence of his participation in the "shoving of the queer." A "stool-pigeon" of these men—a person by the name of Sergeant—was the person selected to entrap Howard—not with the view of arresting him for the crime, but for the purpose of levying blackmail.

Howard met this man by appointment, and having been fully informed as to his designs upon him, after a short conversation agreed to sell him a package of counterfeit money at the rate of two thousand dollars for five hundred. A subsequent meeting was arranged for, and promptly, at the time appointed, both men made their appearance. Without unnecessary delay the quondam detective received his package of spurious notes, and Howard placed in his pocket the five hundred dollars genuine money which he had been promised. No sooner had Sergeant disposed of the notes thus received, about his person, than he attempted to arrest Howard for the offense, but the athletic burglar delivered a powerful blow upon the nose of his assailant and succeeded in escaping.

Considerably damaged and decidedly crest-fallen the detective stool-pigeon repaired to the office of his employers to report the result of his last interview. Here another surprise and disappointment awaited him, for upon opening the package which he had received he discovered that, instead of receiving counterfeit bills, he had expended five hundred dollars of genuine money for ten or fifteen dollars in good bills, which lay upon the top of a very comfortably-sized package of neatly trimmed wrapping paper. The wily Howard had been entirely too "fly" for the gentlemen who found themselves so egregiously duped.

He was afterwards arrested, but in the absence of legitimate proof of his guilt he was discharged.

Just prior to his decease Howard, in partnership with Porter and Irving, was engaged in a silk robbery in the vicinity of New York city. They succeeded in carrying off about six thousand dollars worth of silks, and escaped detection.

The owner of the store was an Irishman of very eccentric habits, and who had no confidence whatever in the security of banks. He, therefore, acted as his own banker, and it was alleged would secrete his money within the folds of the silks which constituted his stock. Upon this particular occasion, it was ascertained, the careful storekeeper had concealed about fifteen hundred dollars in one of the rolls of silk which these burglars succeeded in carrying away.

Many think that Howard found this money, appropriated it to his own use, and declined to divide with his "pals," and by some this action has been regarded as the cause of his death.

Whatever the cause may have been, the man was foully murdered. Whether Shang Draper, in a fit of jealousy, murdered the disturber of his peace, as he is reported to have done in a similar case which occurred previously, or whether Porter and Draper, joining in a common cause in which their "domestic honors" were outraged, slew the suspected cause of it, or, yet again, whether protesting thieves, quarreling over a fair division of the spoils of their criminal ventures and exasperated at the supposed treachery of their comrade, fired the fatal bullet, may never be known.

George Howard has paid the fearful penalty for his crimes, and a disgraced family and a sorrowing wife are alone left to deplore the loss or hail the relief which his murder has occasioned.

LIGHTNING STEALERS

AND

THE DETECTIVE.

CHAPTER I.

Telegraphy and Criminals.

IN these days of energy and push of rapid fortunes and quick disasters, it is an interesting subject to the student of current events, when glancing at the records of the past, he may note the progress that, by comparison, stamps the present century as the most remarkable in the Christian era.

The knowledge of man, within the limits of the past century, nay, within the brief years of the present generation, has been brought to a state of culture never before attainable. Discoveries have been made and appliances perfected which open to the vision of all the avenues to a universal intelligence whose approaches are as various as the appliances themselves.

All the various branches of science within the compass of the human mind have, by the genius which stamps the age, been so developed and so simplified that ignorance is no longer excusable or to be defended, and knowledge, being within the reach of all, has become an open book even to the casual observer.

Perhaps in no other particular has this evidence of advancement and progression been more marked than in the extension of the commerce of the world, and in the invention of those appliances which have brought the nations of the earth, with their great variety of products and manufactures, in close connection. The steamship plows the waves and carries within her broad arm port the interchange of luxuries and necessities between our shores and foreign lands. The railroads which stretch over our vast continent their network of iron and steel, levelling distance, bridging the valleys, climbing the mountains and leaping the flowing rivers, carrying into the far-off western wilds the sturdy emigrant and the ambitious miner, have performed giant labor in the development of the resources and industries of a land richly endowed by nature with all the elements of wealth and sustenance.

The barren prairies have yielded to the plowshare of the husbandman, and vast fields of grain are waving their luxuriant forms, where but a short time before roving herds of animals grazed upon the plains, undisturbed by the crack of the rifle, the click of the mower or the advancing stride of civilization.

From the Atlantic to the Pacific, towns and villages and cities have sprung up almost as miraculously as though under the touch of the wizard's wand: the growing and wide-spreading population have given an added impetus to the inventor and the manufacturer; new industries to supply new wants are continually being developed and utilized for the benefit of mankind.

Delving beneath the surface, the sturdy miner forces from their hidden beds the coal, the iron and the precious metals, thus contributing to the comfort of a people, advancing the progress of invention, and adding to the material wealth of a great and growing nation.

But even these appliances are insufficient to keep pace with this onward march of civilization and of commerce. The means of communication between distant points must be more rapidly and securely established. The systematic transportation of the mails, however expeditious it may be, is no longer available for the practical purposes of trade or the conveyance of intelligence, which must be instantly accomplished in order to be of benefit or value, and to supply this want the inventive minds have been laboring successfully in the production and use of the electric telegraph.

No longer must trade remain inactive, awaiting the ordinary, but somewhat tardy, transmission of intelligence, but with the quickness of thought the electric current darts from continent to continent, over the land and under the sea; and the whole world is now, as it were, within speaking distance and upon speaking terms.

The piping notes of peace or the trumpet blasts of war are heard in our own land simultaneously with their utterance, although the scene of active operations may be thousands of miles away; and the pulse of the American market beats spontaneously with the fluctuations of the London Exchange or the Parisian Bourse. The imaginary girdle of the sprightly Puck has become a living reality; the genius of humanity has "snatched the lightning from the gathering clouds," and the wonderful in nature has succumbed to the wonderful in man.

As the subject of Telegraphy, with its uses and abuses, is to form the basis of the narrative contained in the following pages, a short compendium of the most important phases through which, as a science, it has passed from theory to practice, from speculation to an established and important fact, may not be out of place.

Long before Telegraphy attained its present perfection by the introduction of voltaic electricity as its motive power, individuals and nations were in the habit of communicating information of battles, defeats and victories by means of beacon fires, signals of sounds, of dumb signs, and of lamp signals, as proposed by Æneas.

The flag signals, as universally practiced at sea for communicating between ships, has long been in successful operation, with gratifying results. The " *Tellograph* " of Chappe, invented in 1792, and brought into use during the French Revolution, was another step in the direction of making " conversing at a distance " a practical success. This device consisted simply of a cross-bar, erected on a pole, from which arms were suspended, and by means of ropes the arms were capable of a variety of movements, which, by a systematic arrangement, were easily operated and understood.

From this arose many plans of a Telegraph, notably the " *Semaphore*," a French modification, which came into use in 1816, and is in practical operation to-day on some lines of railroad for signal purposes.

The North American Aborigines made use of regular stations, and spelled words by means of fires of various hues

and substances, and the Indians of the Northwestern Territory made use of these means to convey the information of the approach of General Fremont as he passed through their regions.

But in the meantime, in 1745, Franklin had flown his kite, and had drawn the electricity from the clouds, while Newton and others labored to bring it into general use.

The earliest records of this power of transmitting the electric fluid to any distance, of which we have any knowledge, carries us back to the year 1727, when the annals of science tells us that one Stephen Grey, a pensioner of the Charter House, London, made some random experiments which led to the inference that electricity could be transmitted through strings and wire. He employed a wire about seven hundred feet long, suspended in the air by silk threads, and connected it with an excited glass tube at one end, while another person observed the electrification at the opposite end.

Various attempts were made after that time to ascertain the distance to which the electric fluid could be transmitted by an insulated wire. The inquiry was taken up in 1733 by Dufay and Symner, but no fresh results seem to have been obtained. Then came Franklin, and a little later Dr. Winkler, a German Professor, became identified with researches in physical experiments, but even at this time no one seems to have had the remotest idea of turning it to any practical purpose. In 1746 the "Leyden Jar" was discovered, which tended greatly to assist experiments in the transmission of electric power, and about that period the names of Desaguilliers, a Frenchman, and Dr. Watson, a Welsh Bishop, are recorded as being connected with electricity.

The latter stretched a wire across the river Thames, over

the old Westminster Bridge, in 1747, and at a later period he repeated the experiment by transmitting an electric charge through a wire 2,800 feet long. In the following year he succeeded in operating through 10,000 feet of wire, suspended on wooden poles erected on Shooters' Hill.

Dr. Franklin made similar experiments at Philadelphia in the year 1747 by stretching wires across the Schuylkill River; and Dulac, we are told, experimented in the same year on wires which were extended across the Lake of Geneva; but nobody, not even our own great genius, Dr. Franklin, seems to have harbored the slightest suspicion of the great results to which these early inquiries would ultimately lead.

In the year 1774 Le Sage, a Swiss physician, operated at Geneva on a telegraph comprising twenty-four insulated metallic wires, each wire connected with a pith ball electroscope, which corresponded to one letter of the alphabet. From this, therefore, we must date the ripening into a system of the idea of transmitting intelligible sounds, and to the Swiss doctor is to be accorded the honor of having given it a practical form. This instrument was submitted to Frederick the Great, but found no favor with the Prussian king.

The introduction of the railroad, with its various attendant requirements, peremptorily demanded the speedy development of some practical system of telegraphic communication. A general spirit of inquiry and experiment manifested itself, and an instrument invented by Mr. Wheatstone was in active operation at an early date, on the road between the towns of London and Bristol.

To Professor Samuel F. B. Morse, of New York, however, undoubtedly belongs the title of having been the first inventor

of the art of writing legible characters at a distance by means of electro-magnetism, and to our own time and generation has been left the duty so successfully performed of taming and subduing the fiery electrical current. In 1837 Morse's telegraph was first publicly exhibited in New York, and was at once recognized as the most simple and efficient—though still incomplete —but seven years after, in 1844, it was brought into practical use, and the cities of Washington and Baltimore had actual telegraphic communication.

From that time we may regard the system of telegraphy as a successful and satisfying science, and, yielding to the increased public demand, it has made prodigious and astounding strides. Oceans and territories have been wired by the galvanic thread, and "the uttermost parts of the earth" have been brought within the circle of civilization.

It would seem, to an intelligent observer, that a science so important as this should have thrown around it all the safeguards that are so essentially necessary to protect it from the improper uses of those who may seek to prostitute it to their own purposes, and in the following pages I shall endeavor to portray some of the abuses of this valuable medium of communication, which, even in the absence of restraining and punishing influences, I was enabled to remedy, and, in some respects, to prevent.

CHAPTER II.

Spurious Telegrams and their effect upon " Change."

IN the fall of 1867 the commercial circles of the city of New York were thrown from their usual base of calm and systematic serenity by the frequent reception and publication of telegraphic information, which, upon subsequent examination, would be discovered to be spurious and untruthful. The stock and gold exchanges were being continually agitated by conflicting statements, which, in the excited state of public opinion attendant upon the spirit of reckless speculation, which seemed at that time to have taken possession of the entire community, was accompanied by most disastrous results.

News, apparently authenticated, conveying the intelligence of the burning of railroad bridges, with attendant loss of life, was made the subject of a " Board " movement, which, by depreciating the stock of the corporation alleged to be injured, would compel worthy and needy persons to dispose of their investments at ruinous prices, while the fraudulent operators would thus be enabled to enrich themselves at the expense of those whose limited means did not enable them to incur the risk of holding investments momentarily considered unsafe.

Another point of attack seemed to be the Pacific Mail Steamship Company, and the reported loss of vessels connected with that line was frequently the means of ruining care-ful business men, who had invested in the capital stock of that corporation, while the designing and corrupt manipulators of the "lightning" grew rich upon the spoils.

The gold market perhaps showed greater fluctuations under the influence of these spurious flashes of intelligence than other and more legitimate investments. So precarious was the position of this circulating medium at that time that the slightest rumor, currently reported, would instantly have its effect "on Change," and in a few hours, before the truth or falsity of the report could be discovered, millionaires would find themselves mendicants, and the ruined gambler of to-day would become the wealthy broker of to-morrow.

During the month of October, 1867, a number of these fictitious dispatches were sent over the wires, and, being published in the reliable daily journals, at once obtained credence. The whole wide range of the numberless investments of the capitalists of the country were compelled to submit to the influences which these startling and erroneous reports produced. Steamship and railroad companies, mining enterprises, insurance associations and banking institutions, all came within the scope of the attacks from these unscrupulous, but seemingly well-informed, gamesters.

The evident air of truthfulness and the unquestionable character of the transmission and reception of these messages were unmistakable, and, added to this, a number of dispatches to private parties connected with the corporations, conveying the same information, at once disarmed any suspicion of the genuineness of these evil tidings.

General publicity was immediately given of the alarming

9

news, and the frightened stockholders of these mammoth corporations were filled with dread and consternation at the effect
this would naturally have upon their investments. Millions
of dollars of property would be repoited as lost at one fell
swoop, and this information was usually sufficient to cause intense dismay and to have a seriously depressing influence upon
securities generally looked upon as safe and profitable.

At the "Exchange" the scene frequently was one of excitement and frenzy—the pale, haggard faces of the anxious
individuals who, having unbounded confidence in the safety of
the company, had selected their securities as a profitable investment, and who now contemplated with amazement and alarm
the disasters which foreboded ruin, the completeness of which
they endeavored to ameliorate by a hurried disposition at immense sacrifices. The "Bulls" and the "Bears" of the market, the "*knowing ones*," who, regarding any startling information with delight, were clamoring noisily in their frantic efforts
to buy and sell the doubtful chattels, contributed to the production of a scene at once painful and exciting; while in the
background stood the Machiavelian crew, whose villainy had
produced the general scare, and who now took advantage of
this golden opportunity to enrich themselves at the expense of
their less unscrupulous victims.

To one who has never had the opportunity of witnessing
the wild and extravagant operations of the speculators in
council at a time of rife excitement, but a meager idea can be
given of the tumult and confusion which are its attendant circumstances; and it is probable that in no other condition of excitement do men, as a collective body, so entirely give them-

selves up to the exhibition of passion, and so outrageously and recklessly exhibit their animal propensities.

The scenes at a gambling table, where men of the lowest instincts gather, are not so noisy, so violent, or so repulsive to the better attributes of the man as the riot in the " Board " room. Men at a prize-fight compare favorably to these gentlemen on " Change." A pack of wolves, famished and furious, suddenly come upon blood, is the nearest approach to the howling fight of these men over the fluctuations of the market. Men are fighting to get in, begging to get in, and men are fighting their way out. They are wild with some frenzy that in the cooler atmosphere of life is never awakened, their eyes gleam strangely, their nerves stand out upon their temples and necks, they scream, gesticulate, and thrust each other out of the way, and shake their memoranda at each other like signals of distress.

The momentous importance of the transactions, which, until late years, were never known in these transfers, can be read in the faces of the operators, their principals, and subordinates, and it requires no moralist to discover that here is the quintessence of human avarice and unscrupulousness, or that everything else in the breasts of these men is overborne by the one dominant passion of life, fanned into a roaring flame by the moment's opportunity.

The excitements thus produced were only temporary, for searching inquiry soon developed the fact that the burning of a steamship, or the failure of a company, were fabrications, and that the telegraph had been successfully manipulated to further the designs of those who, taking advantage of the fears created by the information thus conveyed, had been enabled to depreciate marketable securities and purchase the same at the suddenly reduced valuation.

But this is but one side of the picture. It does not tell the story of the troubled hearts and saddened faces of the men who wearily entered their homes when the labors of the day were over ; it does not tell the story of the men who left those homes in the morning in the possession of wealth and came back to them at nightfall bankrupts. Nor does it tell of the after consequences, when luxurious homes were to be given up, and their possessors, after the enjoyment of diligently-acquired wealth, were compelled to buffet against the contending waves of poverty and want.

The situation became alarming ; the telegraph authorities and the community realized the necessity of prompt action in order to discover these frauds, and to prevent their repetition if possible.

The prospect was rendered all the more doubtful from the fact that all the relative circumstances pointed conclusively to the conviction that some one, who either had been or was at the present time in the employ of the Telegraph Company, was in active co-operation with this movement. The manner of transmitting the messages seemed to be regular, the forms were observed with religious truthfulness, and the general correctness of the management of the entire affair clearly demonstrated the fact that the persons interested in this matter were adept in the manipulation of the telegraph, and intelligent observers of the vagaries of the money market.

It was therefore determined that every effort should be made to unearth the scoundrels who were thus preying upon the public, and the Telegraph Company resolved that no stone should be left unturned in the thorough investigation which they decided to make.

Their reputation, and the safety of the financial circles demanded it, and the result of this inquiry will be shown hereafter.

CHAPTER III.

My Services are Engaged—A Visit to the Operating Room—
Suspicions—The Investigation Begun.

IT was at this time that Mr. William Orton was President of
the Western Union Telegraph Company, a position which he
held for a number of years, and the duties of which he fulfilled
with rare ability and fidelity. It may readily be imagined that
these revelations were exceedingly annoying and perplexing to
him, and, as he was held mainly responsible for the proper and
successful management of the affairs of the company, he determined to begin an active inquiry and a vigorous crusade at once.
The manipulators must be discovered, and speedily, and no
efforts should be spared to accomplish this result.

For that purpose he decided to call into energetic co-operation the resources of my detective bureau, and calling upon Mr.
George H. Bangs, my General Superintendent in New York
city, he related to him all the particulars as far as known, of
these operations, and requested him to undertake the task of
tracing them to their inception, and discovering, if possible, the
parties who were identified with them.

From the account thus given it seemed very evident that
these spurious dispatches were manufactured at and transmitted
from some point in the West, where, beyond the reach of suc-

cessful detection, they could tap the wires, and by the use of pocket instruments either receive information of importance and prevent its further passage eastward, or successfully forward the bogus intelligence by preserving all the forms of numbering and cipher necessary to establish perfect confidence in its authenticity.

There also seemed to be indubitable evidences of the fact that some of the employees of the company were actively engaged in this work, as by no other means could the entire machinery of the company be so successfully employed.

Mr. Bangs immediately communicated the result of this interview to me, by a cipher dispatch known only to ourselves, at my main office in Chicago, and together we determined to make a thorough and systematic examination of the various offices of the company, with the view of discovering any suspicious persons who were in their employ, and by that process be enabled to labor intelligently in the work of detecting the guilty parties.

Consequently, on the morning following the receipt of this intelligence, I called at the office of the Telegraph Company in Chicago and had an interview with General Anson Stager, the then Superintendent of the Western Department. I found him fully alive to the importance of the occasion, and disposed to render whatever assistance that was in his power to command to further the object desired. I related to him the information that I had received; stated my opinion as to the complicity of some of the employees of the company, and requested him to conduct me through the operating rooms in order to afford me an opportunity of scrutinizing the various persons in their employ, and perhaps, by that means, be enabled to discover if there was any one employed in that office who was liable to suspicion.

We ascended to the upper story of the building, where we found a large number of operators, both male and female, busily engaged. The steady clicks of the instruments were the only sounds that we heard as the various messages were being received and dispatched, and I thought, as I watched the silent workers, and listened to the methodical and regular ticking, of the wonderful ingenuity of man, and the results achieved by his labor and invention.

Here, perhaps, were flying, as upon the wings of thought, the tidings that would carry to a happy family the clouds of death and disappointment; here the stirring items of a war of men, a story of desolation and of carnage; and there the joyful announcement of a happy marriage, or the depressing news of financial failure. Far and wide over the broad land were speeding these messengers, and yet their only recorders were the dumb, mechanical registers, which worked on regardless of the effect of their operations, or the influence which they exerted upon communities.

Thinking thus, I passed carelessly around, as though engaged in an ordinary examination of the various workings of the company, and actuated by no other motive save that of curiosity. While thus occupied, and engaged in a casual conversation with General Stager, I noticed one young man, as we approached him, turn suddenly around, with a start, slightly change color, and then immediately resume his occupation. Ever and anon, however, I would find his eyes wandering to the direction where we were. I immediately became suspicious; the conscious look of guilt could not be mistaken,

"*I felt reasonably sure that this was one of the individuals I was after*."

and I felt reasonably sure that this was one of the individuals I was in search of.

Long experience in the business of a detective and in dealing with men of all classes and conditions, of all grades and professions, had enabled me to judge very correctly of a man's character by his physiognomy, and I was convinced that this young man was not to be trusted.

"What is that young man's name?" I inquired of Mr. Stager, after we had passed out of the hearing of the individual inquired about.

"Charles Cowdrey," answered Mr. Stager, "and he is an exceedingly smart young operator."

"Has he been in your employ any length of time?"

"Yes, for about three years, and his brother George was with us for nearly seven years."

"Do you know anything about him, aside from his connection with the company?" I asked.

"No, I think not; he was recommended by his brother George, and upon examination he was found to be pretty bright, so we gave him a position."

"What wires does he work on?" I asked.

"On the western wires from Omaha, Salt Lake and San Francisco," replied General Stager, suddenly looking up into my face, as though he began to understand the drift of my questioning.

My suspicions became almost realistic certainties upon the receipt of this information, and I decided to have this young man carefully watched; to place some one in direct communication with him, and, if possible, win his confidence and discover his doings.

9*

After we had gone down stairs I inquired of Mr. Stager, if he had not somebody in his employ whom he could trust implicitly, and who, combining the duties of a telegraph operator with those of an embryotic detective, would be of service in the investigation which I now contemplated.

" Yes," replied Mr. Stager, " I think I have the very person you want; there is a young man at present in this office who is bright, active and trustworthy, and I think, with a proper understanding of his duties, he will answer the purposes you desire."

" Send him to my office then, at seven o'clock this evening, if you can rely upon him," I remarked, " and I will endeavor to make use of him."

After some further inquiries as to the residence of Cowdrey and his general habits, I took my leave of General Stager and returned to my office, determined to impress into the service the person whom he should designate for that purpose, if, upon examination, I should find him sufficiently able and trustworthy.

I dislike exceedingly to depend upon resources and individuals not under my immediate control or in direct connection with my Agencies, but as the only operative upon my force at that time who understood the science of telegraphy, was absent upon another investigation, I was compelled, from the force of circumstances, to avail myself of the opportunity thus afforded of using an employee of the Telegraph Company.

At the time appointed, the young man selected by Mr. Stager made his appearance, accompanied by that gentleman, and announced himself as Frank Osborn. After a few inquiries I found him to be exceedingly bright, intelligent and rather anxious to undertake the novel duties that were designed for him, so I concluded to take him upon trial, and to commence active operations at once.

A long consultation ensued, and it was decided that young Osborn should be discharged upon the morrow from his employment, without any apparent cause, and that he should express himself in unmeasured terms to Cowdrey, with whom he was well acquainted, against the company, and then, if he succeeded in inducing his confidence, to lend himself to the schemes of those with whom he was working, and fully join with them in their undertaking.

I found Mr. Stager to be deeply in earnest in this matter; his long experience and quick foresight enabled him to make many valuable suggestions, which I cheerfully accepted, and between us arrangements were consummated which gave every indication of eventual success. As he was about leaving, Mr. Stager turned to me, saying: "Major, we are upon the right track, and between us these scoundrels will have a hard time; we shall rely faithfully upon your wisdom and determination, and be assured that all the resources in our power shall be placed at your disposal."

The General was evidently in earnest, and with his assistance I entertained no doubts of the result.

CHAPTER IV.

"My Operator" Discharged — A Secret Meeting — I Set up a Branch Office of the Telegraph Company.

THE following morning, according to the plan already formed and understood between General Stager and myself, young Osborn, whose position was immediately adjoining that of Charles Cowdrey's, was summoned to the office of General Stager, and by him informed that his services would not be further required by the company, and Osborn returned to the operating-room, apparently in great anger at the injustice that had been done to him. He related his grievance to Cowdrey, and threatened to repay the company for the injury they had inflicted upon him.

As he was about leaving, Cowdrey called out to him to come back, and, upon his returning, Cowdrey said :

"Frank, meet me to-night at the Randolph Hotel; I want to see you about something particular."

"All right," replied Osborn, "I will be there."

In the evening Osborn repaired to the hotel named, and shortly afterward Charles Cowdrey came in, accompanied by another individual, whom he introduced as George Van Stein.

After indulging in a drink at the bar, Cowdrey proposed that they should take a walk, and, lighting cigars, they sauntered out, and proceeded toward the lake front of the city, when, after walking a short distance, Cowdrey turned to Osborn and said :

"Frank, do you want to make a fortune, and at the same time pay the company the grudge you owe them ?"

"Do I ?" replied Osborn. "Well, as far as making money is concerned, you may be sure of that ; and as for getting even with the company, if I ever have the opportunity, you will see what I will do."

"Well, if you join with us, you will have an opportunity of accomplishing both objects," said Cowdrey.

Osborn immediately signified his readiness to become a party to any operation that would enable him to revenge himself upon the company, and the two others, being convinced of his sincerity, then invited him to the residence of Cowdrey, where they would be free from intrusion, and could talk more unreservedly of their plans.

They then proceeded to a house on Michigan avenue, where Cowdrey informed Osborn he resided, and which was one of the handsomest dwellings in that part of the city; the interior was luxuriously furnished with all the appointments that wealth could purchase, and an air of elegance was manifest throughout. This fact occasioned some surprise to Osborn, as he could scarcely understand how the remuneration of a telegraph operator could procure the comforts which he here saw displayed He forebore to make any remark, however, as the trio ascended the stairway, and, entering one of the chambers on the second floor, locked themselves in.

Being apparently well satisfied with Osborn's sincerity, they proceeded to fully divulge to him their plan of operations;

and, as the particulars of their movements were being related, Osborn's amazement became almost unbounded. So thoroughly were their plans matured, and so carefully were their tracks covered, that detection seemed almost impossible. In almost every main office some employee of the company had been secured who was identified with the scheme, and some of the most prominent brokers in New York city—men whose social standing was above suspicion, and who occupied high places in the community—were found to be the prime movers in this systematic attempt to subvert the telegraph to the base purposes of stock-gambling and respectable robbery.

He discovered also that the so-called Van Stein was no other than George Cowdrey, the brother of the present operator Charles, who was compelled to disguise himself and change his name on account of information previously received that inquiries were being made in regard to former operations.

After identifying himself fully with their prospective schemes and promising to meet them at some future time, when notified, Osborn took his leave and reported at the Agency.

It now became necessary to adopt some measures that would prevent the successful transmission of the messages through the collusion of Charles Cowdrey, and as it was equally necessary that such measures should be taken without exciting the suspicion of any person connected with the Company, I determined, after consultation with General Stager, to convert my private office into a temporary branch of the Telegraph Company, and to have all the messages to and from the West, pass through my hands before reaching the main office and Charles Cowdrey.

To accomplish this object it was necessary that the wires of the Company should be introduced into the building that I then occupied, that all the necessary working machinery should be set up there, and that trusty men should be selected as operators to receive the messages, and subject them to a rigid scrutiny before transmitting them further.

In accordance with these arrangements, the next morning one of my operatives presented a letter at the office of the Company, apparently emanating from General Grant, then acting as Secretary of War, stating that the exigencies of the Government service required that wires should be introduced into my office, and requesting the Company to have the necessary arrangements made to accomplish that object.

Of course this was a fabrication, but I had been so long connected with the Secret Service of the Government, and had been identified with the Government officials in almost every movement relating to the detection of Government malefactors, that the presentation of such a communication occasioned no surprise on the part of the telegraph officials, and the necessity existing was deemed a sufficient palliation for the use of the name of the War Secretary.

That it answered the purpose is undoubted, and in a very short time the wires of the Company opposite to my Agency had been successfully tapped and the intelligent conductors of the lightning were in active motion in an apartment hitherto undisturbed by such noisy visitants.

I have often thought of the varied histories which this little office of mine could unfold, did it possess the power of language. How its walls have echoed to the sounds of laughter and to the moans of despair; to the defiant tones of the desperate criminal brought to bay, and the pleading voice of the young offender, who realized, only when the hands of the law were upon him. the sin that he had committed and the shame that he had brought upon loving friends. Here I have received the magnates of a Nation ; the framers and expounders of its laws, and the trusted officers of Government; and here, too, in a different manner, I have held converse with the brutal murderer, whose badges of infamy were the shackles that encircled his wrists.

Here, too, I have listened to many recitals of crime and criminals, that, in spite of my stern sense of justice, would make the heart feel sad. I have seen strong men bowed to the ground with the weight of degradation which their actions had heaped upon them ; I have heard the prayers of a mother as she pleaded for mercy to her boy, for whom she would have laid down her life. Many, many times I have left this little room, after the close of a day of labor and of trying incidents, sad at heart and wearied in mind, as I reflected upon the crime and the misery with which I was so often brought in contact ; but I was upheld by the sustaining sense that I was rendering a duty to the community in the protection of society, in upholding the laws ; the preservation of the lives of many people, and that through my efforts only the guilty transgressors of the law were brought to punishment, while the virtuous and honorable were protected and sustained.

Now, however, the monotony was to be relieved and varied, and I was soon to be enabled to converse with innumerable people whom I never knew, and without the faintest fear of discovery I was to observe the operations of the gentlemanly rascals whom I intended to make an example of, and to intercept the fictitious items that were intended to operate so startlingly upon the money markets.

CHAPTER V.

Investigations in New York City—" Jimmy " and the " News Stealers "—A Nice Little Plan that was Suddenly Frustrated.

MEANWHILE Mr. Bangs was pursuing his investigations in New York city, and with some degree of success. He had ascertained the name of the party to whom the confirmatory telegrams were usually addressed, and was now engaged in the attempt to discover who the person was.

The telegram was directed to a Robert M. Bronson, at a certain number on Broadway, and an operative was immediately detailed to go to the house, inquire for Bronson, and, under pretense of requesting some information from him, obtain a description of the individual, and thus be enabled to watch his movements.

Upon going to the house mentioned, Mr. Hamilton, the operative, found it occupied by a French family, consisting of a man, and wife and one child, who rented to Bronson the front room on the second floor, and who evidently, by reason of previous instruction, conveniently knew nothing of the gentleman except the fact that he was very seldom in his office; that he only came for his letters, and did not have any particular hours or times for attending to business. It was determined, therefore, that Hamilton should be engaged by the Telegraph Company as a messenger, be intrusted with the delivery of messages, and in that capacity carry a dispatch to the unknown and seemingly unapproachable Bronson.

It is strange, sometimes, how discoveries are made in a direction in which no inquiries have been instituted, and how frequently individuals literally stumble upon knowledge. The man who, climbing a mountain in the West, and slipping in his ascent, caught at a growing bush to save himself from a fall, discovered at the root of the bush which he had unearthed the evidences of a silver mine which made him fabulously wealthy; the painter, who, in the heterogeneous admixture of color in his brush-cleaning liquid, discovered the flesh tint that ravished the beholder and excited the envy of his contemporaries; the musical composer, who, after frequent unsuccessful efforts, accomplished the task of producing upon the piano the effect of a storm at sea, by angrily striking the keys at each extremity of the instrument and bringing his hands rapidly together, are so many evidences of this accidental discovery of materials which have been a benefit to mankind, either in a broad or circumscribed manner, and which have been productive of results unexpected and undreamed of.

Hamilton had not been on duty more than twenty-four hours, when he discovered that he had become an object of regard to some of the larger and older boys.

Having been intrusted with a cable dispatch and instructed to deliver it according to the direction—that of a prominent firm of brokers—Hamilton started off to perform the duty, when, just as he had passed out of sight of the building, he was accosted by a young messenger, who was known to him as

Jimmy Woods—a sporting young fellow, who was also connected with the office. Jimmy was an authority among the
rest of the boys upon all subjects, from a horse-race to the
latest opera; he smoked and chewed tobacco, dressed loud, and
altogether was something of a swell in his limited way.

Jimmy always had money, always was well dressed, and
always had a good word for himself. It was a matter of surprise to many with whom he associated where the revenue
came from, but, as long as Jimmy looked out for himself, nobody seemed to trouble themselves any further about the matter.

Now it seemed that the day before a general revision of
the routes of the messengers had been made, and young Jimmy
found himself transferred to an entirely new locality, while
Hamilton had been assigned to the one formerly taken care of
by Jimmy. Hamilton's curiosity was somewhat excited when
Jimmy accosted him, but, as a shrewd detective, he preferred
to have the other disclose his mission, and he awaited Jimmy's
explanation. After a slight hesitancy it came:

"I say, ' 24 ' " (which was Hamilton's number as messenger), "hadn't I better help you a little this morning?"

"Oh, no!" said Hamilton. "I guess I can make out my
self. I know the city pretty well, and I guess I can get along
fast enough."

"S'pose I take those cables addressed to Morgan & Co. and
Jennings & Bro. I'll do that much to help you along, and I
won't be going out myself for a half hour."

Hamilton detected a shade of anxiety on the countenance
of the persistent Jimmy, and he thought that he appeared a
trifle too willing to be of service on the simple score of good
nature; so assuming a knowing expression, he quietly asked:

"Is there anything in it?"

Jimmy looked up suddenly, and then, with a wink of his eye, he took Hamilton's arm, saying:

"Come in here out of the way, I guess we can *divvy* on this."

On stepping into an open doorway, and concealing themselves from the view of the passers by, Jimmy revealed a state of affairs that occasioned Hamilton considerable surprise.

It appeared that for a long time a systematic scheme had been in operation, by which many so-called *respectable* brokers would become possessed of reliable telegraphic information, prior to its reception by the parties to whom such information was addressed, and at whose expense the same was obtained. The scheme consisted in bribing the messengers, who, upon the reception of information of a character calculated to have any effect upon the markets or the stock board, would deliver the message first to one of the parties to the bribe, and after he had had an opportunity to become possessed of and use the information for his own profit, the messenger would deliver it to the party addressed.

"Now," said Jimmy, "you can make a dollar apiece on each one of these messages, and nobody will know anything about it."

To Hamilton this information seemed almost incredible, and he decided to inform the company of the discovery which he had unexpectedly made, so telling Jimmy that he would think about it, but that he was afraid to do anything of that kind yet, he left him, promising to talk to him again upon the subject.

Upon reporting his information to Mr. Orton on his return, measures were at once taken to discover the extent of this proceeding, and after a diligent inquiry, it was ascertained that a general system of bribery existed, and that no less than fifteen of the messengers were working in collusion with these brokers and supplying them with information designed for other people. Of course these employees were at once discharged, and active measures instituted to prevent a recurrence of such events. Jimmy suddenly found his occupation gone, and there was "weeping and wailing and gnashing of teeth" among the stock gambling fraternity, who found their system of news-stealing suddenly brought to an end.

As the information thus obtained related exclusively to the gold stock and market reports, both foreign and domestic, it can readily be imagined, in these days of speculation, how important a few minutes' anticipation of news might be to those who, taking advantage of any sudden rise or fall in prices, or any intelligence of an unusual nature, would be enabled to profit by their rascality, by the reception of the news thus surreptitiously obtained.

The chief object of the company being to preserve entire secrecy in the transmission of their dispatches, Mr. Orton was exceedingly exercised at this discovery, and he was quite relieved when the measures taken had produced the result desired, although he regretted the absence of any law that would enable him to punish those who had been guilty of this action.

It seems a matter of surprise, that while the statute books are crowded with laws for the protection of almost every right, and for the punishment of almost every crime, nothing could be found which would afford an opportunity of punishing the individuals who were thus engaged in the nefarious operation of stealing news intended for others than themselves, and converting it to their own base uses, and the only safety depended upon increased vigilance on the part of the telegraph officials.

"And soon my little room resounded to the clicking of the instruments as they conveyed far and wide the information they received."

Page 215.

CHAPTER VI.

My Telegraph Office—The Associated Press—The Telegraph as a Detective—A Leak Stopped—A Dispatch from Fort Sedgwick.

THE wires having been duly introduced into my office, and the necessary working machinery having been placed in position and in good running order, I was prepared to hear what other people had to say, without the necessity of being reciprocally communicative.

As Charles Cowdrey was detailed for night duty, and as the daily business of the telegraph company would have been materially interfered with by this interception of intelligence on my part; and as there was no reason to fear that any attempt would be made during the day to use the wires illegitimately, it was decided that my branch office should only be in active operation during the night. Trusted operators were detailed for that purpose, who were to be at their post from six o'clock in the evening and remain until the next morning to receive all messages that came over the wires, detaining such as might be deemed suspicious, and forwarding all the others without delay.

Soon my little room, dedicated to far different uses, resounded to the clicking of the instruments as they conveyed far and wide the information they received.

> " From world to world the couriers fly,
>   Thought winged and shod with fire;
> The angel of the stormy sky
>   Rides down the 'lectric wire."

A very short experience as a superintendent of an improvised telegraph office convinced me of the magnitude of the labor performed by these silent workers, and the wide and rapid and varied dissemination of intelligence through their agency.

I was particularly astonished at the manner in which intelligence of any important item of news was communicated to distant points, and by means of which quick transmission newspapers published in Maine or in California would appear simultaneously with the same items of general intelligence, thus enabling the whole country to be informed, at the same time, of the transaction of any event of general interest—and I was pleased to learn that this astonishment was not confined alone to myself. The telegraphic news reports of the American press, by their remarkable accuracy and the enormous amount of matter daily presented in them, have excited the surprise of the press of all other countries. A single issue of many of our metropolitan journals often contains three or four columns of telegraphic news, which, at the usual rate of charges, would, at the date of which I am writing, amount to at least five hundred dollars—a sum quite beyond the ability of even the leading London newspapers to pay daily. The inquiry then is, by what arrangement, therefore, is the press from Maine to Texas supplied with every important event which transpires in any part of our vast country, within a few minutes of its actual occurrence ?

In 1861, the leading journals in New York city associated themselves together for the purpose of collecting, and sharing in the expense of telegraphing, the most important items of news from all parts of the world. A general agent was appointed to superintend the practical operations of the system to be introduced, whose headquarters were to be in New York. Other agents were located in all the principal cities of the United States, British America, and in many of the European cities. Subsequently to the formation of this association, nearly all the daily newspapers in the United States became connected with it. Everything of interest occurring in any part of this country is telegraphed at once to the general office in New York, copies of the same being dropped at all intermediate points on the route, and the other parts of the country being supplied from the central office.

Of course, the larger share of the press reports come over the wires during the night, commencing about six o'clock and concluding generally about one o'clock in the morning, but not infrequently it has continued as late as four o'clock, and sometimes all night ; and it will thus be seen that mine was no idle office, and the operators, although only working upon the western wires, were kept busy during the hours which they occupied this improvised station.

I have attempted to give some faint idea of the magnitude of this system of telegraphing, but its practical workings must be seen to be appreciated.

In one other respect the telegraph has played an important part, and that is in the detection of crime ; and many instances

10

are upon the record where, but for the agency of the electric current, great criminals would have escaped from justice, and their apprehension would have been a matter of impossibility.

The murderer, after the commission of his crime, seeks safety in flight, and, entering the railroad train, is soon rapidly speeding away from the reach of his pursuers; but, more swiftly than the locomotive, a little messenger is winging its flight along the wires, and just as the guilty man imagines himself free from the law's pursuit, the heavy hand is laid upon his shoulder, and he is in custody. The telegraph, with the rapidity of thought, has anticipated his arrival, and officers, to whom the nature of his crime may be unknown, but to whom a description of his person has been given, arrest him, and he is held for the coming of those who can prove his identity and convict him of his offense.

An incident is told as having occurred in England a few years before the date of our story, though many such have transpired since, which may be worth repeating.

One night at ten o'clock the chief cashier of the Bank of England received a notice from Liverpool, by electric telegraph, to stop certain notes of large amounts. The next morning the descriptions were placed upon a card and given to the proper officer, with instructions to see that no person exchanged them for gold. Within ten minutes they were presented at the counter by an apparent foreigner, who pretended not to speak a word of English. A clerk in the office, who spoke German, interrogated him, when he declared that he had received them on the exchange at Antwerp six weeks before. Upon reference to the books, however, it appeared that the notes had only been issued from the bank about fourteen days and therefore he was detected at once as the utterer of a false-hood. An officer was sent for, who forthwith locked him up, and the notes were detained. A letter was at once written to Liverpool, and the real owner of the notes came up to town on Monday morning. He stated that he was about to sail for America, and that whilst at a hotel he had exhibited the notes. The person now in custody advised him to stow his valuables in his portmanteau, as Liverpool was a very dangerous place for a man to walk about with so much money in his pocket, and the owner of the property had no sooner left the house than his adviser broke open the portmanteau and stole them. The thief was thereupon taken to the Mansion House, but could not make any defense, and as the sessions were going on at the Old Bailey, by a little after ten o'clock the next morn-ing, such was the speed, that not only a true bill was found, but the trial by petit jury was concluded and the thief was sen-tenced to expiate his offense by ten years' transportation.

An amusing incident occurred during this time that is, per-haps, worth noticing in this connection. A jewelry store had been robbed of a large amount in Chicago, and after careful in-vestigation and searching inquiry it was ascertained that the supposed thief had left upon a train going East, but as no def-inite description of the man could be obtained, and as an old black hair trunk was missing from the store, it was supposed that this had been made the receptable of the stolen property, and I, at once, telegraphed along the line to arrest any person having in his possession such an article. At Buffalo, the train was boarded by one of my men, and an examination of the bag-gage car disclosed the black hair trunk, and on reaching New York city the officer stationed himself where he could discover

the individual who claimed it.   Shortly afterwards an individual, well known in crooked circles, but now completely disguised, presented his check for his baggage, when the officer immediately arrested him and took charge of the trunk, which he
directed should be conveyed to my Agency in New York. The
surprise of the thief may well be imagined. He knew that he
had not been suspected prior to leaving Chicago, and that his
trunk should be recognized seemed astounding. Turning to
the officer he said :

"Now, I want to know how you knew that I was on this
train."

"Oh !" replied the officer, " I guessed it."

"Yes, but how did you come to recognize me ; you never
saw me before ?" queried the prisoner.

"Oh, I guessed at that too," said the officer.

"Ah ! that may be," suggested the nonplussed individual ;
"but how in thunder did you come to guess out my old hair
trunk so quickly ?"

The result of the guessing, however, was that all of the
stolen articles were found within the innocent cause of his capture, and the gentleman of the " jimmy and dark lantern " was
remanded back to Chicago for trial.

I made another discovery at this time, which enabled the
Telegraph Company to stop a large leak in their cash receipts,
and to dispense with the services of some of their operators
who were using the wires for their own purposes.

I directed the men engaged in my Agency to keep a record of all messages that were intercepted by them, and this
record was made the basis of a daily report to the Company of
the business done at my branch office. An examination of

this record disclosed the fact that a considerable discrepancy existed between the messages reported as received at the main office and those which actually passed over the wires, and an inquiry was at once instituted as to the cause. Upon investigation it was discovered that some of the operators were in the habit of transmitting messages for their friends without charge, and oftentimes dispatches of great length were sent and received, frequently detaining other more important and more profitable business.

Of course this could not be allowed to continue, and it was decided to make an example of some of the offending operators, which was accordingly done, and prompt discharges were followed by the arrest of one of the parties who was accused of defrauding the Company in this manner. Upon a hearing of the case, however, it was decided by the legal authorities that electricity was not such material as a person could be accused of stealing, and therefore the charge was dismissed.

The evil, however, had been stopped, and no fears were entertained of a repetition of the offense, although it seemed unjust that no laws were in existence to protect the company and their property from appropriation by improper persons and for improper purposes.

Thus matters went on for nearly a week, and nothing was received of a character to awaken suspicion, and nothing had been heard from Osborn, who had suddenly disappeared, when one evening, just as I was about leaving the office, a dispatch was received from him in the cipher agreed upon, as follows :

"Send some one to Fort Sedgwick. I am watched too closely to do anything at all myself. Send some one unknown —send at once.   OSBORN."

This dispatch I took at once to the office of General Stager, and we determined to send my operative, John Conway, a bold, fearless man, and one who could be trusted in any emergency, who had now returned, and was available for this purpose, to the scene of operations at Fort Sedgwick.

The general cordially indorsed this plan, and in a very short time John Conway was upon the road, with full instructions as to his line of duty, and with a determination to perform it at whatever hazard.

CHAPTER VII.

The Wire-Tappers Start Upon Their Expedition—Attempt to Bribe an Operator—The Spurious Dispatch Prepared—The Operation Performed—Captured by Indians.

LET us now follow Frank Osborn in his operations with the Cowdreys, and explain the cause of his failure to report prior to the reception of the dispatch alluded to in the preceding chapter. After leaving the Agency, as has been previously described, he returned to his hotel and prepared to await developments. The next evening, however, just as he was about to retire for the night, he was surprised by the sudden appearance of George Cowdrey, accompanied by another man to him unknown, whose excited manner convinced him that something unusual had occurred. Upon going to Osborn's room Cowdrey immediately closed the door, and, producing a revolver, said threateningly:

"Osborn, when a man's life is in danger there is no use in wasting words. I want you to get ready to go with us at once; do you understand me?"

"Put down that pistol and tell me what is the matter," said Osborn, who was not at all dismayed by the menacing attitude of his companion, but who was anxious to acquire information.

"Never mind what the matter is; you are going with us at

once," replied Cowdrey, but at the same time lowering his pistol.

Osborn, believing it best to comply with the demand of Cowdrey, trusting for some favorable opportunity to communicate with me as to his whereabouts and destination, at once signified his willingness to accompany them whenever and wherever they chose. This prompt acquiescence on the part of Osborn seemed to disarm whatever suspicions Cowdrey may have entertained in regard to him, and his manner became more open and cheerful.

Hastily packing together the various articles composing his wardrobe which he designed taking with him, he announced his readiness to accompany them, and Cowdrey and his companion having previously made all necessary arrangements, they were soon on their way to the great West.

Cowdrey's demeanor toward Osborn, though friendly and seemingly careless, was watchful in the extreme, as though he doubted his sincerity, and was determined that no action of his companion should escape his notice; and Osborn, discovering this, resolved to take no action that would arouse further suspicion, but would yield a ready assent to every proposition made, in order to fully establish that confidence which was absolutely necessary to the success of his plans.

He consequently made no effort to communicate with General Stager or myself, at that time, choosing rather to await an opportunity for doing so when it could be accomplished without the fear of possible detection.

Cowdrey had provided himself with all the necessary implements for tapping the wires, and his provisions were most complete; everything connected with the proper working of a telegraph office had been provided, and opportunity only was lacking to put them into practical operation.

Arriving at the city of Omaha, in Nebraska, they took the Union Pacific Railroad for Julesburg in Colorado, where they disembarked, and, putting up at a hotel in that place, they determined to remain a few days preparatory to starting out upon their campaign of rascality.

What a wonderful transformation this far western country has undergone in a few years! Only a short time before this the great plains and majestic mountains were given up to the roaming bands of Indians, and save the occasional advent of an adventurous miner or hunter, the red man held undisputed sway over the fields and forests; but the steady march of improvement and civilization was ever onward, and in its passage towns and villages sprang up almost miraculously. The broad fields were teeming with their wealth of grain and other products, the railroads stretched their great lengths over the continent; the telegraph flashed from ocean to ocean; the school-house and the chapel reared their modest forms, and the effects of education and well-directed labor were everywhere made wonderfully manifest. Here too followed, as a consequence, the capital of the county; money, that great incentive to ambition, the motive power that stimulates the energies of man, was to be made, and the forms of its manipulation necessarily followed; and here in this far-off locality were found banking institutions, and all the materials of financial and commercial exchange.

The next morning George Cowdrey went to the bank in Julesburg and presented a draft for two hundred and fifty dollars, on J. R. Bronson & Co., which on the second morning following was duly honored, and with the funds thus obtained,

10*

the party proceeded to equip themselves for the journey before them. There was still some danger to be apprehended from roaming bands of Indians, and this fact necessitated the procur ing of rifles and ammunition; and, being provided with these, together with such stores as they needed, on the third day following their arrival the party took the stage for Fort Sedgwick, located upon the stage route a few miles westward.

Here the party alighted, and proceeding to the telegraph office they made inquiries as to communications existing between the Fort and eastern and western cities. Finding that direct communications could be obtained Cowdrey attempted to bribe the operator there to forward a dispatch in reference to the depreciation of mining stocks in Montana. This was met with a prompt refusal on the part of the operator, and as he threatened to have the party arrested if they persisted in their demands or remained in the town, it was thought best to desist and to make a hurried departure from a locality where evidently nothing could be accomplished, and much danger incurred.

Osborn, however, had, unobserved by Cowdrey or his companion, managed to write the dispatch which I afterwards received, and also a note to the operator, explaining the situation to him, containing instructions to whoever came as to the route taken, and requesting him to forward the dispatch to the address named, which note, as they were about leaving, he threw upon the desk without being detected by either of his confederates.

" This is bad business," said Cowdrey, " and now there is no other course left but to depend upon our own resources."

They then proceeded on their way on foot, having provided

themselves with provisions for several days, determined to oper-ate upon the wires at a point where they were assured they would escape detection, and thus the more successfully carry out their nefarious schemes.

Unaccustomed as they were to the hard life they had now to encounter, it may well be imagined that their journey was anything else but pleasant. Tramping all day over the rugged roads, and camping at night with no covering over them but the blue canopy and the bright stars, their experience was decid-edly at variance with the luxurious ease and comfort to which they had been accustomed at home, and had it not been for the inducements held out to them of prospective fortune, they would have retraced their steps and returned home.

But so deeply rooted is this inordinate desire for gain in the minds of men, that almost any hardship will be endured for the purpose of accomplishing it.

The defaulting clerk who sees in the near future the golden fruits of ease and competence and luxury, and so listens to the siren voices that lure him on to destruction and disgrace ; the trusted officer of moneyed institutions, who, to gratify an extrav-agant taste and a desire for the good things of the world, trails his honor in the dust and is at last compelled to face the awful majesty of the law, are not new examples of this theory. The idea of the sudden acquisition of wealth has from the earliest times taken possession of the minds of men and molded their characters and dispositions.

The ancient alchemists, who devoted the best energies of their minds to the vain attempt to produce gold from the baser metals and from minerals, and whose futile efforts to equal the brilliancy and value of the diamond by the carbonizing of other

and _ess valuable materials, are so many evidences of the an-
tiquity of this craving of the mind and heart for wealth which
is not acquired by the slow process of labor and economy.

So, too, with the modern speculators, who are fretting their
souls and shriveling their hearts in the continual battle of
chance, and who are gambling in gold, stocks, grain and every
conceivable article of merchandise, in the hope that by some
lucky turn of the wheel of fortune they will awake some morning and find themselves wealthy.

Go into a faro bank, and look at the anxious faces of the
men assembled there.   All their nerves seem to be strained
to their utmost tension as they watch the turning of the lucky
or the unlucky card; oblivious to all else, their thoughts are
concentrated upon this doctrine of chances, which, eventually,
instead of enriching them, will leave them and their families
beggars.

Go into your prisons and there you will find men of bright
intellects, of clear mental foresight and of good business facul-
ties, who, by the patient process of honest labor, would have
accomplished their heart's desire, but who, yielding to this
golden tempter, have overreached themselves and brought ruin
and disgrace upon all associated with them.

And so, here were these men, having yielded to the base
tempter, suffering privations and enduring hardships which, in
the honest endeavor to make money, would have restrained
harder natures and more determined spirits than they possessed.

Reaching at last, after a toilsome journey of several days, a
remote position between the north fork of the Platte River
and Cooper's Creek, and in direct communication between
Omaha and Salt Lake City, they determined to begin operations

No fears were entertained of discovery, so they carefully unpacked their machinery, resolved to make the attempt upon the morrow, and having prepared the message which they de sired to send, they laid themselves down beside their camp-fire, and, being utterly fatigued, were soon fast asleep.

The point of attack upon this occasion was to be the "Pacific Mail Steamship Company," an extensive corporation whose securities were held by a large number of people, and it was thought that a damaging report would have the effect of suddenly depreciating their stock and enabling the conspirators to realize fortunes from the scare that would naturally be produced. The following is the dispatch prepared to be forwarded:

"San Francisco, Cal., Oct. 1867.

"The special dispatch to the *New York Herald* was full and complete. It stated that the steamer *Great Republic*, of the Pacific Mail Line, which sailed from San Francisco on the third of September, loaded with six hundred and forty tons of freight, and about $1,500,000 of Wells, Fargo & Co.'s treasures, and passengers and crew numbering about eight hundred souls, had been burned at sea; that the captain and officers were intoxicated at the time the fire originated. As near as I can ascertain, about one hundred and fifty of the passengers and crew were lost. The vessel being a total wreck, the crew mutinied, and, taking to the boats, carried off a large portion of the treasure. The steamer *Fire Fly* rescued a large number of the passengers and crew, and has taken them to San Francisco. The steamer *Chrysopolis* has also gone down the harbor to take some passengers off of a vessel there coming up; and that some of the passengers on arriving at San Francisco had made an affidavit before the United States Commissioner to the effect that the captain was intoxicated at the time of the fire, and a warrant has been issued for his arrest."

Prepared as they were with the cipher used in conveying such dispatches, there seemed to be no reason why this should not be successfully wired and attain the results which they confidently expected. The next morning, therefore, they arose, and having appeased their appetites with a very primitive repast, for these city-bred gentlemen were not designed for camping life, and their knowledge of cooking was very limited, they began their preparations for the tapping of the wires.

Being provided with all the appurtenances for the labor before them, and having fully arranged everything for the contemplated work, they spent the remainder of the day in resting and idleness, awaiting the coming of the evening in order that Charley might be on duty to complete the task which they began.

As the time arrived, George, being provided with a pair of climbers, ascended to the top of the pole upon which the lines were suspended, and in a few moments, he had successfully attached the ground-wires to the main line; the electric current was conducted into the earth, and then, applying their pocket instruments, they were enabled to work with all the facility of a regularly-organized office.

Ascertaining the number of the dispatch which would follow, their instrument was soon in operation, and in a very short time the lying dispatch was on its way, and should nothing occur to stop its passage there would be a stir upon the market and "Pacific Mail" would be a fruitful subject for manipulation by the conspirators at the "Board."

Having finished their task, they skillfully removed their attachments, George Cowdrey ascending the pole and performing the labor. He had just finished and was about to descend, when he was startled by an unmistakable yell that foreboded danger.

Immediately turning around and looking in the direction from which the sounds came, he observed a party of twelve or fifteen Indian hunters, about two hundred yards away, running with full speed towards them.

To escape seemed impossible, and to remain where he was involved a danger he did not care to incur, so he quickly descended from his lofty perch and rejoined his frightened companions, who were trembling with fear at this sudden and dangerous interruption of their operations.

On came the Indians, shouting and yelling in a manner which caused the blood to curdle in their veins, and so, without further thought of anything else but safety, the trio of wire tappers gathered up their guns and ammunition and sought to escape their pursuers by flight. It was of no avail, however; the Indians were more fleet of foot than the fugitives; and soon overcoming the distance between them surrounded them; and the others, finding it impossible to resist, succumbed to the inevitable, and quietly allowed themselves to be made prisoners of.

This was a novel and unexpected ending of their hopes of fortune, their dreams of wealth, and instead of reaping the rich reward they had expected, they found themselves in captivity, and oppressed with very painful doubts of their future disposition.

CHAPTER VIII.

The Indian Camp—The Escape of Osborn—The Arrest of Charles Cowdrey.

OSBORN and his companions were securely bound by their dusky captors, who manifested very extravagant symptoms of delight as they performed the operation. Each of them were then placed between two of the Indians, and in this manner they returned to their camp, stopping on the way to take charge of the various articles which had been abandoned by the wire tappers in their hasty attempt at escape.

During that painful march, the minds of the three men were harassed with grave doubts and agonizing fears as to the fate in store for them. Many stories had been circulated of the cruelties of these dusky hunters, and they had every reason to believe that no mercy would be shown to them in this instance.

To Osborn the situation was particularly aggravating—having identified himself with the movement in the interests of justice, and having no share in the prospective gains of the others, he did not regard his present position with any degree of satisfaction or philosophy—and not being either by nature or inclination a coward, he determined to make a bold effort to escape should opportunity occur. His companions seemed,

[232

however, to be utterly broken down; their fate seemed assured, and with the sullenness of despair they submitted to their captors, and anxiously awaited the operation of events that were either to seal their doom or to promise release.

They were conducted back to the camp of the hunters and securely fastened, while the Indians devoted their attentions to the articles they had captured. To them the telegraph had long been a source of wonderment and opposition, and anything connected with it attracted their attention and seemed to excite their anger. Many times they had taken down the lines over which the messages were sent, and the company would thus suddenly find their connections broken off, so that much time would be lost, much labor consumed, and considerable expense incurred in repairing the damage done, aside from the personal danger which those who performed this labor were compelled to incur.

As the darkness of night settled down upon the scene, the prisoners, who were closely pinioned and watched, and whose minds were filled with reflections far from pleasant, were conducted to a small tent, and being placed under the guard of a stalwart Indian, were left to what repose they might be able to take, their captors having previously taken the precaution to bind their feet, in order to prevent any attempt at escape.

Osborn resolved to make the effort that evening, and after his companions had settled themselves apparently to sleep, he silently began to work upon the cords which bound his wrists. By untiring and desperate energy, he at length succeeded in freeing one of his hands, and in a few minutes more both hands were at liberty. He breathed a sigh of intense relief when this result was accomplished, and then set to work to loosen the pinions upon his feet, trembling with fear and anxiety lest he should be discovered, and his rising hopes dashed to the ground. Having the use of his hands, it was not long before he was enabled to remove these bonds, and he found it almost impossible to restrain an expression of his joy at the success which had thus far attended him. But he dared not speak or stir; the silent guardian was seated at the door of the tent, complacently smoking and uncomfortably wakeful, and he could see the rest of the band gathered around their fire a short distance away, engaged in the same solacing occupation. He must wait a more favorable opportunity to make the attempt at escape, and so, settling back upon his blanket, he gave him-self up to a mental consideration of the dangers and difficulties which surrounded him, and of the possibilities of successfully getting away from the vigilant eyes of those who were holding him and his companions in durance. Cowdrey and the other were overcome by the events of the day, and, fatigued both in mind and in body, were lying by his side, and their heavy, regular breathing convinced him that they were asleep. One by one the circle around the fire grew smaller, and finally the dying embers were deserted, and he was left alone with the grim watcher at the door.

The death-like stillness that prevailed was oppressive in the extreme, and to Osborn the time dragged slowly along, as his mind was occupied with conflicting hopes of escape and fears of failure. After watching for some time, his heart gave a leap as he noticed that the head of the Indian jailer was drooping on his breast, and, listening intently, he heard the unmistakable breathing of a sleeper. Quickly and silently he threw off the blanket that covered him, and crawled stealthily to the

"*Moving noiselessly away, he was soon out of hearing of the camp.*"

side of the tent opposite to the entrance; slowly raising the canvas from the ground, he pushed himself partly through, feet foremost, when the sleeping Indian started from his slumber and looked into the tent, to assure himself that all was right within. Osborn did not stir, and the quiet which reigned convinced the watcher that everything was as it should be, and he composed himself for another nap.

After waiting sufficiently long to convince himself of the soundness of the slumber of his unsuspicious guard, Osborn again attempted to withdraw his body from the tent, and by slow, stealthy movements he succeeded in placing himself outside of its enfoldings. All was quiet as the grave; his exit had been unnoticed, and he could have shouted in very joy at the possibility of safety, which now seemed so imminent.

Moving noiselessly away, he was soon out of hearing of the camp which he had left, and he paused a moment to determine upon his course of action. Having full knowledge of the road they had traveled in reaching this place, he determined to return to Fort Sedgwick, in the hope that his surreptitious message from that place had been properly forwarded and received, and that the person desired would, by this time, be found awaiting him, or some knowledge of his movements ascertained.

Meanwhile Conway, in accordance with instructions received from me, had proceeded on his way, and without accident or delay had reached Fort Sedgwick about the time that Osborn was making his escape from the camp of the Indians, and going at once to the telegraph office, informed me of his safe arrival and awaited further orders.

While these events were transpiring my telegraph office was in constant nightly operation, but without discovering anything

of a suspicious character, and the officers of the company were
considering the advisability of removing it, very much against
my earnest remonstrance, when, early one evening, just as I was
preparing to leave, the premonitory signal was given, and in a
short time the message containing the information of the loss of
the steamer *Great Republic*, with all its attendant particulars,
came clicking over the wires.

Admirably done, gentlemen; the regularity of the transmission was perfect, but unfortunately for the success of your
plans my office was in operation, and the cipher by which these
messages were usually sent had been, at my suggestion, changed
ten days previously, and all regular correspondents had been
duly notified of that fact.

Of course, suspicion at once attached itself to this message.
We felt that we had the evidence that would convict the parties of the attempt to tamper with the wires and to forward
the bogus intelligence. The trap had been laid and the unsus-
specting swindlers had fallen into it. I therefore determined
to catch Charles Cowdrey in the act, and for that purpose I immediately dispatched one of my men to inform General Stager
of the state of affairs, and to request his attendance at my
office for consultation. Upon his arrival the facts, as above re-
cited, were communicated to him, and his eyes brightened perceptibly at the recital. After due consideration of the matter,
it was decided to transmit the message received; to have a
watch put upon Charles Cowdrey in order to ascertain what
action he would take in sending it forward, and if he attempted
to do so to arrest him in the act, thus having indubitable proof
against him of complicity.

This action being fully agreed upon, General Stager, accompanied by one of my men, returned to the office of the Telegraph Company, and stationing themselves in close proximity to the operating room, prepared to watch the movements of young Cowdrey.

In a very few moments the quick ear of the General discovered the unmistakable sounds, which indicated the reception of the suspected message, and he also noticed the sudden start given by Charles as he became aware of the nature of the dispatch he was receiving.

Only a short time intervened and Charles Cowdrey's fingers were flying with lightning-like rapidity in forwarding it to its eastern destination, and in a few minutes after that a heavy hand was laid upon his shoulder, and as he turned suddenly around his frightened eyes met the stern gaze of General Stager and the stolid look of the detective. He knew that he had been caught, and he knew at once that his crime and that of his associates was known to the men who stood before him.

" Charles Cowdrey, you will go with this gentleman ; he is an officer of the law, and you are under arrest," said General Stager, sternly.

Without uttering a word he submitted himself to the charge of the detective, and was led away, evidently at a loss to account for the unexpected discovery of his rascality, and in doubt of the whereabouts or disposition of his companions in this enterprise.

A warrant was procured for his arrest for tampering with the wires of the Telegraph Company, and for conspiring to forward bogus intelligence, and upon a hearing being given, in default of bail, he was committed to prison to await a trial for his offense.

CHAPTER IX.

The Discovery of Osborn's Flight—Unsuccessful Pursuit—A Camp Suddenly Deserted—Left to Die—Rescued, but Again made Prisoners.

FRANK OSBORN, worn out with fatigue and almost starving, at length reached Fort Sedgwick, where he found Conway impatiently awaiting him. His escape had not been discovered until he was far out of reach, and he heard nothing to indicate that he was pursued, but his journey had nevertheless been a painful one, and his condition on his arrival at the Fort was most pitiable. The suddenness and secrecy of his getting away prevented his making any preparations for an extended tramp, or of securing any provisions to sustain him upon the way, and consequently he presented a picture of physical and mental fatigue most painful to witness.

However, after being refreshed with a bath, a change of clothing and a good substantial repast, he was conducted to bed, when, after an invigorating sleep of several hours, he felt so much improved and recuperated that he announced himself ready to proceed the next day in company with Conway in the attempt to capture the two individuals with whom he had been associated, and who were now still supposed to be in charge of their dark-skinned captors.

It was decided to request a guard of soldiers from the Fort, as it would be impossible for these two men to successfully cope with the number of Indians who had accomplished their capture, and as the attack had been made by the Indians in violation of the terms of treaty then existing, and of the promises of peaceful behavior, it was thought that a salutary lesson should be taught them for this warlike demonstration.

Major Larkin, who commanded the small body of troops at the Fort, after hearing the particulars of the affair, the object to be attained in recovering the two telegraphic manipulators, and the prompt administration of justice, at once signified his willingness to assist the detective in procuring the release of Cowdrey and his companion, and ordered a guard of eight men, under the command of a sergeant, to accompany them.

Being provided with horses, the party started from the Fort early the next morning, resolved that they would accomplish their mission and return with their prisoners.

Let us now return to the camp which Osborn had so unceremoniously left on the evening of his escape. The sleeping sentinel dozed on at intervals, then, starting up suddenly, would listen to the heavy breathing of the sleepers within, and finally, apparently well satisfied that all was well, would again drop off in slumber. Thus the long night passed away, and as the first faint streaks of morning light came up and illumined the darkness, the camp resumed its usual activity, and preparations were made for the morning's repast. At this time one of the Indians came to the tent for the purpose of relieving the hunter who had stood guard at the tent of the prisoners, and as it was now fully light, his quick eyes at once detected the absence of Osborn. The alarm was given and soon the entire camp was

aroused. Consternation and alarm sat on every face, and instant orders were given for the pursuit and capture of the
runaway.

In a few moments the men were divided into squads, and
they started off in various directions in the hope of overtaking
Osborn and bringing him back to captivity, but at nightfall
they returned unsuccessful, as the reader already is aware of.
No trace had been discovered of the missing Osborn, and the
chase was reluctantly abandoned.

The Indians were now thoroughly alarmed. That Osborn
had escaped was now an assured fact; that his destination must
naturally be the Fort was also undoubted; and if he reached
there in safety and told his story, what would be the result?
Knowing that they had been guilty of wrong-doing, and feeling
that punishment sure and severe would follow, their only alternative was to get away as rapidly as possible. Hastily packing
together their camping utensils and whatever property composed their outfit, and placing them upon the backs of their
ponies, they prepared to leave the place.

A consultation was held, the question of the disposition of
the remaining prisoners was vehemently discussed, and it was
finally decided, in order to prevent their giving any alarm, to
tie them securely to the trees and leave them to be discovered
by whoever should come in search of them.

This being done, and all the preparations being made for
departure, the Indians hurried away, resolved that they would
place as much distance between themselves and the pursuit,
which they felt confident would follow.

The condition of the two men, who were thus left entirely
alone, was a fearful one, and their feelings may well be imag-

ined. Between sentiments of anger at Osborn, for what they considered his desertion of them, and with fears for their safety and sustenance, their minds were filled with many conflicting emotions. Then, too, came the horrible fear that their scheme had been detected, and that, although Osborn might succeed in bringing the troops in time to rescue them from death, they might still be compelled to suffer the punishing influences of the law.

Slowly dragged the long day to its close, each moment as it passed being fraught with intense mental suffering to the two bound men, who, by conversation, endeavored to assist the passage of the far too slowly moving time. As night, with its dark enveloping folds, settled around them, their suffering was augmented, and they vainly attempted to seek some respite from the strain upon their minds in sleep.

Ah, gentlemen! how much easier would have been your position to-night could you have nestled down in the warm coverings of the couches in your city home. How much torment and pain and mental agony you would have been saved, had you refused to listen to the golden tempter that lured you to your ruin, that brought you at last to the dangers of these western wilds, and now has left you to suffer and perhaps to die.

I wonder whether the certainty of punishment will ever operate to prevent crime, and whether the piteous picture of the suffering criminal will ever have a controlling influence in deterring others from the commission of acts that lead to the same results!

I will not linger over the sufferings which these men endured during the days and nights of their horrible and lonely

11

captivity; a captivity which comprised a living death, and which hunger and thirst and mental torture combined to make them wish for death as a release from a life of terror and fear.

It is enough to know that when Osborn and his military escort arrived, they found them utterly exhausted, and only the timely administration of restoratives prevented the flickering lamps of life from expiring.

They were, however, nourished and strengthened, and, after recovering sufficiently, were conducted back to the Fort, the sergeant deciding that pursuit of the Indians would be useless, as they already had three days' start, and to overtake them would be impossible.

The next morning after their arrival, and when they had almost entirely recovered from the effects of their hard experiences, Conway informed these dealers in false information of their arrest, and of his intention to conduct them to Chicago. This was the last blow, and, submitting without a word, they allowed themselves to be pinioned, and, being placed upon the train, they were soon whirling along the road to the city of Chicago, where they were to be tried for their offense.

Before leaving, Osborn and Conway expressed their warmest thanks to the commander of the Fort and his men, who had assisted in the capture of the two prisoners, and for their kind treatment of them while they remained.

CHAPTER X.

In Prison—Legal Questions.

NO event of any importance occurred upon that return journey to Chicago, but to the discomfited and detected operators the time passed heavily and slowly. The returns which they had so ardently expected were not realized, and instead of gaining for themselves the competence they had labored and risked their liberty for, they were now being conducted as prisoners to answer a charge which might involve imprisonment, and certainly carried with it disgrace and dishonor.

Upon arriving in the city they were at once conveyed to my office, and then they seemed for the first time to realize the desperate strait in which they were placed.

"George Cowdrey," said I, after they had been seated, "you are aware by this time that you have been detected in an attempt to tap the wires of the Telegraph Company, and to impose upon the public a dispatch containing false information, which might have resulted in serious consequences to many unsuspecting people. It is equally certain that you were not alone in this movement."

"Does Charley know that I have been arrested?" interrupted George.

"Your brother does not know that you have been arrested, from the fact that he was arrested before you, and while in the very act of transmitting the message you had sent," said I.

"I do not understand. How could he be suspected?" asked George, in evident perplexity.

"Come, come," said I, "there is no occasion for prolonging this interview, but in order to convince you that everything is known, let me show you a telegraph office, which I have established upon my own account," and I pointed to the machinery which had not yet been removed.

George looked in the direction indicated, and realized at once the means that had been employed to secure his detection.

"Now, sir, if you will listen further, you will understand that when your dispatch was received here, but a few moments were necessary to inform General Stager, and but a few more were required to catch your brother in the act of forwarding it," said I, sternly.

"I see it all now," said George dumbly; "we have been fairly caught and must abide by the consequences."

"George," said I to him, "the company know that you have not been acting alone in this matter; they know that behind you are a combination of men with money enough to profit by the scare and anxiety which your dispatch would have occasioned, had it been properly received, and this combination must be broken up. The company are determined upon this, and you can assist them if you will."

"How much will it benefit me if I do so?" he asked, with an eager look in his eyes that convinced me that he would ultimately divulge what he knew, if he was properly handled.

From time out of mind, we have heard the adage repeated about there being " Honor among thieves," and it may be that in remote instances such a virtue has manifested itself, amid such associations; but it will generally be found that when danger attaches itself to the criminal, when he sees the meshes of the law slowly enveloping him, he will, in a large majority of instances, save himself, if possible, at the expense of his confederates. The " honor " referred to being blinked completely out of sight, in view of prospective safety being gained by a timely forgetfulness of its existence.

" George," said I, " I have already told you that the company are determined to suppress this combination; you also know full well by this time that your further connection with them is ended, and you can no longer be of any service to them. You may, however, mitigate the rigor of the prosecution of yourself and brother by a divulgence of the facts which will lead to their exposure, and it depends upon you whether you will accept the clemency thus offered."

" Give me until to-morrow to consider the matter, and you shall have an answer," replied George.

" Take the time you have asked for," said I; " but, if to-morrow passes without this information being forthcoming, I will not be answerable for the consequences. The officers will now take you in charge and you will be duly committed."

George Cowdrey and his companion departed, and I felt reasonably sure that we would hear from him to our advantage upon the morrow.

Upon a consultation being had with eminent counsel, grave doubts were expressed by them of the existence of any law that would reach the offenses of which these parties were charged, and it seemed possible that our labor would be expended for nothing. We had, however, accomplished one object, we had captured the active malefactors, and were in a fair way to expose "the ways which are dark, and the tricks which are vain," of those who had conspired with them in this nefarious work; and, therefore, if no criminal punishment could be meted out to them, we would at least be enabled to prevent a repetition of their dangerous operations.

The opinions expressed were as various and conflicting as could well be imagined, from a purely legal point of view, and there seemed to be an absence of any law that would meet the case at issue.

That such a state of affairs should exist in this age of progression seemed almost astounding, and that an enterprise as far-reaching and important as the telegraph system had grown to be, should at this late day be found to be entirely unprotected, was a discovery as vexatious as it was incomprehensible.

Laws have been enacted for the protection of every conceivable right and industry, and yet we discovered that the telegraph was entirely unprotected. It seemed utterly incredible.

The most stringent laws were in operation for the protection of the mails, and an attack upon a stage-coach carrying the same, had been held by law to be a capital offense. Now the question came naturally—what are the mails? Simply the medium by which the people correspond with each other, and, if necessary, transmit articles of value, such as drafts, bills of exchange, and money. Yet, should these articles be stolen from the mails, no one questions the right of the government to try and to punish the parties who may be convicted of such action.

Now the telegraph, owing to the scientific progressiveness of the human mind, is only another mode of securing such correspondence, and of trafficking in much quicker time with the articles of value already mentioned.

The wires encircle the globe, are used in all the ramifications of business; and are they not entitled to the same protection as a means of communication, as are post roads and the postal facilities of the United States, or of the world? Science is or ought to be protected by the constitution which guarantees to protect inventions and inventors, and is not telegraphy an unquestioned science?

The mind of man is like the waves of the ocean—ever restless, ever in motion; it is ever seeking to solve the causes of creation, and are they not entitled to all the protection possible to secure the fruits of their inventions and discoveries? Common sense answers loudly in the affirmative, but it seems, in this matter at least, the law-making powers answer equally vociferously in the negative.

It was contended by some of these learned men that there could be no property in electricity, because it is one of those subtile elements in which no property can exist. This view seems equally erroneous, as electricity for telegraphic purposes is created by the combination or decomposition of certain mineral substances which are themselves property. Again, it cannot be urged for a moment that there is no property in steam, which is equally as intangible as electricity. Nor can it be asserted that a person would go unpunished who should tap the boiler of his neighbor and appropriate the steam to his own uses. Ether is also a subtile element, but it is a substance, and consequently a matter of property; so also with gas.

The miner, deep in his subterranean cavern, produces the coal which, upon being ignited and subjected to certain influences, produces gas, and, in connection with water, produces steam. Would it be contended for one moment that gas is not property as well as steam? And if electricity is the result of chemical decomposition of certain mineral substances, why should it not be considered property as well as those other intangible elements?

Yet we were informed by these learned minds that not only had no law ever been passed protecting the telegraph, but many gave it as their opinion that no authority was ever vested even in the Congress of the United States to pass any such. In other words, that a man possessing the requisite ability might successfully steal communications from the wires of a telegraph company and escape punishment, while he would be rigorously dealt with should he perform the same action upon the mails.

So conflicting, however, were these legal opinions, that the authorities of the company determined to test the matter by a trial, but in advance of that action, and in view of prospective failure to convict, it was deemed advisable to get, if possible, from George Cowdrey, in advance, the information he possessed, in order to expose the so-called gentlemen who comprised the moneyed portion of this combination, and to prevent their obtaining any further success in their manner of working.

CHAPTER XI.

In Prison—A Woman's Visit—A Confession—A Meeting of Gentlemanly Rascals Interrupted—The Acquittal.

THE following morning I waited upon the captured manipulators in their confined quarters, and found George not quite so desirous as I could have wished to comply with the demand I had made of him on the previous day.

"Well, George," said I, good-humoredly, upon entering, "as you could not come to see me, I thought I would pay you a visit. The old idea of Mahomet and the mountain, you know."

George smiled faintly, but it was evident that he was ill at case. He seemed to have only recently appreciated Osborn's participation in the affair, and yet, knowing full well the position which he occupied, and that, with the information I possessed, his hope of escaping from the charge must be very limited, he hesitated to do what had been required of him.

While we were conversing, the turnkey announced a lady as desiring to see George, and inquired whether he would have her introduced at once.

"What is her name?" inquired George.

"Miss Lizzie Coyan," answered the turnkey.

At the mention of the name George flushed slightly, and.

11*   [249]

thinking that her influence might profitably be exerted upon him, I suggested to him that she be shown up at once.

He hesitated a moment, but finally turned to the keeper and said, " Yes, let her come up now."

In a few minutes a very beautiful looking young lady, very well dressed, and apparently in great distress of mind, entered. She threw herself into the arms of George and sobbed con vulsively, while he in vain attempted to restrain her tears.

I realized at once that this girl would be of incalculable benefit to me, and after she had become subdued, I addressed her. I informed her of the circumstances surrounding George Cowdrey, told her of the necessity of his divulging to me the names of his confederates in New York, and requested her to use her influence in producing the desired result.

I soon ascertained that I had a powerful ally; Lizzie, whom I discovered was of good family, and who loved George with all her heart, and desired to save him from the punishment that seemed to be inevitable, joined with me in the endeavor to induce him to give the names of those who were connected with him, and who were to realize the lion's share of the proceeds of their rascality.

Our joint efforts were too much for the stoicism of George, and at length, yielding his objections to our combined arguments, he confessed the entire conspiracy. I will give the story as he related it.

" Two years ago I was employed in the New York office of the company, having been transferred there from Chicago, and as my position was a good one, my salary was proportionately large. My associates at that time, however, were gentlemen whose incomes were much larger than mine, whose habits

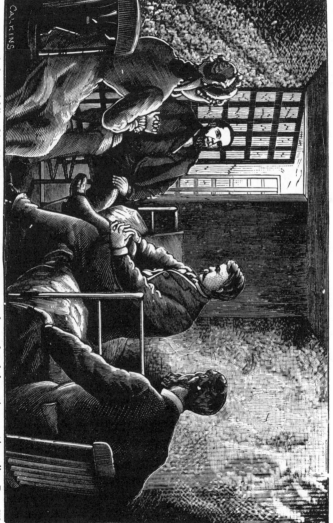

"*At last, yielding his objections to our combined arguments, he confessed the entire conspiracy.*" **Page 250.**

were extravagant, and whose frequent dissipations, in which I as frequently joined, induced the expenditure of a great deal of money—more than my means justified, and I was continually fretting at my lack of funds, and regretting my inability to live in the style of those who were my immediate friends and acquaintances.

"One evening about a year ago, I was sitting disconsolately among a few of my friends at Delmonico's, and while every one else was enjoying himself, my spirits were dulled by this want of money, and my enjoyment dampened by the fact that I could not travel with the rest.

"While thus sitting, an elderly gentleman whom I knew very well, Thomas Fielding by name, a large operator in gold and stocks, and whose wealth was believed to be enormous, approached me and requested a few minutes' private conversation. I immediately went with him to a retired part of the room, where our conversation could not be heard by any one, and signified my disposition to listen to any proposition which he might have to make.

"He then broached the subject of my finances, of which he displayed considerable knowledge, and said that he could place me in a position where I could materially increase my income and command a position of independence. Of course, an offer so tempting as this deserved my attention, and I informed him of my willingness to serve him in any way, by which the results so ardently desired could be arrived at.

"He then informed me of an association of brokers, which had been formed with the view of having messages containing information in reference to certain stocks, come regularly over the wires in order to operate upon the markets, which would be materially affected by the information thus received. He further informed me of the names of several of the party, among whom I recognized several of my most intimate friends at that time, and then he mentioned the fact that I had been selected as the operator to be relied upon, and for whose bene- fit a considerable amount of money had been subscribed.

" This offer was too tempting to be refused, and I at once signified my willingness to join in the movement. My experi- ence as a telegraph operator, during the war, was of such a char- acter that I could tap a telegraphic wire at any point, take off any dispatch I desired, or forward any that was needed, and also repair a wire as neatly as anybody.

" My brother Charley being in Chicago I knew that I could rely upon him, to assist me in forwarding any information I desired, and also to furnish me with the ciphers in use in transmitting the various telegrams which would ordinarily con- vey the information such as was designed to be manufactured and forwarded.

" Thus prepared I at once began my operations, and from many points I was enabled to impose upon the credulity of the people information with no foundation except in the brains of the shrewd brokers and capitalists who profited by these transactions. I was very successful until this last attempt, which you know all about, and which, if it had not been for that infernal Osborn, I would have succeeded in too."

Another ingenious device that had been contemplated by these conspirators was to procure an ordinary telegraph pole, have the same hollowed out through the center, then ship it by a privately chartered vessel to some point upon the Pacific Coast. Arriving at the point designated the pole would be set

up in the place of one of the Telegraph Company's poles in general use, the arms with their wires would then be arranged
upon this hollow pole. The wires would then be conducted
down through the pole thus set up, and carried underground to
a distance of several hundred feet, where these manipulators
were to have erected a wooden shanty supplied with all the apparatus of a regularly appointed telegraph office. From the
batteries thus established wires were to be again run through
the hollow pole and then passed on westward to the terminal
office of the line. By this plan every message that passed over
the wires of the Telegraph Company must necessarily pass
through the improvised office of these lightning stealers, and
no indication would be found upon the outward face of circumstances, which would lead to a discovery of their machinations.

The plan thus suggested was finally abandoned—why, it
was not stated—and to say that I was surprised at the audacious invention, which, had it been carried into effect, might
have been successfully operated, and escaped detection for a
long time, would be but faintly to portray my feelings as I
listened to the narration.

That the plan was feasible there could be no doubt, and my
surprise was augmented as I considered its abandonment.

George Cowdrey was very explicit in his statements, and
from his manner in making the disclosures I entertained no
doubt of their entire truthfulness.

By dint of forcible inquiries I acquired a full knowledge of
the extent of their transactions and of the wide-spread associations which controlled their movements. He gave me a list of

the men who were identified with the combination, and **I was** utterly amazed at the revelation thus made.

Men of undoubted reputation, office-holders of high repute, and, in one case, a Member of Congress—a law maker, and a violator of the laws he assisted in making—were found engaged in this work. The list, however, was undoubted, and I only hesitate to give publicity to the names comprising it from the fact that their publication now would answer no good purpose, and would only tend to bring the blush of shame to faces of their families.

The information was also given of the time at which this select coterie would hold their usual meeting at their principal rendezvous, which appeared to be the office of the J. R. Bronson previously alluded to, and this information I immediately telegraphed to Mr. Orton, the president of the company, who communicated the same to Mr. Bangs, with instructions to wait upon them, inform them of the discovery of their schemes, and warn them against further continuance in their nefarious work.

In accordance with these instructions, Mr. Bangs, on the evening succeeding the reception of this intelligence, which was one of their nights of meeting, in company with one of my operatives, repaired to the place mentioned, and, noticing a light burning in the room reported to be occupied by Bronson, they went up stairs. Upon knocking at the door, Mr. Bronson himself appeared, who stared in astonishment as he saw the imposing figure of my General Superintendent filling up the doorway, with the full glare of the light reflected upon his face. Mr. Bangs, noticing that several gentlemen were present, immediately pushed his way into the room and confronted the surprised individuals, who were at a loss to account for this abrupt intrusion, and were apparently dumbly awaiting an explanation.

"Gentlemen," said Mr. Bangs, "the cause of my visit will be apparent when I inform you that George Cowdrey and his associates have been arrested and are now in prison at Chicago."

There was a simultaneous movement, singularly expressive of astonishment and alarm, manifested upon the announcement of this information, but smothered ejaculations were the only responses that were attempted.

"I have further to inform you," continued Mr. Bangs, "that the name of every gentleman connected with this scheme for furnishing lying information by tapping the wires of the Telegraph Company, are fully known both to myself and to the officers of the company. Every movement of George Cowdrey has been watched, and the fullest knowledge as to his connection with you is also possessed by us."

"Did you come here to insult us?" inquired a pompous, little, red-faced gentleman, whom I will call Mr Jamison, assuming an air of angry importance.

"Not at all, Mr. Jamison," coolly and politely replied Mr. Bangs, "and you least of all—and when I tell you that it was a draft upon you which George Cowdrey had cashed at the bank at Julesburg, you will understand how utterly ridiculous this assumption of anger must appear to me."

Mr. Jamison seemed to comprehend the situation, and his anger, real or assumed, at once subsided. He was not sure how much was known, but he had a pretty well defined idea that our information was undoubted.

"What do you want with us?" at length inquired Mr. Bronson, with an air of indifference he was evidently far from feeling.

" I want to inform you that the Company possesses sufficient information to warrant the arrest of every man present, which of course would not be a very pleasant proceeding for many of you who have reputations to lose; but that they do not care to take such a course at present, and desire simply to warn you against any further attempt of this kind. Should you, however, make any further efforts to tamper with their wires, the law must take its course, and a full expose of your transactions will, at least, be made, if you do not receive a sentence of imprisonment. And now, gentlemen, having accomplished my mission, and given you the information confided to me, I bid you good evening—but beware how you proceed further in this work."

Saying which Mr. Bangs bowed himself politely out, though his fingers itched to pounce upon those rascally well-dressed men whom he knew the law was powerless to punish.

It is needless to say that this visit accomplished all that was desired; the parties interested realized fully their position, and, knowing something of the operations of my Agency, they felt satisfied that further attempts of theirs would be followed by serious results to them. They disbanded at once, and I have heard of no further action of theirs in this direction, which rendered any labor of mine necessary.

The trial of the Cowdrey brothers came on, and upon a bill of exceptions, filed by their attorney, and duly argued, a decision was rendered, which prevented their being tried for the offenses of which they were charged, and they were consequently released.

Their transactions, however, were made public; the nature of their crime was fully known, and, although they did not suffer the penalties of the law, their honorable position in society was gone; they could no longer associate with the friends of the time gone by; their attempts to engage in business were failures, and everywhere amid their old associations they found themselves ostracized and shunned.

The stigma of the criminal was attached to them, and they found no one willing to acknowledge their friendship or to further their interests, and they finally disappeared from the city.

Thus ended the conspiracy which had for a long time convulsed the money markets, and which had contributed in rendering houseless and homeless many deserving people, whose investments were prejudiced by their criminal and illegal transactions.

CHAPTER XII.

Forging by Telegraph—A Bogus Draft for Nine Thousand Dollars Cashed.

AFTER the conclusion of the trial, and although they had failed in being convicted, their disgrace was so publicly known and commented upon as to make their further continuance in Chicago a matter of impossibility. Foiled in the attempt which they had made, and reduced to penury by the result of these transactions, which had failed to yield them the extravagant return they had so fondly hoped for and expected, the situation of these brothers was certainly not an enviable one. Their luxurious home was given up and disposed of, no one would give them employment, and they suddenly disappeared from Chicago. I was inclined to believe that their lesson had been a salutary one, and that nothing further would be heard from them of a nature that would render them amenable to law.

Several months after the events heretofore narrated, however, I was waited upon by General Stager and informed of a successful attempt that had been made to swindle the First National Bank of Emporia, Kansas, the details of which are as follows:

The bank had opened their doors at the usual hour for

business; the clerks were in their places, and the officers busily engaged in the various duties devolving upon them. Money was being received and paid out with the strictest observance of the forms of business, when a young man, well dressed and gentlemanly-looking, entered, and requested to see the president upon business of importance.

Mr. Crosby, the president, was notified of the presence of the stranger, and immediately invited him into his private office. Upon entering, the young gentleman presented a draft for nine thousand dollars, upon a well-known banking institution of New York city, and requested to have the same cashed. The draft was signed by Martin and Edward Paxton, and indorsed by Joseph Paxton, who was represented as the father of the young man.

The interview in every way was pleasant; the young man, who was Martin Paxton, informing Mr. Crosby of their intention to purchase a farm in the vicinity of Emporia and enter into the business of cattle raising, and Mr. Crosby promised to telegraph to the parties in New York, and should the reply be satisfactory he would take pleasure in cashing the same. Mr. Paxton informed the accommodating president that he would not require more than one thousand dollars at the present time, but would take certificates of deposit of the bank for the balance. The manner of the young man was cordial and business-like, and after promising to call upon the following day for an answer, after a short conversation upon general topics, he took his leave.

Mr. Crosby immediately telegraphed to their agent in New York, and also to the banking institution named upon the draft, and before the opening of the bank upon the following morn-

ing answers were duly received—one from the bank, anncnno-
ing the fact that the draft was all right, and one from the agent,
certifying to the responsibility of the parties and the genuineness of the draft.

During that day Mr. Martin Paxton called at the bank, accompanied by his brother Edward, and they received from Mr.
Crosby one thousand dollars in cash and the balance in one-
thousand-dollar certificates of deposit upon the "First National Bank of Emporia."

The draft was duly mailed to their agent for collection at
the New York bank, and its payment expected, as a matter of
course, but what was the surprise of Mr. Crosby when, a few
days afterwards, he received a dispatch, of which the following
is a copy:

"First National Bank, Emporia.
    "Paxton & Sons $9,000, draft not good—have no account
at the bank.
                          "DONALD, SLAWSON & CO."

Mr. Crosby read the message carefully, every word of which
seemed to burn itself into his mind; the perspiration broke in
large beads upon his forehead. Could it be possible that this
information was true? But, no! there must be some mistake.
Did he not have a previous telegram from the bank, certifying
to the correctness of the draft, and did they not also have the
confirmatory evidence of their own agents, Donald, Slawson &
Co., in New York, to the same effect? There must be some
mistake, but evidently a mistake of considerable importance;
and Mr. Crosby, as he laughed lightly at the error committed
by so large and prominent an establishment as the one in New

York was represented to be, could not restrain a cold shiver as he contemplated the possibility of the error being upon the other side of the account.

Putting on his hat he hurried to the telegraph office, and with trembling fingers and anxious heart, he wrote the following, which he dispatched at once:

"DONALD, SLAWSON & Co.,
Broadway, New York.
"You telegraphed us draft and M. and E. Paxton were correct on 16th inst.—we hold the bank for the same.
"H. C. CROSBY."

This dispatch was sent at half-past four o'clock in the after noon, and, of course, no answer could be expected until the following day, and as business was over at the bank, Mr. Crosby, with his mind filled with many conflicting emotions, wended his way slowly homeward. His slumbers that evening were not of that rest-giving nature which had usually been the case with him; the horrible nightmare which beset him seemed to re- solve itself into a hideous distortion of a banker's draft, and the figures $9,000 seemed to be the burden of a song of woe.

The next morning, rising unrefreshed, physically and men tally exhausted, he hurried to the bank, half hoping, half fear- ing for the result. He would soon know the worst, but, of course, there was some mistake; it could not be that they had been deceived by the first information, and the mistake, he was sure, would be rectified in a very short time.

The minutes seemed like hours to the anxious man who counted their passage; the solemn ticking of the clock had an ominous sound, which foreboded danger, and although he endeavored to shake off the feeling of dread and apprehension which overpowered him, he could not rid himself of the fear that the loss threatened wou'd eventually fall upon the bank.

Shortly after two o'clock the messenger boy entered, and on receiving the message, Mr. Crosby, with eager haste, tore off its covering, and upon perusing its contents, sank heavily back in his chair, staring vacantly at the hurriedly written lines before him.

" H. C. Crosby, Emporia, Kansas.
    " We sent no dispatch on the 16th or at any other time, in relation to the parties named, except yesterday. The bank know nothing about the matter.
                    " DONALD, SLAWSON & CO."

Still hoping against the almost certainty that thus presented itself, Mr. Crosby repaired again to the telegraph office and requested an examination of their records, which, upon being duly made, disclosed the fact that his inquiries had been regularly forwarded, and the replies thereto regularly received. There could be no mistake about this, and, somewhat relieved, he requested the operator to inquire at the next principal station whether his message had been received at and forwarded from that point. This was done, and the return message was to the effect that no such dispatch had been received, and no communication had been made, either going or returning, with Messrs. Donald, Slawson & Co., or with a bank in New York city.

Here was a mystery to be solved, but pending its solution the certificates of deposit must be canceled, and the different other banks must be notified of the fact, in order to prevent

their negotiation by the parties who had thus fraudulently obtained them.

It seemed to be evident—and upon no other supposition could the facts be accounted for—that the wires had been tapped, the messages to New York city intercepted, and the bogus information wired to Emporia—and that this had been done at a point between Emporia and Kansas City was also reasonably sure.

The notification was immediately issued to the various banks, prohibiting payment of the certificates, and Mr. Crosby notified General Stager of the situation of affairs, threatening at the same time to hold the Telegraph Company responsible for whatever loss was incurred by these dispatches.

Of course General Stager indignantly repudiated the claim thus set up, unless it could be proven that some employee in the regular service of the Company had perpetrated the fraud; but for the purpose of preventing a repetition of such an attempt, and in order to secure, if possible, the men who had thus imposed upon the bank, and bring them to justice, he determined to unearth the parties, and to put an effectual stop to their schemes of forgery and robbery.

CHAPTER XIII.

Recognizing Old Friends—The Detective on the Trail—Valuable Information.

AFTER listening attentively to the recital of this daring and successful swindle, I at once made up my mind to the fact that George and Charles Cowdrey, and none other, were guilty of the act; and I resolved to hunt them down, and bring them to summary punishment. I communicated my opinion to General Stager, who was somewhat doubtful of the correctness of my surmises, but decidedly anxious that the villains should be arrested. Accordingly, the next morning, I dispatched an operative on my force, Mr. James Rodgers, to the scene of operations, to work up the case.

Mr. Rodgers was a man of fearless courage, and one of the shrewdest and sharpest men in my employ at that time; he had previously been employed as a telegraph operator, and was thoroughly acquainted with the country in and surrounding Emporia.

He was thoroughly instructed as to his course of proceeding, and after providing himself with all necessary articles for his journey, he started West, resolved that upon his return he would be able to report the successful capture of these daring rascals.

Upon reaching Emporia, he called upon Mr. Crosby at the bank, and received from him full particulars of the transaction, which did not differ in any material respect from that furnished by General Stager; and he also obtained an accurate description of the two Paxton brothers, which corresponded exactly with that of the Cowdreys, so that no doubt existed of the identity of the men; and, animated by a desire to show these gentlemen that there was a limit to their immunity from punishment, Rodgers determined that they should be taken, and that every effort of which he was capable should be made to accomplish that result.

In order that Rodgers might fully understand the manner in which these Paxton brothers operated upon the bank, Mr. Crosby produced the telegraph messages originally sent, at the time the draft was presented. Immediately upon the departure of Martin Paxton, after having made arrangements for the cashing of the draft, Mr. Crosby went to the telegraph office, and wrote the following dispatch, which was sent from the office at Emporia.

" To Donald, Slawson & Co.,
    " Broadway, New York.
    " We send you to-day sight draft of Martin and Edward Paxton on Merchant's Exchange Bank for $9,000. Ascertain if good and answer by wire.
                            " H. C. CROSBY, President."

The next morning the following telegram was received:
" H. C. Crosby, President.
    " M. & E. Paxton's sight draft for $9,000 all right.
                        " DONALD, SLAWSON & CO."
12

And one was also received from the bank, conveying the same information.

There could be no doubt of the correctness of these, and accepting them as genuine, the money had been paid as already described to the swindling brothers; since which time nothing had been heard from them or their draft until the unexpected intelligence that the answer to the original telegram was a forgery, and that the first messages had never been delivered, opened the eyes of the bank officials to the astounding fact that they had been made the victims of as precious a pair of scoundrels as ever went unwhipped of justice.

The wrath of Mr. Crosby at the Paxtons was unbounded; he threatened and fumed and cursed them with all the vehemence of his angered heart, and from the depths of his troubled soul. And with little wonder. He had heretofore been regarded as an eminent authority by the trusting depositors of his bank; his word was law among the subordinates in the institution and among the customers outside of it; his opinions upon financial matters were regarded by every one as the utterances of an oracle. But now to find himself outwitted by a pair of inexperienced sharpers, and to have the profits of his little bank for several months thus unceremoniously appropriated, was too much for the dignity of the important president of the important little bank at Emporia. It was no wonder, therefore, that the exuberance of his passion found vent in expletives both loud and deep; and resolved itself into the settled purpose to leave no means untried to bring the swindlers to account.

Mr. Rodgers, being acquainted with the manner of working which these brothers had adopted, and presuming this to have been done by them, of which fact no reasonable doubt seemed possible, determined to discover at first the exact point at which the work was done, and, providing himself with ammunition and provisions for a few days' tramp, he proceeded along the line of the telegraph, in the hope of ascertaining by examination the exact locality at which the tapping of the wires was accomplished.

Leaving Emporia early in the morning, in a very short time he reached Junction City, and, upon inquiring of the operator there, he learned that the two brothers were known to him, they having been engaged in the rather questionable business of trading in horses and ponies of which no previous record could be given.

It seemed that they would come to town periodically with one or two horses or ponies, dispose of them, and then, after a few days of dissipation, would disappear again. Nothing seemed to be known of their whereabouts, but the operator recollected their having been in town during the time that the draft was being negotiated, and he recalled, also, the fact that they had made some inquiries in reference to the messages that were received and dispatched at this office.

Finding that he could not obtain any definite information, Rodgers proceeded on his way, and, when about a mile out from Junction City, he found the unmistakable evidences of their having been at work. The wires had been cut and repaired, a ground wire had been attached, and pieces of copies of old messages were strewn about upon the ground. He also found an envelope directed to "Miss Lizzie Coyan, Kansas City," the remains of a camp-fire, an old jack-knife, and an unopened box of sardines, showing conclusively that the boys

had boarded at their rendezvous and lunched at their im
promptu office.

There could be no doubt of the manner in which this opera
tion was transacted; the telegrams to Donald, Slawson & Co.
and to the bank had never reached a further destination than
this spot, and, by the aid of pocket instruments and an intimate knowledge of telegraphic manipulation, the messages dated
New York city, and carrying assurances of the correctness of
the draft presented, were sent from this place.

Truly a daring scheme, and, as results thus far proved, a
successful one ; but, like all attempts to defraud, while success
may crown the primary efforts, there is a swift and terrible
avenging justice that follows upon the heels of crime, and
eventually brings the offenders to a realizing sense of its punishing influences.

Thus far these rascally brothers had succeeded in accomplishing their object; the bank had been swindled, and they
were in the possession of their ill-gotten gains; but the detective was upon their track ; silently and stealthily he was pursuing the traces of their operations, and, in a moment of fancied security, they were to realize that retribution follows
quickly, and that crime must eventually be discovered and
criminals punished.

Having discovered where the work was done, and with the
directed envelope, which was to form the basis of his investigation of their whereabouts, Rodgers returned to Emporia, and
that evening took the train for Kansas City.

After a few inquiries he ascertained that Lizzie Coyan was
an occupant of a house of ill-fame in the place, kept by a Mrs.
Wilson, and to this house he at once repaired, resolved to get

from her whatever information she possessed of the present hiding-place of the brothers.

Upon being admitted into the house he inquired for the girl, and presently a blooming young woman about twenty-three years of age entered the room, when he instantly recognized her as the young lady who during the trial of Cowdrey had exhibited such a devoted love and self-sacrifice for George, and who at that time was quite a beauty and very much respected in Chicago, but who had evidently fallen from the pale of society—probably through her affection for this man—and was now leading a life of shame.

Speaking familiarly to her, and representing himself as a friend to George Cowdrey, now known as Martin Paxton, and desirous of helping him, he informed her of the fact that he was in danger, and stated that if she would inform him where Martin could be found she would, perhaps, be the means of saving him from being arrested and imprisoned.

"I would lay down my life for George Cowdrey, and anything I can do for him I will willingly do," said the girl, while the tears welled up in her eyes.

She then told Rodgers that the two brothers, whom we will hereafter call by their proper names, in company with some hunters, were encamped upon the Republican River, near Beaver Creek, and that the camp was known as "Honest John's"—a wild desperado, who was the terror of the surrounding country; whose name had been associated with many deeds of violence and bloodshed, and about whom many stories of cruelty and rascality were related.

As the girl related these facts to the detective his mind involuntarily reverted back a short time, when he had last seen her, mingling in good society in the city of Chicago, the center of an admiring circle of friends and acquaintances, and whose face was then lighted with the brightness of purity and happiness; and then contrasted her present position—a resident in a house of prostitution, in a far western country, the sport of rough and hardened men, inured to the roughest experiences of life, and mingling socially with those whose presence and association, a short time ago, would have created only the feelings of loathing and disgust.

However, this is only one of the many phases of human existence, and the dark curtain might be lifted from many lives, revealing many such stories, many such experiences, and the pall of death might be raised from the shroudings of many miserable forms who, in their early youth, gave promises of beauty and purity and goodness.

After ascertaining the place of retreat of the brothers, Rodgers bade the girl good-by, and returned to Emporia. He communicated the result of his discoveries to me from that point, and requested further instructions as to his course of proceedings before attempting any aggressive measures, which would, no doubt, be necessary in order to take the villains in the security of their camp.

I immediately informed General Stager of the results which had thus been arrived at, and also the fact that the Cowdreys and Paxtons were the same parties, and requested further advice from him as to our future movements.

Mr. Rodgers also informed Mr. Crosby of the discoveries he had made, and of the knowledge which he possessed of the hiding-place of the fugitives, and received from him full authority and instructions to attempt their capture; which authority being fully indorsed by General Stager and myself, he immediately began arranging his plan of campaign, and also of providing himself with sufficient aid in case of resistance.

CHAPTER XIV.

In Search of the Forgers—A Gambling Experience—A Trial by Judge Lynch.

THE adventure promised to be one of danger, and in consequence Rodgers found great difficulty in obtaining the services of any one to accompany him. The fame of "Honest John" had circulated far and wide; his unerring aim with the rifle, his indomitable courage, and his reckless disregard of human life, had made him an object to be feared; and most of the hunters whom the detective solicited to undertake the task of capturing the Cowdrey brothers in the camp of this redoubtable man shook their heads dubiously, and finally decided to remain at home.

At length, by dint of offering rewards for the capture of the criminals, and stirring up their courage and pride by the assertion that he would go alone if they were afraid to make the attempt with him, he succeeded in enlisting the services of three stalwart men, who were perfectly acquainted with the country to be traveled, and one of whom had seen the brothers within a few days, and who knew the road to the camp by the shortest route.

To Rodgers the situation was a novel one; his previous experience as a detective had been of a character far different

272]

from what this promised to be. Hitherto he had been engaged in operations which required more skill than courage, more perception of human nature than the rude contact with outlaws, which now seemed inevitable.

The country through which they were required to pass was filled with roaming bands of hunters, many of whom were fugitives from justice, and most of whom were utterly indifferent about the taking of human life. Their time during the hunting season being occupied in shooting the wild animals which abounded in this locality, and at the end of which they bring the skins of the animals they had slain to the nearest market, when, after disposing of them to the traders, they would, with the money so received, indulge in the wildest dissipation, gambling and drinking being the chief amusements to which they devoted themselves, and various wild and strange stories have been told of their recklessness and immorality. Many a sturdy hunter, after a season of hard work, has carried his earnings into the gambling-house, and in one evening the entire sum has disappeared; the man then, maddened by liquor, and desperate at his losses, would, upon some pretext, engage in a fight, and perhaps would be carried out in the morning without the slightest ceremony; a hole would be dug in the ground, his body interred, and the attendants at his funeral would resume their game as though nothing unusual had occurred.

One of the men secured by Rodgers, Bill Byfield by name, but better known as "Tiger Bill," related his experience, while waiting for their team, which conveys some idea of the utter disregard of the value of money, when the demon of play obtains control over the minds of reckless men.

"I had had a pretty good season," said Byfield, "and after
12*

I had counted up my profits, I found I had eight hundred dollars in cash, a good horse, a pack mule, a rifle, two revolvers, a dog and a meerschaum pipe, and I started out to look around the town.   After a while I met a couple of fellows whom I knew, just after I got my cash, and we resolved to have a quiet little game of poker.   Well, sir, I never struck such a streak of bad luck as I did that afternoon.   It was a square game, but if anybody won anything, they naturally meant to keep it.   Well, the first thing I did was to lose five hundred dollars of my money on four queens; it was my deal, and I gave another fellow four kings.   In less than an hour I lost every cent I had, then my horse, then my mule, and then my rifle, revolvers and dog.   I staggered out of the place, and made up my mind to borrow a revolver and shoot myself.

"I walked out to the edge of the town and put my hand to my hip pocket to take my revolver.   I did not find any revolver, but my meerschaum pipe was there, and as soon as I felt that pipe I gave a yell of delight and started off on a run for the house where the boys had won my money.   They were still there.   I got twenty dollars on my pipe, and sat down to play again.   I won a little money, and then my dog, revolvers, rifle, mule and horse.   At last I won twelve hundred dollars in one hand.   The fellow who was betting against me had jacks, but I had the queens.   When I got up from the table it was daylight in the morning, and I had eighteen hundred dollars, besides the things I started with.   I went down to the house, borrowed the landlady's Bible, and took a solemn oath that I would never gamble again as long as I lived.   I never have since, and I never will."

This is but one of hundreds of incidents which might be

told of these sturdy, hardened men, and to Rodgers, his **present** experience was a revelation. He had, however, a mission **to** perform, and he resolved to accomplish it at whatever hazard.

His companions consisted of three hunters of the better class, although one of them was deemed a little unreliable, but he was compelled to accept him, owing to his inability to secure others. The first, Bill Byfield, who has already been spoken of, a tall, broad-shouldered man of immense physical strength, and generally believed to be honest and trustworthy ; the second was a short, stumpy German, whose rightful name was Jack Dumpel, but who generally received the title of " Dumpling Jack," a steady, honest fellow, devoted to the cause, and as brave as a lion. The third was an Indian half-breed, known far and wide as " Friday," a most successful hunter, but not considered of the most trustworthy character, and who was generally regarded with suspicion by his associates.

Securing a mule team and four ponies as the only means of conveyance available, and with all the appurtenances for sleeping and cooking, the detective and his party left Fort Riley, and started on the journey to the camp of " Honest John." They had procured some uniforms at the Fort, and so, disguised as United States regulars on a prospecting tour, they commenced a journey that was as novel to Rodgers as a balloon voyage would have been to the Pilgrims of the *Mayflower*.

Their way led through the wild and beautiful country along the shores of the Republican River, and had the excursion been one of pleasure, it would have been greatly enjoyed by the hunter detective; but his mind was too much occupied with thoughts of the duties that lay before him, and a desire to **be**

successful, to enable him to give much thought to the beauties
of nature that were so lavishly spread before him,

Game was abundant, and "Friday" an excellent cook, so that
the commissary department of this miniature camp was well
taken care of.   Their time was passed in a manner that requires
but little notice, and nothing occurred to break the monotony
of their journey, until one evening, they halted at a large camp
of hunters near to a place called "Eagle Bend," and here the
detective witnessed an episode that will ever live in his
memory.

He had frequently heard of the doings of Judge Lynch, and
the precipitancy of his legal operations was familiar to him
from his reading, but he had never witnessed a practical exem-
plification of the railroad justice that was usually meted out
by this august magnate.

When they arrived late in the afternoon of a beautiful day
in October, there were evident signs of commotion within the
camp.   Something unusual had happened or was about to
occur, and, feeling naturally curious to witness any event that
might be of interest, they halted their team and, fastening their
mules and ponies, pushed their way into the center of the camp,
where they beheld a scene at once startling and ruggedly imposing.

The hunters, numbering about thirty, with flashing eyes
and firm-set lips, were gathered in a semicircle, and in the
middle of this group, between two brawny, armed trappers,
knelt a middle-aged man, with hands upraised as though in
supplication.

Rodgers inquired the meaning of this strange proceeding,
of a person near him, and was informed that the person who

was kneeling there was a horse thief who had been captured that morning, and that he was being tried for his offense.

It appears that the stealing of horses or any other transportable property was not generally considered a grievous crime, if committed upon a stranger, but when a thief entered the sacred precincts of an organized camp, and plied his vocation, the penalty was death, sudden and irrevocable.

The facts of this case appeared to be substantially as follows: One of the hunters, the ostensible leader of the camp, was the possessor of a remarkably fine horse, which was the object of his especial pride and solicitude, and that, returning from a hunt the night before, he had secured the animal to a wagon, and being tired and wearied with the fatigues of the day, had gone immediately to sleep. The barking of a dog disturbed his slumbers about four o'clock in the morning, and remembering his horse, he pulled aside the cover of his wagon and peeped out—the animal was gone. A hurried inspection showed that the fastening had been drawn, and the horse, with a bridle and blanket, had gone off.

Arousing the camp, they hastily mounted their horses and started in hot pursuit of the absent quadruped. A trail was struck, and at a point about half-way to Washington the pursuing hunters espied the horse, and seated upon his back was the individual who was now being so informally tried. The rider made no resistance when he saw the dangerous ends of several pistols looking him square in the face, but suddenly turned the stolen horse around, and rode back to the camp, surrounded by his pursuers.

Upon arriving at the camp, word was immediately given that the thief had been captured, and a crowd of men, and one or two women quickly assembled. A short conference ensued; the delay and uncertainty of the administration of justice in the nearest town was briefly discussed, and then the decision that the thief should be hung forthwith was arrived at without a dissenting voice.

It was at this time that Rodgers and his party appeared, and the sight that met the gaze of the surprised detective was terrifying and grandly impressive. His sentence had been communicated to him by a deep-voiced man, who seemed to be the spokesman of the party, some rope halters were taken from the mules at the corral, spliced and fixed around the neck of the condemned man, while the long end was looped around a crooked limb of a tree over his head, and then the culprit was told to pray.

The mockery of this proceeding struck painfully upon the mind of Rodgers, but he was powerless to interfere; the determined faces of these men denoted a fixed purpose, and that purpose the death of the miserable man who knelt before them. With pale face and faltering speech the poor wretch began his prayer, but not to any one of the many unseen gods was his invocation directed. His face was turned towards those who were about to take away his life, and to them he prayed most piteously. He denied having stolen the horse, and begged for an opportunity to prove that he was not the thief; he asserted that the stolen property found in his possession had been placed there by a man whom he supposed to be its rightful owner, and that he had agreed merely to ride the horse to Washington, where he was to be joined by the owner.

The executioners listened incredulously, but patiently, to

the prayer, and then, after laying their heads together for a few seconds, concluded to let the petitioner live providing he would give the name of the man from whom the stolen property was obtained. This man in the halter refused to save his life by any such cowardly means, and the order was sternly given to hoist him up.

Six men pulled at the rope with sturdy good-will; a shriek rent the air that seemed to affright the very birds of the forest, and which chilled the blood of the detective as he fell back with a sickening sensation at his heart; and then the body of the man was dangling in the air, his face distorted, and his limbs twitching convulsively. Rodgers turned away; he could stand no more. He thought, as he sank to the ground, of this dreadful spectacle which presented itself in the guise of justice, and he endeavored in vain to shut from his mental vision the dreadful sight of that poor victim of man's inhumanity.

Lynch law, that Moloch of civilization, had added another to its long list of victims, and the masquerade of vengeance was over.

CHAPTER XV.

The Brothers Treed—The Attack—The Attempted Escape—The Capture—The Recovery of the Spoil—A Trial and a Sentence.

HEARTSICK and weary Rodgers crawled to the wagon, where he was shortly afterwards joined by his companions, who, throwing themselves down, were soon sound asleep, but to Rodgers sleep came not so readily; the suspended form of that murdered man would come up before him in spite of every effort to efface it from his memory, and the mists of the night were yielding to the soft breaking of the ruddy beams of the morning ere he sank into a restless sleep, and temporarily forgot his painful experience.

The next day they resumed their journey, and at about eight o'clock in the evening "Friday" informed them that they were within a few miles of their place of destination. Rodgers, therefore, determined to encamp for the night, and then, early in the morning, after their ponies had been refreshed by a good night's rest, they would ride down to the camp and attempt the capture.

This proposition was accepted by the rest of the party, and after the discussion of their plans for the morrow, and determining upon their mode of attack, they retired to their wagon and to rest.

They were all astir early in the morning, and after attending to their horses, and partaking of breakfast, they decided to leave the wagon and ride on to the camp of " Honest John," unincumbered by anything except their revolvers, rifles and ammunition.

The morning was beautiful and exhilarating, the river was rippling and dancing in the bright beams of the sun; the leaves of the trees had assumed the beautiful coloring which nowhere else is seen in such rich and varied beauty as in the western forests; their air was balmy, and the sky rolled away in a grand expanse of blue, unflecked by a single cloud. No time, however, was to be given to the admiration of the scenes around them; a duty lay before them, a duty which might involve danger to life and limb; and so, with their minds filled with the task before them, they rode silently onward.

Rodgers noticed a peculiar expression upon " Friday's " face which aroused his suspicions, and he determined to keep a strict watch upon his movements, to prevent any treachery upon his part, and not let him out of his sight until their mission was accomplished. He rode up to Byfield, and communicating his suspicions to him, directed him also to keep his eye upon the half-breed.

After a half hour's brisk ride, they arrived within sight of the camp, which consisted of a large Government tent, and a corral for animals, and without being discovered by any of the occupants, who had not yet, it seemed, made their appearance. Two ponies were fastened outside, which Byfield instantly recognized as belonging to the Cowdreys, and as no other animals appeared in sight, it seemed evident that "Honest John" was not at home. This fact somewhat relieved "Friday," who had been considerably ill at ease during the latter part of the journey, and his countenance brightened perceptibly.

Upon approaching within a short distance of the tent, Rodgers posted his men so as to cover each side of it, in case of an attempt on the part of the persons they were in search of to escape, and then giving the order to advance, they rode quickly down towards the camp.

They had reached the entrance before the alarm had been taken inside, and Rodgers dismounted at the door of the tent just as Charley Cowdrey made his appearance, fully dressed, with revolver in hand. Rodgers advanced, and presenting both his weapons, commanded Charley to throw down his pistol and hold up his hands, and threatened to fire in case of refusal. Charles looked hurriedly around, and finding the tent surrounded and resistance useless, threw his weapon on the ground and did as he was commanded. Rodgers then placed the handcuffs upon his wrists, and proceeded to search his person, leaving the others to prevent the escape of George, who was inside the tent. An examination disclosed about two hundred dollars in money, a watch, a small revolver, and two of the one-thousand-dollar certificates which had been so fraudulently obtained.

Just as he had completed his search he heard a cry from Byfield, and on looking suddenly around, he discovered George Cowdrey running towards the place where the ponies were fastened, he having escaped from the tent on the side guarded by the half-breed "Friday.'

"Instantly there was a fall, and both horse and rider were rolling in the dust."

Rodgers quickly placed the captured man in charge of the German, and calling to Byfield to follow, he started in pursuit of the fugitive George, who, turning around, faced his pursuers, and walked rapidly backward toward the ponies.

"Stop, or I will fire!" exclaimed Rodgers, finding it impossible to reach him in time to prevent his mounting.

"Fire if you will. I won't be taken from here alive, and I will sell my life dearly," answered Cowdrey, desperately.

It was not Rodgers' purpose to resort to extreme measures, the man must be taken alive; and finding Cowdrey disposed to offer resistance, he resolved upon his course of action.

Running to his own pony, which was standing near to the entrance of the tent, he mounted just as George Cowdrey reached his animal, and Rodgers started in pursuit.

His animal being fresh, soon overtook the one ridden by Cowdrey, and when within short range of the escaping criminal, Rodgers drew his revolver and fired twice in rapid succession. Instantly there was a fall, and both horse and rider were rolling in the dust of the road in hopeless entanglement. Rodgers, hastening forward, found that the pony had fallen upon Cowdrey, and pinned him to the ground; he had fired at the animal and thus secured his prisoner. As he approached, Cowdrey reached for his pistol, and threatened to shoot the detective if he advanced, but Rodgers, nothing daunted, steadily approached the man, saying:

"If you attempt to fire, I will kill you!"

Cowdrey, realizing that further resistance would prove fatal to him, as the detective was evidently in earnest, threw down his pistol, and the detective then advanced and took him in charge.

Cowdrey was suffering very much; the pony had fallen upon his leg, and had evidently broken it, the pain from which became excruciating; but the horse was finally removed, with the assistance of Byfield, and the wounded man, who had now fainted, was conveyed to the tent and properly secured and cared for.

After this had been accomplished, Rodgers turned his attention to the half-breed, and, leveling his pistol at him, said threateningly:

"You cowardly traitor, you shall pay for this," and then directed Byfield to handcuff him and shackle his feet.

"Friday" glared at the detective as this was being done, but he realized that he had been detected, and that his half-formed purpose to leave the party and alarm the neighboring camps, in order to attempt a rescue of the prisoners, had been foiled.

On George Cowdrey's person the remaining five certificates were found, and Rodgers, in order to prevent further accident, cut the signatures from them, thus effectually destroying their usefulness. Dumpel was dispatched for the wagon, which, soon arriving, the men were placed therein, and the homeward journey was begun, Rodgers' bosom swelling with honest pride as he thought of the success which had attended his efforts, and of the report which he would be enabled to make upon his return.

Nothing further occurred upon the route, and the party reached Emporia in safety; the two prisoners were transferred to the custody of the officers of the law, and locked up to await a hearing. Rodgers, regretting his inability to deal with the half-breed as he desired, reluctantly allowed him to go his way,

and after thanking the others for the services they had rendered him, he settled with them in accordance with the terms of his contract.

At the next term of the court the two Cowdreys were placed upon trial, and the testimony being overwhelmingly against them, they were convicted and sentenced to a term of imprisonment which will afford them an opportunity for mature thought and the formation of honest resolutions.

The question as to liability was amicably arranged between the bank and the telegraph company, and Mr. Crosby, highly-elated at the successful issue of the matter and the capture of the criminals, was disposed to arrogate to himself the credit of the affair, but in this, however, he did not succeed, as the fame of Pinkerton and his men had been too firmly established to be appropriated so easily.

With the imprisonment of these two brothers the attempts to interfere with the telegraph ceased, no developments of a similar nature having since been made, and although the interposition of the law had been refused, the vigilance of the officers and the integrity of the operators are sufficient to insure the safety and secrecy of any message intrusted to the company for transmission.

To George and Charles Cowdrey it is hoped that the lesson will be salutary and lasting, and that their after life will be devoted to honorable pursuits and honest labor. They have realized what it is to leave a home of comfort for the hardships and exposure of western life, in the hope of illicit gain. They have known what it was to forsake an honorable calling for dishonest practices, and they have seen that home taken away, themselves in want, and they know too surely what it is to bear a felon's name and wear a felon's chain.

Mr. Orton, the valued president of the company, has passed away; the harvest of his life, devoted to the science of telegraphy and to the performance of noble, manly duties, has been gathered in; a brain, wearied with the perplexities of business, and active to a wonderful degree, is at rest, and as I look back to my intercourse with him in connection with the matters here detailed, I pay a tribute of respect and esteem to a great and good man, whom it was a pleasure to meet, a privilege to know, and an honor to be associated with.

General Stager is still an active worker in the service of the company, and bids fair to live many years longer to fulfill the duties which have been so admirably performed by him during a long series of years. I have enjoyed his friendship, and trust that his declining days may be filled with the honors and rewards of a faithful officer and a steadfast friend.

THE EDGEWOOD MYSTERY

AND

THE DETECTIVE.

CHAPTER I.

*The Crime of Murder—Its Prevalence—Its Apparent Increase
—And Some of its Causes.*

WHAT a sad commentary upon the refining and beneficial influences which advancing civilization is supposed to exert upon the hearts and minds of humanity is found in the almost daily incidents of the taking of human life, the frequency of murderous attempts and the reckless disregard of personal safety which are everywhere apparent.

Day after day the newspapers are filled with the horrible particulars of some revolting crime of this nature. Day after day the public mind is appalled by the sickening details of an attempt by reasonable, thinking men, to imbrue their hands in the blood of their fellows, and a limited investigation of the

[287]

criminal calendars of the various courts of justice will convince the most skeptical that this species of crime is alarmingly on the increase.

Nor is the monopoly of this work of human butchery con-fined exclusively to the masculine portion of the community, or to the lowest conditions of society; the hydra-headed monster etxends his slimy fangs through all the ramifications of social regulations, and a record of his deeds and the knowledge of the wide-spread dissemination of his poisonous influences would dismay the casual reader of human events.

Into the palace and the hovel—the peaceful village and the crowded city—the marts of trade and the sanctum of the scholar—he winds his insidious way until all grades of society are placed under contribution to appease this thirst for blood.

The red hand of the murderer is found encased in the delicate glove of the latest foreign importation, quite as frequently as it is discovered to be hard, horny, and a stranger to the niceties of dress or immunity from labor. The gentle-voiced and handsome-faced woman is quite as adept, and often-times quite as reckless in the use of the pistol and the poniard, as are the "desperate characters" who infest our cities and render life unsafe, and a " Smith & Wesson," at short range, has not unfrequently been employed as the active medium in the settlement of a lover's quarrel, the reparation of wounded virtue, or in the determination of a breach of promise of marriage.

Through all grades of society stalks this grim, hideous monster, and in his wake follow hundreds of human creatures, gifted by nature and education with attributes fitted to adorn the highest circles of society; with intellects that would make them leaders of men, walking in close companionship with the brutal ruffian and the debased and ignorant marauder. Eugene Aram linking his arms with those of Bill Sykes—and the dismayed and disheartened communities await in vain the coming of that modern Hercules who shall, with trenchant blows, strike him to the ground, and free them from the horrors of his operations.

To the just reader of current events, or the intelligent observer of the affairs of society, who construe aright the principle of cause and effect, the solution of this vexed question of human depravity is not altogether a mystery.

In my experience of thirty years, spent in the detection of crime and criminals, during which time I have had an intimate acquaintance with the *modus operandi* and the formula of criminal trials as well as criminal transactions, I have often felt utterly disgusted at the maudlin sympathy and mawkish sentimentality which instantly attaches itself to the person of a criminal arraigned for trial.

More particularly is this manifested in the case of the men or women who are placed upon trial for murder. No sooner has the criminal been arraigned and entered the plea of "not guilty" than they are surrounded by a coterie of sympathizers, and that, too, very often, composed of the most respectable portion of our people.

No thought is apparently given to the poor victims who have been hurried out of existence, with no note of warning, and unshriven have been ushered out of this breathing world. No sorrow is manifested for the family thus suddenly deprived of a protector and provider, or the home that has been bereft of a father or a husband; but the low-browed villain, whose

13

hands have committed the damnable deed, and whom the law is seeking to punish for his crime, is held up by these sympathetic addlepates as a victim of persecution, an object of pity, and sometimes as a martyred saint.

Not long since I attended the trial of an individual who had, in a fit of jealous rage, taken the life of his young and handsome wife, and had literally emptied his revolver into her body, and what was my surprise to see the gentlemanly criminal dressed in immaculate style, with bouquet in his buttonhole, and furnished, I was informed, with fresh flowers every day by his admiring and sympathetic friends, for the adornment of his person, the court-room and his cell. Flowers for the murderer, while not a blade of grass was waving over the neglected grave of his victim, the wife whom he had sworn to honor and to cherish!

All the ingenuity of the most talented lawyers is brought into service; all the legal technicalities are resorted to, and every possible device is set up to screen the criminal from the just operation of the law and the proper punishment for his offense; and it is a lamentable fact, that these would-be and self-constituted philanthropists are, perhaps unconsciously, but none the less surely, contributing in a marked degree to the spread of crime by depriving it of its worst features, and screening its deformities with the vail of a maudlin and misdirected sympathy for those who transgress the laws.

Another idea that seems to have great influence, not only in producing popular sympathy, but in forming the verdicts of juries, is the disposition to treat with incredulity the weight and operation of evidence of a circumstantial character. No matter how perfect the chain of proof may be forged; how

correctly and consistently every circumstance may be portrayed;
how distinctly and truthfully every action of the accused may
be traced, or how thoroughly every attendant incident may corroborate the theory of commission of a crime—unless the testimony of eye-witnesses can be procured, who are prepared to
swear that they saw what was intended and artfully designed
to be concealed, and who detected accidentally that which was
carefully planned to escape detection—weak-minded and sympathetic juries will debate very long before accepting the responsibility of a conviction, and the result in many cases is,
that the aggressors escape the punishment they so richly deserve.

Upon the general subject of circumstantial evidence, there
has been, and will continue to be, a diversity of opinion as to
the wisdom of relying implicitly upon such testimony as being
universally sufficient to convict. It is true that the records of
some cases of criminal trials show conclusively that men have
been convicted and sentenced upon evidence adduced of an entirely circumstantial character, and that years afterwards the
true history of the crime has been revealed, which proved beyond doubt that the person thus punished was entirely guiltless; and it is also a cause for serious regret that men have
been executed upon such testimony, who were afterwards
proven to have had no knowledge of the crime. But in the
great majority of these instances, and their numbers are happily very few, it will be shown that such convictions were the
result of a great moral excitement, in which an insatiate public
appetite for justice must be appeased, at whatever cost.

These instances, however, form the notable exception to
the general rule, and the fact is patent to all, that in the great

preponderance of cases particularly that of the taking of human life, the evidence of a perfect and conclusive circumstantial character must inevitably be relied upon, and being of a thorough and convincing nature, have produced the conviction of the real offender.

In the following pages I shall attempt to depict a crime, the detection and punishment of which clearly illustrates the important nature of circumstantial evidence, in the development of a theory of criminal action, in which no *positive* proof could be adduced upon which to base an examination or to construct a theory of operation.

In placing before the reader the facts of this case ; the discovery of the murdered body ; the subsequent identification ; the tracking of the murderer and his final conviction, I shall endeavor to show the importance of this much-abused, but none the less effective agency of detection, and which eventually resulted in the vindication of outraged law, and the punishment of the guilty.

CHAPTER II.

Edgewood—The Finding of the Body—The Excitement of the People—A Religious Ceremony Interrupted.

THE romantic little village of Edgewood was situated on the line of the Erie Railway, in the State of New Jersey, and but a few miles distant from New York city. It was a beautiful and picturesque spot, and being in close proximity to the great metropolis, of easy access, and combining all the advantages and refinements of city life with the invigorating and healthful influences of a rural residence, it was largely peopled by mercantile gentlemen from New York, who with their families made this delightful locality their place of permanent abode. In addition to these, the inhabitants also comprised some of the oldest and wealthiest families of the State, whose large and commodious residences, broad fields, luxuriant orchards, sloping lawns and noble old trees all contributed to render Edgewood a scene of rural beauty seldom witnessed.

Here, in the peacefulness and luxury of rural repose, dwelt a community of refinement and wealth; all being socially equal, the congenial and affable associations of all were assured, and, undisturbed by those foolish and vexatious questions of *caste* and *status*, which the residents of large cities are continually being exercised about, the time passed happily and pleasantly along.

Crime was comparatively unknown, and save as the information was conveyed to them through the medium of the news journals, their lives would have floated on in calm serenity and moral repose, untainted by the contaminating influences of an association with evil-doers.

On the Sabbath day the little village church was the scene of many a pleasant greeting and hearty hand-shake; friends separated for a week gathered in little knots around the door-ways and discussed, with the gravity of legislators, the important social events of the preceding days. Young men with bright eyes and glowing cheeks, home, perhaps, from some distant educational institution, would recount their experiences. Coy maidens would blushingly and shyly descant upon the merits of the various swains with whom they were acquainted, and with quiet, mischievous badinage would force the modest little victim of their raillery to confess, with hesitating speech, the object of her preference.

Thus would the time be passed until the solemn bell summoned the gathered crowds to assemble for the daily worship; then with hushed voices and noiseless steps they entered the chapel, joined in the songs of praise, listened to the words of wisdom, and separated for their homes upon its conclusion, with the inward solace of the morning's benisons.

But I desire to speak of another Sabbath that dawned upon this quiet, happy little village.

On the fourteenth of March, in the year eighteen hundred and sixty-nine, the people had assembled for evening worship in the little church. The opening hymn had been sung, the

"There, upon the white snow glistening in the pale moonlight, lay the body of a young man, still and cold in death."

pleading, earnest prayer had been uttered, and the village Dominie had just announced his text, when the solemn stillness was broken by the sudden entrance of a well-known citizen of the place, whose blanched face and agitated manner at once conveyed the intelligence that something dreadful had happened.

"A man has been found dead on the common near the church!" was his startling ejaculation.

Immediately the congregation were upon their feet, eager questions and hurried answers followed, and then, in utter disregard of the unfinished religious ceremony, the entire assem bly, with one accord, hurried out of the building and hastened to the scene.

It was, alas, too true. There, in close proximity to the church, upon the white snow, glistening in the moonlight, with face upturned and rigid, lay the body of a young man, still and cold in death.

The discovery had been made by a Mr. B. A. Jessup, an estimable gentleman, who, in company with two others, were wending their way to the chapel for the purpose of attending service, and, being somewhat belated, they concluded to shorten the distance by taking a diagonal pathway across the open common which intervened between the road and the church. When about midway across, Mr. Jessup, who was in the advance, tripped accidentally over some object, which, at first, was thought to be a lay figure, which the farmers designate as a "scare-crow," but, on stooping to make a closer examination, the horrible discovery was made that the "object" was the lifeless form of a human being. Horrified by the discovery, and realizing the necessity of communicating the intelligence to some one who could act advisedly and with authority in the matter, or, perhaps, acting upon impulse and with no definite object in view, Mr. Jessup ran quickly to the church, and, without preliminary or introduction, conveyed the startling intelligence which had so suddenly alarmed the assembled worshipers and brought them so hurriedly and affrightedly to the spot.

The appearance of death at any time is sad and appalling. The cold, white face, and eyes that seem to be staring wildly into futurity, and which loving hands will gently close, ever fill the heart with sorrow; and it is not strange in this instance, when those who were gathered around, who had so suddenly been called from a scene of peace and quiet happiness and brought to stand face to face with this dread monitor in its ghastliest form, that a thrill of awe and fear should pervade the entire group. Strong men stood momentarily irresolute, while the young people clung to each other in affright, and some time elapsed before any one could sufficiently recover to attempt the investigation necessary to the discovery of the full facts of the case.

An examination, however, being had, disclosed the fact that the body was that of a man entirely unknown to the villagers, of evident foreign extraction, probably German, fine-looking, and apparently about twenty-eight years of age. It had been stripped of its outer clothing, and was clad only in vest, shirt, drawers stockings and shoes. The vest was of good material and well made, the shirt of fine linen, and the underwear of excellent quality; the shoes were of no ordinary manufacture, were shapely, and fitted neatly to the feet.

The unknown victim thus discovered was endowed with finely shaped hands and limbs, was possessed of a handsome face, surmounted by curling locks of dark-brown hair, and the upper lip was concealed by a drooping, dark mustache. In fact, everything about the body gave unmistakable evi‐ dence that the unfortunate man was a gentleman and a for‐ eigner, but nothing was discovered that would, in the slightest degree, throw a ray of light upon the question of his identity.

Upon lifting from the head a small, low-crowned, narrow-rimmed felt hat, of light pearl color, stained with blood upon the inside, several wounds was discovered, which had evidently produced his death. The skull was fractured and the brain was contused ; great, ugly marks were found upon his forehead, as though produced by the heavy blows of some blunt instru‐ ment, and the fingers were lacerated as though the unfortunate man had struggled desperately for his life.

While these evidences of a brutal murder were so plainfully apparent, it was also discovered that life had been extinct for some time, probably several days ; that the clothing of the de‐ ceased entirely free from blood-stains, and that the wounds upon the head had been carefully cleansed.

An examination of the ground in the vicinity of the find‐ ing of the body also disclosed the foot-prints of a man, who had evidently carried the body from a strip of woods, some two hundred feet distant, and an oaken barrel-stave, found near the body, led to the reasonable theory that the body had been thrown over it, and by that means had been carried from the place where the murder had been committed, to the locality where it was discovered.

The excitement produced by this event, even in this quiet little village, was intense ; the information spread with meteor-like rapidity, and the entire community became imbued with the determination to allow neither expense, time or trouble to

13*

be spared in the effort of ferreting out this mysterious crime, securing a vindication of the outraged laws of the land, and discovering, if possible, who the unfortunate man was, who had thus met a violent and untimely death.

Of course, as is usual in such cases, the wildest rumors were circulated, the imagination largely supplied the deficiency of facts, and the varied accounts of the occurrence differed as widely as the antipodes. Great crowds gathered around the village store the following morning, and many and surprising were the opinions offered and the suggestions made.

The inquest was held on Monday morning; but no evidence was elicited that would dispel the doubt and uncertainty as to the identity of the murdered man, or of those who had caused his death; and at last, finding it impossible with the limited information then possessed or accessible to proceed to a successful determination, the jury were discharged, the head of the murdered man was severed from the body by an eminent physician, placed in a hermetically-sealed jar of spirits for identification, and the body was interred.

A meeting of the citizens was called, and a committee was appointed of the most influential and wealthy gentlemen to prosecute the inquiry; money was liberally subscribed, and it was resolved to at once employ the services of "the best detectives in the country" in unearthing the dreadful mystery.

The feeling of alarm and indignation was so intense that the young and more exuberant spirits threatened the formation of a vigilance committee; but yielding to the wisdom of older heads, the excitement resolved itself into a deep seated determination to discover the murderer, and bring him to justice through the legal channels and by the recognized legal means.

CHAPTER III.

*The Agency is Employed—An Examination of the Field—The
Initials upon the Garment—General Suspicions.*

ON the eighteenth day of March, four days succeeding the
discovery of the body of the murdered man, as related in
the preceding chapter, Mr. George H. Bangs, my very able
and efficient General Superintendent, and my son Robert A.
Pinkerton, who was then and is now in charge of my New
York office, were seated in the private office of the Agency,
when three gentlemen were announced as desiring an interview
upon an important matter. The proper direction being given
they were admitted, and upon presenting their cards were
discovered to be a Mr. Thomas Sharpless, Henry Thornton, and
B. A. Jessup, members of the committee appointed by the
citizens of Edgewood, and instructed to secure the services of
the Agency in discovering the identity of the unknown man,
the cause and manner of his death, and, if possible, the arrest
and punishment of the party or parties who should be found
to be implicated in the dreadful affair.

" Well, gentlemen," said Mr. Bangs, " please relate to us as
clearly as you can, all the circumstances attending this affair."

It has always been my rule, and that of all persons connected with my Agencies, to require from every one who either

desire my services, or who is engaged under my direction, **to** give full and explicit accounts of whatever transpires in connection with any matter with which they are identified. I have frequently found that some apparently unimportant incident, some half-remembered fragment of conversation, or some trifling, ill-considered remark have been the means of affording a perfect clue, and very often have enabled me to construct a theory, which, but for these "trifles light as air," would never have approached a definite determination; hence the direction of Mr. Bangs to the gentlemen present to be explicit in detailing the circumstances attending the object of their visit.

Mr. Thomas Sharpless, who was an attorney at law who resided at Edgewood, and who had volunteered to assist the prosecuting attorney of the county in the investigation of this matter, and who seemed to be the spokesman of the committee, at once complied with the request. He detailed at length the finding of the body by Mr. Jessup; the alarm at the church; the unsuccessful investigation by the Coroner; the inability to ascertain who the murdered man was, and the entire absence of any clew as to the place where the murder was committed, or any trace of those who might have perpetrated the deed. After adjusting the necessary preliminary arrangements, Mr. Bangs agreed to take charge of the matter and give to it his personal supervision, the gentlemen retired, leaving heir addresses in case their presence should be required at any time.

The outlook was certainly not very promising, it must be confessed, and in this confession both of the gentlemen soberly, and with evident sincerity, coincided. There seemed to be no starting-place, no point of attack, and so, without further consideration, they determined to visit the locality, examine the ground, question the villagers, and then they would be the better qualified to act intelligently in the investigation of this seeming mystery.

On the following morning, therefore, Mr. Bangs, accompanied by Robert A. Pinkerton, left New York, and in a short time found themselves in the pretty little village of Edgewood, and also found Mr. Sharpless awaiting their arrival, who conducted them immediately to the scene of operations. Upon an examination it was found that the place where the body was found was within a short distance of a piece of woods, and within a quarter of a mile of the railroad depot; but the footprints which were said to have been discovered on the Sunday evening had been completely obliterated by the crowds who had thronged to the place upon the fact being made known, and who had thus destroyed one opportunity which possibly might have afforded some weight in the discovery of the murderers.

The doctor who made the post-mortem examination of the body of the deceased was next interviewed, and gave them his opinion, founded upon the results of his personal and scientific inquiry, that one of the wounds had been caused by a sharp instrument, and the others by a blunt one, probably by the barrel-stave that was found near the body; that the skull was fractured in two places; that the right eye had been forced out, and that the victim must have been dead over forty-eight hours at the time of the finding of the body, and that the wounds were sufficient to have caused death.

They then made the acquaintance of some of the villagers, and very quaint and curious was the information they received

It seemed as though every man had resolved himself into an amateur detective, every one had a particular theory of his own, and between the recital of what they knew and what they imagined, it was almost impossible to arrive at any definite information. After repeated inquiries of numerous individuals, they at last found something tangible, and which approached something like information. Mr. Aaron Bronson, who accompanied Mr. Jessup when the body was discovered, informed them that he saw the tracks of a man going from, and returning to, the woods, about thirty yards distant from where the body was found; that the tracks coming from the wood were long, and deeply imbedded in the ground, as though the parties who made them were burdened and hurried, and that those made in returning were lighter. He also informed them that upon an examination of the clothing of the deceased he found the sum of thirty-five dollars in the pocket of the vest, which seemed to him to be conclusive evidence that robbery was not the cause of his death.

Mr. Jessup and his companion both confirmed this statement.

It was also ascertained that several of the residents had remarked a noticeable resemblance between the deceased and a person who, on the Friday preceding, had inquired of them the proper direction to a public house, kept by Jacob Gross; which house, it was ascertained upon inquiry, did not bear an enviable reputation, and was frequented, principally, by serving men and peddlers. The proprietor was known to be a man of no character or principle, a gamester and a drunkard, and was shunned by the residents of Edgewood. His wife was a vulgar termagant, whose violent temper and coarse language

were well known, and universally condemned. Popular opinion and a general suspicion seemed to attach to this couple, as
being in some way implicated in the mystery, and the fact of
the deceased having made inquiries for Gross's Hotel becoming
known, convinced many that they had some knowledge of the
occurrence, which they could reveal, if they were so disposed ;
several other circumstances of a suspicious character were related in reference to this hotel-keeper, Gross, and his amiable
wife, which were deemed of importance by the embryotic
detectives, whose name was legion, and which seemed to them
to point unequivocally to them as the perpetrators of the
crime.

Not feeling at all convinced of the force or weight of such
information, but desiring to derive all the information possible
from every available source, Mr. Bangs determined to inquire
into the movements of the two Gross's, but in a manner that
would occasion no suspicion of his intention, and by persons
entirely unknown to the villagers, and disconnected, apparently,
from any operations with which the detectives were supposed
to have anything to do.

It has always been an undeviating practice with this Agency,
never to neglect the slightest point of information connected
with any operation in hand, that may be received ; and,
although I may be convinced in my own mind, that the result
of such inquiry will not shed the faintest ray of light upon a
dark and seemingly hopeless investigation, yet I have very
often, by pursuing these devious ways to the fountain of
truth, discovered traces which have eventually led me to complete success in the right direction.

Mr. Bangs, therefore, selected from my force of operatives

a young man, Henry Brockman by name, and directed him to assume the role of a journeyman painter, to take up his residence temporarily at Edgewood, and to gather whatever information he possibly could, in reference to the suspected man, Gross, and his wife; to get into conversation with them, and to endeavor to ascertain from them all the facts which they were supposed to be in possession of, in regard to the movements of the person who had inquired for his hotel, and who was believed to be the person who was afterwards found murdered, as previously detailed.

But the most important question yet remained unsolved, viz., the identity of the murdered man. The discovery of his name, his place of residence, his occupation, all seemed to defy the efforts of those who had previously attempted to arrive at any information in reference to the said affair; and after four days of inquiry they had given the matter up in despair, and the question seemed now as completely enveloped in mystery as ever.

Of the hundreds of people who, attracted by the publication of so unwonted a crime in that peaceful locality, had thronged to view the body, not one was able to say who he was, or that they could distinctly remember ever having seen him before.

This information Mr. Bangs was determined to obtain at first, as he felt confident that without this knowledge the detection of the guilty parties would be utterly impossible, and that with it he would be enabled to proceed with confidence and with assumed certainty of eventual success.

The two gentlemen, Mr. Bangs and my son, therefore made a careful examination of the clothing found upon the body of the murdered man, and the only thing that was found, that would in any manner serve as a mark of identification, was that the letters "A. B." were worked in embroidery upon the shirt which the deceased wore; and this fact, it was resolved, should be the foundation-stone of the structure of their inquiry.

With this information obtained, and after having made a complete survey of the ground, they returned to New York city.

CHAPTER IV.

The Value of Little Things—The Identification of the Murdered Man and Discovery of his Residence.

IT is a remarkable subject of consideration what small and apparently insignificant causes will oftentimes produce wonderful and revolutionizing effects; and yet the world's history contains many marked evidences of the great forces which have sometimes grown from and been produced by comparatively trifling inceptions and circumstances. The swinging of a chandelier in a Romish church in Italy, which suggested to Galileo the idea of the pendulum in the measurement and indication of time; the falling of the apple from the tree, which conveyed to Isaac Newton the theory of gravitation; the hissing of the tea-kettle, which led to the employment of steam as a motive power; the irregular and crude but phenomenal charcoal pencilings of the little boy in the quiet farm-house kitchen, which gave promise of the future greatness of the painter, Benjamin West, are so many irrefutable evidences of the correctness of this declaration. The same thing is also true in reference to the operations of every-day life in society or business. Often in my own experience I have been led by the most unimportant facts to the establishment of undoubted evidences. and by the most trifling circumstances to the most conclusive results.

Such was the experience in the solution of the mystery attaching to the personality of the unfortunate man who was found at Edgewood, and in the detection and punishment of whose assailants, my officers were then engaged.

A few days after their return to New York, Mr. Bangs caused the following notice to appear in the "Personal" column of the various papers of note in the city.

"INFORMATION WANTED—of an unknown man, evidently a German, having 'A. B.' marked upon his clothing, who was found murdered at Edgewood, N. J., on March 14. Address Box ——, N. York Post Office."

The little bark was sent adrift upon the waves of public journalism, in the hope that in due season it would return freighted with the knowledge so much needed, and with the information so essentially requisite. Being naturally possessed of a hopeful, sanguine temperament, Mr. Bangs felt assured that good would result from this measure, and that in a very short time he would be furnished with some tangible information that would enable him to act intelligently in the matter in hand. Nor was he disappointed, for the mail that very day brought a reply to the advertisement, signed by Jacob Kuenzle, in which the writer requested an interview, as he fully believed that he could identify the person referred to, as a gentleman who was known to him, and who had been missing for several days.

An appointment was made, and on the following morning a person, very gentlemanly in appearance, and a German, was announced as desiring an interview, and upon his entrance, proceeded at once to the matter in hand, and his narrative is concisely as follows:

In the month of October last (1868), a young German artist, answering to the description that was given to him of the murdered man, engaged a room from him on the second floor of the house in which he (Kuenzle) lived; that the young man informed him that he had just arrived from Strasbourg the day previous, and had been recommended to Mr. Kuenzle by some friends of his, whom he became acquainted with on the steamer in coming over; that he had occupied the room until the eleventh day of the present month (March), when he left home without having apparently made any preparations for an extended or protracted journey, and that since that time, neither he nor his family had seen or heard anything of him. Upon reading the notice in the papers, the letters with which the clothing of the murdered man was marked attracted his attention, and as the name of the gentleman who lodged with him was Adolph Bohner, it seemed to him at once to be reasonably possible that they might belong to the missing occupant of his room.

Having previously taken possession of the clothing of the deceased, it was produced, and immediately identified by Mr. Kuenzle as belonging to Adolph Bohner, except the hat which was found upon his head, which he did not recognize as ever having been worn by him. Thus the question of identity was settled beyond doubt, and bright sunlight of success began to dawn upon the vision of Mr. Bangs, so long obscured by doubts and aggravating perplexities.

While these revelations were being made, and the unraveling of the tangled web was becoming more easy and certain of accomplishment, quite a different scene was being enacted in Edgewood.

From the very commencement of the legal investigation into the facts of the case, the inhabitants of the village and environs seemed to have resolved themselves into a joint stock company for the wholesale manufacture of wild and exciting rumors. Most of these, however, were bubbles so transparent and so manifestly the invention of an overstrained imagination, that the sensations created were of short life, and they quickly passed out of notice to make way for others not less imaginary and no less ridiculous.

The important, self-constituted, and inexperienced detectives, so-called, with which the place seemed instantly to swarm, dazzled by the reward offered, had been carrying matters with a high hand in that hitherto undisturbed and peaceful locality.

And here let me say, by way of parenthesis, that I never work for rewards; my labor, time, or skill are not expended upon the possibility of obtaining the sum offered by a citizen or a community for the detection and punishment of a criminal, but my operations are based entirely upon a distinct understanding and agreement of a business character, and the acceptance of my terms for such services.

Chief among the gentlemen ambitious to achieve the renown and greatness of a successful detective was Mr. James Byerly, the sheriff of the county, and it must be confessed that his intellectual acquirements (he could not write his own name) eminently fitted him for the duties he so magnanimously took upon himself; linked with this, an experience of two long years spent in the arduous occupation of serving warrants and legal notices had, as he fondly imagined, furnished him with all the legal knowledge and natural sagacity necessary for success, and, added to these, the self-sufficiency of the individual amply supplied all other defects, real or imagined.

This gentleman determined that something ought to be done, and that he, of course, was just the man to do it, and he at once began to make things lively, very lively, for the suspected parties at Edgewood. Gross and his wife were arrested at once, and, as might have been expected, in the absence of any proofs adduced upon the hearing—for the reason that no time was given for their production, even should any exist—they were as quickly discharged. A boy who had run away from Gross on account of bad treatment, was next pounced upon; he was traced to New York, brought back, and, notwithstanding Mr. Byerly, with a sagacious shake of his empty head, declared that he possessed the unmistakable air and manner of a murderer, the authorities were compelled to release him for lack of any evidence whatever to hold him. Mr. Byerly's ardor was by no means subdued by these unsuccessful efforts, and this boy having stated that he spent the night of the Saturday preceding the finding of the body at the house of an inoffensive, hard-working Dane named Hans Schreiber, the undaunted and ambitious *detective* discovered in that fact undoubted evidence of the poor weak-minded Dane's complicity in the foul crime. (I verily believe that, had the boy slept in a cow-shed, the pertinacious criminal-hunter would have procured a warrant for the arrest of the inoffensive bovines upon the morrow.)

Consequently, acting upon this undoubted and, to him, infallible evidence of guilt, the doughty sheriff at once descended upon the unsuspicious object of persecution and locked him up for a hearing: but in this master-stroke he was doomed to another disappointment, while the consequences of this rash arrest were nearly fatal to his victim.

In the middle of the night the prison authorities were awakened by loud cries emanating from the cell where Schreibei was confined, and upon hurriedly donning his clothes and hastening to the spot, the poor man was found in an alarming condition of mental excitement; crying, groaning, frantically clasping his hands, tearing his hair, and muttering in his native language. A physician was at once sent for, and also the rector of the village church, who was conversant with the language spoken by the prisoner. Upon their arrival the distress of the poor man seemed pitiful in the extreme; he smote his breast, and with his eyes upturned towards heaven, uttered passionate prayers and lamentations.

"My God! Why am I suspected? My heart is clear!" He said it was impossible to eat or sleep, or even to think, and that wherever he went the people would point to him, and say, "There goes the Dane, who killed that man!"

The physician stated that, unless some measures were taken immediately, he despaired of the man's reason, and earnestly urged the authorities to take such steps as would secure an early hearing, and if no evidence could be produced, that he be discharged. Accordingly, the next morning, an examination took place, and not a particle of evidence was presented that in the faintest degree implicated the nearly-crazed prisoner with the murder of the then unknown man.

The Dane was at once released, but it was a long time before he regained his wonted vigor, either of mind or body, and he never afterwards seemed to be the same blithe, cheerful **and** happy man that he was once known to be.

Of course these proceedings entirely prevented my opera-**tive**, Mr. Brockman, from obtaining any reliable information **up** to this time, and as these suspicions were formed and arrests made upon the presumption that the body found on that Sabbath evening was that of a German peddler, who had appeared once in the neighborhood, plying his usual trade, and who by some was thought to resemble him in several particulars, the results obtained were of no importance whatever

The unpleasant result of his last adventurous attempt at criminal detection produced rather a dampening effect upon Mr. High-Sheriff Byerly, and he very dejectedly and reluctantly gave up the further prosecution of the case. He heaved a sigh of disappointment as he thought of the glittering reward so far beyond the reach of his limited powers; and as he sorrowfully resumed the routine duty of serving notices, all Edgewood breathed a sigh of relief.

"Mr. Kuenzle with tearful eyes at once recognized the features of his unfortunate lodger."

Page 312.

CHAPTER V.

The Murdered Man.

O N the day following the visit of Mr. Jacob Kuenzle to the office, in company with that gentleman Mr. Bangs went to Edgewood, in order to afford Mr. Kuenzle an opportunity of viewing the head of the supposed Adolph Bohner, which was still in charge of the Coroner, in order to place the matter of identification beyond doubt.

Upon its being shown to him, Mr. Kuenzle, with tearful eyes, at once recognized the features of his unfortunate lodger, and thus the question as to who the murdered man was became definitely settled, and the work of tracing the perpetrators of the awful deed, their detection and punishment, was intelligently commenced.

On returning to New York city, they proceeded to the residence of Mr. Kuenzle, and thence to the apartment formerly occupied by Adolph Bohner, for the purpose of examining his effects in the hope that something would be found that would give fuller information of the young man, furnish some knowledge of his associates, and by that means enable them to form some opinion of the possible cause of his death.

Mr. Kuenzle, having a duplicate key, unlocked the door,

and, upon entering the room and throwing open the shutters, the bright sunshine revealed a very comfortably furnished apartment; the arrangements were very neat and attractive, and gave evidence of the habits and tastes of a gentleman of education and refinement. In the center of the chamber stood a table, on which was a student's reading-lamp, and surround-ing it were a number of books, all of an advanced character, and showing evidences of having been frequently used, and among them was found a large diary, written in the German language, which seemed to contain a very fully written account of the writer's movements, his daily transactions, and the various thoughts that occupied his mind. On opening this book, it was found that the last entry had been made on the tenth day of March, and concluded with the following sen-tence, which seemed to have been written just previous to the gentleman's retirement to bed: " *To-morrow will go to Edge-wood, N. J., to meet August Franssen, who promises to pay his indebtedness to me.*"

Ah! Adolph Bohner, how little did you think when in the peacefulness of your own pleasant chamber you penned those words, that a stranger's hand would be the next to open your little book, and a stranger's eye would read the story of your life; little did you think as you wrote those promises for the morrow, what that morrow was to bring forth; still less did it occur to you that the visit so innocently planned, and so pleas-antly anticipated, would be to the locality of your death; and that when your head pressed the downy pillows that evening, and you resigned yourself to repose, that the next sleep that visited you would be that long sleep that knows no waking!

This last entry in the diary of Bohner was thought to be

sufficiently important to investigate, and Mr. Bangs inquired of Mr. Kuenzle ·

"Did you ever see this man, August Franssen, or do you know anything about him?"

"Yes," said Mr. Kuenzle; "I know him very well, but I have not seen him for two or three months."

" Were he and Mr. Bohner very intimate friends?" asked Mr. Bangs.

"At one time they were quite friendly," was the reply; "but Franssen got into bad company, was very dissipated, extravagant and lazy; he was thrown out of employment, then began to borrow money of his friends, and among the number was Mr. Bohner, who helped him on several occasions."

"Do you know of their ever having quarreled?"

"Oh, no!" replied Mr. Kuenzle, "I don't think they ever quarreled, but Mr. Bohner, getting tired of lending Franssen money without getting it back again, at last concluded to stop, and upon the next request, he refused to lend him any more."

"Did you see Franssen here after Bohner had refused to continue his loans?" asked Mr. Bangs.

"No, sir," replied Mr. Kuenzle, "he did not come again, and Mr. Bohner told me shortly afterwards, that he had gone away from the city, was working in some country town, and, he thought, was trying to do better."

"How did they become acquainted with each other?"

" Why, they came to this country in the same steamer; they were acquainted in the old country, and, I think, went to school together there; but this Franssen was a wild, bad fellow, and, I believe, did several times run away from home, and gave his parents much trouble."

Mr. Bangs at once felt assured that this man Franssen was connected in some way with the murder of Mr. Bohner. The fact of his borrowing money from his friend, and being refused further favors, his going away, the description given of his habits and disposition, and the fact that Bohner was to visit him on the day following, being his last appearance in New York, all seemed to favor the theory that Franssen was in some way connected with the affair.

Mr. Bangs determined to discover Franssen's whereabouts, and watch him pretty closely, and, in the meantime, to carefully read the diary of Mr. Bohner, in order to ascertain the full particulars of his antecedents, and the extent of his connection with Franssen.

CHAPTER VI.

The History of Adolph Bohner—His Connection with Frans-
sen and Their Departure for America.

THE story of Adolph Bohner, as learned from his diary,
was quite a romantic one. He was born in Strasbourg,
the capital city of Alsace-Lorraine, in the year 1844. Strasbourg was then in the French department of the Bas-Rhin,
but through the operations of the Franco-Prussian war and
the treaty of peace at Versailles in 1871, is now connected
with and made a province of Germany. This beautiful town
is situated on the River Ill, one of the tributaries of the Rhine,
and is built upon a level plain nearly six miles in circuit. It
is surrounded by a great wall with all the military accompani-
ments of bastions, ditches and outworks, and its famous clock,
built by Isaac Habrecht about 1570, is renowned as one of the
greatest works of its kind.

The river, with its many branches, flows through the town,
and is crossed by innumerable wooden bridges, contributes to
the healthfulness of the locality, and the people generally are
a hearty, healthy and somewhat independent community.

The father of Adolph was an extensive manufacturer of
woollen goods, who had by his own efforts and the economy of
his household—a proverbial element of German domestic rule

[317]

—succeeded in accumulating a sufficient competence for the support of himself and family. He was thus enabled to confer upon his children all the advantages which education affords, and young Adolph's boyhood passed amid the comforts of home and the acquisition of such useful knowledge as would fit him for an active struggle with the world.

The family of old Herr Bohner was one of the happiest in Strasbourg; nowhere within the seven gates of the town could there be found more real domestic pleasure and happiness than under the steep roof of the lofty, well-built house, where every evening could be seen the jolly old father, with his pipe and his tankard of beer; his happy, round-faced and round-bodied *frau,* and the noisy, chattering, playful children, who made the old house resound with their merry peals of laughter.

Adolph had early given evidence of a genius for painting, and some of his crude sketches were held up by his proud and doting mother as perfect treasures of art. As the boy grew older, his ideas and ambitions became more expanded, and it was found necessary to foster this precocious talent by the guiding hand of a skillful teacher. His progress was quite rapid, and a brilliant future was predicted for him by those to whom his success was a matter of pride and himself an object of affection.

Thus the time passed until the boy was old enough to perform military duty, when, according to the laws then existing, he was required to serve three years in the standing army under the emperor.

This was the first sorrow that had come to him, for it necessitated a parting from those who were dear to him, and in addition to this the young painter had taken it into his head to fall in love with a beautiful young Alsatian maiden, who returned his passion with all the intensity of her warm German nature, and the separation was all the more painful on this account. The parting between the young lovers was affecting and sorrowful, and with a heavy heart Adolph shouldered his musket and went off to the camp, while Rosa returned weeping to her daily household tasks.

Among the associates of young Bohner was a fellow-student by the name of August Franssen, a wild, reckless boy, whose willfulness and incorrigible temper had been a source of great solicitude and anxiety to his parents, and whose frequent outbursts of anger and exhibitions of precocious cruelty had rendered him obnoxious to his schoolmates and companions. Several years before Adolph's entrance into the army, August Franssen had ran away from home, and after a life of vagabondage and lawlessness had returned to his native place but a short time before Adolph's departure.

His life had been a precarious one, and not very well calculated to exercise a restraining influence upon the evil elements of his nature. He had floated through the most of Europe even at this youthful age. He had lived alternately in Paris, in the Isle Napoleon; had been a member of a gang of doubtful characters in Naples; a soldier in the Swiss Guard at Rome; then deserting, had led a roaming gypsy life in and around Constantinople, and, finally, after a life full of adventure, and not of a character calculated to advance the peacefulness of his disposition, he returned home, and was welcomed by his parents with some of the joyfulness that is said to have been associated with the home-coming of the "prodigal son."

Franssen too, it seemed, had cast his eyes and set his

affections upon the lovely Rosa; but she, knowing his early history and his questionable career, and also, it must be confessed, entertaining a profound regard and affection for Adolph, refused to listen to the vows of the nomadic August. This repulse filled his heart with bitterness, his soul with anger and resentment, and he vowed to be revenged upon his more successful rival.

It could not well be expected, after the restless, aimless life he had been leading for several years, that young Franssen would settle quietly down to the dull routine of a shoemaker's life—his father was a prominent maker of shoes in Strasbourg, and desired his son to follow in his paternal footsteps—and consequently he hailed with delight the information that he was required in the ranks of his country's defenders.

Coming from the same locality, the two young men were assigned to the same company, and an intimacy sprang up between them, which ripened into a sort of quiescent friendship on the part of the quiet, thoughtful, undemonstrative Bohner, for the wild and reckless vagabond Franssen, which was repaid by the other with a secret dislike and envy, which was carefully concealed by an assumed demeanor of friendliness and confidence.

Amid the scenes of camp life, military maneuvers, and the stirring incidents of a soldier's life, varied by an occasional leave of absence, which they would spend at home among the old folks at Strasbourg, the time passed away, and at the end of their three years of service, the two young men returned joyfully homeward.

The meeting between Adolph and Rosa, upon the return of her lover, which was of the most loving and demonstrative kind, was witnessed by August Franssen, and was the first open demonstration of affection which he had seen. He became very much exasperated, and, unable to control himself, he fled from the spot, uttering imprecations upon the devoted heads of the unconscious lovers, who were too much absorbed in the happiness of each other's society to pay any attention to what was transpiring around them.

Time passed on, life seemed to be very happy and bright to the young couple ; no outward evidence was discovered of Franssen's jealous passion, and nothing occurred to mar the pleasure of their existence or the fulfillment of the bright promises of the future.

One day young Bohner received a letter from some of his friends who had emigrated to America, who were now in business there, and whose flattering accounts of the New World filled him with a desire to visit this great continent, to judge for himself of the attractions of this " El Dorado," and if he was satisfied with the survey to return for his bride, and then together they would begin their marital existence in that land of liberty and independence of which he had heard so much.

Adolph made his wishes known to his indulgent father, who, being desirous of pleasing his boy and affording him every opportunity to " see the world," and to better his fortunes, at once acceded to the young man's request, and bade him prepare for the journey.

When August Franssen learned of the intentions of young Bohner to visit America, he immediately conceived the idea of accompanying him, and began a systematic course of worrying his old father into a consent to his wishes, and the furtherance

14*

of his plans.   But the old gentleman was too stanch a
German, and too thoroughly a shoemaker, to listen either
with patience or approval to his son's schemes, and he peremptorily refused to allow him to go, or to be at any expense
for his traveling about, and informed the young gentleman
that he must settle himself to business at home, in order that
he might become what his father was, a good shoemaker.   The
old gentleman, you see, was an implicit believer in the old
maxim, that "a shoemaker should stick to his last."

This denial of his request, and the dashing of his hopes for
adventure, aroused the wild spirit of the willful young man,
and he determined to go whether his father consented or not;
and, of course, as the consent was out of the question, he must
needs go without it.

Ascertaining the day on which Bohner was to take his departure, he quietly made all the arrangements necessary for
leaving, and not being very scrupulous in his moral proclivities,
he did not hesitate to rob his father, and to steal from him the
amount that he considered necessary for his purpose.   He
therefore secretly made his way to Havre, and was safely on
board the steamer before young Bohner, accompanied by his
father, mother, and sweetheart, arrived.

Of course, the scene between these loving people who were
about to be separated for a long time was affecting in the extreme; but over the horizon of their hopes of a speedy and
happy return there came no premonition of the terrible fate
in store for their loved one, and no vision of the lonely grave
in that far-off land of strangers.

"He felt a sharp tap upon his shoulder, and upon turning suddenly around, he found himself face to face with August Franssen."

CHAPTER VII.

The Surprise—The Voyage—Sea-sickness and Safe Arrival.

THE surprise of young Bohner may well be imagined, when, after the vessel was comfortably under way, and he was standing by the side, looking gloomily and disconsolately at the almost indistinct and rapidly disappearing figures upon the shore, he felt a sharp tap upon his shoulder, and upon turning suddenly around, he found himself face to face with Franssen.

Explanations followed, and although Adolph by no means justified the faults of his companion, or was disposed to be very grateful for his society, he was compelled to accept the situation, and be as friendly as possible.

The voyage was an uneventful one, and except so far as concerns the two persons with whom our story has to do, unworthy of record. Neither of them having had a great deal of experience in traveling upon the sea, they were not hardened to the tossing of the waves, the lurching of the vessel, and the general feeling of discomfort that began to take possession of their inmost souls. A slight storm, shortly after the ship had left port, completed their misery, and very soon they both succumbed to that dreadful disorder known as sea-sick ness.

The bright dreams of ambition that had floated through the imagination of the enthusiastic young artist; the golden visions of the glorious and happy future which had dazzled his eyes and encouraged his hopes, now faded away before the dreadful reality of the failure to keep anything on his stomach. However, his trials were of short duration, and, after the observance of the correct rules of diet, his digestives triumphed, and he was soon enabled to enjoy the novelty and beauty of an ocean voyage, undisturbed by anything more serious than occasional thoughts of home and those he had left behind him.

Not so, however, with his more highly tempered and bilious companion, who, not being very considerate in his mode of living at home, and paying but little attention to the laws of diet, became an easy prey to that " destroyer of hope and producer of melancholy." Many a time, as he lay groaning and sighing upon his bunk, cursing his fate and everything else in general, he was disposed to regret that he had ever attempted the journey he was now making, and for a time, too, perhaps, he forgot the evil thoughts that filled his mind towards his more successful rival, who ministered to his wants, endeavored to cheer his disconsolate spirits, and who used every means in his power to make him comfortable and contented. It was not, however, until the voyage was nearly over, and the waves and weather became more calm, that he was able to trust himself to visit the deck and enjoy the fresh breezes and the beauties of ocean grandeur.

Better would it have been for Adolph if his companion had not lived to reach the shore, and far better for Franssen would it have been, if the dark waves had washed over his body and covered the grave of a man with no stain of human blood upon his soul.

Such was not to be his fate, however, and they both arrived safely in New York and landed upon the shores of the great metropolis. Bohner at once sought the abode of Jacob Kuenzle, to whom he had been recommended, and Franssen, whose means were limited and whose future was undecided, located at Castle Garden, until he could definitely arrange his plan of action.

In a short time he was enabled to secure employment in his distasteful occupation of a shoemaker, but not having paid any attention to his work at home, he found it very difficult to retain a position for any length of time. By nature indolent and extravagant, and possessed of a wandering, reckless disposition, his earnings disappeared as rapidly as acquired, and his friend Bohner was frequently called upon for loans to assist him out of his pecuniary embarrassments, and to afford him opportunities for gratifying his tastes for dissipation. At last this became burdensome, and Bohner refused emphatically to advance any further sums for such purposes, without any return being made, or any prospect, however remote, of its ever being done.

Franssen then left the city, obtained employment in the country, and almost entirely disappeared from Bohner's notice, until, after several months' absence, he suddenly appeared and requested Bohner to visit him at Edgewood, when he would repay him the amount that was due him. What followed that fatal visit, the reader has already been made acquainted with.

CHAPTER VIII.

On the Trail—A Yellow Dog—" Thou art so Near, and yet so Far."

THE reading of this history fully strengthened the theory already formed, that Franssen was the guilty man, or, at least, was concerned in the murder of his friend, and steps were immediately taken to obtain information of his whereabouts, and to secure, if possible, such evidence as would place beyond doubt the question of his perpetration of, or complicity in, the mysterious crime.

Public justice required the apprehension of the murderer, and having been intrusted by the authorities with the duty of his detection, Mr. Bangs at once proceeded to act upon the evidence he had received, and to attempt the task of vindicating the outraged law.

At that time there was in my employ a young German, by the name of Joseph Mendelsohn, a very bright, active young man, who had once been engaged in shoemaking, who could converse fluently in both the French and German languages and he was deputized for the purpose of discovering the whereabouts of the suspected man.

Assuming the garb of a mechanic, he was instructed to visit the workshop of a Mr. Schneider, in New York, in whose employ Franssen had once been, to ascertain his usual haunts at the time he worked there, and, if possible, to learn who were his associates.

Mr. Schneider was at his place of business when Mendelsohn called, and upon his inquiring if August Franssen was employed by him, was answered in the negative. Mr. Schneider informed Mendelsohn that Franssen was an idle and dissipated fellow and a poor workman; that most of his time was spent in the company of bad men and women, and that he was compelled at last to discharge him; he was discharged about three months before, since which time he had not seen or heard of him, until about a week ago he met him, and Franssen told him he was going home to Europe; that he had no money, but would work for his passage over. After receiving from Mr. Schneider the names of some of the places that Franssen frequented, he took his leave.

He next proceeded to a saloon kept by a German widow, fair, fat and any age you pleased. Upon entering he called for a glass of beer, and invited the blooming and corpulent widow to join him, which she did very willingly, and after indulging in a couple of glasses of the beverage, the landlady became quite good-natured and communicative.

Mendelsohn asked her if Franssen had been there lately, saying at the same time, that he would like to see him, as he was from the same part of the country where he came from.

" Ach!" replied the elephantine widow, " dot Franssen, he was a leetle black beast. He have not here been for two or tree week. He make me a debt of him for two dollars, und den he no comes around anymore."

" Do you know where I could see him?" inquired Mendelsohn.

"Nein, I don't can tell," she replied; "he got a gal Louisa, by der house of de corner round, but maybe she don't can't tell neider, I don't know."

After receiving full information of the residence of the fair Louisa, Mendelsohn took his departure and proceeded to hunt her up. Upon inquiring at the "house of de corner round," he was informed that Louisa had removed a few days ago to Jamaica, on Long Island, and was living on a farm. He determined to see her, and taking the train therefor, Mendelsohn late in the afternoon found himself in that beautiful farming district in close proximity to New York.

The large, comfortable, and well-built houses, and the capacious farm buildings, were very attractive. The well-cultivated and fruitful fields were already beginning to put on their robes of green, and were looking beautiful in the light of the descending sun upon an April day.

Ascertaining that the house where Louisa lived was about a mile and a half from the railroad station, Mendelsohn in vain endeavored to hire a conveyance for the purpose, and was at last compelled to travel the distance on foot.

He trudged along merrily, contentedly admiring the beauties of nature everywhere spread before him, and enjoying the recreation which the walk afforded, when suddenly he heard a stifled sort of yell behind him, and turning around, discovered a large and savage-looking yellow dog in full run, and evidently possessed with the intention of devouring him. Now, if there was one thing that Mendelsohn detested more than another, it was a yellow dog—yellow dogs were a perfect nightmare to him. It was said that his father had been a maker of sausages at one time, and that in consequence yellow dogs had sworn eter

nal enmity to the whole race of Mendelsohns. However **true**
that was, there was no doubt of the enmity of the one behind
him, and without indulging in any very extended reflections
upon the duties of the hour, he materially hastened his pace
and endeavored to seek safety in flight. It was of no avail;
the infuriated yellow dog was a better runner than the fright
ened detective, and Mendelsohn in sheer desperation was forced
to try his agility in climbing a tree that grew by the roadside.
He had just succeeded in catching hold of one of the lower
branches, and was in the act of drawing his body up beyond
the reach of harm, when he felt a sudden snap behind, and
realized, with a thrill of horror, that the yellow dog and his
coat-tails had formed an intimate acquaintance; giving himself
a strong and desperate pull, which lifted the animal some three
feet in the air, he reached a position of safety, and the dog, not
being of the " iron-jawed " species, unable to hold himself above
ground by the strength of his teeth, relinquished his hold and
fell to the ground, and Mendelsohn rejoiced that the strength
of his garments had prevented the beast from lunching upon
cassimere and buttons. Not to be defrauded of his victim in
this manner, the dog squatted himself under the tree, and by
repeated and savage barking, gave assurance of his intention
"to fight it out on this line if it took all summer."

The position was a very provoking one to the poor detective,
but happily was destined to be of short duration, for very soon
he heard footsteps approaching, and the dog, finding other and
more available game, left his guard and proceeded to attack the
intruder. But this time he found an enemy who proved too
much for him, and who, after promptly administering a few
well-directed blows with a heavy stick which he carried, com

pelled the canine aggressor to beat a hasty and yelping re·
treat.

"Hello, mister!" said the stranger, "I guess you vas come
town now, de dog don't vas here any more."

Mendelsohn, who had already begun his descent, instantly
dropped himself to the ground, and thanked the new-comer for
the unexpected but very grateful relief he had afforded him.

He proceeded on his way without further molestation, and
arrived at last at the house where the girl Louisa was domiciled,
and upon inquiring for her he was shown into the kitchen,
where the young lady was engaged in the domestic occupation
of preparing supper. She greeted Mendelsohn with a frightened, shy, and suspicious look, and in a constrained manner,
and no wonder, poor girl; she had been leading a wild and
dissolute life in New York; had been an inmate of a house of
ill-fame, led to it, she said, by the death of her parents, and her
inability to support herself otherwise; but at last becoming
tired and disgusted with her mode of living, she had engaged
herself with the gentleman at whose house she was then working, determined to reform, to leave behind her the shame and
misery of her past career, and to strive to walk in the path of
rectitude and right. It is not to be wondered at, then, that she
should feel suspicious of a person who had inquired for her by
name, and who was entirely unknown to her.

Mendelsohn, feeling the delicacy of his position, and desiring to obtain the required information without exciting the
suspicion of the young lady as to his true intentions, informed
her that he was a friend, and at one time a fellow-workman,
of Franssen, who desired to serve him; that he had obtained
for him an excellent situation in the shop in which he himself

was engaged, but that he could not find out where he was in
order to communicate with him, and that, learning that Franssen was paying attentions to her, he had come for the purpose
of inquiring from her where he could find him.

"Why," said the girl, in astonishment, "he has just left
here, and if you came from the station, you must have passed
him on the road; he has not been gone twenty minutes."

Mendelsohn's chagrin at this piece of news may well be
imagined; he cursed that yellow dog in his inmost soul, and
when he thought that it must have been the man he was looking
for who drove the beast away and invited him to come down
out of the tree, his vexation was unbounded.

To think that he was conversing with the very man he was
in search of, and that he could not recognize him, was provoking in the extreme; but it settled conclusively one question,
and that was that Franssen had not departed for Europe; that
he could be found; and that fact was some consolation, even
in his great and aggravating disappointment.

He hastened to inform Louisa that he had missed his way,
and must have passed this house without recognizing it, and
had to retrace his steps, which accounted for his failure to meet
his friend.

"Where is he living now?" then inquired Mendelsohn.

"I don't know, and I don't care," replied the girl.

"You have not quarreled, I hope?" said he.

"Yes, we have, and I hope we have parted forever. He
is a mean little beast, and I never did like him. He knew
that I wanted to get away from the life I was leading, that
I wanted to be a better girl and live an honest life, and he
came out here for the simple purpose of getting me to go back

to the old way of living. He says he has got some **money**
now but money or no money, I will never be again what I
have been, and I never want to see him again!"

"Don't you know where I can find him?"

"No," replied the girl, "I did not ask him, and I did not
want to know; but if you go to Egbert's beer saloon, on For-
syth street, you can find out all about him."

Mendelsohn, finding that he could gain nothing further
from the girl, and satisfied as to her truthfulness, took his
leave, hoping that he would be in time to catch Franssen at
the station and, by accompanying him on the train, be enabled
to form his acquaintance, or to find out his place of abode.

In this, however, he was disappointed, for the train had
left when he reached the station, and he was compelled to wait
impatiently an hour for the next train, which he took and returned to New York, not entirely unsuccessful, but disappointed at the opportunity which he had missed, of finding
the person he was in search of, and rendering further efforts **in**
that direction unnecessary.

CHAPTER IX.

Egbert's Saloon—" Old Sledge "—Traces of the Murderer.

THE following day, by direction of Mr. Bangs, Mendelsohn proceeded to the saloon of Jacob Egbert, and upon entering, found quite a motley assemblage gathered together. The place seemed to be the resort of idle mechanics of all trades and branches, who, however varied their occupations might be, united upon one subject at least—the love of drink.

Mendelsohn ordered a glass of beer, and seated himself at one of the many tables that stood around the room, in order to survey the scenes around him before commencing operations. A strange medley of human beings was presented, and over the ceremonies presided the fat, red-faced and quick-sighted landlord, ever on the alert for the many calls upon his fluid resources, and equally quick-sighted as to the coppers of the poor devils, who spent their earnings for his beer, while their families were starving at home.

He noticed one man who seemed to be acquainted with everybody, and whom everybody seemed to be acquainted with. He was greeted with a certain reserved, grudgingly-bestowed good-nature by the tipplers, but the good-nature seemed to be of a forced character, as though they felt that their salutations were necessary, yet they would prefer to let him alone.

Leaning over to a man who was sitting opposite to him, half asleep and probably half intoxicated, Mendelsohn inquired of him who the individual was who seemed to be so well acquainted and so much at home.

The stranger thus accosted turned round, and distinguishing the person pointed out, said:

" Why, that's ' Old Sledge,' the rummest old duffer about. He knows all the boys, he does."

" What is his business ?" inquired Mendelsohn.

" Well, if you've got a watch, or old clothes, or any old furniture that you don't want, and if you can't get anything to drink, which you do want, that old cove will take 'em off your hands, and won't give you too much for 'em either."

Mendelsohn thought that this fellow must know something, if anybody did, of the man he was after, and so, sauntering carelessly across the room, he sat down alongside of him. After a few minutes, in which he took a mental survey of the individual, he carelessly asked him in German :

" Has August Franssen been here to-day, do you know ?"

" No, sir," replied the gentleman addressed, " I'm waiting for him; he promised to meet me here this evening, and I want to see him."

" I want to see him too," replied Mendelsohn, " I want to find out something from him; won't you take a glass of beer ?"

Mr. Schlentz—for that was his name—accepted the invitation very readily, and they soon became engaged in general conversation.

As the time wore on and Franssen did not make his appearance, Mr. Schlentz began to grow impatient, and finally got very angry at his delinquent debtor, for so Franssen proved to be, and denounced him in unmeasured terms.

"When did you see him last?" at length inquired Mendelsohn.

"Last night—he came to my place about twelve o'clock. I was in bed, but he woke me up and wanted to sleep there all night. Well, I let him do so, as he could not get in where he worked, and this morning he borrowed two dollars from me, which he promised to pay to-night, or bring something as security."

"Where does he work?"

"I don't know, or else I would go after him there," replied the "Old Sledge."

Mendelsohn discovered that this "Old Sledge," as he was called, was one of those individuals who would advance anybody money who had something to pledge for its value; that his trade was quite extensive, as the people with whom he dealt were an improvident set, were idle and dissipated, and that Schlentz, it was suspected, was not, as a general thing, very particular in inquiring into the question of ownership of any article that was brought to him as collateral for money desired.

"Has Franssen borrowed money of you before?" asked Mendelsohn.

"Yes, often,' replied Schlentz. "The last time was about the eleventh of March last. He borrowed some money to go to the country to look for work, he said. He returned on the next evening very late, and said that he could not get any work, but that he had met a man there who had a gold watch and chain, a pair of pantaloons and a coat, which he had bargained for, and which he would give me. I told him not to bring such things to my house, at which he seemed to get angry, and shortly afterwards went to bed. I did not see him again after the next morning until last evening."

"Did he bring you the things he promised?" asked Mendelsohn.

"No," replied Schlentz. "I asked him last evening what the prospects were about those things, and he told me he was afraid to bring them just yet."

Mendelsohn felt as though he had at last struck the trail, and that, by following up this money-lender, Schlentz, he would be enabled to finally discover Franssen, and learn what he wanted to know. After a few remarks, he excused himself and left the place, intending to keep a sharp look-out upon Schlentz, to see with whom he left the place, and then to follow them.

Meanwhile Brockman, in his capacity of house painter, was pursuing his investigations at Edgewood and the surrounding country. He learned that Franssen, or a man answering to his description, had been employed for a short time in a small town a few miles distant, and he immediately proceeded to the place mentioned, took up his quarters there, and instituted inquiries.

He found that the shoemaker of the village was named Thomas Hitner, and, on going to his shop, found the gentleman disengaged and disposed for conversation.

He inquired if a man named August Franssen had been in his employ, and was answered that such a person had worked for him, but that he had left, and he did not know what had become of him.

Mrs. Hitner, who was one of those talkative creatures, and who rejoiced in every opportunity to tell what she knew, told Brockman the full particulars of Franssen's connection with them. She said that Franssen came there to work for them on March 13th (the Saturday before the body of the murdered man was discovered); that he worked for them until the 22d, since which time they had not seen nor heard anything of him. She also stated that the same evening, in the course of conversation, he inquired how far Edgewood was from there, and said he had heard in New York, where he had just come from, that a young man had been murdered at Edgewood, who had no clothes on when found; and inquired if it was true. He said he was told about it by a young man whom he had met in a saloon in New York.

This was a piece of information valuable indeed. The fact that Franssen should have heard of the murder nearly twenty-four hours before the body was discovered, was conclusive evidence that he knew something of the occurrence, and was another link in the chain that was being forged, which was eventually destined to drag the miserable man to justice.

15

CHAPTER X.

Franssen is Discovered—The Detective is Employed as a Shoe-maker—A Nightmare—The Ownership of the Blood-stained Hat Decided.

MENDELSOHN continued his watching of the Forsyth street saloon, and in about an hour afterwards he saw a man answering the description of Franssen enter; he therefore crossed the street, and looking through the blinds that were hung at the windows, he observed him advance directly to the table where Schlentz was seated, and, accosting him familiarly, sit down opposite to him and engage in conversation.

Their colloquy lasted but a few minutes, when, drinking a glass of beer, they arose and came out together. They walked briskly, and Mendelsohn followed stealthily; they traveled a few blocks and halted in front of a dark, somber-looking struct-ure, over the door of which appeared the name of JOSEPH SCHLENTZ, Junk Dealer.

Schlentz opened the door and they entered, and after re-maining inside a few minutes, Franssen came out alone, and bidding Schlentz good-night, started off.

Mendelsohn followed him unobserved, until he came to a store on Greenwich street, occupied by Jacob Gehring, as a boot and shoe store and dwelling—and, opening the side door of which with a latch-key, Franssen entered.

Feeling satisfied that Franssen was then engaged in the employ of Mr. Gehring, and could be found upon the following morning, Mendelsohn returned to the Agency, and finding my son, Robert A. Pinkerton, the Superintendent, still there, having been detained by some important night service, he communicated his intelligence to him, and was directed to go to Gehring's on the following morning and solicit work as a shoemaker, and by that means endeavor to cultivate the acquaintance of Franssen.

Accordingly, on the next morning Mendelsohn presented himself at Gehring's store and solicited employment. He was fortunate enough to find a bench vacant, and upon his statement of his ability to perform the labor required, and expressing his willingness to commence his duties at once, he was conducted to the workroom, where, donning the leather apron, he was soon engaged in an occupation he had fondly hoped that he had relinquished forever.

Mendlesohn's first day at shoe-making was a very long one, and when at last the time arrived to lay aside his work for the day, he did so with a sigh of relief which was as genuine as it was profound. During the day he had, however, managed to get into conversation with Franssen, and knowing his weakness for the female sex, he had related some curious and amusing incidents in relation to his experience with them, which pleased Franssen immensely, and on leaving the workshop that evening he invited Mendelsohn to take a glass of beer with him, which was accepted, and they proceeded to a saloon in the neighborhood for the purpose of indulging in the favorite beverage.

Having made arrangements to lodge with Mr. Gehring, and by that means to be nearer to Franssen, he was rejoiced to find that he was to occupy the same room with him, and would thus be enabled to watch his every movement. Mendelsohn, therefore, began the active operations of the campaign.

The evening passed away without any eventful incident; Mendelsohn and Franssen strolled about together, imbibed a glass of beer, and then returned to their home, when, feeling very much fatigued and sleepy after his hard and unusual day's work, Mendelsohn disrobed and retired; Franssen followed shortly afterwards, and they were both soon wrapped in repose.

About midnight Mendelsohn was awakened by a loud noise, which resembled the cries of a man in distress, and which, he found, were uttered by his room-mate Franssen, who was evidently the victim of an alarming attack of "nightmare." Upon going noiselessly to the bedside of the troubled sleeper, he found Franssen with his eyes distended, his face distorted as if with fear, gesticulating with his arms, and crying :

"Oh, my God, Rosa, do not look at me so! I cannot bring him back to you. He is dead! I saw him! He is dead! I see him now lying upon the snow. My God! my God! I can see him now!"

He turned suddenly and awoke with a shudder, when his eyes, glassy and with an expression of abject terror, met the gaze of the astonished Mendelsohn, who was standing beside him. Quick as thought he jumped from the bed, and, with a tiger-like spring, flew at the amazed detective and grasped him by the throat.

"What did you see? What did you hear? By God, I will kill *you!*" he exclaimed.

Mendelsohn, recovering somewhat from the surprise which this sudden movement had occasioned, and being desirous of avoiding any suspicion of his having discovered anything from his assailant, answered:

"What the devil do you mean? Are you crazy? I have seen nothing and heard nothing. What ails you?"

Franssen looked searchingly into the face of Mendelsohn, who bore the scrutiny without flinching, and then, with an assumed laugh, but with an evident air of relief, withdrew his hands from the throat of the detective.

"What does all this mean?" inquired Mendelsohn; "pulling a man by the throat because he happens to hear you struggling in your sleep, and tries to relieve you."

"Oh, nothing," said Franssen; "I must have been dreaming, and a horrible dream it was too," and he shuddered as he spoke. "I hope you will forgive me. I did not mean anything, and I am sorry that I touched you."

"All right," said Mendelsohn, jumping into bed; "and now go to sleep again, but don't repeat that dream, if you please."

Mendelsohn settled himself again for slumber, but it was a long time before his companion became quiet again; he rolled and tossed uneasily upon his couch, swearing to himself, and finally settled into a troubled sleep.

On awaking in the morning he appeared to be nervous and excited--his face was pale and haggard, and his eyes were bloodshot. It was very evident that his slumbers had not been of that rest-giving nature which comes to easy minds.

Having some time to spare before their labors commenced

for the day, they strolled out, and, after walking a short distance, Franssen was hailed by a young man with whom he had previously worked, whom he had not seen for some time, and who was introduced to Mendelsohn as John Knowlton. After the usual salutations, a proposal was made and accepted to indulge in a morning drink, and the trio repaired to a neighboring saloon for that purpose. While they were partaking of the beverage, Knowlton carelessly asked:

"Franssen, what did you do with that light hat you bought of me some time ago?"

Franssen looked up suddenly, and his face flushed, but, hastily recovering himself, answered as indifferently as he could:

"Oh, I traded it for this one," holding out the one he wore, which was a black felt of good quality, and nearly new.

"You made money by the trade, I guess," said Knowlton.

Franssen evidently desired to change the conversation, and so, with the remark that the profit was not very large, he said that he must go to work, as it was getting to be time for the shop to be opened, and he and Mendelsohn bade Knowlton good-morning, and went back to Gehring's and to work.

At noon Mendelsohn reported at the office, and upon learning of the conversation in regard to the hat, Mr. Bangs, remembering that Mr. Kuenzle was unable to recognize the hat found upon the body of Bohner, he resolved to visit him and learn from him what kind of a hat Bohner wore when he left home. He also instructed Mendelsohn to take the hat found, to find out where Knowlton worked, and to ascertain from him, without exciting suspicion, whether he could recognize it as the one he had sold to Franssen, and which he had inquired about.

Mr. Kuenzle, upon being questioned by Mr. Bangs, distinctly recollected that Bohner had worn a new black felt hat, which he had recently purchased, and had not worn very frequently.

Mendelsohn returned to his work, and secreting the hat which had been furnished him in his trunk, interrogated Franssen in regard to the man they had met that morning. Franssen informed him that Knowlton worked for Mr. Schneider, where he himself had been engaged some time ago, and as Mendelsohn knew where Schneider's place of business was, having been there inquiring for Franssen, he determined to go that evening, and interview Mr. Knowlton.

Accordingly, after supper, taking the hat with him, he went to a store where he was acquainted, and leaving his own hat, he put on the light one, which had only been stained on the inside, and repaired to Schneider's shop, where, fortunately, he found Knowlton standing in the doorway smoking.

He accosted him familiarly, and after a few minutes' conversation, invited him to take a walk, which Knowlton assented to, and they proceeded on their way; after walking a little while they entered a saloon, seated themselves at a table, and called for their drinks.

In touching their glasses, which is a proverbial custom among Germans, Knowlton noticed the hat which Mendelsohn wore, and after drinking remarked, laughingly,

"So you're the fellow Franssen stuck with my old hat, are you?"

"Was this your hat that I traded with Franssen for my black one?" inquired Mendelsohn.

"It looks very much like it; let me see it," said Knowlton.

Mendelsohn removed the hat from his head, and handed it to Knowlton, who, after examining it carefully, said emphatically,

"Why, of course it was mine. I'd know it among a thousand!"

This unquestionably decided the identity of the hats, and was another proof of Franssen's connection with the murder of his friend.

Aye! restless and uneasy you well may be, poor, dream-haunted victim of your own vile deeds, for conscience is an ever active and ever present accuser. How many times as, laboring at your daily toil, and with whistle and song, you attempted to shut out the thoughts that would come in spite of you, has the pale face of that boyhood friend come up before your startled vision. How many times has your empty laugh of maudlin mirth been silenced by the sight of that ghastly face, that, in defiance of all you could do, would come in between you and the foaming liquid with which you endeavored to drown remembrance; and when the shades of night are gathered around your sleepless couch, when all the earth seems "wrapt in dark and dreamful ease," and you seek in vain for "nature's sweet restorer," those cruel wounds, bleeding afresh, will come before your view, crying out for justice and for vengeance!

Crouch and cower as you may, the dreadful spirit will not down, but, like the ghost of the murdered Banquo, will fret your soul, until your days become a burden, and your nights a living horror.

CHAPTER XI.

The Detective in Love—A Pair of Gloves and a Job of Paint-
ing— Gross Becomes Communicative and is a Victim of
Wifely Government.

WHILE these incidents were transpiring in the city of
New York, Henry Brockman was pursuing his investigations in the vicinity of the village where the murdered man
was found.

Being invited to remain at the residence of Mr. Hitner to
tea, he cheerfully accepted the hospitalities so kindly offered,
in the hopes of receiving further information of Franssen's
doings while there, and was soon engaged in social converse
with the shoemaker and his loquacious wife. Mrs. Hitner was
a decided and an unremitting talker; her information was as
varied as the inhabitants of the place were numerous, and poor
Brockman's ears fairly ached with the deluge of information
that was poured into them. In the short half hour that intervened before the table was prepared for the evening meal, he
was made as thoroughly acquainted with the entire neighborhood as though he had lived there during the whole of his
life. He learned from her that Franssen, during the time he
was working for them, became intimately acquainted with the
servant girl, Julia; that he had taken her out on several occa-

15*   [345]

sions and that shortly before he left he had given her a pair
of kid gloves, nearly new, and which he said were too small
for him.

Julia, the girl, was a neat, comely-looking maiden of about
two-and-twenty years, and who had already cast her friendly
eyes upon the good-looking detective, and Brockman determined to pay some attention to her, in order to get a look, if
possible, at the gloves which Franssen had given her. He,
therefore, began to talk to Hitner about some necessary painting, and upon his offering to perform the labor at a remarkably
low price, he was engaged to paint the outside front of the
house; and he also arranged to lodge with them until the job
was completed.

Julia was a young girl who was very susceptible to flattery,
and Brockman soon won his way to her good opinion by a few
well-timed compliments of her cooking and the neatness with
which everything about the house was arranged. She was
rather vain, too, of her handsome face, and Brockman, pursuing
the victory he had already gained, did not fail during the evening to quietly inform the young lady of his admiration for her
beauty

After the usual household duties for the day had been performed, Mrs. Hitner desired Julia to go to the store, a short
distance away, and Brockman immediately offered to accompany her, which offer was most graciously accepted by the
blushing young damsel, who evidently felt highly flattered by
the very marked attentions of the gallant young painter, whose
good looks had already served as a passport to her youthful
affections.

The evening was a very beautiful one; the moon was shin

ing brightly, and the stars twinkled in their far-off setting of blue ; the grass and trees were putting on their spring suit of green, and, basking in the beauty of these surroundings, the young detective and the blushing housemaid wended their way to the village store.

The life of a detective it will be seen, is not always associated with the hardened criminal and the details of his crime. There are many bright spots in his existence, and, although he may be engaged in an investigation which contains within itself all of the depressing influences of depraved human nature, while he may be required to be intimate with the violators of the law, and to greet socially the suspected thief and murderer ; yet there are constantly recurring incidents of a pleasing and happy nature, in which the bright sides of life are shown to him in all their vividness of coloring and sweetness of existence.

So it was this evening, while walking with this young and blooming girl, whose love of flattery was, perhaps, her only fault, and whose heart was as pure as the skies above, that Brockman felt pleased and happy at the lot that had fallen to him, and endeavored by cheerful conversation to contribute to the enjoyment of the occasion.

From Julia he learned that Franssen was disposed to be very attentive to her, but that, forming an instinctive dislike to him, she had endeavored to repel his advances, which, however, never assuming an offensive form, gave her no occasion for treating him in any way other than friendly. She said that he had accompanied her twice on short visits to friends, and that on one occasion he had given her a pair of kid gloves, but slightly worn, and which he said were too small for him.

Thus the evening passed pleasantly away, and Brockman congratulated himself upon the prospective success of his mission.

The following day being Sunday, Brockman invited the young lady to accompany him to church in the evening, in the hope that she would wear the gloves and thus afford him an opportunity of examining them, and, if possible, having them identified; nor was he doomed to disappointment, for, as Julia came down stairs arrayed in her "best bib and tucker," look ing very charming indeed, she brought in her hands the gloves which she designed to wear, and walking to the mirror to arrange her bonnet—a failing that all of the sex are believed to be afflicted with—she carelessly threw them upon a table, while she performed the momentous operation.

Brockman as carelessly picked them up and lightly examined them; they were of a light brown shade, of good quality, and had evidently not been purchased by Franssen for his own use. Upon turning them over, he noticed with intense satisfaction that the letters " A. B." were marked upon the inside, thus convincing him that another of the missing articles of the murdered man's wardrobe had been traced to the custody of his late companion, who had no doubt been his murderer.

Upon returning from the church, Brockman turned the conversation upon the gloves, and remarking that they were too large for her, and that he was going to New York in the morning for his tools, offered to present her with another pair. This she blushingly, and with evident pleasure, accepted, and Brockman, under the pretense of matching the color, which she admired very much, obtained possession of them upon their reaching the house.   The next morning they were brought to the Agency, and Brockman returned to **Hitner's** house prepared to finish his job of painting, and carrying with him a new pair of gloves to adorn the hands of the pretty Julia.

Having accomplished the object of his visit, and finishing the job of painting, which he had engaged to do, to the satisfaction of Mr. Hitner, Brockman received his pay, and with a sly kiss from Julia, and a promise to come and see her soon again, he took his departure from the hospitable residence of the friendly shoemaker.

He then returned to Edgewood, and took up his quarters at the hotel kept by Jacob Gross, according to the direction of Mr. Bangs, who had a firm belief that Franssen must have stopped there, prior to the commission of the deed. These people, owing possibly to their precipitate arrest, and the unsuccessful attempt to connect them with the crime, when the investigation was so aggressively begun by the indefatigable and indiscreet Sheriff Byerly, had maintained a rigid silence about everything connected with the murder. This action was, in itself, suspicious, and Mr. Brockman was directed to operate skillfully upon the shiftless landlord and his ill-tempered wife.

It has been very truly said, temper is a very good thing in a woman; so good a thing, indeed, that she should never lose it; and I am seriously inclined to this belief. It is a matter of doubt, however, whether Mrs. Gross had ever heard this fact stated before; but, if so, she had evidently forgotten it long since, for the ease with which she continually lost hers was wonderful. The frequency with which her outbursts occurred, and the slight causes which produced such terrific results, were a marvel to poor Gross, who was usually the victim of her ill-humor, and upon whose devoted head she generally emptied the vials of her wrath.

Since their arrest, the slightest allusion to that occurrence was sufficient to arouse the latent passions of the inn-keeper's wife, and fearing to vent their expression upon her customers or friends, her unlucky spouse became the target of her invectives and the recipient of her spleen.

Fully aware of this weakness of the amiable lady, Brockman proceeded cautiously with the conversation, in order that he might lead up accidentally to the forbidden subject. He, accordingly, after tea, invited the landlord and his wife to join with him in drinking a glass of beer, and as both of them were very fond of that liquid, his invitation was cheerfully accepted.

Under the influence of frequent potations of the home-brewed beer of the henpecked Gross, the conversation became friendly and communicative in the extreme, and Brockman, after speaking about his business, and his not being able to obtain as much work as he would like, and soliciting a job from the landlord, which he finally succeeded in securing, carelessly inquired:

"What is all this talk about a murder in this neighborhood, that I hear?"

"Oh," replied Gross, a man was found down by the church last month, and nobody can tell who he was or who killed him."

"But don't they suspect anybody?" asked Brockman.

"Suspect anybody?" broke in the wife, "well, I should say they did; they suspected everybody; they even arrested me and my old man here, and he is such a fool, that I was afraid he would get us both into trouble with his nonsense."

"Is that so?" said Brockman, "why, what could they have against you?"

"That's just it, "again spoke the wife; "because we keep a hotel and some Jew peddler was known to have inquired the way to our house a few days before the man was found, that nunbskull of a sheriff had us arrested for killing him."

"Yes, and that ain't all," interposed Gross, "the people, who were crazy about the affair, came down here in a body, and they went through my house, searching for evidence; but they paid more attention to my beer and cigars than they did to anything else; but they've got to pay for it yet, I tell you."

Mrs. Gross was here called away to attend to some customers at the bar, and the conversation was continued by the two men.

"Were there no suspicious characters around here about that time that you noticed?" asked Brockman.

"Yes, there was one man, he came here to supper on Friday night, and he went away without paying for it, too," replied Gross; "but I was so mad about being arrested myself, that I would not tell the darned fools anything about that!"

"What kind of a looking man was he?" inquired Brockman.

"Well," said Gross, "he was a small-sized, dark-complexioned fellow, with black hair and mustache; he had on a *light felt hat,* and said he was a shoemaker, and that he was going to New York to get work. I don't believe that, though; I believe he was nothing but a regular tramp; he didn't pay for his supper, and left about seven o'clock and I haven't seen him since."

"What are you talking about, you old fool?" yelled out the shrill voice of the enraged landlady, who had returned and heard the latter part of her husband's reply; "do you want to have us both in prison again? Will you never learn any sense? you ought to be sent to a lunatic asylum, and I believe there are plenty there that have got more brains and better sense than you have!"

Here the good lady's anger got the best of her judgment, and she railed at the unfortunate man with all the vigor and force of a "Five Point" virago.

It was in vain to attempt to stop her. Once her passion was excited it became a perfect whirlwind of wordy abuse, and Gross knew better than to interpose, for on more than one occasion he had felt the force of her strong right arm, which she had a dangerous way of using, when aroused.

Brockman, however, having obtained all he wanted to know, and having no desire to interfere in a quarrel of so domestic a nature, made his escape from the room, and long after he had retired to bed he could hear the shrill notes of the old lady's voice, as she berated soundly her too communicative spouse. He had obtained a description of Franssen, and could locate him when desired, and with that result accomplished he composed himself to slumber and was soon in the land of dreams.

CHAPTER XII.

The Home of Bohner—A Happy Gathering—Dreadful Tidings—The Detective's Letter.

WHILE these investigations were being made and these damning proofs against Franssen were being gathered together, we will turn to another scene, where the hearts of parents and loving friends were being tortured and torn by the tidings of the death of the loved one, for whose safe and happy return they had so often and so fervently prayed.

After the discovery of the identity of the murdered man, the knowledge of his parents and their residence, Mr. Bangs felt the necessity of informing them of the fate of their son, and wrote to them a letter conveying as gently as possible the sorrowful tidings of his death, the fact of his having been murdered, and also the efforts that were being made to discover the guilty parties, but carefully omitting to mention the suspicion that was attached to August Franssen.

We will precede the letter upon its journey, and await its reception in the home of the Bohners.

Since the departure of their son, the parents had pursued the even tenor of their way. The old father attended to his business with the regularity of a town-clock, and in the evening smoked his pipe and drank his beer with all the composure and happiness of a lord, and the good wife went about her daily duties happy and contented with her lot, and every now and then would think lovingly of her absent boy, and long for his return. In the evenings she would sit beside her husband, and between the stitches of the warm socks she was knitting would weave also a bright dream of the future; her boy's return, his happy marriage, his fame as a painter, and the comfort and happiness which was to surround them all in the bright days to come.

And then Rosa would come tripping in, her beautiful face aglow with thoughts of the love of the young artist; and during the cozy evenings she and *Frau* Bohner would build wonderful castles in the air, bright with the beauty of loving thoughts, and strong in its foundation of loving hearts.

Upon a delightful evening, late in April, the happy family were gathered together—the father pompous and expectant, the mother hopeful and anxious, the children quiet, and evidently knowing that something was to follow the return of the servant from the post-office. A steamer had arrived the day before, and a letter from Adolph was anxiously awaited. A knock at the outer door gave notice of a visitor, and soon after old Herr Franssen was announced, who, failing to be favored with letters from his own son, came to hear through his good old neighbor the intelligence he so ardently desired.

The usual greetings over, Herr Franssen fills his pipe, and joins the happy and expectant group. After a while a gentle footstep is heard, and Rosa, accompanied by a younger brother, makes her appearance. She cannot wait the dawning of the morrow for the news, but must anticipate the message by coming herself to hear from her beloved to-night.

Every face beams with the radiance of expectancy, and

every eye is sparkling with the pleasure of anticipation, **when** the door is opened, and the servant, whose arrival has been **so** anxiously awaited, enters with a countenance far from assuring.

"Well, sir," asked Herr Bohner, "where are the letters **?** Be quick, sir, we are impatient."

The servant mechanically presents the packet to the old gentleman, who hurriedly scans their superscriptions. A shade of disappointment crosses his face—he fails to discover the handwriting of his son, and the influence of that disappointment is at once communicated to the assembled group.

"Is there no letter from Adolph?" anxiously inquired the fair Rosa, upon whose face the lines are sharply drawn, and whose breath comes quickly.

"None, my dear," replies the father, as he endeavors to conceal the emotions which are almost overpowering him.

But stay, what is this large, official-looking envelope, whose post-mark is New York, and whose writing is so unfamiliar? Adolph must be ill, and unable to write, and in order to prevent useless worriment to the dear ones at home, has procured the services of a friend to transmit the message; with hurried hands he removes the covering, and with anxious eyes peruses the contents. He does not read far, however—his face turns pale, and with a prayerful cry of "My God! My God!" the paper drops from his nerveless grasp—he falls back in his chair and seems to lose the power of action.

He is instantly surrounded by the startled, wonder-stricken members of his family, who with blanched faces inquire the cause of this sudden emotion. Fears press heavily upon the hearts of all; forebodings dark and dreadful fill theirs minds, **and in** the excitement and agony of the moment, none have the courage to read the fatal paper and solve the awful mystery.

Presently old Herr Franssen, who has been an interested, though silent spectator of the scene, slowly rises, picks up the fallen missive, and silently reads the mournful information. He is visibly affected as he reads, and when the conclusion is reached, the duty devolving upon him becomes apparent, and bidding the frightened family be calm, he gently breaks the stillness, and with a quivering voice informs the loving people of the news which the letter contains.

How strange and inscrutable are the ways of life! What curious circumstances are woven by the warp and woof of fate! And here, in this distant German home, the knowledge of a son's foul murder is communicated to a stricken family by the lips of the man whom the murderer calls by the tender name of father.

The effect of this revelation may be imagined; it cannot be described. The father, whose every hope was centered in his boy, and to whom his letters were a never-failing source of pleasure; the mother, whose clinging arms had held him to her loving breast, who had watched his path through life, and who had loved him as only a mother can love; the fair maiden, who was so soon to have called him by the tender name of husband, and whose future seemed so bright and promising—all thoughts, all feelings, all emotions seemed to blend in one common oppressive sense of despairing sorrow and grief.

The children, too, though still too young to fully appreciate the solemnity of the occasion, were awed into silence by the events that were transpiring, and huddled together with startled eyes and wondering faces.

"Herr Franssen with quivering voice informs the loving people of the news which the fatal letter contains." **Page 358.**

Herr Franssen, too, who realized fully the anguish of the gentle people who surrounded him, and who sympathized so acutely with their sorrowing, seemed utterly powerless to render any service, but stood by as though deprived of speech, and silently wiped away the twinkling tears that would fall in spite of all his efforts to repress them.

We will not linger over the painful scene, nor attempt to depict the anguish which settled upon the hearts of all as they realized that they had for the last time looked upon the face of their darling, and whose loved form was laid away in a strange land and in an unknown grave.

The father went about his daily duties, solemn and thoughtful; the mother, who had grown old in a single night, performed mechanically, but with breaking heart, her household labors; and Rosa, whose hope in life had departed, and who had, with tottering feet, groped her weary way homeward on that fatal night, had lost the charm of healthful beauty, and went about her home like one bereft of reason.

Something must be done, however, and after writing to Mr. Bangs and thanking him for the information so delicately conveyed, and for the efforts he was making to discover the murderer, the old father decided to come to America himself, visit the grave of his son, and, if possible, to render whatever aid lay in his power toward the apprehension of the slayer of his boy.

CHAPTER XIII.

The Murderer and the Detective—Remorse—Tired of Life—An
Attempt at Suicide.

LET us leave the aged and sorrowing father, who, bidding
adieu to the home he had thought would be a haven of
rest and happiness in his declining years, is sailing over the
seas, to the land that had proven so fatal to his hopes, and
follow the movements of the crime-stained Franssen, who is
being so closely watched by his fellow-workman, the detective
Mendelsohn.

The closer their intimacy became, the greater became the
disgust of Mendelsohn at the brutal mind and low instincts of
his companion, yet, as his association with him was necessary
for the public good, he disguised his abhorrence under the
vail of seeming friendship, and the two became seemingly firm
friends.

I know that the idea is too widely prevalent, that the life
of a detective, from his immediate association with crime and
criminals, must naturally partake of the grosser elements of
that association, and in the opinion of a great many people,
whose judgment and knowledge are, on many subjects, worthy
of consideration, a detective must necessarily be an adept in
crime, in order to become an expert in its detection—but from

my own experience of nearly thirty years, and in the management of the detective force connected with my Agencies, I
have no hesitation in pronouncing such judgments fallacious
and unjust.

It is true, that in many cities of the Old World the leading
tenet of detective belief seems to be that "to set a thief to
catch a thief" is the true secret of success; and consequently
the entire machinery of the detective service in France is
worked by those who have either suffered the penalty of
crime, or who, from the operation of judicial clemency, have
espoused the cause of justice and law, when they should rightfully be suffering its penalties. The result of this practice,
however, has generally been that only the little criminals are
punished, while the great ones labor on unmolested, and it is
not an unusual occurrence, that a share of their ill-gotten gains
finds its way into the pockets of the individuals who are supposed to be exercising their ingenuity in the detection of the
crime, from which they are reaping their harvest of bribery.

This practice, does not, however, affect the true theory of
criminal detection as carried into successful practice, and I
have yet to employ the first criminal as an operative on my
force, and have yet to fail of success when success was possible.

A detective, to be at all successful in his calling, is required
to be of a well-developed mind, to possess a clear and compre-
hensive understanding, and to be able at all times to assume
any position that may be requisite for the accomplishment of
the object he has in view, and he must also be prepared to
sacrifice, for the time being, his finer sensibilities, in order to
cope successfully with those who have rendered themselves

amenable to law, and who are destined to suffer its punishing inflictions.

It is not to be wondered at, therefore, that Mendelsohn should feel a wholesome disgust at the low brutality of the man with whom he was then associated, and with whom he was required to be on such intimate terms of acquaintance; but the cause demanded it, and, making a virtue of necessity, he performed his duty, and with what eventual result will hereafter be shown.

Several days passed without any event transpiring that furnished any additional facts in relation to Franssen's connection with the murder. He performed his labor in a dull, mechanical way, and his evenings were spent in saloons and in beer drinking. Mendelsohn had endeavored by every possible means to win his friendship and inspire his confidence, but thus far was only partially successful, Franssen seeming indisposed to be at all communicative, and averse to conversation. A dull, heavy melancholy seemed to have settled upon him, and oftentimes while at work the vigilant eye of the detective would observe him start suddenly from some deep reverie and shake himself, as though endeavoring to throw off some heavy burden that was weighing upon his mind.

Thus matters went on, until one day Mr. Schneider, whom Franssen, it will be remembered, had at one time worked for, called at the shop and delivered a letter to Franssen, which had been sent to him in care of his former employer. Franssen's dark face turned to a deathly sallow hue, and his hand trembled nervously as he broke the seal. His eyes glared in a frightened, devilish manner as he read the contents, nor did he lift them from the paper until the last line was completed.

A strange fascination seemed to overcome him, and, as though spell-bound by the information which he was reading, not a muscle of his frame seemed to move, and only the increasing deadly pallor of his face gave token that the message was of a character far from agreeable.

The letter was from his father, and informed his son of the sad news of poor Bohner's death; alas! no news to the guilty man, who, conscience-stricken and cowed with fear, now read of the sorrow and grief his hand had brought upon that loving family at home.

For some minutes after he had finished the reading of the letter, Franssen continued dumbly staring at the silent messenger of death, then dropping the paper from his hands, he got up from his bench, and with a muttered curse, strode about the room.

" What's the matter, Franssen, any bad news?" asked Mendelsohn.

Franssen stopped suddenly in front of the detective, and with a look of intense fear and agony, such as one seldom sees, save upon the faces of the dying, " Matter enough to make a man wish that he was dead!" he answered in a voice as hard as iron.

" What is it about?" inquired Mendelsohn, in the hope that in his mental excitement Franssen would divulge something of his guilt.

But not so. That hardened man, whose mind, blunted by his association with crime, and his soul harrowed by the great fear that now overcame him, had no words to utter, and Mendelsohn waited in vain for a reply.

Until this time he had rested quietly in the belief that Bohner had not been recognized; until this time he had in-

16

dulged in the security of believing that no one but himself knew who he was or where he was from.

That belief had been so tightly hugged to his breast, had been even in his loneliest hours an anchor of hope to his despairing heart, and it had been so suddenly and so strangely dispelled and taken away from him, that he was left powerless from surprise and fear, and, it must be confessed, from remorse.

Let us do this miserable man the scanty justice that he deserves. His life had been a wild and reckless one; his associates, although of his own choosing, had been of a lawless and disreputable character, and however much he may have transgressed the laws of society and of government, I do not believe that until that time his hands had been stained with blood. It is not strange, therefore, that, linked with the sleep-disturbing visions that had made his slumbers far from peaceful—the day-dreams of that upturned face that ever and anon appeared to him, even in the fancied security of his position—that this dreadful information of the recognition of the murdered man, this knowledge that search was being made for the murderer, should fall upon him like an avalanche that buried beneath it all his hopes of safety and plunged him at once into

> "Regions of sorrow: doleful shades, where peace
> And rest can never dwell; hope never come."

Without answering his companion's question, he walked back to his bench, picked up the letter, and crushing it in his hands, thrust it into his pocket.

During the remainder of that day no word escaped his lips; silent and grim, he labored on, and when the day's work was finished he laid aside his tools in a dazed sort of way, as though his mind was far away, and his thoughts were occupied with other things than implements of trade.

The same reticence was observed at the table, and as he arose, after an ineffectual effort to eat, Mendelsohn caught a glimpse of his face, which caused him to start back in horror. There was something in the expression of his eyes and in the firm set of his lips which he had never seen there before, and which gave token either of a deep despair, or of some fixed resolve.

Mendelsohn at once made up his mind not to lose sight of him, and so, hurriedly rising from the table, he hastened out and found Franssen putting on his hat as though about to leave the house. Mendelsohn then passed, and as soon as Franssen went out he followed him, keeping sufficiently in his rear to escape his notice, and determined that he should not elude his watchful eyes.

Franssen went directly to a saloon, and walking up to the bar, filled his glass with whisky, a liquid which Mendelsohn had never seen him take before, and drained it to the dregs; then, leaving the place, he started on a brisk walk towards the lower part of the city. Soon they came to the wharves and piers that lined the dark shore of the rolling river, but on, on they went, passing the numerous vessels that lay quietly and firmly at their docks; past the thronged and lighted ferries, where laughing and contented people were coming and going upon their own missions of pleasure or engagement; stopping once again to drain another glass of the fiery liquor—then on and on they went, until the open square of what is known as the Battery was reached, Franssen in advance, and his shadow following swiftly and noiselessly.

Only a short distance away loomed that circular structure which he had made his home when first his feet touched the shores of what was then to him a foreign land, and where he had parted from his boyhood friend, who now was sleeping in the arms of death.

I wonder did that pale, bleeding face beckon him on, or was it the cowardly devil working within him that led him hither, and brought him to this lonesome, dreary spot, where, at his feet, were rolling the dark and sullen waters.

Whatever the influence, their operations were short though powerfully impelling, for, stopping but a few minutes upon the brink of the river, he prepared himself for the leap. His design was apparent enough now, and Mendelsohn sprang forward and caught him by the arms, crying :

"Stop! What, in God's name, are you going to do?"

Franssen, startled and surprised, turned around and, recognizing his fellow-workman, struggled desperately to shake himself free from the vice-like grasp.

"Let me go!" he cried; but his struggles were not so fierce as before; the devil had evidently been weakened by this sudden interposition, the tempter of his brutal courage had been subdued, and he finally submitted quietly to the restraining arms of the detective.

"What does all this mean?" asked Mendelsohn, when he had grown quiet and stood sullenly before him.

"It means that I am tired of life, and that I thought to have ended it *there*," said Franssen, pointing doggedly to the water.

"Are you crazy?" exclaimed Mendelsohn.

Franssen laughed, a harsh, grating laugh, and shuddered as he answered: "I was, I believe, but it is over now."

Yes, the devil within him was quite dead now; the forced courage which had sustained his coward heart had quite subsided, and he walked subdued and silent beside Mendelsohn on their return to the residence of Mr. Gehring.

Not yet shall death claim thee for her own. Justice has an account to settle with thee, and the trial balance will soon be drawn.

CHAPTER XIV.

THE conversation between these two men, so strangely associated, and who had so recently been actors in a drama of so serious a character, upon their walk home, was neither animated nor interesting. Mendelsohn in vain tried to induce his companion to unburden himself of the weight of anxiety and mental distress which had led him to the rash act, but Franssen was too thoroughly occupied with his own thoughts to be drawn out, or to join in the conference which the other sought to engage him in.

He experienced, it must be confessed, a feeling of relief in escaping from the consequences of his temporary freak of insanity; but with that consciousness of relief there came also a deep sense of fear and dejection. One thought would recur to him amid the chaos of his meditations, one impulse seemed to rule the entire nature of his reflections, and one fact was dreadfully apparent to his troubled mind. He could not remain in New York; he must get away from everything that would tend to connect him with the murder of Bohner, and he must place between himself and that sorrowing old father a distance that would prevent the possibility of their meeting. Then, too, with a quaking heart he thought of the law's pursuit should he be suspected; yes, he must go away; there could be no rest or safety in this crowded city; he must seek some refuge that would hide him from the vigilant search of the detective and the iron grasp of the law. There must be safety in flight, but to remain longer where he was would be dangerous and fatal.

These thoughts were continually filling the mind of this hardened man, who but a short time before had been so intent upon self-destruction, and under the influence of this prospect of safety and this imagined immunity from punishment his spirits arose, and he seemed disposed to throw off the burden which had so fearfully oppressed him, and to be more cheerful and companionable.

In this transition from despair to hopefulness, from his mental depression to buoyancy and spirits, Franssen only illustrated, in his ignorant and brutal manner, the changes in temperament that take place in the minds of all evil-doers, whether intellectual or uncultured.

The conviction that comes to everyone who is guilty of crime, that they are deserving of punishment because of their transgression of the law, is universal; high or low, ignorant or profound, they cannot escape the painful emotions which are the offspring of remorse, and which, to finer natures, are so violent and tormenting as to be equivalent to the severest punishment of guilt.

In the operations of conscience the element of remorse is the one which most distinctly comes into consciousness; its lessons are being constantly forced upon the mind by the events which are daily transpiring around them, and which inevitably tread upon the heels of crime. Hence a universal conviction pervades the entire race of criminals that a man's "sins will find him out," and however successful he may be in concealing his guilt from his fellow-men, and however fortunate he may imagine himself to be in escaping their censure or punishment, there is an inward intelligence he cannot evade, a power within himself from which he cannot escape, and in this condition of mind he is, according to Aristotle, "neither brute enough to enjoy his appetites, nor man enough to govern them."

It is not to be considered strange, therefore, that this man, brutal and ignorant as he was, should so easily yield to a frailty which is common to all, and that, after a temporary experience of vanity and woe, in which his animal nature had been "worn to the stumps," he should so naturally change from a desire for death to a dread of its consequences and a longing for life and safety.

Linking his arm in that of Mendelsohn, they walked along the lighted streets, and at length, feeling the necessity of making some explanation of his strange conduct, in order to disguise the real intentions that animated him, and to secure the secrecy of the only man who knew anything about the transactions of the evening, he addressed the detective:

"What do you think of my crazy fit awhile ago?" said he, assuming a carelessness he was far from feeling.

"What do I think? Well, I think you must have been hard hit by something, to lead you to such an act. What is the matter, is there any trouble over in the old country? or anybody dead?"

"No, no,' quickly answered Franssen, "nobody dead in
the old country—but—but—things are not going right with
me here, and I must get away."

"What is the matter, some love scrape?" asked Mendelsohn.

"Oh, no," answered Franssen, in a troubled, perplexed
manner, "nothing of that kind; but I don't get along at all,
my mind is troubled, and I can't be contented here."

They were now passing a brilliantly-illuminated saloon,
from which issued the sounds of music, of clinking of glasses,
and of gay laughter, and Franssen, partly with the view of
turning the conversation from the channel into which, in spite
of himself, it was drifting, proposed that they should go in.

On entering, an animated scene was presented to the view;
tables and chairs were liberally distributed around the gayly
decorated room, a bar resplendent with all the gaudy furniture
of many colored glasses, and embellished with large mirrors,
which reflected in duplicate the gay panorama in front, and
crowds of men and women were gathered together engaged in
conversation and in drinking. At the end of the saloon a
stage was erected, which, supplied with all the appurtenances
of scenery and footlights, formed a very close resemblance to a
miniature theater.

It required no very close examination of the place to convince Mendelsohn of its character. Many times before, he
had been within these very walls upon duties connected with
his profession, and the glare and glitter of his surroundings produced no effect upon him, save that of disgust and
curiosity.

Only a short time previous, he had been there upon a very
16*

different errand from that which brought him hither to-night.
A young man, handsome, highly educated, and of staid, quiet
family connections, had been lured to the downward path of
vice by the seductive smiles of one of the painted devils of
society, and forgetting the duties which he owed to himself,
and the respect due to his family and friends, had yielded to
the temptations so attractively displayed before him, and was
pursuing a life of profligacy and immorality.

At last, having exhausted his means, but by no means his
appetite for the base pleasures of the debauchee, he was led to
rob his trusting employer of the money necessary to gratify his
thirst for pleasure and his desire for sinful amusements, and in
this very den of licentious enjoyments he had been found by
Mendelsohn, and was remanded to the protecting arms of the
law.   It is the old story; and now between the narrow walls
of a prison cell he bitterly meditates upon the folly and crime
which are invariably incidental to a life of sinful pleasure and
dissipation, while his family are compelled to bear the burden
of shame and ignominy which his conduct and its punishment
has brought upon them.

To many of those who were seated around the various
tables, men and women, Franssen seemed not to be an entire
stranger, and many rough nods of recognition from the men
and vulgar winks from the women attested the character of
the acquaintance, as he and his companion pushed their way to
a position near to the stage, seated themselves at a side-table,
and gave their orders for the required drinkables.

The performances at this place were neither of the most refined or artistic nature, as was evinced by the obscene jokes of
the male performers and the cracked voices of the female

artistes, while the discordant harmony of the orchestra contributed in no small degree to confirm this opinion. Franssen, however, enjoyed the maneuvers of the actors, or appeared to do so, for his laugh was among the loudest, his hand-clapping the noisiest, of the motley assemblage, and as the frequency of his potations began to have their effect upon him, he became one of the most interested and appreciative spectators, and his interest was manifested in a decidedly vociferous manner. He seemed to have entirely forgotten that but a short time before he had attempted to take his own life and end his troubles, which at that time seemed heavier than he could bear.

At length there appeared upon the stage a young woman, that is, a woman young in years, but upon whose once beautiful face the marks of dissipation were too deeply laid to yield to the operation of paint and powder, which had been very lavishly applied. She was dressed in rather scanty but very gaudy costume, which afforded an ample display of shoulders and limbs of no mean dimensions, and with a smirking smile that was intended to be seductive and captivating, she sang, in a voice that had evidently seen better days, a ballad of doleful plaintiveness, whose refrain was, "We have parted from each other," which induced Mendelsohn to mentally congratulate the departed, whoever he was, upon having succeeded in getting safely away from the false lights that had temporarily dazzled him.

Upon Franssen the effect of her appearance was of the most animating character. His eyes brightened, and he eagerly devoured every one of the false notes and shrill octaves with most intense enjoyment, and at the finish his applause was unbounded.

Mendelsohn had several times endeavored to engage his companion in conversation with regard to his departure, but without avail, his only reply being that he would tell him further about it when they reached home. With this he, of course, was compelled to rest contented, and although he would much rather have preferred to get Franssen alone in order that he might obtain the information he desired, he reluctantly submitted to his will, and pretended to participate in the enjoyments of a scene that was uninteresting and decidedly distasteful.

Scarcely had the applause attendant upon the exit of the repining songstress ceased, when Franssen, slapping the detective familiarly upon the shoulder, exclaimed :

"What do you think of that, old fellow ; ain't she a stunner ?"

Mendelsohn was constrained to reply truthfully and literally that she was indeed a "stunner."

"That's my girl," added Franssen, "and after she gets through, I will introduce yo ."

"Your girl!" said Mendelsohn ; "why, do you know her?"

"Of course I do, and so shall you, if you behave yourself," replied Franssen.

A short time afterwards a woman, faded and wrinkled, but with the remains of evident beauty upon her face, came up to where they sitting and quietly took a seat beside Franssen.

"Why, Adelaide, how do you do?" was Franssen's greeting, as he extended his hand. "I have not seen you for some time, but you did splendidly to-night."

Mendelsohn looked at the lady in astonishment. Could it be possible that this girl, old before her time, dressed in gar ments that had once been handsome and stylish, but which now showed unmistakably the result of long usage, whose pale and faded countenance told too plainly of a fast and dissolute life, be the charming, painted fairy, who had but a few minutes previously skipped so lightly upon the stage, and whose cheeks, thanks to the artificial bloom upon them, glowed with the rosy hue of apparent health? And yet such was the case. Adelaide Smith, who now sat down to her glass of beer, and " Mdlle. Anita Colonna," as she appeared upon the bills, were one and the same person.

Franssen awkwardly and brusquely introduced the singer to Mendlesohn, and then, ignoring his presence altogether, engaged the girl in conversation upon matters which related entirely to himself, which, soon proving to be of a character that was important, induced Mendelsohn to become a silent but interested listener.

They seemed to be very good friends indeed, although it must be confessed that the affection seemed to exist entirely on the part of Franssen, the girl listening carelessly to his compliments, and answering his questions in a listless, indifferent manner.

" Addie, I'm going away from here, and came to say good-by," said Franssen, after the usual preliminaries were gone through with.

" Where are you going to ?" inquired the girl, without evincing any great concern at the announcement.

" I don't know yet," replied Franssen. " I haven't made up my mind yet, but I can't get along here, and I am going to get out."

" Well, I wish you luck," carelessly said the girl, as though his movements were not of the slightest importance to her.

" Ad, have you got any money? I'm dead broke," suddenly asked Franssen, as though he wanted to get to business at once.

" Where would I get any money from?" she laughingly answered. " You must think I'm wealthy."

" No, I don't think that," said Franssen, " but I thought you might give a fellow a lift when he is hard up."

" What did you do with all the money you had last month? You seemed to have plenty then," impatiently asked the young lady.

" Sh— !" ejaculated Franssen, changing color, and looking nervously around, " don't talk so loud."

" I'm not talking loud," said the girl, " and you seemed to have lots of money then, and now you say you are broke."

This was important news to Mendelsohn, and he jotted it down carefully in his mental note-book. The fact that Franssen, who never earned more than enough money to make both ends meet, should have had " plenty" the month previously, was a confirmatory proof that it had come from some illegitimate source.

" Well, if I did have it last month," exclaimed Franssen, " nobody knows that better than you, it was a harvest for you; but that's not the question ; have you got any now? I must have some."

" No, I haven't got any, and can't let you have any, that's flat !"

" Well !" said Franssen, angrily, starting to his feet, " if you won't, you wont, and that's all about it," and then, turning to Mendelsohn, he said, " Come, comrade, we've had enovgh of this, let's go home."

And so, without paying any further attention to the young woman, and without the civility of a parting word, Franssen stalked angrily out of the saloon, followed by the detective, who quietly informed the girl that he would see her again.

Upon reaching home, and going to their room, Franssen began impetuously to collect his belongings together, as though to engage in the momentous task of packing up ; then turning suddenly to Mendelsohn, as though he had thoroughly made up his mind to do what he now proposed, he asked :

" Have you got any money, Mendelsohn ?"

" Yes, I've got a little," replied the detective.

" Well, look here," said Franssen, " I must have some, and I haven't got any ; how much have you got ?"

" Haven't you got any friends you can borrow from ?" hesitatingly inquired Mendelsohn.

" No, I have nobody that I could ask," replied Franssen, who knew too well, that by frequent borrowing and never paying, he had exhausted the confidence of what few friends he had.

" Well, I don't know about it," said Mendelsohn, " you see, we have not been together long, and you are going away; how do I know that I will ever get my money back again."

Franssen studied awhile, as though impressed with the correctness of this view, and in doubt as to what he should do —then he slowly drew his wallet from his pocket, and took from it a folded paper. He seemed to be doubtfully considering his action, and finally, having reached a conclusion, he

came to where Mendelsohn was sitting, and presented the
paper to him, saying :

" This is all that I've got, and you will do me a great favor
if you will take it and loan me five dollars.   I must have some
money, and this is all I can give you for it."

Mendelsohn took the paper, and as he unfolded it he could
scarcely repress an exclamation of surprise, for the offered
security was nothing more nor less than a pawn ticket, dated
the thirteenth of March, for a coat and pair of pantaloons, and
these articles, he had every reason to believe, had once been
the property of the murdered man.

" I got three dollars and a half on these, you see, and they
are fully worth the extra money that I want for them, and I
must get the money somehow."

Mendelsohn pretended to hesitate about loaning such an
amount upon the collateral offered, but finally agreed to do so,
and told Franssen that he would give him the money on the
following morning.

This seemed to satisfy him, and he quietly undressed himself and lay down in his bed, Mendelsohn following his
example, and they were soon sound asleep.

Ah ! sleep well and sleep soundly to-night, Franssen, for
the days will be long and dreary, and the nights dark and
gloomy, ere your head will again press the pillows in fancied
security, or your lungs inhale the air of liberty

CHAPTER XV.

The Flight Intercepted—The Arrest of Franssen.

MENDELSOHN arose early the next morning, but, early as it was, Franssen was astir before him, and was busily engaged in packing up the various articles that composed his scanty wardrobe, a proceeding which gave unmistakable indications of his intention to depart as soon as possible.

"Hello!" called Mendelsohn, starting up in bed. "What are you doing?"

"I'm packing up, don't you see?" replied his companion, without looking up or pausing in his occupation.

"You seem to be in a hurry," said the detective. "When do you intend to leave?"

"I must go to-day," doggedly answered Franssen; "and I would like to have that money as soon as you can get it."

"Which way are you going?"

"Well, I don't know exactly, but I think I will go to Buffalo first, and then try to work my way out West."

Mendelsohn dressed himself as quickly as possible, and then, telling Franssen that he would return with the money as soon as he had seen his friend, he came immediately to the Agency and reported to Mr. Bangs the information that he had received, and placed in his hands the pawn ticket, which he had accepted as security for his loan.

He was furnished with the required amount of money and instructed not to lose sight of Franssen, but to keep careful watch of all his movements, after which he returned to the shop, where he found Franssen, who, having notified his employer of his intended departure, and arranged for the receipt of such money as was due him, was engaged upon some work that had previously been commenced, and which he was required to finish before his pay would be forthcoming. He gave him the money, and then went to his own bench and to work.

Mr. Bangs immediately dispatched an employee to redeem the articles mentioned upon the pawn-ticket, and sent for Mr. Kuenzle, whose presence he desired for the purpose of identification. In a short time the young man returned with the clothing, and very soon afterward Mr. Kuenzle appeared, who, upon the garments being shown to him, immediately recognized them, and pronounced them to be the property of Adolph Bohner, and declared that they were the same which he had worn when he left home on that fatal day.

Mr. Bangs, therefore, determined to have Franssen arrested at once, deeming the evidence thus far collected to be of such a convincing character as to leave no reasonable doubt of his conviction for the murder of his friend. He therefore notified Mr. Sharpless, who was acting for the committee of citizens, and who, being an attorney, had also been engaged by the district attorney to assist in the prosecution of the criminal, of his intention thus to act. Mr. Sharpless had, under the direction of Mr. Bangs, also previously prepared all the legal papers necessary for the arrest, when the time should prove propitious.

This gentleman, whose office was in the city, upon receiving the information of Mr. Bangs's intended action, hastened to the Agency, and the two together proceeded to fulfill their part of the programme; Mr. Sharpless becoming very enthusiastic about being " in at the death," as he termed it.

Franssen, meanwhile, indulging in the brightness of the prospect before him, worked on with excellent good-humor, and occasionally broke forth in snatches of German song.

Seneca says "most people imagine themselves innocent of those crimes of which they cannot be convicted," and it may be that this man, red-handed as he was, with the fear of punishment coming unbidden to him, and beyond any force within himself, compelling him to flee from the coming of the father of his friend, and deceiving himself with the immediate prospect of escape from capture or conviction, may have lulled his coward conscience to sleep, may have succeeded in convincing himself that he was not so guilty as he had at first believed, and so, stifling his remorse, and crowding out of his view the vision of an avenging justice, may, for the time being at least, have been singing from the lightness of his heart—a heart whose very lightness was the evidence of a low and debased mind, and of a reckless and murderous disposition. But in this he forgot the truthfulness and power of Emerson's words: " There is no den in the wide world to hide a rogue," and that when a crime is committed, " it seems as if a coat of snow had fallen on the ground, such as reveals in the woods the track of every partridge and fox and squirrel and mole."

To Mendelsohn this exhibition of levity was disgusting,

and, knowing what he did, he determined to try the effect of mentioning the murder in a manner that would not excite any suspicion on the part of Franssen.

Taking up an old paper which contained an account of the murder of Bohner, and which he had in his possession, he perused it silently for some time, and then, turning to Franssen, carelessly said:

" That was a strange thing, that murder over at Edgewood, wasn't it ?"

The merry song ceased, and Franssen, with a scared, blanched face, looked up quickly and inquiringly into the eyes of the detective, but he saw there no evidence of suspicion— only the quiet, easy expression of one who was asking an unimportant question of a person who was supposed to have no interest in the answer.

" Y—yes," stammered Franssen, in reply, "but they don't know who did it, do they ?"

" Well, you can't tell about that," said Mendelsohn. "You see, those detectives don't tell everything they know, and the paper only says that they have information which will lead to the arrest of the murderer, but don't say what that information is."

Franssen seemed visibly affected, and did not answer immediately, while Mendelsohn, seeing his agitation, said solemnly:

" I would not like to be the man who did it, for as sure as fate he will be found out, and then somebody will be hung."

Franssen dropped the hammer he was using, and, on stooping to pick it up, Mendelsohn saw by the expression of his face that the blow had struck home.   His hands trembled, and for a short time he was powerless to speak, but at length recovering himself by a strong effort, he said, lightly laughing, but with faltering voice:

"Yes, I suppose so, and I don't think I would like to stand in his shoes."

"No," replied Mendelsohn, "neither would I. I would not stand in that man's place for all the money that could be offered to me. He may never be found out—he may evade every suspicion and escape every danger—he may never be called to account for what he has done before a court of justice—but is there no other punishment but this? Do you think that any man who has killed another can ever realize what happiness is again? No, no; every hour in the day, in the darkness of the night, when in company or alone, that dead face will glare out from some unexpected quarter, and the guilty man, starting with affright, will hear, ringing in his ears, as the deathly fingers are pointed at him, the fearful charge of *Murderer !* No, no, I would not be that man for all the world!"

During this speech of Mendelsohn's, Franssen's face was a perfect study. As he spoke of the possibility of escaping detection his face lighted up, and he listened eagerly, but as he reverted to the visions which remorse would conjure up in the mind his face became livid, his eyes stared wildly, and when Mendelsohn had finished he sank back and his work fell from his lap unnoticed.

He did not attempt to answer, but after sitting awhile he again resumed his labor; the merry song, however, did not come to his lips again, as he mechanically finished the work in hand.

Mendelsohn then changed the conversation and began to talk of Franssen's departure, expressing his regrets at losing his companion, and wishing him good luck and a safe journey.

At length the job was finished, and Franssen, receiving the wages that were due to him, bade his companions good-by, which occasioned no very serious regrets on their part, for his manners and habits had not gained him many friends among his fellow-workmen, and no sorrowful words were spoken as he started to go out. "Hold on, Franssen!" cried out Mendelsohn, taking off his apron, "I'll go with you part of the way—it's too bad to have a fellow go off alone."

Franssen accepted the offer, not very graciously, however; but Mendelsohn could not afford to stand upon ceremony now; he was rather anxious to know of the whereabouts of Mr. Bangs, and also to obey his instructions not to lose sight of his fellow-workman.

As they passed the saloon where he had spent a great deal of his time and the greater part of his money, Franssen proposed that they should go in and take a parting drink, which, being assented to by Mendelsohn, the two entered the "Hall of Gambrinus."

They had not been gone a great length of time from the residence of Mr. Gehring, when Mr. Bangs and Mr. Sharpless appeared, and upon entering the store and inquiring for Franssen, were informed of his departure. This occasioned no uneasiness, however, for Mr. Bangs knew that the prospective prisoner was in good hands, and that there was ample time to reach the train, which he must take if he was going in the direction which he informed Mendelsohn, and that he was fully provided with everything necessary for taking him either in New York or New Jersey.

"Franssen uttered a shrill, frightened, and despairing cry, and dropping his satchel attempted to *run away*"   Page 383.

They therefore proceeded to Chambers street ferry, and taking the boat were soon landed in Jersey City, at which place the depot of the Erie Railroad was situated.

Franssen and the detective having quenched their thirst and their sorrow at parting in the foaming glass, then started for the ferry, where, purchasing a ticket for Buffalo, they went on board the boat, which conveyed them across the river.

Mendelsohn began to grow uneasy; it lacked only fifteen minutes of train time, and as yet he had seen no indication of the parties whom he expected. He was debating in his own mind the course that had better be pursued, when, as they were walking through the long, covered way that led to the cars, Mr. Bangs suddenly stepped out from one of the door-ways that opened into the street, and stopping immediately in front of them, addressed the shoemaker :

" Your name is August Franssen, I believe ?"

Franssen, thus suddenly accosted, was unable to do anything but stammer out an affirmative.

" Then," said Mr. Bangs, sternly, " I arrest you for the murder of Adolph Bohner !"

Franssen uttered a shrill, frightened and despairing cry, and dropping his sachel, attempted to run away, but the iron grasp was upon his shoulder, and escape was impossible. Finding that further efforts were useless, with a smothered groan he submitted quietly and without further effort to the officer, who slipped upon his wrists the badge of dishonor—the shackles of the criminal.

The journey that followed was very different from the one that he had planned for himself, and its destination quite foreign to the locality named upon his ticket.

Instead of flying swiftly from the danger which he imagined had threatened him—and which proved, alas, too real—or
of finding the security he had fondly hoped to realize in
flight, ere the shades of night had fallen over the land he
was an inmate of a prison cell, the mark of Cain upon his
brow, and surrounded by the darkness and gloom of mental
agony and despair.

CHAPTER XVI.

The Inquest—The Trial—The Conviction—Intervention of Maudlin Sympathizers—The Triumph of Justice and the Sentence of the Prisoner.

ON the following morning the first act of the drama, so important to this unhappy man, was performed. The news had been published the evening previous, and the village was in a fever of excitement and expectation.

"The murderer has been taken" seemed to be the burden of every salutation, and at almost every fireside this important subject formed the topic of conversation, usurping, it is feared, more elevating and more praiseworthy subjects.

What the night's reflection or the restless slumber brought to the prisoner is beyond the reach of human ken; what thoughts may have come to him in "the dead silentness of the midnight hour;" what phantoms may have been conjured up by the disordered brain of the luckless man over whom was hanging the dreadful charge, will never be known; but when the morning dawned, and the crowds had assembled to witness the preliminary steps in this legal course of retribution, no step was firmer, no form more erect, no glance more unflinching than were those of the man who stood there on trial for his life.

17 [385]

He had evidently determined to face the worst that could befall him, and with that iron nerve, which oftentimes sustains the basest human, he looked upon that gaping assembly, who had come to hear the inquest, without the shrinking of an eye or the trembling of a muscle.

The opening proceedings of the coroner's inquest were in nowise different from those which characterize such hearings everywhere. The jury were impaneled in the usual form, the testimony was taken in the prescribed manner, and no event of any importance occurred until the prisoner himself was called to the stand.

The silence at this time became almost oppressive; a painful stillness seemed suddenly to fall upon that gathered throng. Every ear was strained to catch his faintest utterance, and every eye was fixed upon him with the intensity almost of fascination.

Reader, have you ever, while sailing over the boundless ocean, experienced that awful calm, that terrible quiet, which precedes the coming storm? The air becomes oppressively heavy; the dull leaden sky seems to have suddenly closed in upon the scene; the dashing waves that but a short time before were surging around the ship, rocking it to and fro upon their bosom, have subsided, and the mighty deep stretches far and wide around you in one unbroken, even surface, mirror like in its placid smoothness. The sails are clinging to the masts, and the vessel stands seemingly motionless. The heaviness of the atmosphere communicates itself to those on board; the faces of the crew and passengers insensibly assume that appearance of solemn inactivity with which the sea and air seem charged, and in that awful moment, when the great voice of nature is hushed and ominously silent, when sky and sea are filled with that intensity of depression which burdens the heart, we realize the wonderful nature of existence, and feel the dreadful solemnity of unerring and impending death.

Such was the stillness that filled the over crowded room, as the lips of the accused man profaned the Holy Book, and he swore to give "the truth, and nothing but the truth."

I will not attempt to give here the details of his testimony —testimony which reliable witnesses disproved and denied— in which he attempted to account for his actions, and the possession of the articles which had been traced to him. At last the head of the murdered man, carefully preserved, but showing through the transparent glass of the receptacle that contained it the marks of the cruel blows that had beaten out his young life; the lips colorless, but almost smiling into the face of the miserable man who had been his companion, and who had slain him, was presented to him for recognition. With a stolid look he gazed at the face of the man who had so often befriended him, and who, in return, he had hated so intensely, and then turning to his interrogator, in a voice which contained no sign of tremor or fear, answered unhesitatingly :

"I don't know that man, I have never seen him before!"

It may seem incredible, but such was the answer that was given, and no further questioning could induce him to change his denial, or to identify the features as those of his friend. He had schooled himself thoroughly, and nothing could shake the stability of his inward teaching.

That this was a mistake will readily appear, for gathered around him were several persons, among them Mr. Kuenzle, who had frequently seen them together, who knew of their

intimacy, and who were horrified at the disclaimer which was
then so coolly and imperturbably made.

The evidence, however, was conclusive, although circumstantial, and the verdict of the jury was that

"Adolph Bohner came to his death from the effect of
blows, administered by the hands of August Franssen," and
the miserable man was duly committed for trial.

It is unnecessary to weary the reader with the details of
the trial, which eventually took place, and which resulted in
the conviction of the accused.   Suffice it to say, that the evidence presented formed one unbroken chain of circumstantial
proof, which even the doubtful and hesitating jury failed to
discover any weakness in, and they were reluctantly compelled
to render a verdict of "Guilty."

The prisoner was proven to have made an engagement to
meet Bohner at Edgewood; he was shown to have been at
Gross's Hotel on the evening when the murder was committed,
and to have suddenly disappeared therefrom.

His residence at Hitner's was testified to, and his knowledge
of the murder in advance of its discovery fully shown; the
gloves which he had given to Julia, the servant maid, were
produced and identified; the hat that was found upon the
head of the murdered man was proven to have belonged to
Franssen; the pawning of the coat and pants of the unfortunate Bohner were unquestionably traced to Franssen, and the
concert singer, Adelaide Smith, who had been hunted up by
Mendelsohn, testified (rather reluctantly, however) to his
having a considerable amount of money at that time, and
especially to a twenty-franc gold piece, which Mr. Kuenzle remembered having seen in Bohner's possession; all these things

pointed so directly and conclusively to the guilt of the Alsatian, that notwithstanding the firmness of the prisoner's denial
(although he failed to account for his movements on the days
in question), the apparently well-concocted and well-defined
theory of the defense, and the evident reluctance of the jury,
Franssen was duly convicted of willful and premedittaed murder, and was sentenced to "be hung by the neck until he was
dead."

Thus far the majesty of the law had been upheld; thus far
the supremacy of justice had been maintained, and thus far
the ability of the detective had made itself manifest in producing this result. A crime that at first seemed shrouded in
impenetrable mystery, and that had defied the efforts of less
experienced men, had, through the operations of my officers
and by the skill and energy displayed by them, been successfully unearthed and the criminal brought to the bar of justice
and condemned to suffer the penalty for his evil doings.

And yet, no sooner was this result accomplished, than the
maudlin sympathizers, with strong minds and weak heads,
came to the front in unusual numbers. They winked entirely
out of sight the damning facts which so conclusively and so
firmly placed the load of guilt upon the shoulders of the ungrateful Franssen, and were loud in their denunciations of the
judge and jury, the attorneys and the witnesses, and, as may
be assured, the poor detectives were not allowed to escape their
venom or evade their assaults.

The diplomatic service was brought into requisition, and
the French consul was induced to interest himself in the attempt to procure a new trial, for the reason that Franssen was
not yet a naturalized citizen of the United States. No efforts

were spared, no means were left untried, that would tend in any degree toward striking the shackles from this convicted felon, and sending him forth a free man, free to pursue his work, and perhaps to repeat his crime.

The enormity of his offense was completely overlooked by these philanthropic imbeciles in their ardor to save the condemned man from suffering the penalty of his crime ; eminent legal counsel were secured, a stay of proceedings obtained, and reasons for a new trial were filed and argued with an ability worthy of a better cause. Finally, upon the important fact being discovered, that during the deliberations of the jury which tried the case they had come into court for instructions upon some point of evidence or law about which a doubt existed, and the judge, in answering the questions, failed to have the prisoner present at the time—a new trial was ordered, the county charged with the expense of another suit, and a hope of safety held out to the miserable man who so richly deserved his doom.

It may be that the testimony of that old, broken-hearted man who had sailed across the seas, and who had arrived in time to take a mournful part in the second act of the sad drama which had so fearfully destroyed the happiness of his family, and rendered his home so desolate, had some effect upon the wavering minds of the jury ; it may be that the sight of that agonized face and the tears that fell from the heavy eyes of the sorrowing father, as he sat silent and comfortless during the continuance of this second trial, had some influence in breaking down the firm stolidity of the murderer, and rendering him less hopeful, less confident, and more ill at ease ; but certain it is, that instead of receiving his acquittal, the jury, in spite of their reluctance, were forced to make a treaty with conscience, and to render a verdict of "murder in the second degree," and instead of hanging, the "*persecuted gentleman*" was sentenced to a long term of imprisonment.

The chain was too strongly forged to yield to the efforts of those who sought to break it, and in the end justice triumphed, the law was vindicated, and the guilty man painfully realized that "the way of the transgressor is hard."

The body of Adolph Bohner was interred in the graveyard of the little village church, and over the green mound, where in summer the roses bloom, and the snow lies heavy and deep in the dreary winter, a little white stone is all that tells of the fate of him who, burning with ambitious hopes, whose heart was filled with happiness and joy, came from his far-off home and lay down here to rest—a victim of a friend's foul crime. In the after time, perhaps, as the children play in merry sport at hide-and-seek, amid the "monuments of departed dust" which lie around, the laughter will be hushed, little faces will grow pale, and little eyes be dimmed with tears, as they listen to the story, so sorrowful in its details, of the young artist, who had been found dead and murdered, lying upon the snow-cov ered ground on that peaceful Sabbath evening.

CHAPTER XVII.

*The Home of the Bohners and the Prison Cell—The Sorrowing
Family and the Maniac Criminal—The Fall of the Curtain.*

TWO more scenes and our story is told.

After the trial was over, and Franssen was conducted
to his lonely cell, public excitement died away, and the world
moved on in that easy-going, forgetful manner that the world
has had since the day of creation.

The first scene is far away; old Herr Bohner has returned
to his home in the city of Strasbourg. Sorrow-stricken and
heart-broken he sits at the fireside, as with trembling lips he
tells the story of his journey to those assembled—nearly the
same group which we have mentioned before—all are there
but one. Herr Franssen is not of the number; he had heard
of the part his son had played in the tragedy, and he could not
meet the sorrowful faces of the family whose fireside had
been made desolate, and whose lives had been darkened by his
unworthy offspring.

Mute in their agony, tearful in their sorrow, they listen to
the words as they fall from the faltering lips of the father.
He tells them all the story—that pale sad face with the marks
of cruel blows upon the fair forehead—the trial—the demeanor

of the prisoner—the conviction—and then of the little grave under the maples in that village churchyard.

When he has finished, a silence like that of the grave falls upon them—a silence, broken only by the convulsive sobs of the fair Rosa, who tearfully and lovingly presses to her lips a tress of brown hair, cut from the bruised forehead of her dead lover.

And in that solemn silence we will leave them.

Let us draw the curtain and look upon another scene, far different in its import.

It is night, and in the prison the stern-faced keepers have gone their rounds, and securely fastened the iron bars that stretch their forms between the prisoners and liberty, and are preparing for an evening's enjoyment, entirely undisturbed by the scenes of misery and crime which they had so recently left behind them.

Let us look into the narrow room where lies the recumbent form of one of the prisoners. It is August Franssen. Changed, ah, so greatly! No longer do we see the careless indifference that marked his demeanor upon the trial, but pale, haggard, and distressed, he lies here now, restlessly dreaming and tossing from side to side. Suddenly starting from the bed, his eyes gleaming even through the darkness, staring wildly and fixedly at the distant corner, and with hands outstretched as though to keep off some hideous object that threatened him, he cries:

"No! no! don't come near me! Your hands are bloody, and your face—ah! keep off! keep off! You came between me and the girl I loved. You had money and I had none, but now you are—dead! I see it all—that lonely night! You whistled as you came along, but you did not know who was

17*

behind you, you did not see that upraised arm—but the blow fell, and you were down upon the ground! Ha! ha! you will never love again, and your money now is mine! Sh——! do not speak, they will hear you! Do not come any nearer. De not touch me with those cold and clammy hands! I saw them clasped before me that night, as you cried out: 'Would you kill me?' Kill you? yes, damn you! But it is all right now. Rosa will be mine, and you will be forgotten! Ha! ha! I have won!" and he sinks back exhausted upon the couch, laughing wildly.

Ah! dreadful sight. The reason has fled, and in its place a wild insanity. Verily, his sins have found him out—a fearful retribution—and we will look no further.

Reader, our story is done. The detective has performed his mission; the weight of punishment has fallen upon the guilty transgressor, and now we draw the curtain upon the last scenes of a history, alas! not rare in these degenerate days, but which has proven with all the intensity and convincing force of unerring judgment, that "he who sows to the wind, shall reap the whirlwind."

BOOMING LOGS AND THE DETECTIVE.

CHAPTER I.

The City of Raceford.

THE proprietors of one of the most extensively-known Lumber Manufacturing and Booming Companies in the western country engaged my services, some years ago, to discover, if possible, who the persons might be that were employed in stealing their saw logs and cutting them into lumber suitable for the St. Louis and Dubuque markets. It had for a long time been the unvarying experience of the managers of the corporation named, that, however closely and unremittingly they might watch the store booms of the mills, however industriously they might labor to invent and then use all the known checks upon the tows coming down the river, the product still continued to fall short, and the raw material to mysteriously disappear. The net annual losses were necessarily quite heavy and the directorship of the company desired, whatever might be the cost, to decrease, if not entirely stop, this drain upon their resources. It was not only injuring their business in the present, but must prove their financial ruin, in the future, if permitted to continue. The problem to be solved was, "Who were the depredators?"

Although business of a far different and more absorbing nature was at that period enchaining a good portion of my attention, and freely draining upon the men and resources of the Agencies, I at once determined that this new task should be undertaken. In order that I might work understandingly in the inception of the case, Superintendent Warner was instructed to proceed to the locality, make a survey of the situation, and, upon his return, we would be enabled quickly to decide as to the proper course to pursue. The distance from Chicago to Raceford, the location of the mill property, was considerable, and it was not until more than a week had elapsed that we were fully prepared to begin energetically the real business of the operation. Mr. Warner had well performed his duty, and personally inspected the town and adjacent country, the pine lands, from which the logs were taken, the water-course, down which the rafting was done, and the structures in which the material was converted into clear lumber, siding, flooring, studding, joist, scantling, fencing, common stock boards, culls, and framing timber of various lengths and dimensions. Ostensibly in search of ties to be employed in the superstructure of a railroad then in course of construction not far from the neighborhood, he made close examination of everything of interest to us. With his report to aid, the groundwork of the plan was comparatively easy of formation.

In the commencement, I dispatched Jasper Root, an ex

perienced operative, who had long been in the employ of the
Agency, to Raceford, with orders to find suitable work on the
docks, in rafting or milling, nigh the vicinity, and then to look
out sharply for information which might lead us to some of
the thieves. He was to report to me, day by day, through the
medium of the mail. To cover his identity and prevent sus
picion resting upon him through writing, he was supplied with
a cipher and key, and a manner of receiving and sending letters, the particulars of which I need not dwell upon.

Raceford, at the time of which I write, was a city containing nearly two thousand inhabitants. Picturesquely dotting a
handsome site, extending across and embracing both banks of
the Lotus river, which is navigable for smaller craft a number
of miles from its mouth, to the eastward, the land gradually
sloped down to the edge of the forest of pine. In the west
rose abruptly a low range of tree-clad hills. The bridge
spanning the deep, swift-flowing waters of the river was of
rustic build and material, but a thoroughly stanch and reliable
structure, capable of being swung open at its center arch to
give unobstructed passage to rafts, and such small propellers
and steam-tugs as were used by the lumbermen in transporting
lumber to market, and importing necessary stores and supplies.
About the city, and extending along the country, between the
Lotus and another large stream, for more than a hundred
miles, was an immense forest of Norway pine. From its
mazy depths the sturdy arm of the woodman had already
drawn almost priceless treasure, and there yet remained much
valuable timber to be thus appropriated.

The principal street of the town stretched to the westward
and eastward, starting from the bridge. There were other

thoroughfares parallel with, and at either side of it, but they seemed mostly devoted to residence purposes, and were not as evenly graded or carefully worked as the main road. Avenues —many of them handsomely shaded by spreading tamaracks, elm and honey-locust trees, intersected the streets at right-angles. On two of these were situated the village school-houses—one in the western part of the city, and one in the eastern—both built of red brick, and each one surmounted by a dome and the inevitable copper-tipped lightning-rod. There was the West Side School and the East Side School, as there were the West Side Merchants and the East Side Merchants, the West Side Doctors and Lawyers, and the East Side Doctors and Lawyers; in fact, there was the West Side best Society and the East Side best Society, and, as in other similarly situated and divided places, there existed a wide diversity of opinion in the minds of the West Side Citizens from those of the East Side Citizens. Both sections had their churches and their favorite ministers. Both sides attended re-ligious services; both sides sent their boys and girls to school. Raceford had two banking-houses, a score of drinking places, billiard-saloons and bowling-alleys, with two rival hotels, the West Side Hotel and the East Side Hotel. The grog-shops were about equally apportioned in the city, and every West Side dealer was said to dispense better liquor than any East Side man could boast, and *vice versa*.

When the sawyers, raftsmen, and boomsmen were not em-ployed at their business, they passed a part of their time, and spent much of their money, with the proprietors of the saloons and bowling establishments.

The old citizens of Raceford formed, and they still form, a

thrifty, industrious, and well-behaved community. They labored arduously during six days of the week, and on the seventh rested and devoted themselves to their religious duties and the digestion of their Sunday discourse and dinners. They gave liberally of their means for the enlightenment of the distant heathen, and the West Side contested, in this regard, with the East Side, each striving to carry off the palm by donating more than the other to the missionary cause.

The ladies held their sewing circles, and, as a matter of course, there was the West Side Martha Washington and the East Side Martha Washington Sociable. The Oolong consumed at the one was, by its drinkers, pronounced far superior to the Gunpowder of its opponents; and the scandals discussed by the West Side Martha Washingtonites were claimed to be much more racy than those dwelt upon by the Martha Washingtonites of the East Side.

There was but one Masonic, and but one Odd Fellows' Lodge. The West Side Masons and Odd Fellows and the East Side Masons and Odd Fellows "dwelt together in unity," which fact gave great cause for complaint on the part of the chief fomenters of discord throughout Raceford. It was the mystery of mysteries, and the anti-secret-society people of both parts of the town shook their sage heads knowingly, and urged significantly that there must exist some vast inherent wickedness in the midnight councils of the brother Masons and Odd Fellows, because they failed to keep up and feed the prevailing village feuds. The members of these societies, however, said nothing in reply, but continued to live harmoniously—at least, as far as the outer world could judge.

Raceford, from its location in the midst of, and surrounded

by, the almost exhaustless lumbering district, was a place of considerable importance. A principal manufactory of, and shipping point for, the immense product of the great pineries, and a grand *entrepot* for goods of all kinds consumed in a wide range of territory, it bid fair shortly to become a sort of north-western metropolis of boards.

It had its small East Side and West Side newspaper, the first called *The East Side Bugle of Liberty*, and the other *The West Side Bird of Freedom*. The editor of the *Bugle* was very bald, squinted fearfully out of one eye, and could not see well with the other. He was short, squabbish, spoffish, and cynical, and never, excepting by mistake, said a civil word of anything or anybody from across the Lotus. His devil (or apprentice) was disgraced one day, because, during Skoob's absence, he inadvertently admitted to the columns of the paper a local paragraph alluding to a newly-arrived West Side milliner as " capable of adorning a hat with taste and skill almost equal to that of Miss Myrtle of the East Side Ladies' Emporium of Fashion." Skoob abjectly apologized for the insertion of the objectionable sentiment in the ensuing number of the *Bugle*, and wrote, complacently, that " that particular imp of darkness had been impaled upon the office shears, and then ignominously consigned to the lowest depths of the ink-keg, whence he should issue no more forever." Of course, the excuse was accepted, and the *Bugle* lost not a single patron on the West Side.

The leading spirit in the editorial sanctum of *The Bird of Freedom* was long, lean, gaunt, facetious, and bore the proud name of Jobson. He cut up Skoob unmercifully in his journal, but usually laughed at, and refused to reply to, his adversary's fierce philippics, failing to find any pith or point in them. Jobson let fly his *Bird of Freedom*, without stint or reserve, at every East Side person, thing, or institution, and was continually urging the residents of that benighted and unwholesome district to "come over to Jordan's happy land," meaning thereby the West Side. The two sheets fought hotly-contested battles upon every local issue, and, when other subjects failed, metaphorically knocked the heads and chief pillars of the churches together to keep up the interest. When these pastimes palled on the public taste, Skoob turned to engraving, with his keen pen-knife, ludicrous caricatures of Jobson. One, which had several times done service in the *Bugle*, was the picture of a thin, starveling donkey, with broad leather-apron ears, behind one of which monstrous appendages rested the editorial quill of *The Bird of Liberty*. Beneath the illustration was printed the legend: "The *Bird* Gone to Grass!" This sometimes brought forth a rejoinder, in kind, from Jobson, who also wielded the graver as well as the pen, in the shape of an overgrown calf, with the identical head and bald pate of Skoob. Under the caricature would be found these caustic and descriptive words: "The Meandering Idiot of the *Bugle* Looking for His Ma!" These gentle and harmless diversions, which excited the citizens to the highest pitch, never culminated in editorial duels or rencontres. Skoob was afraid to fight and Jobson did not dare to; the reader will probably suggest an impalpable distinction without perceptible difference.

From the sample of contents already given it will be conceded that the Raceford newspapers were conducted, at least, with spirit and energy, if not with stateliness and grandeur.

The fall was not far advanced, and the emerald hue still rested undimmed upon hillside and lawn. A subtle perfume from the resinous forest trees pleased the senses, and the hum of industry arose from the town and was borne on every passing breeze. The mills were in motion, and the whir of the busy saws and the rattle of swift-running machinery made the city seem, as it really was, the center of a great and material industry.

Of Root's journey to Raceford little need be said. He went first to Trafton, where he left his baggage, and, clad in a rough suit, took cars over the North Central Railway to a point on the Lotus, not far from Junction City, and the remainder of the trip was performed upon the good though diminutive steamer *Orient*, Captain Perkins. The river ride was an entirely novel one to the young man, and he greatly enjoyed the seemingly endless panorama of gorgeous scenery which was unrolled to view as the craft advanced further and further up the narrow and serpentine stream. He managed to strike up a friendship with the chief officer while *en route*. Having served several years on shipboard, in different capacities, Root was quite at home on the water, and, unasked, lent a hand when necessary to the correct working of the craft, thus securing the good-will of the commander and his subordinates.

The detective had been for many seasons off the sea, doing shore duty. Having in view the task before him, he rightly conjectured that a little natural bronze-tint added to his complexion, and some strength lent to his muscles would not come amiss; hence, during the several days passed on the river, he remained mostly forward on the lower deck, although he had prepaid full cabin passage. He aided in receiving and putting off freight during the making of the different stoppages, helped take on wood, and in shoving out and hauling in the gang-plank, making himself generally and agreeably useful. It was a term of excellent training for work that he supposed he would soon have to do. At night, enveloping himself in a blanket, he preferred to sleep on the captain's deck, forward and near the great bell, which was surmounted by a huge pair of elk-horns. With a chair-back for a pillow, he slumbered soundly, only awakened now and then by the grating of the keel upon the gravelly river bottom, or the sudden silence of the machinery incident to a landing. The result was that he soon became as tawny as a Spaniard, and as tough, to look upon, as a Sandwich Islander.

Once during the trip, when the steamer rested on a bar from which, for a time, it seemed impossible to extricate her, Root worked like a hero in the capacity of second mate, that officer being disabled with a sprained ankle, and the captain remarked that he handled tools and managed men with the skill of an old sailor. He also insisted, when the *Orient* once more moved up stream, that the volunteer should accept pay for his labor, but the operative declined, saying that he saw how short-handed he was and had therefore assisted a little, but in reality any true river man would have done the same for another in distress.

In the course of a conversation which he held with the captain during one of the last days of the trip, Root confidentially informed his new-found friend that he had been forced to flee from Trafton, because of a little difference which had arisen betwixt himself and the government authorities, connected with certain Canadian blankets that he had *imported* during the previous winter.

"That accounts for the absence of baggage, when you boarded the *Orient* at the Point."

"Yes. I left a United States detective in the lurch at Trafton. He had been after me for several days, but I found him out, took leave of my landlord from a rear door of the hotel, gained the train, already in motion, and succeeded in reaching Junction just as you were leaving the shore. Raceford is your destination ; so it's mine too! All places are alike to me, if they are away from the crowded cities. Of course, I don't want everybody to know my story."

"Depend upon me," said the captain, "for keeping your secret. I don't love the revenue fellows any too well myself, though I take special care never to fall into their clutches. If there is anything I can do for you, command me."

"I know of nothing now, thank ye. When we are ashore I may ask a good word from you in getting work."

"You shall have it, sir. And a hint from me is worth something with the company and with the people of Raceford."

Root returned thanks, and there the conversation was interrupted by the call for dinner. The agent knew his place, and ate with the mates and pilots well forward, while other passengers partook of their meals at the captain's table, abaft in the little cabin.

During the same afternoon the detective had an interview with the second mate of the steamer, in his part of the texas, or hurricane, deck, where he was found prostrate, and suffering great pain from the injured limb. An application of cold water, made by the visitor, gave the mate some relief, and, after awhile, he was communicative. Without particularly desiring the man to keep his revelations to himself, Root gave out the same intimation as to smuggling that he had presented to the captain. The mate also promised any assistance he could give when Raceford should be reached. Root left the deck with the impression that the injured man would not be slow in telling his story to some of his chums in port. It was what the detective desired. Then, if he failed in securing employment, he could have a valid excuse, ready-made, for remaining in the pinery, and, at the same time, avoiding any suspicion that he had an eye upon those engaged in swindling the manufacturing company. He was aware of the fact that he might find many among the logsmen and raftsmen who were in reality hiding from the officers of justice, and this hint, which the captain or mate would naturally set afloat, might serve as an introduction to their confidence. When the tired detective spread his blanket for sleep that night, the steamer was some thirty miles below the falls and but twenty miles from Raceford.

CHAPTER II.

Mrs. Buxton's Hotel.

THE *Orient* was alongside the wooden wharf at Raceford, ready to receive her freight of lumber, lath, and shingles, when the detective awoke the ensuing morning. After a late breakfast, consisting, in part, of fried fish, coffee, and biscuit, he desired to see the city, in company with the captain, but, having purposely left his luggage in Trafton, to aid in giving shadow of confirmation to his previously concocted story of a recent escape from the government officials, he was restrained through lack of clean linen and other necessary clothing. It would not do, he thought, to make his *debut* that cheerful Sabbath forenoon on the congregation-crowded streets of the (as the captain had hinted) hypercritical city of Raceford, wearing garments, never very elegant, and clad in which he had performed the entire voyage from Chicago. He made application to Captain Perkins, asking how he should extricate himself from this dilemma. With characteristic promptitude, he immediately invited the passenger to his stateroom, and, exhibiting a well-filled wardrobe, informed Root that he was at liberty to select and use anything that it contained. Thus instructed, the operative proceeded to make himself at least presentable. There was little difficulty in enveloping himself in

Perkins' shirt, the only trouble arising in finding pins with which to fasten the neck-band, that encircled his by no means slender throat, with several inches of cloth to be spared. But the question as to waistcoat and pantaloons presented an insur mountable difficulty. None of these articles to be found in the captain's collection would do. They fitted him too much A linen coat, made rather scant in the body for its owner's use as an under garment, the detective at last managed to employ as a loose duster. The greater propoition of the contents of the closet were far too broad and expansive for convenience, the smaller kinds, even, hanging from his bony frame like the storied "shirt on a bean-pole." He promised his friend that, if he could possibly find the needed articles for sale in the city, he would procure a temporary outfit and return those which he wore that very day. There was a too-evident disregard of the cost of cloth in the duster and the shirt to comport with his ideas on personal economy, but he was compelled to take the things. After a bath, a touch of the razor to his face, and decking himself in his borrowed costume, Root saw, by the cabin glass, that he was greatly improved in outer appearance. He was no longer ashamed to enter the town with the captain. It was well that he had waived the attempt to supply himself with clothing by purchase. The stores were all closed. Not even the most enterprising merchant on the West Side, or on the East Side, would venture to open his warehouse doors for the transaction of business on a Sunday. The proprietors of the saloons and corner groceries were not so particular.

"Now," said the captain, "I'll take you to the best board ing-house, for a laboring man, in all Raceford."

"I shall be greatly your debtor!" answered Root.

After a considerable walk the two men came to Mrs. Buxton's residence and entered. The house was by no means large or showy, but seemed to be well kept in every respect. Its hostess was not "fair, fat, and forty," but some years younger than that, and far from beautiful. She was florid as to face and pock-marked; had fiery red hair; was angular in frame and in temper, and spoke as fine and broad a brogue as any lady ever brought to America from the northward of the Green Isle of Erin. Still, she was not particularly ugly. When presented for the first time to the view of the agent, Mrs. Buxton was engaged, her head enveloped in a bandana handkerchief of many colors, and her skirts unfashionably pinned back, furiously dusting the furniture of the public sitting-room with a big, black turkey-wing.

"An' is it there you are, captain?" was her pleased ejaculation, as soon as she beheld the portly figure of Perkins in the doorway. Pausing in her labor she advanced toward the gentlemen and continued: "How has it sped wid ye, since the age that you've bin away?"

"Very well, indeed," responded the captain, glancing about him. "You are tidying up the old house, as usual, I see. These lumber boys *do* play havoc with your rooms!"

"Yes, sir; they're not *very* particular; but, when they hev the money, they always pays well an' promptly!"

At this juncture the captain brought forward his companion.

"This is Mr. Root," he said, "who is newly arrived in these parts; was a passenger on the *Orient*. Of course, immediately upon making Raceford he commenced looking for your house, which, I must tell you, is famous wherever steamboats——"

"There! That is quite enough an' to spare, Mr. Perkins, an' it plaze ye! You've kissed the blarney stone, sure, an' I knows your tricks, thankin' ye all the same fur the compliment intended."

"Well, the house *is* a good one, and the landlady a kind-hearted woman, tho' I do say it in her presence, and I have urged Mr. Root to secure board and lodging here. I suppose that you can accommodate him? He'll suit you, and the persons you have here. He's an old sailor, tho' not too far in years to make an excellent husband for as young a lass as Mrs. Betsy Buxton."

"Arrah, now; ould Nick fly away wid ye for a regular novelist! Let's have no more on *that* subject, if ye plaze."

Mrs. Buxton's face and hair, for a brief period, were of the same glowing color.

"I was saying," resumed her tormentor, evidently content with having caused her some slight annoyance, "that Mr. Root is a sailor, at present out of employment, and has come here to seek work. He is fairly honest, I think, and will not be long in securing something to keep him from eating the bread of idleness."

"You are quite welcome, sir. The little good me mother and I have, you and the rest shall share wid us!"

Mrs. Buxton preceded the two men to the sitting-room.

"You can stow me away almost anywhere. I don't carry a great amount of luggage at the present time, but have sent for my kit, which will arrive in a few days. Put me in the garret, or in the cellar, or in the kitchen, for the occasion, until you see a chance to change me for the better. I'm not at all hard to please."

18

"As for the matther of that, we hev all the space that is needed."

Excusing herself, when she saw her reflection in the mirror, the widow left the room, but soon returned, with her red hair smoothed down, and her skirts in better trim.

"The house is not crowded," resumed Mrs. Buxton, "an' we've an iligant room on the second floor front, that nades a tinant; an' as fur males to ate—I niver saw the time when praties wor so raisonable or so fine! Wid a roast duck, from the lake, now an' thin, I'm sure we'll be able to kape ye from starvin' enthirely!"

The landlady was evidently desirous of making a favorable impression upon the young man, so fairly spoken of by the captain, whose recommendation carried great weight with her. On the other hand, Root was disposed to like her and her house. As Perkins was about to take his leave, having business connected with the steamer to attend to, he turned to the widow, and, with a mock-severe tone, remarked:

"When I call again of a Sabbath morning, Mrs. Buxton, I shall expect to find you engaged in meditation, and not in house-cleaning."

"Go away wid ye now! An' how could I help it, Captin? Mother and I are cooks, chambermaids, and iverything; and wasn't the ould lady preparin' to be off betimes to church! Oh, the dust it was that broke the Sabbath, and not me own good turkey wing!"

The captain laughed heartily, and bade the lady adieu.

Root, after some moments of pleasant conversation with Mrs. Buxton, retired to his room, which he found quite cleanly and comfortable. He spent the day at the house, making the acquaintance of his fellow-boarders. There were ten or twelve men in the place, all hard-fisted laborers, devoted to rough work, employing rough language, and forming a rough community. But they were generally good-hearted, jovial persons, and, when off duty, quite companionable—even convivial.

As concerned the matter of employment, Root early learned that real work was over for the season, and apparently the only chance left for him was in rafting, piling or loading lumber, or accepting a subordinate position about some of the mills. It was a dull season, taken at its best, and several of his new acquaintances residing with Mrs. Buxton, and who were themselves resting, from lack of demand for their services, thought that he might possibly remain in the vicinity an entire month without labor which would realize even a bare subsistence. As for saving any money, they were unanimous that it was simply out of the question.

Monday came, bright and balmy, and Root made the purchases necessary to keep him in raiment until the arrival of his valise. He then visited the *Orient*, and returned the costume he had borrowed of the captain, with thanks for the accommodation. Perkins heartily made him welcome, but, as he was deeply engaged in stowing away his cargo, the operative did not remain long on board. He left the steamer, and strolled about the town, taking bearings in the West Side and the East Side.

A "drive" of logs was expected down the river before many days, and Root hoped that, when it arrived, he might at least secure a few days' occupation. He thought that he would find an opportunity to try his luck in "riding" a saw-log without getting "dipped." An old logsman volunteered the remark, that, if he could preform this difficult feat, con stant labor in the busy season would be easily attainable.

At all of the numerous places visited, he received an un· varying negative, in response to his application for even a temporary job. The boss sawyers had more help than they needed, and there were loafing upon the wharf dozens of old and experienced hands, who found nothing to do. All were " wait- ing for something to turn up." There was no course left for Root but to assume the role of convivialist, await the coming of his things as patiently as possible, and make preparations for such service to the Agency as he could best put in.

It was not long before he found that, as he had hoped, his friend, the mate of the *Orient*, had very thoroughly circulated the information concerning the new arrival at Mrs. Buxton's being engaged in the smuggling line, and concealing himself from the officers of the law. Of course this gave him good standing at once with those who chanced to find themselves in the same condition, and paved the way to his becoming well acquainted with all who were employed in anything out of the honest way in the lively little community. He therefore passed considerable time in the drinking places and bowling saloons ; treated his companions often enough to be deemed no bar-room sponge ; drank as largely of the liquor dispensed as the stomach might bear without turning in open rebellion, and soon acquired the reputation he coveted, and which would fall in with his designs.

Among the earliest to attract Root's attention was a man called Big Bill Groom, one of a ring of reckless persons of the same kindred, and regarding whom he had listened to consid erable discussion at his boarding place. Bill was of towering and Herculean form, bloated by gross indulgencies, with dark and forbidding features, and general demeanor to match. Grouped with his brother and cousin, they formed a clan bearing a hard reputation in Raceford, however impossible it had been to trace any really criminal acts to their doors. Big Bill had the ague in its chronic form, and was mostly to be found at a French saloon, where Root first met him, in the attempt to drive off the chills with frequent and heavy draughts of fiery liquor. He drank and shook, and shook and drank, until it was quite impossible for him to decide which he had done most of. At night he had many times retired to his bed completely broken down, not infrequently assisted to reach home by some of his chance companions. The detective also learned that, previous to the date of the death of his wife, which event had occurred two years previously, Big Bill held the reputation in the community of a correct, industrious and honest man. The same could not be truthfully said of some of his relatives. He had seldom drank, and never been known to indulge to excess. But when the good woman, the mother of his children, the bride of his younger and better days, was taken away, strength and good resolution seemed to have found burial with her remains. Bill gradually neglected his duty, grew untidy in habit, reckless in language and behavior, and finally lapsed into the unresisting victim of intoxication. He had formerly filled positions of trust and emolument under the direction of the superintendent of the company, but was no longer given work requiring promptitude or undivided attention.

Thinking that a man, who had for so many years been an inhabitant of the town, might know some things necessary for him to become acquainted with, Root approached Big Bill, one day, when that individual was suffering from a "shake" of more than ordinary severity, and, speaking compassionately, inquired how long he had been a victim of the disease.

"Oh, a year or two," responded the sufferer, between his closed teeth, which involuntarily rattled and made his utterances spasmodic and almost unintelligible. "I don't remember a single week that I've missed m' regular chill, since a year ago last month. An' I can say to ye, stranger, if ever ary man tells yer it's fun ter hev th' ager, yer may tell him fur me he's a liar. I'll back yer in't."

It is simply impossible to describe on paper the jerky, hitchity-hitchy, petulant and half-uncourteous style in which the short-clipped words came from the blue lips of the sick man. His whole person was convulsed as though from internal commotion, and he vainly attempted to control his muscles and nerves while he spoke. The effect was to exhaust the patient, and cause the hearer to experience mixed feelings of mirth and commiseration.

"Yes," returned Root, struggling against an almost uncontrollable desire to laugh, "I can feel for you, Mr. —— What may I call your name?"

"Groom—Wil-l'am Groom—but, here'bouts, I'm best known as Bill—Big Bill Groom—ter dis-tin-guish me from a cousin, cal-l'd Lit-tle Bill Groom—curse him!"

"I can pity you, Mr. Groom."

It was a long, long time since Bill had been addressed as "Mr. Groom," and his large, dull gray eyes brightened under the momentary inspiration.

"I can feel for you, Mr. Groom," continued the new

comer. " I have been in the same boat myself, and know it is anything but pleasant. By the way, I'm something of a doctor—tho' more seaman than doctor—and, if you'll come with me for a moment to the nearest drug store, I'll see if I can't fix something that'll relieve you."

Big Bill was inclined to accept, but hesitated.

" No !" he finally replied, " I can't 'low ye t' do it ! I've no money t' fool 'way on med'c'ns ! Really, I think ther's not a bit of hope ! I'm bound t' shake 'til I die !"

" Money makes no difference, shipmate, nor the want of it, either ! I have a little in the locker still, and while a sailor has a dollar he can't see a human being suffer ! So come with me !"

Reluctantly Bill accompanied the sailor to the nearest pharmacy. A few shillings' worth of pure brandy, with a mixture of quinine and cayenne pepper, were procured, and of the preparation Bill swallowed a goodly dose. After a couple of hours had elapsed, he took another, and declared, with more intelligible utterance, that he " felt better." The succeeding stage of the disease was more mild than usual, and the excruciating pain in the bones was perceptibly diminished. The next day, under continued administration of the remedy, Big Bill shook himself cheerily, when asked how he felt, and replied :

" Jist like a water spaniel after a swim—first rate !"

He was subsequently heard to remark, that no man in the diggings need be found saying anything agin the sailor chap, " unless they wanted Big Bill down on 'em !"

CHAPTER III.

Evidence of Striking Regard.

A FEW days later, when Big Bill had in a measure regained his good nature, and a proportion, at least, of his physical strength, Root, at the end of a short search, came upon him on a Saturday night in company with his brother Jo and cousin Little Bill Groom, at Brott's saloon, on the West Side, drinking very liberally and playing bluff and poker rather recklessly. All were more or less influenced by the liquor they had imbibed, and, therefore, equally ready for a fight, or an exhibition of friendly regard. Upon the agent's appearance in their midst, he was seized by Big Bill, who grasped his arm and almost dragged him toward the bar, where he bluntly introduced him to those present as his "friend Root, a newcomer in Raceford, an old sailor, and a right jovial fellow." Of course, the stranger "was glad to meet the company," so he expressed himself, and was by no means laggard in improving the opportunity to corroborate the exalted opinion which had been formed of him through Big Bill's complimentary mention. It was expected, and the freshly arrived man did not disappoint the general understanding, that he would invite the persons in the room to indulge in refreshments at his ex-

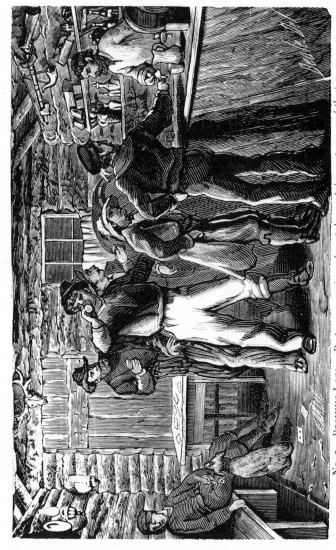

No. 2.   BOOMING LOGS.   *Root was unanimously rated one of the company, and the peer of any "sport" in Raceford.*

Page 417.

pense. Had he taken any other course, it would have been considered uncivil treatment of his companions.

It was remarked that the "sailor chap" accomplished the agreeable task with an exceeding grace, almost proclaiming that he had been accustomed to treating from his boyhood. Not a man refused the proffered glass. On the contrary, all partook with as positive a zest as though rum had been a stranger to their lips for a month. This preliminary once performed, Root was unanimously voted one of the company, and the peer of any "sport" in Raceford.

Jo Groom, the observer soon discovered, was an entirely different individual from Big Bill, his elder brother. Two persons could hardly have been found in the State more dissimilar in figure, face, complexion, and temperament. They presented few outward signs that they were even remote branches of the same family tree. Jo was slimly, yet strongly built; well shaped—in truth, handsomely formed—of about the medium height, had black hair, piercing dark eyes, and finely-molded features. His visage was of that pink-tinged olive which gives the possessor an appearance of having been nurtured under fair Italy's cloudless skies. Wearing a long mustache of silky fineness and raven hue, the remainder of his face was close shaven. A crescent-shaped scar, which, at some period of his life he had received upon the left cheek, marred the general effect of a countenance in other respects remarkably attractive and agreeable.

Clad in his roughly-fashioned attire, which, from its style, showed that in this particular he was peculiarly fastidious, and which set off his graceful figure to an advantage; with a soft, felt hat set jauntily on one side of his head, Jo Groom was,

18+

when fully himself, a man who, had he been transferred to and brought up in a more healthy moral atmosphere, and given a fair opportunity, must have made his mark high above the best of those among whom he moved. An observant person would not pass him upon the street without a second glance. Jo had been tolerably well educated, and was more refined, when he so desired, in the use of language, than his brother, or any of his male relatives. He had enjoyed no special opportunities above those given Big Bill, but had better improved his chances and more industriously cultivated his mind, while the other lad—their parents had but two sons and a daughter, and the latter died in her infancy—walked in a different path, much preferring the gun, dog and game-bag, to masters, books and the rural academy. However well he outwardly appeared, Root was but a short time in learning Jo Groom was a more reckless, more thoroughly unprincipled, man than the larger and more openly wicked Big Bill Groom. For years the younger of the brothers had been the intimate associate of gamblers, addicted to their pursuits, and it was hinted that to his general reputation of gamester and frequenter of haunts of vice might be added that of sensualist and libertine. Drink and evil company had completed his moral wreck long before Root formed his acquaintance.

Little Bill Groom, first cousin of Jo and Big Bill, was a young person whose company was by no means sought by the reputable ladies and gentleman comprising good society in Raceford. He was repudiated by the *elite* of the West Side as well as by that of the East Side. In his diminutive body were centered, crystallized and intensified all the meannesses, vices and crimes of his cousins Bill and Jo, without the least scintilla of manhood, honesty, or rectitude of purpose, for their amelioration or regulation. Where Big Bill and Jo were bad, Little Bill was simply satanic. Where they exhibited littlenesses he was wicked. Where they had odd streaks of virtue in their composition, he gave out only physical turpitude and mental malignity. He was, to employ an aphorism circulating in the town and describing him, "Little Bill, but big villain." He abounded in nerve and pluck and had lived twenty years, dur-ing fifteen of which, at least, he had been a constant terror to all the inhabitants of his neighborhood. Nothing very cruel could occur but it was charged to him. Yet no real crime had been fastened to his skirts. That he was guilty of about two-thirds of the aggregate mischief perpetrated in the place was implicitly believed.

After the first drinks had been taken, Big Bill waxed communicative, drew Root aside, and informed him that he knew something of the trouble his hearer was hiding from, very truly remarking that he held a fellow-feeling for all who were similarly situated, and more especially for one who was good enough to befriend him when down with the shakes, and it was his self-imposed task to go about among the employees and see if he could not find work for a companion. If he secured it, Root was the one who would be benefited. Mr. Slayton, Superintendent for the Raceford Manufacturing Com-pany, was not sure but he would soon require more help, and if so, promised to call upon Big Bill. Jo exerted a powerful influence over Slayton, through the medium of the manager's spouse, who was accused of undue partiality for the handsome woodman, and that power should be employed in Root's be-half. It could be but a few days, he believed, before his comrade would have as good a situation as there was in Raceford. Root was naturally thankful for the efforts put forth to aid him, and made known his feelings in appropriate terms, concluding with the usual proposition to once more treat the company. It was accepted, and the fluids were duly dispensed and absorbed. Subsequently cards were introduced, and Root, who, at home, was looked upon as a fair player, joined in a game, the stake being but a small sum. At first Jo and his brother carried off the honors and the cash, in a majority of instances. This cemented the friendship that the Groom family had conceived for the new-comer. Luck seemed set against Mr. Root. Still he would not give it up. Presently he began to realize winnings. This continued until he had retrieved a portion of his former losses. Meanwhile, the frequent pilgrimages the Grooms had made to the bar told heav ily upon them, and each member of the trio was more or less intoxicated when Root withdrew from the card-table, giving place to an entire stranger, who said his name was Bates, from Canada. For some hours he had been sitting near, an interested spectator, occasionally expressing a desire to participate in the amusement. Bill and Jo Groom, from the moment that he discovered the latter had money about him, seemed to absorb most of his attention. He had watched their movements very narrowly. Bates was a tall, heavily-built man of thirty years, with long, brown hair, bushy whiskers, and small, shrill voice—the latter so disproportionate in volume, when contrasted with his muscular development, as to attract immediate observation. He had arrived in town the preceding day, as he said, to secure work, as a sawyer, in one of the company's mills.

There was something in the stranger's manner and general

appearance that Root did not like from the first, and the style in which he noted the words and actions of the two drunken men, prompted the detective to keep an eye upon him. Bates's early success in the game was good. At first he gained. Then he seemed to lose, but parted with very small sums of money. Finally the tide of fortune appeared to change, and Big Bill, the more deeply intoxicated of the brothers, was the winner, the spoils always coming from Jo, who, having just received his month's wages, was in funds Bates was evidently playing, for some purpose of his own, into Big Bill's hands and against Jo Groom, but so deftly was his work performed that the bystanders could only judge by results, having no ocular evidence that there was any cheating being done.

Root saw as much of the trick as any one, and had his suspicions, but said nothing. He thought that the brothers would settle their matters peaceably on the morrow, without great damage to one or the other; and it was a puzzle to him, at first, why Bates should waste his time on such foolishness when he certainly had a chance to fairly win Jo's funds. He was evidently a proficient in the mysteries of poker, whether truly a sawyer or not. Jo Groom finally grew excited over his brother's unusual good fortune, and raised the "ante" considerably. Big Bill "saw" him and "went fifty dollars better." Jo covered the advance—and lost, his brother holding four deuces. This ended the course, Jo declaring that he was "too drunk to play with even a worse drunkard than himself." Bates grumbled somewhat, but was careful not to go too far, being really quite content to quit where he stood.

It was then two hours into the morning of the Sabbath, and Brott, the saloon-keeper, insisted upon closing the place, in deference to the church-going people, he said, but, as Root thought, because he saw premonitions of a storm brewing between the members of the Groom family. Big Bill was particularly far gone in drink, perceptibly flushed with success, and not sparing of words in coarsely taunting Jo with his want of skill. They were finally separated, and left the saloon, each person pursuing his own route homeward.

Big Bill, as the detective saw, rolled and tossed, making slow progress, like a fishing-smack in a chopping sea. Something suspicious in the movements of Bates caused Root to follow in his wake. He managed to do this without pressing too near him, and in a manner to conceal his proximity from any third party that might be in the neighborhood. His movements were noiseless. The night was very dark, excepting when, at long intervals, the black clouds were removed from before the face of the moon, but the operative kept within ear-shot of his man, and was soon rewarded, as they were passing through a dense grove of pines, by hearing some person conversing with Big Bill.

He was about to leave the trail and return, thinking that Groom had encountered one of his neighbors, when the peculiarly shrill voice of Bates distinctly met his ear. He quickly changed his mind and hastened rapidly forward to prevent any game which might be meditated by the stranger. Before he could gain the locality, however, there came a muffled, crushing sound, followed by a dull thud upon the earth, seemingly caused by some heavy falling body. Starting on a rapid run, the agent soon became satisfied, though all was silent, that he was nigh the spot whence the noise had proceeded. The moon gave light at this moment, and in his pathway he saw Bates, bending over the prostrate form of Big Bill.

The meeting with Root was a startling surprise to Bates, who attempted to escape. Drawing his heavy revolver, the detective struck the villain a stinging blow over the head. It was a glancing stroke, however, and only stunned its recipient, producing an ugly and bleeding scalp-wound. It was sufficient to give Root the advantage, which he improved by pouncing upon the thief. Bates soon recovered his coolness, and attempted to break from his opponent's grasp, but, failing, he was quiet physically, saying:

"I'll be even with you for this."

The remark was accompanied by a movement of the right hand toward the hip, as though to draw a pistol or other weapon. His antagonist was prepared for this, and, by the light of the moon, Bates soon saw the forbidding dark muzzle of a pistol in uncomfortable proximity to his head. Recognizing his powerlessness under the circumstances, he sullenly dropped his hands by his side. "I give it up. Don't fire. I surrender," he said.

"Then throw down your weapon," commanded Root.

Bates let fall his pistol, which he had secured from the pocket and previously held, partly concealed, in his right hand, cocked and ready to be discharged.

"Now stop where you are, or it will go hard with you."

Root continued for a moment to hold his weapon pointed in Bates's direction, while he gently touched Big Bill with the toe of his boot.

"What have you done to him?"

Bates made no response, neither did Bill move or speak.

"What's up, Bill? Answer your friend. Tell me you are not killed." And the operative lowered his revolver, while he felt of the neck of the prostrate man. The artery responded to his touch, but with a weak, fluttering beat, as though life within the body were faintly struggling with almost victorious death. Shaking the supine form rather rudely, he sought to recall the man to consciousness. In the meantime the captive stood still, making no second effort to get away, knowing that he was closely watched by Root.

Presently Big Bill moved, turned uneasily on his side, opened his eyes, and, recognizing his friend, as well as the surroundings, he said :

"Guess I'm almost killed."

"Where are you hurt ?"

"On the head—it's worse nor the agur !"

Big Bill was evidently recovering very fast.

"What did he hit you with ?"

"His fist, I guess, tho' 'twas harder nor my head."

"See if your money is safe."

After several fruitless efforts, Big Bill at last sat up, searched his pockets, and, looking scowlingly upon the thief, said :

"It's all gone ! He's got it !"

"Can you find strength to search him ? I'll hold him powerless."

"I'll try !"

Big Bill finally arose, his limbs making many uncertain movements, and, with unsteady gait, walked up to Bates.

"Give me back my money," he said, in a thick voice, "give it me, or, by ——, I'll kill you !"

Before the thief could respond, seeing the discarded pistol lying glittering in the grass, Big Bill stooped, picked up the weapon, and would have shot Bates, unarmed as he was, upon the spot, had not Root promptly struck up his hand.

"Hold! Don't fire!" he said. "We must deliver the rascal to the officials! He deserves killing, but let the law take its course!"

Then pointing to Groom, who stood, fairly trembling with rage, his hand holding the weapon extended, Root continued:

"Bates, turn that money over to its owner!"

Thus persuaded, the stranger gave back to Bill his roll of currency.

Upon searching Bates's person, brass knuckles, bearing sanguinary evidences of having been recently used, were discovered. It was with that deadly instrument the blow prostrating Big Bill had been given. Happily, Groom's skull was unnaturally thick, otherwise the stroke would have resulted in death. Binding up his hurts as well as possible, Root tied Bates's hands securely behind, and the three personages proceeded to the county jail, where the would-be assassin was given in charge of the proper officer.

After visiting a drug store and a surgeon with Bill, and seeing that his cuts received proper attention, Root accompanied the now thoroughly sobered woodman to his residence. Big Bill's gratitude knew no limit. But for Root's interference he might have been murdered, as well as robbed. But for Root the dastardly scoundrel would have made his escape—not to speak of the relief his medicine had previously brought when he was down with the ague.

"I'll not forget you, neither will Jo! And Jo *is* a man of

influence here, if he *is* my brother, and if, as I believe, I *am* nobody!"

Bidding the injured man "good-morning"—for the East was growing gray with the coming dawn—Root returned to his boarding-house, his room, and slept.

CHAPTER IV.

Root Makes a Discovery.

IT is not strange that Big Bill awoke at a late hour Sunday morning, suffering from pain which he not very elegantly described as a " shocking bad headache." He said he thought the shakes were bad enough, but the knocks he had received with the brass knuckles, from the hands of Bates, had left behind sensations with which, in range of discomfort, those accompanying fever and ague were not at all comparable. Dr. Gallup, who was called in, looked exceedingly wise, after examining the wounds, which were happily on the thicker portion of the very thick skull, and, shaking his head sagely a number of times, exclaimed that there had possibly been con tusion of the outer walls of the cranium, and there was immi- nent danger that congestion might supervene and communicate to the brain proper, from the abraded *dura mater*, or substance covering the contents of the cranial cavities. Should his fears be confirmed, recovery would be doubtful. The condition of the patient's physical system made inflammation easy. How- ever, were the symptoms to abate during the night, when he would come again, there might then arise hopes that the injuries to the delicate membrane had been slight, and the man would soon be as well as ever.

[427]

Big Bill listened to the venerable physician's learned disquisition, barely able to grasp but a small portion of his meaning, and replied :

" I hope so, for the ague's better nor these pains, which cut both ways at onst !"

Towards evening the patient lapsed into a calm and peaceful slumber, which lasted for several hours, and, when he awoke, the blood-shot eyes were perceptibly cleared up ; the pinched and anxious expression of the countenance was gone, the skin feeling moist and warm, and the heart beating naturally and regularly.   The reaction had taken place, and, as yet, no symptoms of brain disease presented themselves.   Nigh midnight Dr. Gallup came in, and Bill surprised him with :

" Well, Doctor, the Drum-major is all correct, isn't it ?"

He intended to throw back at the physician one of his half-remembered terms, " *dura mater*," and the man of drugs and herbs laughed heartily over the confusion of ideas, which he did not pause to correct, but continued his examination of the patient's pulse, and then said :

" You're better !   We may even safely say that the crisis has been passed, and from this time forward, with good nursing, you will gradually convalesce."

It was true, Big Bill was in no present danger.

Root also slept longer than usual, but had no hurts to recover from, excepting those inflicted upon the stomach and brain through a debauch, to which it is customary to give little, if any, heed, and he arose, comparatively well, in good season for dinner.   According to custom, he was honored with a chair near that of the landlady, who invariably sat at the head of the board and poured the coffee, with which every dinner in that house was prefaced, while the remainder of the dishes were passed from hand to hand, in the good, old-fashioned, backwoods fashion.

The new arrival was already a favorite with nearly all the boarders; more from the fact, however, that he always had a smile and a cheerful word with which to greet every one, than from the general understanding that Mrs. Buxton was occasionally caught casting her blue eyes in his direction. In truth, Jones, the "oldest boarder," who had zealously courted the widow for more than a year, to the no small disgust of others, who were themselves anxious to take the same course, felt that Root was in a fair way to cut him out; hence the aforesaid Jones put on a sour expression, looked as surly as his round and expressionless face and milk-and-water eyes would permit, and usually sought to pick flaws in the sailor's general deportment.

But Root kept his allotted place near the head of the table, and only laughed the more and tried the harder to treat the acrid fellow, who kept a small grocery store almost opposite Mrs. Buxton's house, with courtesy and cordiality. Under this regimen, Jones was first very mad, then madder, then maddest. But the widow and the new-comer seemed to care little, and even pretended not to notice the mental pangs and jealous tortures of the disappointed suitor. Others were not so lenient, however, and did see. They poked fun at Jones unmercifully.

On this particular Sunday, Root did not look or really feel as well as was natural with him. He was not precisely ill, but there lurked a sense of unrest about his mind, and a remnant of bad whisky in his system, which tended to less joviality than usually characterized him. He saw at a glance, when he entered the long, low dining-hall, that his connection with the late affair between Big Bill and Bates had just been under discussion, and he determined not to be the first to recall the subject. He therefore commenced to talk to the disaffected Jones about duck-hunting, of which the dealer in molasses and green tea knew about as much as Root did of the profession of preaching. Jones retorted by a sickly grin, intended to be sarcastic, and said he didn't hunt. He "was a man of peace, and didn't believe in shooting harmless water-fowl."

"But you eat ducks, when cooked?" asked the operative.

"Yes; but that's another thing," responded Jones. " I drink tea, but I don't kill Chinamen!"

"An' phat is it you are talking about?" asked Mrs. Buxton. "Whativer it is, all of us want to hear something else Let us know who wor killed an' wounded this mornin'!"

"What was it that you were remarking?" asked Root, assuming an air of innocence.

"Oh, the murther an' the robbery, an' all that! Sure, an it's yourself that knows what we mane, so don't ye kape us starvin' fur all the worruld like so many ducks waitin' fur to be fed."

Root acknowledged that he knew of no murder. True, there had been a robbery in the place; it had been found out; the person stolen from had recovered his money; Big Bill was in bed with a sore head; a man named Bates was in jail with another battered pate, the last-mentioned personage being charged with crime, and having before him a prospect of doing the State some service in the penitentiary.

"Jist hear him, now!" exclaimed Mrs. Buxton's mother, an elderly dame, who always sat at the landlady's right hand, "the most tidy, fidgety little woman" that ever wore white lace cap and smoked a clay pipe in the chimney nob. "Oh, hear him! he was there! an' there was no murder, afther all! Did ye iver see sich a wicked falsifier as that same Andy Burch, who wasn't there, but said he wur, an' who comes here this blissid day an' tells us that Mr. Root had clane kilt the robbin' thafe of the worruld, an' helped to bury him afther midnight! Worra! worra! did I ever hear such a liar? The future punishment of some persons nade be hard above the common. An' there was no murder, afther all?"

"No, Mrs. McCarty, there was no person killed."

"Musha! An' Raceford is to be baten by that miserable Rockton, which had an enthire suicide, all to itself, only a wake ago it was last Wednesday!"

And the nervous old lady wiped her eyes and threw back the wide ruffles of her new cap, adorned with the lavender ribbons, as though very indignant that somebody had not been put out of the way. She "wondered why Rockton should have a monopoly of such things, leaving its rival, Raceford, behind?" Still Mrs. McCarty was the kindest-hearted old lady in the place, and would shed tears over an accident to a neighbor's pet kitten.

"Whisht, now, mother," said Mrs. Buxton. "We are glad to learn, so we are, that no person was mortally injured."

"An' to be sure we are—but that lying spalpeen, Andy Burch! Jist wait till he comes forninst me again!"

Here the conversation became general, and various topics were discussed, but the talk was constrained and uninteresting until Root had related, in a modest way, the truth of the affair in which he had participated. It was noticed by Jones, who seemed to watch narrowly to see the effect, that when the

young man spoke of the pistol which Bates had purposed using upon him, the widow turned pale, and her hand trembled
perceptibly as she prepared a second cup of coffee for some
one. Mrs. McCarty grew powerfully excited, and had to be
quieted by her daughter. Jones looked on, a glum, sulky and
lowering individual. " Poor Jones !" This was the mental
remark of all who appreciated his uncomfortable condition.

After dinner, in the widow's own sitting-room, to which he
had been invited by both ladies, Root entered more fully into
particulars. The result was that Mrs. Buxton mildly rebuked
him for " kaping such company," and said, feelingly :

" It is a shame so dacint a young gintleman should be afther
roaming about the streets of Raceford at the dead hour of
night wid such a bad, mane set as the Grooms, who are the
divil's own imps—especially Jo and Little Bill."

The new-comer was advised to steer clear of the entire
crew. As the contrary course was in the exact line of his
duty, however, Root, after patiently listening to his landlady's
remarks, promised he would " think of it." He did so, and
arrived at the conclusion that he was compelled to continue
the acquaintance so auspiciously commenced. While Big Bill,
Jo and Little Bill Groom might have nothing to do with stealing logs, or selling such as had been stolen to the mills, and
although they might not, in person, drive iron dogs into timber to break costly saws and endanger valuable lives, they were
of the exact class of men who undoubtedly would know something about these transactions, and as to the identity of the
persons engaged in their perpetration. Undoubtedly it was
Root's task to keep up his intimacy with the Groom family.

Wandering down the main street of the place, a little later

the same Sunday afternoon, the operative encountered Jo Groom, sauntering leisurely along, dressed in his best, toward Mr. Slayton's residence, where he sometimes passed an hour or two of a Sabbath evening. Whether his visits were agreeable to Mr. Slayton, or the contrary, Mrs. Slayton, as the scandal-mongers of the West Side, as well as those of the East Side, were united in saying, was not averse to his presence.

Root was received by Jo with more than usual cordiality, and his hand was shaken with fraternal warmth. Jo had heard the particulars of the attempted robbery from Big Bill, to whom, upon learning of his troubles, he had paid an early visit, and he was keenly touched by the evidences of the devotion of this new-found friend, which he had received from his brother's lips. He was greatly beholden to Root. He would never forget him for saving Bill's life, and shrewdly thwarting the villain, Bates. Again he proffered his assistance in securing anything that was attainable in Raceford. He was on his way to Slayton's house to secure something for his friend to do. Root was pleased, in turn, and spent some time in agreeable conversation, when it was finally arranged that, Tuesday of the same week, they should take a trip to Pine Log Bridge, some distance up the course of the Lotus, in company, and shoot duck, there reputed very plentiful. Monday they would not be able to leave, as Bates's examination had been fixed for that date, but the next day they could go as well as not, both being for that time unemployed.

Jo volunteered to secure the loan of Slayton's gun for his own immediate use, and allow Root to carry his, which was a considerable exhibition of friendship on Jo's part, as he seldom

19

permitted any one to hunt with his fowling-piece, by which he set great store.

Then the two men separated, Jo walking away, setting his hat more jauntily than ever on one side of his head, taking the direct route to Slayton's elegant mansion, while the detective, still unknown as such to all in Raceford, passed on to the river, and thence southward, along the edge of one of the races, or auxiliary mill-courses, from which the town had received its name, to the neighborhood of Ligon's Mill. The trip was taken, partly to find out if the *Orient* still remained in port, and partly for another purpose, connected with his business in the locality. He discovered that the steamer was gone, having departed during the previous night, and was not expected back for several weeks.

After looking about him in a seemingly careless manner, Root discovered something worthy of examination, and sat down, in the shade cast by a huge pile of lumber, near Ligon's Mill, to study over the thing he had seen. It was an enjoyable position, cooled by the fresh breeze which, that day, floated down the valley watered by the river. While thus reposing, he was joined by Little Bill Groom, who had been engaged in fishing for rock-bass some distance further down the Lotus. Root, while none too well pleased by the interruption, civilly invited the young reprobate to take a seat near him.

"Don't care if I do," said Bill the little, with his big *basso profundo* tone—a voice so deep and strong as to be notable when contrasted with the size of the speaker—who was small, active, wiry and weasel-like. He had the vocal compass found in the heavier pipes of the church organ. One expected to see the form of the young man quiver and perhaps burst asunder in giving utterance to his words. "Don't care if I do," said Little Bill, as he rested himself not far from the operative. "Bin out fishin'. Got a few shiners. But they don't bite well to day How are you, anyhow, since the rampagings and hittings of last night?"

Little Bill was informed of Root's very good health, and also of the fact that Jo had just been encountered on his way to Slayton's. Little Bill received the last-mentioned item of intelligence with a shrewd and slightly contemptuous shrug of his little rounded shoulders, and remarked, in his big, sonorous voice:

"I don't half like Jo's going to Slayton's so much. He's already got hisself inter one bloody muss there, bin told his room's better nor his company, an' I should think he'd know enough to stay away. But seems as how he won't take no sort of a hint, without a kick, an' I'm thinkin' that 'fore many days, like's not old man Slayton'll give him both hint an' kick, an' the kick 'll come fust. But Jo's tender place is wimmen. Mine and Big Bill's is whisky. I s'pose Mrs. Slayton, who's some years younger nor her husband, has taken a sort o' notion to Jo, an' it's got to be the talk of the town, both sides the river, an' I wouldn't be surprised to come afoul o' Jo's dead body, some mornin' early, when I'm out arter the cows, with a charge o' buckshot in the head. I tell yer, stranger, 'tain't no nice thing fur to go foolin' round arter none of these yer rapid married ladies, even tho' they sets a trap fur ye. It's a dangerous game. Fur my part, give me ducks and fishes. They don't never go back on a feller, and fishes 'specially allus bites when they're hungry, an' when it rains, an' flies and sich is scarce. I've warned Jo mor'n wonst. If he can't take the warnin', he'll hev to suffer the consikinses."

Suddenly Little Bill dropped his fishing-pole, pointed with his finger in the direction of some lumber, and exclaimed:

"By ——, look there!"

Many of the boards were resting on the ground, just as they were dumped from the feed-carriage of the saw-mill, consequently they held about the relative positions they had occupied while in the log.

"I don't see anything! What is it?" innocently queried Root.

"I didn't know that the Ligons belonged to the gang," said Little Bill, in response. "But, look there! Do you see that di'mond H? It's Hi Hooker's mark, an' Ligon's mill's been cuttin' up Hooker's logs, or I'm a pesky muskrat!"

"Well," returned Root, with apparent unconcern, "I don't doubt that the Ligons have bought the logs, or that they got into their boom quite accidentally!"

"'Bought 'em!' 'Accident!' All in yer eye, Mr. Root! Old Ligon buy other men's logs? He's not so green, when he can git 'em fur almost nuthin'! No!—Yet that ar' log with the di'mond H onto its end was Hooker's property—but I'll not say anything about it! 'Twont pay!"

"As for me," returned Root, "I'm sure that I've got no interest in mentioning what I've seen! But I can't imagine how those little marks on the ends of the boards show that the log was stolen!"

This was said as a feeler, to cause Little Bill to talk, and it had the intended effect.

"You see them creases on the ends of the boards? Well,

they're made with a scratcher, suthin like a gouge on the end of one leg of a pair of dividers, which makes straight or crooked lines on the butt-end of the saw-log when first cut and scaled. Each mill-owner has his reg'lar mark, which is recorded in the nearest magestrate's office, an' law purtects 'em in owner-ship of all logs as has their sign onto 'em. Now pile eight or ten o' them widest boards a-top of each other an' you'll find they'll fit together, an', barrin what's bin cut away by the saws, will make up the 'rig'n'l log, with the di'mond H on to its end."

Root saw very readily that Little Bill's description, while it was not so complete as the one that Mr. Warner had previously given him of the same process, was quite correct. Before him was truly some stolen lumber. He made mental note of the fact. After Bill had exhausted his store of information concerning marking and scaling (measuring) logs, with the usual processes of obliterating the characters by sledge-hammers, or sawing off the butts of the log and then re-marking them, and been listened to by Root—who, judging from his actions, must have considered his revelations of very little interest—he arose, gathered his fishing-tackle together, bid the stranger " good evening," and waddled away homeward, for his supper. With rod over one shoulder, a small string of bass in the left hand, and the right swinging carelessly at his side; a big bunch of his straight, black hair sticking from the dilapidated crown of his straw hat and fluttering in the breeze; with dirty, bare feet; pantaloons turned up from their bottoms half-way to the wear-er's knees, and a long and spacious, much-tattered and soiled, but once brown linen coat, nearly sweeping the ground and bulging out behind in the wind, as he walked, he presented a picture of active, rugged rascality that an artist would have delighted in portraying. Little Bill of the big voice had been comparatively successful that afternoon, hence was uncommonly cheerful, and, while he plodded on toward the house that he called his home, seeking some of the less-frequented streets, probably from deference to the church-going residents of the West Side, he hummed the quaint and ancient ballad, each stanza of which closed:

> "My name is Captain Kidd,
> As I sail, as I sail!"

When left alone, Root, without making himself particu larly noticeable—in fact, quite the reverse—found, through rapid personal examination, that Ligon's mill had not only worked up Hooker's logs into boards, but had served those belonging to and bearing the marks of several other proprietors in the same manner. Among these the detective succeeded in jotting down on a stray bit of paper the following: Four marked ⟨H⟩ ; one marked (B) (Raceford Booming & Manu-facturing Company's design); four marked Ɛ̄ ; three marked F ; one marked ⚇ ; two marked X ; one marked ⚹ ; and others, not bearing their own sign, L^N. Of course, the majority of the boards in the yard rightfully belonged there.

Here was one point gained. Root returned unobserved to Mrs. Buxton's house, and, at a late hour that night, wrote and mailed to me a report, detailing the circumstances related in this chapter. It is unnecessary to say that the earlier part of the night had been passed in Widow Buxton's little back parlor.

Poor Jones!

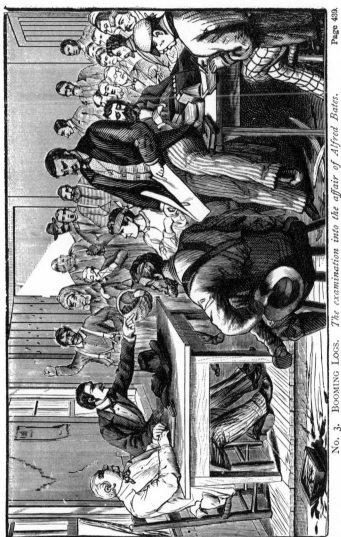

No. 3.   Booming Logs.   *The examination into the affair of Alfred Bates.*

Page 439.

CHAPTER V.

Raceford Justice.

THE examination into the affair of Alfred Bates, charged upon affidavit of Big Bill, otherwise William Groom, and Jasper Root, with the high crimes of robbery and assault with intent to commit murder, under the State statutes, was necessarily held before two magistrates of competent jurisdiction. Justice Simmons, the West Side official, summoned to his assistance Elihu Tillman, the East Side magnate, and at ten A. M. the Monday following the trouble, they jointly occupied the little, tabled and slightly elevated platform at one end of the small, dingy court-room, sitting upon the two high-backed, splint-bottomed office chairs, denominated, for the nonce, the judges' bench.

Mr. Simmons was stout, stumpy, florid, blue-eyed and red-haired. He had formerly consumed brandy habitually, thus providing a rubicund wrapper for his jolly, big bottle-nose, and many a flaming carbuncle upon either rosy cheek. He was now a temperate man. He dressed carelessly, spoke gruffly and stutteringly, and usually decided suits justly. Wanting in scholarship and writing with hesitancy, as for inditing a correct legal document he could no more accomplish that feat than " squeeze himself through an alderman's ring."

[439]

The impediment in his speech detracted materially from the lucidity of his legal decisions and marred the solemnity befitting nuptial ceremonies. In the latter he was frequently obliged to officiate. He was also subject to seasons of mental abstraction—absent-mindedness. In one of these he so badly blundered as to pronounce the newly-wedded pair " m-m-m-an and w-w-wife—and m-m-may G-g-g-od h-have m-m-ercy on your s-s-souls !" He was thinking of a convict that Judge Wallow would have to sentence to be hanged during the next month. But, withal, " 'Squire Simmons," as he was usually called, comported himself like the upright, honorable man that he was, and certainly became a good judge of the distilled uice of the grape, sometimes described as " old Cognac "—so good a judge that he quit the use of it—if not of the points in a complicated suit at law.

Justice Tillman, of the East Side, was thin and lath-like in figure, and finical as to dress and demeanor. Not very tall, but mentally and physically a prodigious man—in his own mature and deliberate estimation. With stiff, dark hair, brushed backward and upward from a low, narrow forehead, and carefully tucked behind a prominent pair of flabby, amply-spreading ears ; with small, suspicious black eyes ; with bushy brows, which came together across the root of a turned-up nose, which seemed always to be snuffing some bad odor in the atmosphere ; with no beard upon his jaundiced face ; with thin, pursed-up lips, and sharp, squirrel teeth ; long visage and a mock-majestic mien, the Justice of the Peace from the East Side was oracular, opinionated, high-flown in language, and a graduate of the academy at Yorkville. Quite Chester-fieldian in his written style, in his own judgment and understanding, he articulated hoarsely and with a muscular effort, as though perpetually suffering from a " frog in the throat." One great point that he usually made in the delivery of his opinions or findings in cases, was to flourish an immaculate pocket-handkerchief and blow his musical proboscis violently, as though to give point and emphasis to his sonorous sentences. He was always anxious to have Skoob, the editor of the *East Side Bugle of Liberty*, present, and nigh at hand, to make extended note of his legal utterances, especially those styled by their author covering " the civil aspects of the subject."

Simmons did not " care a Continental," he sometimes stutteringly remarked, " for the Press, and dried-up old Jobson, of the *West Side Bird of Freedom*, might come and hear, or stay away, whichever suited him best. As for Skoob and his East Side penny trumpet, whatever he or it reported he did not mind, and no sensible person in Raceford would for a moment seriously consider." Simmons also used a handkerchief, and his proboscis was more trumpet-toned than Tillman's. In this they were alike. In all other things different.

The hour had arrived.

Deputy Sheriff Babb opened Court in his usual style, which was nothing if not informal, and the two magistrates sat, alert and stiffly erect, behind their primitive pine table.

At the left, and before the justices, was the witness box, an old, ill-used, splint-bottom chair, without a vestige of a back, and suffering from one shaky leg. To the right was the prisoner's bar, another wreck of a common chair, with a broad shingle replacing the worn-out seat, and both of its forward supports very unreliable. Across the remainder of the apartment were ranged tiers of rough, wooden benches, without

19*

bars or rests for the occupants' spines, unplaned and un
painted, yet by no means wanting in color; in truth, much
tobacco-juice and smoke had stained them of a dirty yellow
from end to end, and their upper surfaces had acquired polish
from frequent contact with posterior portions of numberless
coarse pairs of pantaloons. In front of the judge's desk ran a
narrow shelf, for the use of attorneys. At one extremity,
next to the prisoner, who was in his place, stolid, unkempt
and sullen, appeared Mr. Little, a prominent criminal lawyer
of the place, who had been retained by Bates for his defense.
Little whittled away upon a bit of soft wood, with his pen-
knife, and worked his corkscrew face into divers and sundry
fantastic but unhandsome shapes, as he mentally reviewed the
intricate paths through which he must lead his client if they
shunned the highway to the penitentiary.

Mr. Jacobs, the District Attorney, rested quietly at the
other end of the shelf, or stand. He was gentlemanly, placid,
fresh-looking, and reputed a sound, sensible lawyer.

Little was towering in stature, bony in build, unprincipled
in character, as well as generally brutal and abusive in his
treatment of witnesses and opposing counsel, although possessing a flow of native eloquence which he could employ when
absorbed in a particularly knotty case. Bates's matter was
believed, by those who knew Little intimately, to be a hard
one to handle, judging from the many eccentric curves and
grimaces into which the lawyer wrought his features, and the
diligence with which he slashed away at his pine stick, fashion-
ing nothing, but throwing off large shavings, recklessly and
nervously.

Skoob sat at one end of the lawyers' table, wide awake,

note-book in hand and spectacles on nose. Jobson was in his place, at the opposite side of the smoke-begrimed court-room, more than half asleep, as Horace Greeley is said often to have been when attending meetings, but taking in, at the same time, and mentally jotting down, all that transpired about him, thinking up a sensational heading for an article in preparation for his paper, which, in his elegant way of describing it, "should make Rome (Raceford) howl again !"

Judge Simmons, the crime having been committed within his district, called out :

" L-l-l-little B-b-b-bill G-g-g-groom !"

Little Bill swaggered forward, his long, coarse, black hair sticking out in almost every direction, and seated himself uneasily and sidewise upon the witness chair. His testimony did not amount to much, and was given in his own peculiarly crooked and disjointed manner, his bass voice causing the windows to rattle. He knew little of the main circumstances, excepting that Bates played in Big Bill's interest, as against Jo. He thought such conduct very " sing'l'r !" Little Bill left the stand.

" B-b-b-big B-b-b-bill G-g-g-groom !" was then the call made by Squire Simmons, and that personage, very pale, his head bandaged, rough-whiskered and shaky of leg, limped along the hall, making the floor quake, and very cautiously occupied the witness seat, having due knowledge of the frailty and uncertainty of the structure. He related the substance of the circumstances attending the robbery, adding that Bates, when he had first overtaken him, Sunday morning, pretended that he wished to help, in a friendly way, to bring him to his home. The next moment Bates had struck the drunken man over the head with the intention of maiming, if not killing, and then robbing him. Big Bill was not very closely cross-examined by Little. After Brott, the saloon keeper, had given in testimony, principally bearing upon occurrences at his place, Justice Sim-mons called:

"J-j-j-jasper R-r-r-root!" and that individual filled the vacant chair. It was observed by some that, at this stage of proceedings, Little sharpened his pencil and prepared to note down something; Tillman brightened up; Simmons grew a shade more crimson in the face; Skoob turned over a new leaf; Jobson ceased his snoring; Babb, the deputy, walked nearer to his prisoner, and the spectators hitched about uneasily on the benches, while a number coughed and cleared their throats ex-citedly. Root naturally remarked these unusual symptoms, and wondered what might be in the wind. He was very soon enlightened.

Justice Tillman, assisted and directed by Jacobs, first inter-rogated the witness; and all went smoothly enough until it came Little's time for cross-examination. The lawyer correctly concluding that, if he could break down this part of the testi-mony, he might yet succeed in winning his case, had held his chief forces in reserve, to dash them, as he expected, with crushing effect upon the sailor's devoted head. He commenced in a harsh and arrogant manner by proposing unimportant and even impertinent questions, perhaps to test the metal of his subject. Encounter succeeded encounter, and in every one the lawyer came off only second best. This had consumed some minutes, when Root noticed Jones, "Poor Jones!" sitting in one corner, a deeply-interested and apparently delighted audi-tor. Then the plot instantaneously flashed through the operative's brain. The jealous-pated grocer was at the bottom of the annoyances that Little had been giving and was preparing for him. Having the key, however, the witness believed he could solve the riddle to his own satisfaction, if not to that of the entire assemblage.

"You say, Mr. Root," queried Little, in a softened and would-be-insinuating tone of voice, "that you suspected the defendant, and therefore followed him. Be so kind as to inform the Court *why* you suspected Bates!"

"He played into Big Bill's hands—Bill being very drunk —when he (Bates) had shown, by an exhibition of superior skill, that he could easily have won the money himself. Second, Bates had previously watched Bill and Jo, and particularly noticed the size of Jo's pile of money. Third, the prisoner left the saloon ahead of the rest, and stopped, after walking a little distance, waiting, on Big Bill's direct route homeward. Fourth, as I moved along, before reaching the grove, I heard footsteps near, and they were not made by Groom, but sounded like those of the prisoner."

"That'll do, Mr. Root. You were not called here to make a speech! Tell the Court where you were born."

"In Edinburgh, Scotland."

"Your age?"

"Twenty-eight."

"How long have you resided in this country?"

"Twelve years."

"Were you ever convicted of any crime?"

"No! And I never had an occasion for employing a pettifogger for any purpose whatever."

Applause from the audience told the witness that he had

struck the right chord. Mr. Justice Simmons attempted to cry "Order in the Court!" but had hardly reached his third stuttering repetition of "Or-," when Justice Tillman came to his assistance, and completed the sentence with a profoundly audible "der in the Court!" followed by a resounding note from his nasal trumpet, partly muffled by the white pocket-handkerchief, which startled the citizens and restored silence. Mr. Little whittled away still more vigorously at his piece of shingle, and started on a new tack.

"Mr. Root, tell the Court where you lived before coming to Raceford."

"For a couple of days, at Trafton."

"Where before going to Trafton?"

"Chicago."

"In what business?"

"Sailing."

"On what vessel?"

"The schooner *Maria*, Charles Walker, owner, Captain Boyer, master."

"What is your business here?"

"To enter upon some employment."

"Had you any other calling, while a resident of Chicago, other than sailing?"

"Yes. I was, for a time, porter in Smith, Walker & Co.'s wholesale grocery house, on South Water street, where Jones, of this city, formerly bought his stock. Just before I left, however, Jones's credit gave out, and the firm refused to trust him for any more goods——"

"Stop! stop!" interrupted Little. "I protest! I appeal to the Court if the witness has not exceeded his bounds!"

"But Mr. Little seems to have no bounds, as concerns his questions," explained Root.

Upon hearing the allusion to Jones, attention was so gener ally concentrated upon the grocer, that his malicious enjoyment was brought to a sudden conclusion; he soon sneaked out of the room, and was seen no more during the continuance of the investigation. It had chanced, just at the very moment Root's mind reverted to the Chicago wholesale firm, that he remembered where he first saw the jealous Jones, whose face had, all along, been strangely familiar to him. The operative had been engaged upon peculiar service, ostensibly as Smith, Walker & Co.'s porter, for several months, and he did not fear further recognition, hence could not resist the temptation to repay Jones for setting Little after him.

Order was soon restored, and Little once more changed his course.

"You say that you found Big Bill lying upon the ground, insensible, and the defendant stooping over him. What was the color of Bates's clothing?"

"He now wears the same things—the Court can judge of their color."

"It was a dark night?"

"When the moon did not shine."

"What did Bates do when you arrived?"

"Tried to run off."

"What did you do?"

"Caught him by the coat collar, and then thumped his head gently with my pistol."

"Do you carry pistols?"

"When I happen to be with a thief."

A sensation in the crowd informed the witness that his words and acts were again approved.

"Couldn't Bates have been captured without being pounded?"

"Couldn't he have robbed Big Bill without hammering him?"

"That's not answering my question. Were you compelled to strike the prisoner?"

"I was. He prepared to draw a weapon; and you wouldn't have a man stand still and be shot, would you?"

"Did he produce a pistol?"

"He did, but quickly saw that it would be of no use, as the muzzle of my repeater was close to his cheek, and he wilted."

"Wilted?"

"Yes."

"And, pray, what is that?"

"It's about what you did, Mr. Little—begging pardon of the Court—when I spoke of Grocery Jones, awhile ago. You shouldn't have lent yourself to badger me, because Jones dislikes me and wanted you to."

Little was cornered again. There was a roar of laughter from the direction of the seats, and Babb, the Deputy Sheriff, had to cram nearly all of his pocket-handkerchief into his mouth to keep from joining in the same sort of disturbance. Both justices shouted "Order! Order!" in their respective and strangely dissonant voices, and presently comparative silence was secured.

"None of your impudence, witness, if you please; but a clear and direct answer to my questions."

"Certainly, sir."

" Did Bates really make any attempt to kill you ?"

" He drew his weapon and held it, cocked, ready for use, in a threatening attitude. You may call that an attack, if you wish. It was as nigh one as I desire a man like Bates to get when I'm around !"

" How do you know the lock of the pistol was set ?"

" It was at full-cock when Big Bill picked it up, and is so still. That's the pistol—the one upon the table before you."

Here was another halting-place for Little. Skoob started spasmodically, and dropped his note-book ; Jobson opened his eyes ; even the magistrates were interested, and the prisoner, who had previously been gazing upon vacancy, looked up at Little and seemed to be talking lowly to himself, his words sounding somewhat different from those of a heartfelt bene-diction.

Little began again :

"Mr. Root, did you see the prisoner take Big Bill's money ?"

" I did not. As I said before—— "

" Never mind what you 'said before'! *Did* you see Bates searching Bill's pockets ?"

" As I said before—again begging pardon of the Court—I did not. Bates was bending over, and his hands resting upon Bill's body. I can't say he was searching his pockets, but I do say he was neither choking him nor pulling off his boots, and his hands were in the vicinity of the hip pocket, in which, but a few moments earlier, at Brott's saloon, I had seen Groom deposit a considerable roll of currency."

" What did Bill do when he arose ? "

" Well, Bill was naturally very mad ; I was not at all

pleased, and—'as I said before'—by our united exertions **we** induced Bates to restore the money he had stolen—at least, some bank notes which were recognized as Bill's property. They were folded up in a bit of the *West Side Bird of Freedom*, which had Groom's name written on its margin."

Skoob dropped his note-book again.

After a long and tedious examination, resulting in no disadvantage to the prosecution, Little gave the sailor up as a hard case, with the remark :

" That's all—you are a sharp witness ! "

" I'm glad you think so ! Wish I could say the same of you, regarding your capabilities as an attorney, but I can't ! "

Again the building was shaken, even to its foundations, with illy-suppressed evidences of appreciation from the backwoodsmen. Root took his former seat, the lawyers had their say, closing very briefly, and, after a few minutes' consultation, both magistrates united in holding the defendant in two thousand dollars bail for trial at the ensuing term of the Circuit Court. As he could not make up the bond, he had to remain in the sheriff's custody.

CHAPTER VI.

Diamond Cut Diamond.

THE character Root had been instructed to assume, he now thought very clearly established in Raceford. While his social standing was certainly none of the best, when strictly classified, it seemed well calculated to further my designs, and bring to light the mysterious depredators. In fact, some tangible evidence in the proper direction had already been elicited, which would prove valuable in the future; but it could not be openly employed until something additional had been found to go with it. So the search must be continued.

The extent of the losses of the Manufacturing Company, through the annual disappearance of its saw-logs alone, can hardly be estimated or appreciated by those unacquainted with the details of the rafting and lumber-producing industry. I was informed by the manager, that probably thirty thousand dollars a year would fall short of reimbursing the corporation for the heavy drain upon their resources caused by thieving and roguery in its myriad shapes, and the stated yearly deficit from this source was actually increasing with the lapse of time. Powerful efforts were now to be made to permanently put aside all opportunities for the continuance of robberies.

Root had received minute instructions from me, before leaving Chicago, to endeavor to enter Raceford under some real or assumed cover, in order that the parties engaged in illegal acts in that vicinity might receive him with open arms —and no fraternity in all the world are more ready to accord room in their midst, or a place in their esteem, to members of the same clan, than the extended guild of guilt and crime.

How perfectly the officer had been taught this, and how carefully obeyed my directions, has already been developed. He was safely on the ground; was well acquainted, in some respects, with the men who knew, if anybody in the neighborhood knew, all the windings and intricacies of the business to be worked upon; was measurably popular, and occupying the very position, in most regards, that I had desired he should occupy. The publicity necessarily given him in the robbery, the preliminary trial and accompanying events, was not precisely as I could have wished, but, as the act of befriending and probably saving the life of Big Bill had indelibly stamped his merits upon the minds of that family, as their particular friend and champion, aside from Root's supposed fellow-feeling for them, and, as the incident was one of those quite common in detective and other experience, which could not well be avoided, provided for in advance, or guarded against, I found no fault, but accepted the results with as good a grace as possible, and ordered the operative to continue his labors.

Satisfied that Root's connection with the Agency was im- penetrably hidden, the remainder was not difficult to bear. The "sailor chap" was a firm favorite with the rough portion of the inhabitants of Raceford. His fame as a sharp, shrewd, reckless, as well as brave and formidable man, had reached even to the environs of the West Side and of the East Side, while there were some who looked upon him as no better than the vagabond family with whose members he passed much of his time. I cannot say that even the respectable people in Raceford were all prepared to shun him, as undoubtedly they were prepared in the case of the Grooms.

So industriously did the mate of the steamer *Orient* circulate his story, saying that Root was flying from the United States authorities, and working in the pinery merely to hide himself, that the sailor had only been a couple of weeks a resident of the place before he was made aware of the fact that he was watched and followed by some one. Had he lacked visual and auricular evidence, which he did not, Big Bill had given him the information that a stranger, calling himself Riggs, and apparently from Trafton, had lately been making inquiries about him. Root, having but one thing to conceal, was not fearful of arrest, but he thought it best to get rid of his shadower. Pretending to have urgent business at different and widely-separated points in the town, he tested the capabilities, patience and muscle of the official to the uttermost.

The officer hailing from Trafton had not succeeded in following him without a break, and one particularly dark night, after losing his party several times and then picking him up again, he seemed determined to trace him to his home, or to a meeting with his supposed confederates. It was nearly ten o'clock. My operative distinctly heard the stealthy footsteps following after him. Walking for a time very fast, Root gained several rods the start, and then, by cutting through by-places unknown to the officer, returned and came suddenly behind his pursuer, thus doubling upon him. Even this did not cause the revenue man to drop his game. Passing by, pretending not to notice his shadower, Root continued his trip homeward, the other following as rapidly in his wake. Up street and down street, across vacant lots, through cornfields and gardens, over fences and under raking, tearing thorn bushes, the supposed smuggler led the now thoroughly mystified and exhausted myrmidon of the law.

At last, reaching the boarding-house, Root sprang nimbly up the stairs, quickly opened and passed within the entrance, leaving the door partly ajar. Very soon he heard his following friend coming after, probably to examine and learn the name on the panel. Just as that jaded and disappointed individual reached the upper step and had bent himself forward to read the words on the plate, by the light of a lucifer match that he had ignited, Root suddenly flung back the heavy door and stood facing his late pursuer.

"Look here, my friend, whoever and whatever you are!" exclaimed the angry operative, "get out from this! Go, or you'll run against something from this"—producing and cocking his revolver—"which may hurt you! If Little has hired you to waylay me, tell him it can't be done! Go, now, or it will be the worse for you! Get out!"

The still blazing match dropped from the trembling hand of the affrighted, thunder-stricken personage, and, without uttering a single word, he retreated from the spot. Root listened until his footsteps no longer met his ear, and then re-entered his boarding place and retired.

"An' who was it that I heard ye talkin' wid, last night?" asked the lively widow, at the breakfast table, the next morning. "I thought that you wur mad! You said some mighty hard words!"

"Talkin', was I?" responded the detective, as he deliberately poured his coffee into the saucer; "Oh, yes! I remember! A cur had followed me, in the dark, an' I just scolded him away!"

"Was that it? Sure, an' I thought I heard you say somethin' about 'Mr. Little'! But I must have been dramin'!"

"Poor Jones" looked up sheepishly and beseechingly at Mrs. Buxton, and scalded his mouth with the hot liquid he unwittingly swallowed, but made no complaint.

This was all that was said on the subject.

And the revenue detective took a steamer, that very day, for home, and was seen no more in the vicinity.

Justice Simmons, with whom Root, after the trial, had become rather intimate, when made familiar with the night adventure, laughed heartily, at first, then assumed an air of solemnity.

"I don't know much about these detectives," remarked Root, with earnestness, "and must say that the little I have read and heard of them prompts me not to seek their acquaintance, but it would seem that if this fellow is one of the class, they are not all as shrewd or successful as they might be. In fact, whoever employed him has been egregiously swindled. A greater blockhead never entered public or private service!"

"You're r-r-right, s-s-sir," stuttered the magistrate. "I'm of your op-p-p-pinion! The G-g-government b-b-better get rid of all s-s-such f-f-fellows!"

Here Mr. Simmons brought his voice down to a hoarse stage whisper, and advised his visitor to look out for that scoundrel, Little. He suggested that, if he did not, the unprincipled lawyer might do him some bodily harm. The operative thanked the judge for his counsel, but did not see how the attorney, if that way inclined, could work him any damage. It was explained to him that Little was a bad man, held temper like an Indian, and had never been known to quit an enemy until he had been severely punished. He would hardly attack Root in open daylight, or in a fair field, but, in time, manage to press him into close quarters and then apply the law, the lash, or some unfair form of violence without mercy. Dealing in ambuscades, thrusts in the dark at character or life, he did not hesitate to hire and pay for injury to the body or property of his foe. Controlling the East Side newspaper, and owning its editor, body and soul, as the people said, he used both dexterously and unscrupulously to the accomplishment of his evil ends and purposes. Such was the general reputation of the party that Root had deeply offended.

After thanking the justice, and promising to be on the lookout, the operative agreed, upon receiving a cordial invitation from the kind-hearted Simmons, to call again, and then took his leave.

Jo Groom was found by Root, at least two hours before noon, that day, in what was then known as "the Frenchman's bowling saloon," so badly under the influence of liquor that he concluded not to say a word about their proposed hunting excursion. Big Bill was not yet well enough to go, and Little Bill far from the kind of companion he desired on any occasion, much less as a fellow-occupant of a frail skiff, with two loaded shot-guns. Besides, Little Bill was less in the detective's confidence than either of his cousins. This being the situation, he was compelled to defer the trip, and seek other companionship and employment. He found the latter in looking over the newspapers, which, it being Saturday, were issued that afternoon, and they were, to him and to others, more than ordinarily interesting.

It being the week following the examination and committal of Bates, every resident of the place wanted to know what the *Bird* and the *Bugle* would have to say about that matter. Whatever Skoob should remark, Jobson was confidently expected to contradict—and *vice versa.* Both papers were issued from their respective offices at three o'clock Saturdays, and each sturdy carrier ran down his respective and dusty staircase at as nearly as possible the same moment, to reach the nearest subscribers if practicable, before his opponent could get there. The East Side read its *Bugle of Liberty* first, and the opposing *Bird of Freedom* second; the West-Side read its *Bird of Freedom* first, and immediately afterward its opposing *Bugle of Liberty.* Both sheets were very carefully studied, even to the last advertisement of a stray ox, or the latest patent medicine notice. And the journalists prospered in purse accordingly. It was even hinted by wiseacres that the editors continually fanned the embers of discord in the place that they might profit by the interest excited. I hope this was a slander upon the noble profession to which they belonged. The West-Siders subscribed for their bitter adversary and the East-Siders subscribed for the paper printed on the other bank of the river, much upon the principle, it is believed, that most men and women are desirous of hearing or seeing the criticisms which their enemies may pass upon them. At any rate, this rule applied to Raceford. The two merely news accounts of the trial I need not give in these pages, but the editorial remarks, supposed to be founded upon the facts, seem so clearly to show the temper of the editors,

20

and hence the temper of the worthy citizens of Raceford, that I may not refrain from placing them before the reader in their entirety. Here is the comment made by the *West Side Bird*, etc. :

THE BATES-GROOM AFFAIR.

In another column we this week give a very full and explicit report of the circumstances attending the attempted robbery of one of our citizens, Mr. Wm. Groom, by a burly cut-throat, calling himself Bates. It is enough, in the shape of comment, to observe, that a more deliberate and willful trial to crown craven theft with bloody murder was never made in any place, and we are induced to wonder that the citizens of Raceford, proverbially peaceful and law-abiding, as they are, did not, when the facts were first made known, rise in their awful majesty, and summarily hang the scoundrel to the first tree. Justice, though sometimes a little slow in reaching a conclusion, is sure to be made apparent in the end, and,

> "Though the mills of God grind slowly,
> Yet they grind exceeding small ;
> Though He stands and waits with patience,
> With exactness grinds He all."

And Graves will, after the next sitting of the Circuit Court, probably have an opportunity to see the outer world as others see it, who gaze through the iron-barred casement of a State Prison. We heartily commend the act of Judge Simmons, in holding Bates under heavy bonds, that he may no longer roam at large. Were the prisoner, in truth, to appear upon the streets, he would be sure of meeting violence at the hands of a justly enraged people. But what shall be said of a lawyer, of the surpassing genius of a Little, who so prostitutes his learning, his talents and his profession as to lend his aid in shielding such a man as Bates from condign punishment? He places himself simply beneath contempt, and his reward will be the scorn of all honorable West Side citizens. What deserves to be written of a section of our fair country which harbors within its limits so disgusting a creature as Little? The verdict might well be: "*Anathema maranatha!*" The mystery is that the heavens do not fall and extinguish that immoral portion of this people, or the outrage dearth, which they cumber, open wide its jaws and swallow them up in the midst their wickedness. We intended speaking at length, in this connection, of the part taken by that stranger among us, Mr. Root, but only space remains in which to say that he acquitted himself handsomely and exhibited the fact that he was more than a match for the mendacious Little, in a battle of words, as he had previously been for Bates in the handling of carnal weapons.

The article in the *East Side Bugle*, etc., was somewhat dissimilar from the foregoing in matter, manner and conception. It employed the following extraordinary language:

MUCH ADO ABOUT NOTHING!

After a careful perusal of an extended and minute report of the facts connected with a recent occurrence on the West Side, the attentive reader will be quite prepared to render a determination, equal in solemnity to that which we have reached, and this conclusion will undoubtedly be that no greater scoundrel, at the present time, in this country or in any other country, remains unwhipped of justice than the man, William Groom, generally denominated by his vile associates, "Big Bill Groom." If there crawls, under the blessed sky, a more despicable brute and villain than Groom, it is that personage called Root, who appeared, in the trumped up case alluded to, as chief witness for the people, under the too-evident tutorship of that acme of all that is Satanic, Jacobs, the

Prosecuting Attorney. United and almost superhuman efforts, aided by—we grieve to say it—Justice Simmons, were put forth by Big Bill Groom and his quondam friend, Root—*par nobile fratrum*—to extinguish or crush out our worthy Mr. Little.

By false-swearing, which was palpable to the most careless hearer, they endeavored to show that the man, Bates, a poor, friendless orphan, just from the East, and one whose good character had never before known blot or stain, was a groveling plunderer and would-be shedder of human blood! A darker and more atrocious calumny was never sought to be forced down the throats of the goodly people of East Raceford. An uglier and more brazen falsehood never issued from the prejudiced lips of lying West Siders, and that is saying considerable. But all they could do was not sufficient to silence Mr. Little or convict his client. By Mr. Little's wondrous skill as a criminal lawyer; by his scathing sarcasm; by his powerful and unanswerable logic, the witnesses for the prosecution were thunderstruck and theoretically annihilated! Their ready perjuries were spiked; their batteries turned against themselves. Mr. Little, it is the unanimous remark of all who heard him, covered himself as with a halo of glory, and brought the accusations of the false-swearers to naught, returning their poisoned shafts full upon their own breasts. Mr. Bates would to-day have been a free man but for the cowardly zeal of Mr. Simmons, who insisted that he should go to jail, that that popinjay, Jacobs, might have at least one case for prosecution before the grand jury. He thus urged, in the very face of stern facts, all of which were against him, and Judge Tillman had to consent. But of one thing the people of this great and glorious republic and of the East Side may rest well assured: no grand jury to be collected in the county of Sodus can or will be impaneled which can or will indict the innocent and much-abused Bates. After the next sitting of the Circuit Court, he will roam these forests and plains as free as the air we breathe this day.

So mote it be!

Here was a sensation; here was richness! Here something for Mr. Root to think about!

These two articles, so widely divergent in conception, execution and conclusions reached, starting from premises which were identical, were productive of more than the usual amount of discussion in the town. Each journal numbered its partisans, and naturally both phases of the reports had their zealous adherents. The result was, that feeling in the streets, hotels and boarding-houses ran high, and not a few of the inhabitants of the East Side and the West Side nearly came to blows; even the ministers of the gospel felt compelled to refer to the subject in their sermons, the ensuing day.

The following Wednesday afternoon, the Martha Washingtonites of the West Side and the Martha Washingtonites of the East Side had to quarrel over the same matter. It engrossed the attention of bar-room hangers-on and dock loafers. In fact, Raceford had not been so thoroughly convulsed upon any single issue, or topic, since the almost unprecedented rise of 1854, when the waters of the river swept away the bridge, actually cutting in twain the town which had so long been theoretically divided. Old men and young men wagged their tongues over the case; old ladies and young ladies sipped their tea with both newspapers spread before them, discussing spiritedly the pros and cons, and the possibilities and impossibilities of the thing. More than one man and wife dreamed about it, having fallen asleep differing as to the innocence or guilt of the parties in the suit.

Big Bill, the man who had suffered most in the trouble, and Root, who was put to some discomfort through it, both kept quiet. Bill remarked, at the outset, that he'd "got enough of it, and wasn't goin' ter make a fool of hisself ary more in that direction!" While Root, who was free to remark what he pleased, was pleased to remark nothing.

The excitement passed over, "like a summer's cloud," producing no permanent evil consequences, and the fever finally died out. Other incidents arose; other matters of difference came up, which, for their brief season, monopolized public attention.

CHAPTER VII.

Long Pine Bridge.

SEVERAL days subsequent to the occurrence of the events related in the preceding chapter, while Root was passing from the lath-mill, in which, for a short time, he had been employed, attending to and feeding a rapacious circular saw, and going toward his home, the wearisome labors of the day well ended, he encountered Big Bill, sitting on a lumber pile, alone, his face buried despondently in his hands, and once more shaking painfully with the ague. Walking up to the sick man he saluted him:

"Halloo! Groom! What's the matter now?"

"Matter enough! Got the shakes agin! I tole yer the agur was bound ter carry me off, sooner or later!"

And Bill's words become almost unintelligible, they were so chewed and cut up by his chattering teeth, while his entire body quaked and quivered as though he suffered from palsy. At last he continued:

"I've jus' made up m' mind there's no use a tryin' no longer! I'm a gone coon! Ain't of no use for myself nor no one else! Slayton's just discharged me, 'caus' h' foun' m' 'sleep under th' shade of er pile 'f boards, yesserd'y! He said I wur settin' a bad 'zample to th' other men! An' now I'm outer work, outer money, outer clothes, outer everythin'—

[463]

'cept agur—got more 'f that than's necessary! Don' **care a** copper! Slayton's a ol' hippercrit, anyhow, an' he'll git 'is pay some time! But I'm gone up er spout! Liquor's got the better of me, an' I can't help myse'f! I was jis goin' up to yer house, ter load my gun an' blow my cuss'd brains out, and everlastingly end my wretched life! Life's no use ter me! I'm no use ter nobody!"

"This is all stuff and nonsense!" earnestly returned Root. "At your time in life, you should not think or talk like that. Come! Cheer up, comrade! Take some more of the medicine that I ordered! Go home and early to bed, sleep well to-night, come out all correct to-morrow, and then have a trip with me to Grass Lake! I'm not to be employed for some days, and would like no better sport than to help you pull your canoe to Long Pine Bridge. That'll bring you out of the dumps! That'll make you content, 'spite of yourself! Jo Groom won't allow you to be long without work, if he can prevent, and they say that he's considerable influence with Slayton. He'll make the old man give you a better job than you ever had!"

"Yes, I know Jo's got some power ther', but I'm under the belief that he'll have his walkin' papers, too, one o' these days. He's gettin' more forrard than he orter. He'll carry things with a high hand fur a while, when Slayton 'll pluck up courage t' discharge 'im—then th' fat 'll be inter the fire, an' ther'll be a fuss in Slayton's fam'ly, an' some one 'll git hurt!"

"But what is the use dwellin' on the dark side? Look at the other for a while! Come, let's see if these shakes can't be cured!"

The companions adjourned to the nearest drug store—Bill

staggering along like a drunken man—where a second mixture was made and a dose of it taken. Then, with the guidance and aid of Root, Big Bill managed to get home, all thoughts of self-destruction having been banished from his befuddled brain. Before separating, it was arranged that Jo's fowling-piece should be borrowed for Root, and that they would meet at an early hour the next morning, well prepared for a day's absence, duck-hunting, up the river.

Bill was, much to the surprise of the operative, promptly on the spot at the hour selected, the guns and plenty of ammunition, lunches, etc., in fine order. The boat had been cleaned from stem to stern, and Big Bill was himself appearing more happy and cheerful than he had been for some weeks. He thought himself sure of at least one day's relief from his dreaded foe, fever and ague.

Entering the yawl, Root assisted in propelling her up the river. It was a cool, delightful morning, and everything along both sides of the Lotus wore an appearance of Sunday quiet and repose. After passing to the northward four or five miles, guided by Big Bill, they struck into a narrow, crooked stream, which bore the rather pretentious name of Goose River. Following the channel—at times almost hidden in reeds, bushes, and tall grass—they pulled steadily at the oars for an hour or more, when they arrived at Long Pine Bridge. This structure had been built for the accommodation of farmers and choppers, in going to and from Raceford, and was just far enough above the water to permit a man, by bending low, to glide through in a small boat. Bill and his companion landed before essaying the passage, and, after a brief breathing-spell under the shade of a tree, partook of their dinner, for which violent exercise

20*

had given good appetites. A black bottle, which Root had taken care to provide, was also appealed to on more than one occasion. It contained "good liquor," as Big Bill remarked, and "should not be allowed to remain idle." But neither indulged sufficiently to sensibly feel the effects of what they drank. Then, re-entering the skiff, they shot safely under the massive timbers of the structure, applied themselves industriously to the oars for half an hour, and found themselves in one of those inland tamarack swamps, abounding in that part of the State. In the center of the impenetrable maze of straight, bushy-topped trees was a clear space a mile or more in circumference, where the water was deep and clear, and was bordered by high grass and green, waving flags.

This was Grass Lake, which, from general report and usual indications, the hunters believed to be plentifully stocked with wild-fowl. Pushing about the boat with a pole, as noiselessly as possible, so as not to frighten the game, the search began. It was continued for several hours with good success, Big Bill proving himself a very water-dog, upon occasion, and Root making many excellent and telling shots. Early in the afternoon they were ready to start upon the return trip, loaded down with game. Big Bill, by this time, was jubilant. He had forgotten his fevers and chills, and overflowed with fun and rough humor While they sat side by side, bending to the work of rowing, guided. but by no means forced on by Root, he whiled away the moments by relating many instances in which the company had been swindled, but without entering into details as to the precise manner in which, or by whom, the various jobs had been done. He betrayed considerable bitterness toward the directors of the Manufacturing Company, charg.ng some of them with having connived at his recent discharge by Slayton. He would not confess to his confidant, though given every cautious and reasonable opportunity, that he had personally enacted a part in any of the many irregularities occurring in the vicinity. He evinced faith in Root, believed him to be in every respect as bad as himself, and the author of as many criminal acts, yet at first very shrewdly attempted to cover his own connection with anything criminal. Before he was through with it, however, he let out enough to convince the detective, as well as the most skeptical attorney, that he was really connected with those who had performed the deeds spoken of. He left a very vivid impression that he and his friends had appropriated logs and other property, and would do so again when opportunity presented.

"Is there nothing to be made in this way, now?" queried Root, carelessly.

"Not a dollar," answered Big Bill, with one of his broadest oaths. "The Company keeps too close watch of logs, booms and mills. It was not so two years ago! Some of the boys then made more than a hundred dollars a month above their regular pay."

Root desired to ask how it had been done, but prudently refrained, remaining silent, while Bill rambled on, in his unconnected, jerky way, as he pulled at his oar:

"I tell you, them wur *the* times! We had good profits and less hard work than now!"

"I suppose there was a chance for speculation? The boys bought logs, above, on their own account, and, rafting them down, sold out at a large advance, eh?"

"Do you think so?" questioned Big Bill, giving a contemptuous bob of his bushy head, and turning toward his companion; "not much! I'll tell you, one of these yer days, how 'twas done! Haven't time now! Jis look over yon way! Do you see that ar' skiff?"

Root turned his eyes in the direction indicated, and said he did see a boat.

"Les' go to it, an' find if there's anything there worth the havin'."

Soon they were alongside the other boat, which was chained and padlocked to a small tree that grew near the water's edge. In it rested, covered by an old coat, a quantity of log-chains, and iron dogs, hammers, and other raftsmen's implements.

"Dogs," Bill explained, "are used ter fasten logs together, in the raft, by means of ther chains. I'll jus' fasten ter these ere things; none of 'em is marked, so they're common property, an' I takes 'em! I'll show yer, if you keep mum, within a month, what I'll do with 'em!"

Root could easily perceive that his free-and-easy companion was in the act of committing a larceny, but he took no part in the proceeding, merely passing a remark upon the danger of discovery.

"Danger!" said Bill, as they resumed their seats and sped swiftly down with the current; "there's no sort o' danger. Them chains aren't marked with the company's big 'B,' an' none others hereabouts are marked at all. A month hence no man will be able to identify them. Wait a bit."

In about half an hour the skiff, now heavily loaded, was run into shallow water on the west side of the river. Big Bill then selected a suitable spot, were there were but a few inches of water above the muddy bottom, and there deposited the property he had stolen, leaving only a wooden hammer-handle, which might easily be taken for a broken limb of a tree, remaining above the surface. This done, once more the prow of the boat was pointed toward Raceford.

After a few minutes Root said :

" I suppose you'll get at least a dollar or two for those things planted there in the water."

" A dollar ! More nor that, pardner. We'll not part with 'em for a cent less nor ten dollars, an' they're worth at the least twenty in the market. You'll get as much as five dollars for your half."

" That won't make this so bad a day's work, after all," said Root, knowing that it would not do, under the circumstances, to express hesitation or unwillingness. " If there were only chances enough like this, life, even in the pinery, might be made quite endurable. And if more chains were lost, we might realize a tolerable little pocket in the course of a year."

" Yes. I tell yer, before the ——— Company got so ——— sharp and commenced marking every link of every new chain, and every dog, hammer and sledge, with a steel die, you can bet the boys made heaps of money by *finding* those yer things an' sellin' 'em. You've seen these tradin' barges tying up ter bank of the river at odd times ? They purtend to take in fish, an' sell whisky an' bacon an' sugar an' merlasses to the lumbermen and raftsmen ; but I knows as how they're up ter a different racket nor that, principerally buyin' up, secretin' an' then sellin', in Trafton or Chicago or some other place, such things as can be *found*, an' for which they will pay a small price, an' fur which they can git a big rate elsewhere. They makes more money after midnight than durin' all the rest of the day."

Throughout the remainder of the trip, stimulated by the profitable voyage and the liquor he had consumed, Big Bill kept his thick tongue running, explaining to his friend, among other things, how, when the workmen were more than usually excited against any particular mill-owner or boss, they could wreak their vengeance for real or fancied injuries, or take reparation for acts that fell heavily upon them. It was generally through "loading" their logs so that valuable property would be destroyed.

This process was performed in the following manner : selecting some unusually dark night, the disaffected boys, to the number of two or three,—never more than three—would enter the store boom of the miller to be punished, bring forward a medium-sized log and fill it with files, well driven in by a wooden maul, to avoid unnecessary noise. These files were then sunk deeper in the wood, which closed over and concealed the apertures. When finished, the "loaded" log was towed back to the store boom, near the chute, whence it would, the next day, at the latest, find its way within the mill. For upright saws the files were driven into the sides of the log. For circular saws, it was easier to use smaller files, or the broken iron dogs, well driven in at either butt. When such a log was once on the way, or carriage, and securely fastened to the bed, it produced dire confusion. The saws, run with great speed, in gangs, would penetrate rapidly, finally strike the steel impediments, there would be heard a crash, a rending of the machinery, and the result would be that a loss, in ruined saws alone, would fall upon the mill, of from five hundred to eight hundred dollars. Frequently sawyers were wounded, or killed, by this sort of treachery. Suspension of work, delay in contracts, and replacing injured property, sometimes swelled the losses to more than five thousand dollars. Meanwhile the miscreants who had wrought the villainy stood by, secure from harm, and exulting in the success of their plans. It could only be told that somebody had held a grudge against that particular mill. Proffered rewards for the discovery of the perpetrators did no good. Thus far, although there had been a number of such occurrences, no man had ever been arrested for the crime. The old blacksmith, Leonard, who for years carried on a thriving trade in the town, repairing, re-cutting and setting old and broken saws, and putting in new ones, was, at one time, suspected of having some share in the mischievous business, but, after a careful investigation, it was generally conceded that he was guiltless. The responsibility was not fastened upon any person, and, finally, when animosities were once buried, and strikes quieted down, the occurrences became more rare, and then ceased altogether. Better than a year had elapsed since a "loaded" log had been struck by saws in Raceford.

Bill concluded his relation with an oath, and saying:

"There's more than one way of getting even with them!"

Whether this was intended as a threat or not, Root was unable to determine, but he was prompted to keep a watch over certain things which, thus far, had been overlooked.

Darkness had already set in, when Root and his comrade fastened and locked the painter of their boat to a spile, under cover of the dock above the Company's store boom, shouldered their guns and game, and wended their way to their homes.

Root, as in duty bound, made a present of his ducks to the landlady, receiving, in return, a grateful glance from a pair of blue eyes and "many thanks" from a pair of lips that the hunter had begun to think were not so ugly after all. After a hearty supper, an hour's talk, while he smoked, with the raftsmen and lumbermen, the weary operative retired to his room—not to sleep, but to write a report, which, the ensuing day, was on its route to the Agency.

CHAPTER VIII.

Jones's Little Scheme.

THE ducks which Root had shot furnished an excellent breakfast and dinner, the ensuing day, for the occupants of Mrs. Buxton's boarding-house. All were fond of wild fowl, not excepting the landlady in person. While most of those at the table partook of the food with relish, it was noticed that Jones, when some one cruelly remarked that Root was "a duck of a fellow," nearly choked over the tenderest portion of a flyer with which he had been regaling his sharp-set appetite. The grocer spluttered, turned red in the face, and swore several fierce but inaudible oaths directed upon handsome sailors in general and the one apparently fast supplanting him in the widow's affections in particular. But he swallowed his food and his jealousy at the same time, managing to conclude the meal without absolutely committing himself to anything more than ordinarily foolish. His confusion was marked by his companions, however, and several who were in the secret of its origin laughed heartily over it during the enjoyment of the after-dinner pipe on the shady piazza. Jones was there pronounced "soft" by the majority of his friends, and his particular weakness was believed to be Widow Buxton. Any man who paid her more than merely commonplace attention was sure to secure his mortal enmity. Root was therefore set down as his inveterate foe. Nor was Jones satisfied in his own mind, that the opposition, in this instance, had not the advantage of possession, which he thought nine points of the law. Of one thing he was very sure, since Root's sudden advent in Raceford, Mrs. Buxton had not heartily praised the butter, tea, and coffee from Jones's stock more than three or four times, and on at least twenty different occasions had she actually found fault with goods in his line which the grocer had doled out to her as the very best to be purchased in any American market. This was evidence to the man's jaundiced mind that somebody stood between Mrs. Buxton and Mr. Jones, and that identical somebody the groceryman was prone to believe was the sailor who had donated the birds they had that day been consuming. No wonder that the food stuck in his throat and he found it unpleasant to the taste.

But Jones's openly-exhibited jealousy and ill-temper only made the widow the more disgusted with him, and caused her to look with more favor upon her latest gentleman lodger. Friends even hinted that, thus early, he was her favorite among all who made their home at her house. Be this as it may, when, the next week, both the *Bird* and the *Bugle* made the announcement that the grand theatrical combination of Messrs. Langrishe and Alwater, with a new drama entitled 'Black Hawk," written by a young lady of literary attainments residing at Fond du Lac, and introducing the inimitable comedian, John Dillon, then just commencing his successful career on the stage, was to give a series of six entertainments at Masonic Hall, and Root had invited the widow to attend at the opening in his company, everybody knowing the fact thought their engagement as good as settled, and the sensitive heart of the

pensive dealer in wet and dry groceries was completely pulver-
ized. He learned the fact, the stupendous fact, the, to him,
soul-harrowing fact, the irrevocable fact, when he early sought
Mrs. Buxton's kitchen, and offered himself to escort that lady
to the exhibition. The reply of the landlady, returned with a
smile, " I hev promised to go wid Mr. Root," fell upon his
senses like a stroke of lightning from a cloudless sky, and he
felt that his enemy might have knocked him down with a
feather.

" Very well !" was his tart rejoinder. " I suppose you'll
become a member of the Groom family next. Root and Big
Bill, Little Bill and Jo Groom are as thick as forty peas in a
pod."

" It makes no whit uv differance to me, Mr. Jones," replied the widow. " I'm afther plazin' meself who I goes to
the theater wid, an' perhaps even the Grooms might be as
acceptable company as some that I knows of !"

" I dare say ! I dare say ! Well—well—good-morning !"

Thus ejaculating, and hardly knowing what he said or did,
the discomfited grocer, with lips compressed, and a greenish
glitter in his eyes, withdrew from a portion of the house in
which his absence was certainly more desirable than his
presence, returned to his store and sulked during the remainder
of the day. The poor lad, Tom Bosker, whose duty it was to
deliver packages from the establishment to the houses of its
patrons, was made the victim of Jones's pent-up spleen. Upon
his devoted head he emptied the vials of his wrath, ending by
belaboring him with a broom-stick, until the boy ran home for
his life, saying he'd never more enter the place.

" That man Jones is perfectly awful," explained Tom to

his mother. "I only wanted a quarter to go to the theater with"—and he rubbed his head, back and shoulders, where the broom-handle had fallen heaviest—"when he ran at me, like a mad wild-cat, swore at me, jerked the basket out of my hand, and then cut me over the head with a stick! I truly believe that he's gone ravin' crazy since Mrs. Buxton sent to Smith for sugar, dried peaches and tea! An' I thought I was doin' him a favor in tellin' him, just after Smith's boy told me of it!"

Mrs. Bosker, who was also a widow, and strong-armed as well as strong-minded, put brown paper, wet in vinegar, on Tom's hurts, while her lips worked spasmodically, and her breath came and went hurriedly. She was evidently very angry. As soon as Tom felt a little better, his mother told him to mind the bread in the oven, and see that it did not burn, while she made a call upon a neighbor. When she returned Mrs. Bosker carried a basket of things on her right arm, a heavy bundle under her left, and she walked with a proud step.

"I've seen Mr. Jones," said the woman to her son, when they sat at supper, devouring that person's provender, "and he has begged my pardon, an' says, says he, if you'll go back an' carry the parcels again he'll never so far forget hisself as to use an uncivil word, much less a blow, upon you! I think he'll keep his word. So, to-morrow, you can go back to the store!"

This was conclusive. Tom Bosker resumed his position, and Jones told him to take an apple from the barrel whenever he felt like it. The lad noticed that Mr. Jones wore a handkerchief over one eye and the side of his head, but asked no questions, and, like an obedient son of a mother capable of

enforcing her rights, went about his business as usual. Jones's
sore eye was several days in course of recovery, and when it
was finally uncovered, the cheek under it had three neat little
indentations traversing its surface, all of livid hue, which were
not made by Dr. Pillsbury's cupping instrument. Some of
those at the boarding-house thought they might have been the
result of contact with sharp finger-nails. But nobody said
anything. Jones himself declared he had not seen them until
the doctor scarified the skin before cupping to reduce the inflammation about the affected eye.

This was only adding fuel to Jones's hatred of Root.

The theatrical season opened and closed with equal bril
liance. The people of both sides of the river in Raceford, and
the two newspapers, were united in praising the plays, the ac-
tresses and actors, and the scenery. Still, Jones had not secured
Mrs. Buxton's companionship for even one night's entertainment at Masonic Hall. More than this, he learned that she
had sent another order for dried fruit to an opposition establishment on the same street. Tom did not give the information, however, as he had been sufficiently instructed by the
blows received never to know anything in the future not connected with his department of the business. Once he had
known too much. Mrs. Buxton might have had divers and
sundry live reasons for not preferring to cook Jones's desiccated
peaches, apples, and Turkish prunes, still, the interested grocer
could not behold them. He never ate such preparations. He
could not understand why Smith's store got her money when
he kept such superlatively excellent goods in that line.

"That sailor, Root, has set her up to it, I'll bet a hundred
dollars," said Jones to himself. "I'll have to stop that fellow's

game, or he'll soon have the widow's fortune under his control."

The theater had gone—the circus had come, held its stereo-
typed performances, carried off its several hundreds of dollars,
and the tattered and no longer wonderful show-bills fluttered
from the fences and walls, already things of the forgotten past.
Still Root remained in Raceford, and Jones fretted and stewed
until he seemed absolutely growing consumptive. Mrs. Buxton
had not entirely ceased trading with Jones, and he continued
to receive his daily sustenance at her table. But the truth
could no longer be concealed. Smith, the married man, and
sole proprietor of the small store with the yellow front and
single show window, received the greater proportion of the
widow's money expended for edibles. Jones grew thin, pale,
cadaverous, and his bristling hair changed to a gray color in a
few months—because he failed to renovate it regularly—while
his peaked nose grew sharper, and his watery eyes of a greener
hue. Root had not married Mrs. Buxton, but it was evident,
to the eye of jealousy, at least, that it was only necessary that
he should pop the momentous question for the lady to accept.
Jones looked about him and endeavored to find some instrument with which he might send Root out of the way. Who
he lighted upon, the context will sufficiently explain.

Jones and Lawyer Little held a conference in the old, tum-
ble-down grocery store, one night, after most honest folks were
in their beds. As Root was passing the place he noted a
light shining through a hole in the rough shutter. Just before,
he had seen Little descend the stairs from his dingy office,
sneak off through a side street, and finally enter Jones's building by a rear way In truth, thinking that Little must have

had something to do with the watch somebody had not long before put upon himself, in the shape of the *quasi* revenue detective, my operative for some weeks kept a close nightly shadow of the unprincipled attorney. Until the date in question, his industry met no substantial reward. Now, however, two of his enemies were in council. How should he hear what they said? Such men as Jones and the lawyer, having naturally so little in common, could hardly find it necessary to converse secretly after midnight, without something momentous or criminal being on the carpet. Root moved noiselessly to the window at the side of the building, applied one ear to the crevice from which the ray of illumination issued, and plainly heard Jones remark:

"Little Bill is just the fellow!"

"I think of no one more easily to be persuaded with a proper reward," answered Little.

"We must, as you say, keep within the law; but I still want that fellow punished for the public exposure he has made of my failing credit!"

"Be sure of your policies," rejoined the attorney, in a hoarse whisper, "and leave the rest to Little Bill and Little — me!"

"I'll see Bill the first thing to-morrow!"

"Good night!"

The last words were from the attorney, and Root had no time to spare in leaping nimbly aside, and throwing himself flat in the gutter at the edge of the building, thus securing a complete cover in the darkness, before the door opened and Little emerged. The heart of the detective beat fast and loud,

despite his efforts to keep it still, as the lawyer, almost touch
ing him with his foot, brushed past and soon disappeared.

"I think this is certainly the muddiest place I was ever
in!" said Root to Mrs. Buxton, the next morning, as he visited
her particular domain, the kitchen, to beg the loan of her wisp-
broom with which to cleanse the soiled coat that he held in his
hand. "And the slipperiness of some of the sidewalks is something perfectly wonderful! I tripped and fell, last night, while
coming home, and was nigh breaking my precious neck at
the crossing from Jones's grocery!"

"Faith, an' no wonder in the worruld, wid the whisky an'
the ill company ye kapes!" And Mrs. Buxton looked really
in earnest. "I've more'n half the mind to scold ye roundly for
your goings-on! But I can't. Here's the brush! Take your
self to the backyard, where ye kin scrape off the mud widout injury to me clane carpets and nately-oiled furniture! What's the
raison, now, ye will not follow me good advice, quit them blath-
erin' Grooms—the gamblin', drinkin', thavin' ruffians of the
town that they are—sign the pledge, kape it, an' become a da-
center an' a happier man?"

"I'd do almost anythin' within reason for your sake, Mrs.
Buxton, but I have sufficient reason for askin' to be excused
from that pledge at present. Still, as I'm not at all well, I may
tell you the doctor has prescribed that I shall take but little
liquor hereafter, which may make a difference with me. Never
fear, Mrs. Buxton, I can mate with even worse than the
Groom family and still retain my self-respect and honesty!
Now you know I have regard for you——"

"Get out o' this, now!" interrupted the widow, her hair
redder than ever, and her cheeks of even a deeper crimson than

her hair. "Take yourself away, before I sinds me broom forninst yer face! Bad luck to ye for a gay decaiver of a man that ye are!"

Root made a hasty exit from the kitchen, laughing immoderately to behold the flustration evident in the features of his landlady, and attended to the soiled garment. The reader will know it was bedraggled while secreting himself from Little, and not from the occurrence of any mere accident.

The widow proved correct in one thing, if not in others. The young man really was forced, from close association with the Grooms and the rough men by whom he was surrounded, to take into his system more liquor than was perfectly agreeable or conducive to his physical health. Hence, the ruse he had adopted of pretending to be ill, and forcing from the good physician the recommendation that, until perfectly recovered, the whisky-bottle should no more visit his lips. It was a hard prescription to implicitly follow and affect the companionship of the parties he was working upon, but the operative tried to put it in practice, and partially succeeded. He had no doubt, from the words he had heard in Jones's store, that the grocery-keeper and the lawyer were hatching some rascality of which he was the intended victim, and in which they would essay to hire Little Bill Groom to enact a leading *role*. His position required a cool head. That he was determined to have, as well as a keen eye upon the movements of the two conspirators, who, he felt convinced, were intending to work him some bodily harm.

Justice Simmons, with whom Root was by this time upon quite friendly terms, advised the new-comer in Raceford that something was going wrong with Little. The lawyer's apartments adjoined those of the magistrate, and the latter

21

could generally tell when the former was planning something of more than usual interest through the attorney's habit of nervously marching back and forth upon his office floor, which was uncarpeted, an operation which he sometimes kept up for hours upon a stretch, when his mind was more than usually pre-occupied. During several days past, Simmons said he had heard those quick, stealthy steps, betokening the fact that somebody within Little's knowledge was concocting some devil's broth, or about to do some ugly act. Simmons naturally thought of Root and the supposed anger Little had shown upon the close of the investigation of the man Bates, and warned the opera-ive to beware of the movements of the wily villain. Without referring to the portion of an interview between Jones and Little, to which he had so recently listened, Root promised the kind-hearted justice that he would keep his eyes open, and went his way, as usual.

It was during the same afternoon that the detective, while visiting the mill of Stephen Rogers, in the outskirts of the town, was a participant in a transaction of a very sensational character. This saw-mill, singularly enough, had been left in charge of one man, and a worthless, drunken fellow at that, who had several times fallen victim to delirium tremens, and, during a few weeks past, more than once attempted suicide by drowning, when more than usually under sway of the fantastic worm of the still.

As Root approached the side of the building, his attention was drawn in the direction of the door by the loud screams of the drunken sawyer's little boy, who had, but a moment earlier, been happily playing and kicking up his heels in the sawdust. The child was not more than six or seven years of age, but displayed a wonderful development of lungs for one of his years, and shrieked for "help" with remarkable vigor. Thinking it possible the boy had been snake-bitten, or some other accident had harpened to him, the active young man ran quickly to the place.

"Look at dad! look at dad!" yelled the boy, turning and pointing, in great fright, toward the interior of the mill.

Root did look, and a scene was presented to his view, the companion piece of which he hoped never to be so unfortunate as to behold. The heavy gang of upright saws was running at the full speed of the engine, and, lying across the body of the pine saw-log then being cut into two-inch plank, and which was at least four feet in diameter, was the body of the sawyer, Ludwig by name, his head hanging down at one side and his feet at the other, with arms composedly folded over the breast, eyes closed, awaiting death, which was near at hand in its most terrible form. The sharp, tearing blades of steel, their teeth glittering in the sunlight, were ascending and descending within a few inches of the man's chest. The thought flashed through the brain of the startled spectator of the act that the drunkard, urged on by the demons which, in his imagination, were pursuing him everywhere, armed with red-hot pincers, and seeking to tear his already bleeding flesh, had made his preparations for a novel but certainly effective suicide. The operative shouted for Ludwig to save himself, while yet there was time, but the stupid glance given by the maniac upon unclosing his eyelids, without the utterance of a word, satisfied Root of the man's intention, and that, if he did not desire to witness a cruel and horrible tragedy, he must do the saving in person. Running quickly to the lever used for throwing the revolving belt from the pulley carrying the crank to which the upper part of the saw frame hung, he exerted all his strength to turn it, but the madman's cunning had been before him. The bar was fastened to its place with a coil of tarred rope-yarn, and his best efforts, he soon realized, would never suffice to unloosen it. " My knife !" was his first thought ; " where is it ?" the second. After a search of all his pockets it was not to be found. Then he remembered leaving the implement at his room.

Meanwhile precious time was being wasted. The savage, ripping saws still ascended and descended, giving forth a peculiar crunching, rasping sound, and throwing out a little fountain of yellow dust, as the log and its human burden were rapidly hitched up, notch by notch, by the clicking ratchet wheel of the carriage, nearer and nearer to their sharp and deadly teeth. Ludwig watched the young man's every motion, appreciated his powerlessness, and the air fairly rung with his maniac laugh when he saw that nothing could be done to prevent the progress of his machinery of death. It was too late to think of turning off the steam and thus stopping the entire mill. The gibbering lunatic could not be thrown from his bed on the log without falling into the mesh of fast-revolving and uncovered machinery under him, and thence to the smothering dust pit. What should he do? In less than two minutes it would be too late for anything. Driven to the verge of desperation, Root looked wildly about him for a sharp instrument which would sever the cords securing the shifting-bar. The saws must be clogged, or stopped at once. The gang-carriage must be brought to a stand-still in some way. But how? That was the all-important question. His eye lighted, at this juncture, upon the massive mall, used in sinking the dogs in the ends of the logs, thus fastening them to the movable carriage. He seized the heavy instrument. One blow from it upon the cast-iron arm of the lever and the latter was shattered in pieces below the knotted rope. Another second, and the belt was thrown off, the arbor ceased rotation, the great upright saws trembled, slowly raised and fell once or twice, and the log ended its forward movement. All was still. The man was saved, but not an instant too soon. The sleeve of his coat had been touched. In a minute more his whole body would have been cleft in a dozen places, and his blood have flown from his severed arteries.

It required all the agent's remaining muscle to place a plank where it would be useful, and then wrest the insane Ludwig from his resting-place. But at last this was accomplished, and he dragged the German outside the mill, where they were soon joined by half a dozen sawyers and raftsmen, who volunteered their assistance. The steam of the engine was blown off, all made secure, and then the men bore the mad fellow, screaming and howling, uttering alternate prayers and execrations, to his home, where, through the exertion of force, he was placed on his bed in an easy position and confined with straps, there to remain until the violence of his mania should pass away.

The gratitude of Mrs. Ludwig, a respectable, hard-working German woman, and of her children, knew no bounds, and was lavishly expressed when the family learned how the young stranger had saved the life of the husband and father. The little Ludwig, whose loud cries had first riveted Root's attention, was particularly in earnest in his simply-expressed praise of this new-found friend. It was with extreme difficulty that the sailor, some hours later, separated from the children of the man he had helped to a life that he was so anxious to part with.

Meanwhile Ludwig was easier, and, under the care of a physician, and through the influence of a powerful opiate, soon fell into a peaceful slumber. His disease had evidently reached its crisis, passed the fatal point, and there was a reasonable probability that, thenceforward, he would be upon the mend, and gradually recover.

The evening of the same day the agent once more found himself in the presence of Jo Groom, to whom he related a fictitious tale concerning his own adventures with the schooner *Fenton*, saying, among other things, that, during one short season he had succeeded, with the help of a picked crew, in *finding* several cargoes of lumber along the Michigan shore, for which he had realized the market prices in Milwaukee and Chicago. Why could not some such operation be made to succeed in these pineries? Jo admitted that similar tricks had been profitably performed in that locality, in the past, and the companies largely swindled, but they could be played no more. Too careful watch was now kept, and any one attempting the game was almost sure of capture and prompt punishment.

It was plain, from the manner as well as words of Groom, that he had conceived a liking for Root, not deeper, but perhaps resting upon more disinterested grounds than the esteem held for the same individual by Big Bill. Jo was quite open and free in his professions of regard, and profuse in his promises to use every possible influence in his friend's behalf.

"You are no bummer, and I like you!" was one of Jo's favorite expressions. He even went so far as to relate many exciting incidents of the past, without entering into particulars, showing the sailor that he had been an industrious participant in the wholesale thievery of the preceding few years in the lumber region. If he could only come down to a specification of dates, names, dollars and cents, his stories would prove of great value to the hearer; but, however adroitly a stimulant was put in here, a suggestion there, and a half-way careless query made elsewhere, Jo failed to recall or speak of the needed data.

He, at first, gave merely the skeleton of the fact, a plain narrative, setting vaguely forth that "a certain day, which was indefinite, 'we' ran a whole raft of floaters into a store-boom; they staid there; the owner of the boom paid 'us' a round hundred dollars. That was not a bad night's work for three or four?" This is a fair sample of his earlier confidences, amounting in the aggregate to just nothing at all. Something had been done by somebody somewhere, and at a date not given, was the sum and substance of the young fellow's earliest confessions. Portions of the stories were not without interest. Occasionally the men ran narrow chances. Again, they would be passing a watchman, lie low between the logs in the water and thus escape detection. Then, again, they were nearly caught, only getting off by swimming like ducks, diving under the surface, coming out in a shaded place, then heading for shore, leaving their valuable plunder to take care of itself. At one time two men were actually drowned, having been knocked off a raft by those attempting their arrest, and the bodies were never recovered. This was an isolated instance, however, and generally the encounters of the log-stealers, though far from harmless, were without fatal results.

As time passed and Root remained in Raceford, somewhat ill in health, as he reported, working a little now and then, when he found opportunity, and frequently receiving letters containing remittances from his partner in Trafton—but really from the Agency in Chicago—Jo Groom gradually thawed out, grew more intimate, finally cast aside all reserve and, as far as it was possible to do, gave himself away to the detective. Root spent his income generously, but not foolishly, among the woodsmen. He even promised Jo, if he proved discreet and behaved himself properly, that he would, during the following season, admit him to membership in his firm, upon the payment of a fixed sum of money, and allow him to draw one-third of the profits of the business, which would be considerably better than working for day's wages and lying idle half the time. Thus flattered, Jo voluntarily gave the sailor information concerning almost everything going on in the vicinity. The only difficulty with Groom was he had no cash capital, being impecunious to a degree. He had formerly possessed some money, which he swore that the mill-owners, to whom he had been selling floating logs, had cheated him out of. He was determined to be even with them. Sometimes he loudly cursed his late partners and accused them of arrant cowardice, terribly bad faith, and all manner of abuse and deceit as practiced by them upon himself. According to his own understanding of the matter Jo was an innocent, unsophisticated, ill-used individual. And Root was always ready with words of sympathy and commiseration. The words cost nothing, and they cemented Jo's friendship for and confidence in their employer.

Growing gradually more confidential, Jo related, on one occasion, all the circumstances connected with a run of two hundred logs in one raft, which he and two others had contracted to put into a convenient store-boom at a late hour of one moonless night, two years before. When they were well down the stream, the wind, which had previously been assisting them, suddenly died away, and their progress was so tardy that they could not hope to succeed in properly securing their booty until after sunrise. By tying up in a secluded place, and waiting until the next night, they might get all in and realize their profit, but one of the partners, saying he was " not going to Waupun State prison for all the pine lumber in Wisconsin," dropped his pole, jumped into the river, and swam ashore, just within a few miles of their port, at an hour before sunrise. The second accomplice followed, and nothing remained for Jo but to do the same thing. He was simply powerless, and the large gains were transformed into actual losses. Subsequently he took another partner, who got drunk on the eve of an interesting job, told his wife what he expected to do, the wife informed somebody else, and in a few hours the whole town was aware of the facts. So that chance was spoiled, and all his pain and trouble came to naught. It was not long before Jo began to call Root by his first name, Dave, and it seemed his constant wish to be always with his friend, when not more profitably employed. Sometimes he even neglected the lady before alluded to, in order that he might meet and talk with Dave. The two men were as sociable and companionable as two of the sterner sex well could be, much to the surprise of the agent, who, from Jo's long reticence, was hardly prepared to return his suddenly-formed attachment.

Among several other projects for plundering others and easily earning money, Jo brought forward one in which a small stern-wheel steamer should play a conspicuous part, and with which, he averred, lumber might easily be taken from one of the numerous docks, situated in out-of-the-way places, late at night, while owners and employees soundly slept in their beds. He said that he controlled men forming a proper crew for such a piratical craft, and they would, with proper caution and a good leader, manage things successfully that very season. He thought, by using his influence over Slayton, he could himself secure the captaincy of one of the Booming Company's steam tugs, then play into the hands of his associates, almost any night, bring their steamboat noiselessly to the loading-place, and then, after putting on part of a cargo, tow her to a hiding spot.

In a few nights, acting in this way, a full freight might be secured and the steamer could then drop easily down the stream, until in a safe locality, get up steam and go to a port where the loot would meet ready sale for cash. Root saw that, although it was a specious, yet it was, from the nature of the surroundings, a perfectly impracticable plan ; still he professed his admiration of the scheme and his eagerness to enter upon its execution as soon as the steamer could be purchased and opportunity offered.

One day, while out shooting squirrels with Jo, Root pointed out, from the shore, the spot where Big Bill had secreted the chains previously stolen from the skiff.

" That is all right !" answered Jo. " We need not meddle with the booty ! Bill will take care of it when the time comes ! He never forgets anything of that sort !"

From this it appeared to the agent that Bill and Jo were at least in partnership in the chain-stealing business, if in no other department. And neither of the twain placed any confidence in Little Bill. Their secrets were not committed to his care. Why was this so ? Was William the Small too grasping, too great a rascal, or too honest for their partnership ? Time might solve the inquiry. But could Root afford to wait ? He thought not. Having in mind the use to which lawyer Little and grocer Jones were trying to put Little Bill, the sailor determined, as he had the opportunity, and Jo was in one of his communicative humors, to learn more as to the character of this personage with the big voice and small proportions. By the employment of apparently careless interrogatories, gentle hints and innuendoes, Jo was finally prompted to give his tongue the rein about as follows :

" Little Bill is a bundle of contradictions," said Jo, " and is afraid of no living thing, excepting it may be a cat. He will stand up before most kinds of danger like a man. As long as he can know what is before him, he's all right. But let a secret foe approach, and he's like the skittish horse, he wants to run away. If he could see the shape of the thing he'd stand as firm as the Rock of Ages.

" I can't account for the fellow's hatred of cats ! Large or small, old or young, Billy shoots them whenever and wherever he can find them. If one crosses his track during daylight, he'll follow after, leaving any other work he may be engaged upon, however important, and hunt the animal down if he can.

Never, by any sort of chance, does he touch the fur of a mem
ber of the tribe. He even hates rabbits because they look like
cats, and, if he knows it, will not eat the finest, fattest squirrel,
from the same reason, tho' in the latter case I can't see the resemblance. To me, squirrels are squirrels, an' rabbits are rabbits! To Billy they are all of the cat tribe, and he'll have
none of 'em! I truly think, if you were once to throw a
harmless kitten in Bill's face, or put it on his knee, and he was
in a place he couldn't get out of, he'd faint away, or have a
cataleptic fit, or something of the sort! When he was a mere
boy, I once playfully threw a cat at him, and he did not recover from the shock for several months. Few in the town are
aware of the real cause of Little Bill's constant hunt after cats.
It is from his dread of their comin' afore him at night. A cat-
call, or an imitation of the mewing of a kitten, would scare
Little Bill sooner than the sound of a musket at his ear, and a
cat with arched back and tail a wavin', comin' at him, makes
him run like a frightened fawn!"

"It is certainly a very strange case," said the operative

"His other failings follow this. One is the thirst for money,
which has always been his poison an' always will be! For my
part, I love a pretty girl above all the cash in the country.
But put a five-dollar bill before Billy, and he'll no sooner look
at a handsome face and figure than at an enraged tom-cat.
The 'fiver' will blind him to almost anything. Every principle the fellow has seems submissive to the power of avarice.
Many a scrape has his greed for lucre brought him into. His
weakness in this regard is well understood, and of course if
Billy's services are wanted in anything, the people know they
can be had for pay. I've often warned the lad that a ten-dol-

lar note will be the signing of his death-warrant one of these days. But to such cautions he gives no heed, and goes on as before. What he does with his money, excepting occasionally to pander to his other appetite—that for gambling—is more'n I can tell, and is beyond the conjectures of any of his friends and relatives. Billy is a curious chap! There's no tellin' what he'll come to when he gets his growth! I'm afraid it'll be nothing very good!"

"He is a remarkable character, at least, and, as far as voice is concerned, would make a fortune as a *basso profundo* to an opera or negro minstrel troupe!"

"Perhaps so," replied Jo. "But he'd never try to learn music, or anything useful. The only instrument he has the least liking for is the fiddle, and those who have brought him up—his father and mother are both dead—say that even this partiality arises from the fact that he knows the innards of the cat furnish strings for violins, and he is in favor of anything that has a tendency to diminish the number of those hated animals!"

Here the conversation was changed, and, having learned sufficient of Little Bill's character to satisfy his desires in that direction, Root pursued inquiry no further.

That night, while sitting in his room, after the completion of his report, the agent ruminated upon the circumstances by which he was surrounded. What sort of a plot were Little and Jones engaged in forming? What might they not do to ruin his quickly-acquired reputation in Raceford? Whatever they could do he was sure would be done, no matter how cruel and unmanly. They doubtless desired to drive him from the place. He must, he concluded, therefore, observe the utmost vigilance;

have the greatest care when abroad at night; be continually on
the alert, and always prepared for tricks and pitfalls. His own
work must go on. He was satisfied that stupendous frauds had
been, in years past, perpetrated upon the company, but was not
so sure that anything was at present being done in that direction. If so, the gains were small, and the losses to the capitalists comparatively light. That he had struck up a friendship
with the ringleaders in all that was dishonest, in the persons
constituting the Groom family, he was well satisfied. Who
their coadjutors were he had yet to determine.

CHAPTER IX.

Conspiracy Developed.

FROM this time forward the detective kept an eye upon Little Bill, when he could, while also looking after the meetings of Jones and Little. The morning of the day on which my last chapter ends, he saw the grocer start off in the direction of Little Bill's home, which was then at the house of his cousin, Big Bill. When, later in the day, he met and talked with the latter personage, he learned, without asking any direct questions, that Jones had actually hired Billy to act as an assistant in cleaning up and renovating the store building, which sadly needed overhauling and repairing. Billy was especially engaged to paint the front part of the weather-beaten structure and also to whitewash the remainder of its outer walls. As the agent went back to Mrs. Buxton's for dinner, Little Bill was just descending the step-ladder, bearing a paint-bucket in one hand and holding the wooden end of the paint-brush between his teeth, using the right hand to steady himself while he came down to the ground. Root stopped and spoke to the lad, asking him pleasantly how he progressed in his job.

"Oh, right smartly!" responded Little Bill, his voice seeming to sound more deeply and beautifully bass than ever before. "Only I don't exactly like the business! Much pleasanter

employment, accordin' to my way of thinking, up at Long
Pine Bridge, after fish an' game! Don't think I was exactly
cut out for a house painter. I'm too short. Makes me dizzy-
like, standin' so high up above the sidewalk. More'n that,
there's the biggest heap of cats about this 'ere place that ever I
seen anywhere! Cats! I'll take my solemn oath there's hundreds of 'em under the old shell at this very minute! They
are of all sorts, sizes, ages, colors, and both sexes! For my
part, I don't see how Jones stands their continual nightly
caterwauling, and think he's sensible in taking up his lodgin'
at Mrs. Buxton's while I clean up a bit, inside and out!
Needs it, don't it? It's so infernally foul, people can't hardly
stomach the goods coming out of it!"

Bill ran on in this way for some minutes, meanwhile preparing to go to his dinner. He appeared to want to talk more
than usual. Root surmised that he might possibly feel a measure of confusion upon meeting him at the store, and was
using his voice and a long string of useless words to cover it.
However this may have been, Little Bill continued his talk,
hardly allowing the agent to put in a single sentence, until he
was ready for the start homeward, when he abruptly concluded
by saying: "Guess I'm goin' to be late! I'm off for dinner!"

And Little Bill started. But just in his pathway was
stretched a large, fat, sleepy-eyed tom-cat, lazily sunning himself by the side of a fence. The youth looked all around, to
find if he was observed by any one, thought he was not, picked
up a heavy club and ran off after the now thoroughly frightened feline. Little Bill lost his dinner, as Big Bill subsequently said, while attending to an errand for Jones, but as
Root was leaving home, after enjoying his noonday meal, the

same day, he saw the young fellow climbing the ladder, brush between teeth, and paint-pot in hand, as before, but he was, judging from appearances, very weak and weary, and ascended the wooden rounds with an exhibition of less than his usual elasticity and vigor of muscle. The operative, who had witnessed the inception of the cat-chase, made sure in his own mind there was certainly one less rat-catcher in the world than there had been an hour earlier, and that, without having eaten a morsel of food, Little Bill was resuming his tedious work on the weather-boarding of Jones's store.

Nothing worthy of mention transpired during the ensuing few days. Root still kept track of the journeyings of Little, Jones and Company, but had learned nothing which warned him what the job upon him would be.

The summer, meanwhile, had passed, and fall was approaching. Operations at the mills had nearly closed, the product of the forests having been almost exhausted. Preparations were being made for the winter campaign, the scene of which would naturally be transferred to the timbered country a hundred miles in the interior, and consist in cutting down, squaring, scaling, and preparing immense rafts of logs to be run down the stream when the spring's high waters rose. It was evident that if the detective desired to trace the robberies to their true source, and then follow them, step by step, until they reached accomplishment at the mills, he must form some combination which should give him access to the camps of the woodsmen and raftsmen in the pineries during the coming winter months. He therefore began to seriously talk up the arrangement, previously hinted at, of purchasing a steamer to be used in *finding*, picking up, or filching, cargoes along the lake shore or the banks of the river. Jo was his particular confidant in this business, as well as prospective participator in the venture. Provided with a good rifle, and sufficient ammunition, Root made known his intention of going, as soon as the first snow fell, on a deer-hunting expedition, expecting, before he returned, to pass a few weeks with his friends, the Grooms, in the section of the pinery where they were to find employment. He had spoken to Jo on the subject, and, with his full concurrence, or advice, was first to repair to Trafton or Milwaukee, and make sale of, or trade off, his mythical schooner, and in some way secure a steamer, or propeller, suitable for navigation of inland waters and for the peculiar sort of traffic in which, during the next season, they proposed to embark. After the completion of his trade, he proposed returning to Raceford, taking up the trail to the pine country, with his gun, going to the logging camp, and there meeting and further conferring with Jo Groom. It would be time enough, this cautious person said, to let the remainder into the secret when everything would be ready. He thought that, acting as a salaried and licensed scaler for the Company, and embracing other chances which would present for turning an honest penny, he might lay up, by the ensuing spring, at least a cool thousand dollars, which he could invest in the contemplated business as a member of the firm.

Learning these facts through my agent's reports, and seeing no absolute necessity for keeping a man in Raceford during the dull season, I had written Root to close up matters, so that they could be easily resumed, and report as quickly as consistent at the Chicago Agency. The operative had everything ready for a start, when an incident occurred making it necessary that, for a time at least, he should remain where he was. In fact, that individual was detained, and could not depart if he so desired. Some days elapsed before I learned the full particulars connected with his delay. But at last the reports, from which I condense the following, came to hand.

Jones had, with Little Bill's assistance, finished the repairs on the store, and, the following day, was to remove from Mrs. Buxton's house, where he was lodging as well as taking his meals while his own rooms were being rejuvenated, and everything about the place appeared to be prospering. Still the widow refrained from smiling upon the efforts of the grocer to secure her regard. She could not like him, and would not try to. But the zealous and jealous dealer in groceries and provisions persevered. Assuming to have forgotten his grudge against Root, Jones endeavored, in various ways, to meet him upon more amicable terms than before. Besides, he had just received, by the latest steamer—and the last one that could reach the place that winter—a choice invoice of new goods, from which the landlady had, with her own hands, made selections of a bill amounting to a considerable sum. Good customers now filled the store from morning until night, and the boy, with his well-laden basket, was seen to fly from house to house with uncommon speed, and people whispered that the affairs of Jones must be decidedly progressing. His sales were larger, his stock better, and the warehouse neater and cleaner than for some years before.

It was late that night, as usual, when Root found himself returning from a saloon in which he had passed several hours with Jo and Big Bill Groom—and later from a watch upon Little—thinking how much easier he would feel, on the morrow, if Jones should, as he proposed, take up his old quarters, and thus rid the widow's house of his presence. Truth to say, the operative had enjoyed few hours of unbroken repose since that man took up his abode in the best room in the house, next adjoining his own. While yet in the vicinity of Jones's store, the moon appeared from a mass of clouds, revealing the figure of a man just ahead of him. It turned out to be Mr. Slayton. The two paused upon the sidewalk and chatted for a moment upon different topics, then separated, and Root immediately crossed the street, entered Mrs. Buxton's house and was soon in his bed. But he was not destined long to sleep undisturbed. Perhaps an hour after midnight he heard the startling cry of ' fire!'' Accustomed to false alarms, several of which had occurred within a few weeks in Raceford, at first he gave little heed to the sound, and was fast relapsing into a somnolent condition, when some one knocked loudly at his chamber door, shouting : '' Get up ! Jones's store is on fire !''

'' This is Little Bill's work,'' he thought, but said nothing. His half dormant energies were quickly aroused. Hurriedly dressing himself, the operative rushed out of the room just in time to behold Jones, with a white, frightened face, flying down the stairway, shouting, '' fire ! fire !'' at every step. With the others, Root followed to the store building. But all were too late. When the crowd of half-clad, wholly excited men and women reached the front of the warehouse, and Jones, trembling all over like an aspen leaf in the wind, applied the key and opened the door, the hungry flames burst forth, scorching the grocer's hair and eyebrows, and driving those accompanying him away to a more comfortable distance.

'' I'm a ruined man ! I'm a ruined man !'' cried Jones,

rnnning to the middle of the street, where he stopped, wring-
ing h's hands, and gazing upon the wild scene before him.
"Everything I've got in this world is going!" he added.
"Ruined! ruined! ruined!" He met much sympathy from
the citizens, and men and women gathered about him to learn
the circumstances under which he had left the store.

"Everything was safe—no fire left in the store—no light
anywhere! I can't think how it could have caught, excepting
some one went iu at a rear window, which I now remember I
failed to fasten, and started it! Oh, I'm ruined! ruined!"

Every effort was made to enter the place, but no one could
succeed. The entire interior was a mass of flames when the
entrance was opened. This gave a further draft, and fire soon
came through the roof and siding in many places, showing
conclusively that the torch had been applied long before the
evidences of a conflagration were discovered. Soon the upper
floor went down with a crash, then came the roof, followed, a
little later, by the front and side walls and chimney. Then
the red flames leaped high in the air, as if desirous of reaching
the star-lit sky, burnt fiercely for half an hour, with a bright,
intense heat, then gradually fell and settled down, as the firemen, with two hand-engines, got streams of water upon the
seething mass. Luckily the wind came from the northward,
driving the shower of brands and bits of burning timber upon
an unoccupied space of land south of the store. The fire was
confined to Jones's building. Had the stiff breeze then prevailing come from the South, Mrs. Buxton's dwelling must
certainly have been consumed. Root volunteered to aid in
working one of the engines, and labored hard, with the rest,
to save the property. All was of no avail. In a few hours,

where had stood the warehouse, was only a heap of smoldering rubbish. Not an article of value, apparently, had been
spared. The iron safe, containing Jones's private books and
papers, and standing in one corner, where the desk had been,
had gone through the floor into the cellar, where it rested on
its side, among over-baked potatoes, turnips, carrots and cab-
bages, awaiting removal and examination. It was probable
that its contents were in a fair state of preservation.

Considerable excitement was occasioned by the fire, as is
always the case in small places, and with communities little accustomed to deal with such things. Little Bill was early on
the ground, completely dressed, as if he had not retired when
the news of the occurrence reached him. Root noticed that he
was acting very mysteriously, first talking excitedly to one man
and then to another, pointing with his hand toward the burning pile. Doubtless, he was rejoicing that so many cats were
either burnt up or deprived of their accustomed rendezvous.
Presently the young fellow disappeared. Subsequently, while
Root was standing in the doorway of his boarding-house, wiping the water from his face and hands, and when the confusion
and turmoil seemed to have subsided with the flames, he was
approached by the sheriff, who said :

"Mr. Root, I am sorry to say I have a warrant for your
arrest ! You must come with me !"

' My arrest ?"

" Yes !"

"And pray what am I accused of ? Why am I taken at
this unseasonable hour ?"

"You are charged with incendiarism, in setting fire to
Jones's store ! Little Bill Groom is your accuser !"

No. 5. Booming Logs. "*I have a warrant for your arrest!*"

Page 502.

Then the conspiracy of the three persons, Little Bill, Little and Jones, was at last explained. Their game stood fully exposed to the gaze of their victim. But there was no present help.

"It's impossible they should accuse me of that thing! It is abominable! It's a malicious lie!" But realizing that words would do no good, and perceiving that they were surrounded by a mob of unsympathizing people, excited to the belief in his guilt, doubtless, by the tales of Little Bill, Jones and his legal adviser, he deemed it best to say no more, but quietly submit to the sheriff's demands.

"I think," said that official, in a low voice, "from the prevailing sentiment, I had better take you at once to the jail, where you will be safe. I'll defend you to the last. The people have been tampered with by some one, and threaten Lynch law. Still they have no evidence of your guilt."

Mrs. Buxton appeared the only one who dare proclaim a belief in his innocence. After saying as much she remained silent.

It may truly be said that these impressive incidents, following each other in such rapid succession, had partly dazed and bewildered the detective. He knew that he was guiltless; he thought he could prove himself so. But the knowledge he had of the men among whom he lived taught him that, during the present sway of popular excitement, it would be sheer folly to attempt forcing a conviction in their minds of his innocence. He therefore made no resistance, but walked along, still protesting, however, that he knew nothing whatever of the origin of the fire.

"As God is my judge, gentlemen, I had no more to do in starting it than that child in its mother's arms."

"Faith, an' I belave ye," whispered Mrs. Buxton, as the sheriff and his posse, among the latter being Jo and Big Bill Groom, accompanied the prisoner to jail, where he was fated to pass the remainder of that night at least. The two Grooms —to their credit be it said—behaved themselves discreetly, and while they were determined to aid in protecting their friend from violence at hazard of their lives, if need be, they ventured few words, probably knowing that anything coming from their lips, under the circumstances, would hardly have any effect in removing the onus of the allegations against Root. They therefore contented themselves with standing near, and by their acts more than by any particular language used, exhibiting their confidence in the young man's want of guilt. A few more, among the foremost being Mr. Slayton and Justice Simmons, accompanied the sheriff, with a constable and a few firemen, keeping back the crowd, with which was seen Little Bill, seemingly hungry for the blood of the helpless man. The jail was finally reached without the occurrence of any violent outbreak, and the mob had to employ itself in hurling curses, shouts of derision and scorn after the prisoner, as he disappeared within the haven of safety.

"I can't understand this," said Slayton, at the cell door, after Root had been placed in charge of the turnkey. "I parted from you, I remember, a little better than an hour before the alarm was sounded, where we had been talking, and distinctly saw you enter the boarding-house. I can't fathom the mystery. But, my friend, I am as sure you did not do the deed as I am that I live."

"Thank you!" said Root, deeply affected. "It will all be explained some day. At present I'm as deeply mystified as any one. What my suspicions may be perhaps I had best keep to myself! you can rest assured I am not guilty, but the victim of as damnable a plot as was ever hatched to injure man in the world! Never mind! To-morrow I trust I may be able to get bail until the examination, which I shall demand must take place directly!"

Leaving the prisoner to pass the hours as best he could, his companions remained on guard outside the prison, still fearing a forcible demonstration from the prejudiced and enraged citizens, until the sun had risen for another day, and, better counsel having prevailed, the crowd had quietly dispersed. Everything was soon as quiet and peaceful as ever in Raceford. But there were some in the place who did not find rest. This was not the case with the tired operative, who slumbered as sweetly and as calmly on his iron bedstead and husk mattress as he could have done had he been in his more luxurious couch under Widow Buxton's hospitable roof. Exhausted by the mental troubles of the night, with his efforts at the brakes of the engine, attempting to extinguish the fire, it was an hour past sunrise when he awoke.

Part of my information regarding the circumstances just related came to the Agency in the shape of a letter, written by Root, while in jail, directed to his cousin at Trafton, as he explained to the jailer, who did not ask to examine the contents, but having upon its envelope the number of a post-office box, the matter in which I controlled, unknown to all excepting the special Agent of the department. I very naturally desired to know more. Situated as I was, and as my agent must be,

22

however, it would not do to make direct inquiries by letter, nor could Root safely write all I wanted to know; I thought best to send a cousin to Root; at least, a substitute for one, in the person of operative Gross, who started for Raceford the ensuing day. The second detective was especially instructed to co-operate with Root, under cover of their supposed relationship, and make himself useful, if possible, in hunting up the perpetrators of crimes in that particular locality. Gross was a sharp-eyed, quick-witted, industrious man, and I knew he would play his part well. He was supplied with funds, to be used, if necessary, in retaining reliable legal talent for his *quasi* cousin's defense, before the magistrates.

The first reports from Gross were awaited impatiently. At last, a package arrived. By its contents I was informed of events succeeding the night of the destruction of Jones's store. It appears that Mr. Slayton, who, it was understood, would be put on the stand as a witness for the prosecution, from the fact that he had parted from Root only a short time before the smoke and fire began to pour from the roof of the building, had been one of the first to come forward and offer to serve as one of the accused man's sureties, the bail having been placed at ten thousand dollars, for his appearance at the preliminary examination before Justices Simmons and Tillman. He was quickly followed by Dr. Pillsbury and Justin Roberts, the latter a well-known attorney, and about the opposite of Little in almost every respect. These were three of the most respectable and most wealthy residents of Raceford, and none were stockholders in or officers of the Booming Company, excepting Mr. Slayton, and he was merely a superintendent, and had been purposely kept in ignorance that the Agency had an operative

at work in the lumber region. He was not even aware that detectives were ever consulted regarding the robberies in that portion of the State. The bond was presented, declared satis· factory, accepted, and Root immediately set at liberty. This event occurred the day succeeding the one witnessing the arrival of the prisoner's cousin in the town. There was now much work to be done. After the two men had held an interesting and confidential conversation, in Root's apartment, during which Root imparted the suspicions he held of the real perpetrators of the incendiarism—it was without doubt an intentional fire—and repeated the portion of a conference to which he had listened between Jones and Little, it was determined to remain merely upon the defensive, unless something new was discovered, until the holding of the preparatory trial, and the line of prosecution intended to be pursued by Little should be fully developed. It was believed that Little Bill would be brought forward to testify that he had seen Root in the very act of setting fire to the store. In no other way could such a charge for one moment be sustained, incendiarism constituting one of the number of crimes in which purely circumstantial evidence produces but little effect upon a juryman's mind. Was it possible, through the aid of Big Bill and Jo Groom, to bring this unsupported testimony to naught? They thought it was; at least they would, when the time came, give it a trial. Should the perjured witness fix upon any precise moment when he had, or would falsely swear he had, seen Root make his exit from the store, and that time should agree with the one on which Mr. Slayton and the operative were actually engaged in conversation near the doomed building, it would naturally fall to the ground. If placed at any particular mo·

ment later than that, Root could prove an *alibi* through at least half-a-dozen lodgers at Mrs. Buxton's, who had been aware of his presence in the house and carefully noted the hour. One of the number had even seen him enter his bed-room and lock the door after him. Should the young perjurer arrange the decisive moment as previous to the hour specified— that of the meeting with Slayton—there was a hiatus which only Root himself could fill, and his lips would be sealed. During over an hour of that period he was shadowing the lawyer, Lit-tle, following him from his office to his residence, and then walking leisurely to the point where he encountered Slayton. Previous to the beginning of this hour he had passed the en-tire evening in the companionship of Little Bill's two cousins; a fact regarding which Little Bill had probably no knowledge, excepting he obtained it after the commission of the crime. These matters must be looked into. They were intrusted to the care of operative Gross.

Two days thereafter, while, as Simmons said, Little was in the midst of the work of preparing his testimony for the sitting of the two magistrates, Gross shadowed Little Bill to the lawyer's office. He knew where to find Root, and at once informed him, when, together, they visited the apartments of the jus-tice, which, as before related, adjoined those of Little, on the same floor of the same building. The worthy magistrate was at home, as friendly as ever, and greeted them cordially. They quickly detailed the circumstances connected with the work going on in the next room, and inquired if there was any available way in which the conversation between the attor-ney and Little Bill could be overheard. It was an uncommon thing to ask, they were aware, and an uncommon thing to do, with them, but the crisis seemed to demand the use of any means, unusual or usual, in checkmating the villainy they knew to be going on. Simmons at first shook his head, then thought over the subject a moment, and finally answered:

"Perhaps so! Yes! It is in the interests of law and justice! Yes! I'll do it!"

The magistrate then explained that there was close at hand a sort of closet, in which, for many years, he had stored away old records, newspapers, bundles of musty law papers and documents, cast-off clothing and the like, which was only separated from Little's inner office by a thin partition of boards, covered on the lawyer's side by common wall-paper. The lumber had shrunk considerably, parted in places, and torn the paper, and he had recently discovered, he said, while a blush overspread his honest face, that a dialogue, carried on in Little's sanctum, even in a cautiously-low tone of voice, could be distinctly heard by standing nigh and listening at the wall in the little closet.

"But for the great importance of the emergency, I would never have imparted this information to any person. It may be used as an instrument in the accomplishment of the ends of justice!"

Simmons was considerably confused, and seemed to suffer from the ordeal through which he was passing. He was quickly assured by his visitors that they appreciated his feelings, and no advantage would be taken of his secret, without his voluntary consent. Meanwhile, what they did had to be done quickly, or the conference between the conspirators would be concluded. The way was then exhibited. The magistrate, saying that Root could not be a witness in his own case, determined to accompany Gross, and from that moment he forgot to blow his nose resoundingly. The office doors were locked and bolted, as they always were at night when the judge and a select party whiled away the hours at a game of euchre, and the men took the further precaution of removing their heavy boots.

"Now," said Simmons, standing before the narrow door of the recess, which was only secured by a primitive wooden button, "not a word must be said, not a noise made by us while within, as they can hear us just as distinctly as we can hear them. Root, you can stay here and hold the door shut until you hear us coming, then carefully open it for us. If I hear what I expect to hear, we will know what to do toward ending and punishing the originators of one of the most diabolical conspiracies ever hatched in the State. And I'll do my share, be the consequences what they may!"

"I am satisfied with the arrangement," said Root.

The small panel door was quietly opened, without giving forth a single creak of the hinges, which the detective saw had recently been well oiled, and the justice and detective entered. Then Root shut the door and put his foot against it. He was not quite certain that sufficient air could gain access to the cupboard for the sustenance of life, but, reasoning that, possibly, Simmons, while greasing the hinges, would naturally provide for the rest of the surroundings, he sat in his chair ready for the coming of the searchers after knowledge. He had not long to wait. Soon he felt a soft pressure against the toe of his boot, he removed the obstacle, and the men emerged from their corner, presenting a sight which, had he not had his risibles under excellent command, must have caused the operative to

laugh long, loud and heartily. As it was, and near the headquarters of the enemy as they were, he could not repress a smile,
and was internally convulsed, to the extent that his handkerchief was employed to close up his mouth to prevent chance of
an explosion, of which there was imminent danger. Simmons's
long, fiery red hair was plentifully sprinkled with dust and
soot, until changed to the color of a singed cat, and his face
bore a striking resemblance to that of a half-washed Ethiopian
serenader, while his hands, of whose whiteness he was usually
very proud, were smirched and begrimed like those of a chim-
ney-sweep. Gross, who was naturally a light-complexioned,
white-haired, Celtic-looking individual, was transformed into a
tolerable Othello, excepting the curling wig, his poll being fan-
tastically decked with odd strips of white paper, cobwebs and
lampblack, forming a head-gear more ridiculous, if that were
possible, than those usually affected by poor representatives of
King Lear, or those of the other sex, in personating the mad
maiden lover of Hamlet, fair Ophelia, upon the mimic stage.
The clothing of both gentlemen was fashioned, by added
spiders' nests, filaments of twine and lint, into a costume of
pepper and salt, and their lungs were so choked with powdered
abominations of every sort, that some moments necessarily
elapsed before they could raise their voices so as to be heard.
Their peculiar personal appearance was explained, but not until
Simmons had donned his spectacles, and, with an air of conscious satisfaction, seated himself in the chair of office. The
consequent merriment became general, though suppressed, as
Little Bill and the attorney had not had time to vacate the
building. It was continued for some minutes, Root gazing
upon his two companions in utter amazement, and they looking

at each other with equal suprise, but finally Simmons stuttered:

"C-come, l-let us g-get out of this f-f-fix before some
f-f-fool wants to come in."

The Justice sounded his nasal trumpet sonorously, to clear it
from accumulated dust, and then proceeded to apply cold water
to his person and brushes to his habiliments, soon making himself once more presentable. Gross followed his example with
a similar result. In a few minutes a chance visitor would not
have recognized them as the same personages who had just
emerged from the magistrate's mysterious pantry.

It was well for all concerned that this cleansing process was
early attended to, as the outside doors of the little court-room
had not been many minutes unfastened when Jo Groom entered, searching for Root, whose companionship he had sadly
missed since the fire and succeeding arrest. The Agent was
not particularly well pleased with the untimely visit, but saw
the necessity for appearing so, put on a pleasant face, dissem-
bled a little, and gave Joe a cordial welcome. Gross had previously been made acquainted with Joe, as the operative's
cousin from Trafton. He was also pleased to see Jo Groom,
and, without hearing the result of the excursion into Simmons's
cupboard, Root felt compelled to invite Jo and Gross and Simmons over to an adjacent beer saloon. But the magistrate,
being still a temperance man, refused. Then the three others
left the Justice alone and went to the ale house by themselves.
Of course, the observances that followed kept Root and Gross
engaged the remainder of the afternoon. By sunset they had
reason for leaving, it being their supper time.

At a late hour that night, however, Root and his

cousin, Gross, might have been seen issuing from the building in which was situated Simmons's office. They were walking fast, talking cheerfully, and one of the number evidently felt more happy than usual. Root sat and smoked his pipe, and wrote on his reports until past midnight. Still, the labor done seemed a labor of love, not a task or hardship.

The ensuing morning, two days before the date appointed for Root's examination upon the charge of incendiarism, at about ten o'clock, the city of Raceford was completely electrified through a public announcement by the sheriff of the county that he had just turned the key on Jones, Little and Little Bill, all of whom were charged, upon affidavit of Willis Gross, with conspiracy to defraud certain fire insurance companies out of five thousand dollars, the amount of policies which Jones held upon his building, stock and fixtures; and on a second charge of incendiarism on the part of Little Bill, with Jones and the lawyer as accessories before and after the fact. The investigation would take place the following day, agents of the insurance companies having been sent for.

This news spread like wild-fire through the town, and by noon the inhabitants on both sides of the river were in a state of bewildering excitement. People could not see how, if Root was the man who set fire to Jones's store, there could be any truth in allegations made against two well-known citizens, lawyer Little and Billy Groom. But before the day for the examination arrived the agitation had raged, surged, gained fever heat, and then quickly subsided, leaving the troubled waters as calm as before.

"But I can't fur the life of me understand how their arrests are to effect Mr. Root's case!" exclaimed Mrs. Buxton, when

22*

she heard of the allegations made against Little Bill, Jones and the lawyer Little.

"It is easy enough," replied Gross, who was sitting at a window reading a newspaper, but looked up as the lady concluded. "You see, Mrs. Buxton, if the men now in jail set fire to the store, an' it can be proven, then Root couldn't possibly have done it! More especially as all the testimony there is against my cousin consists in a lying affidavit, made out by Little and sworn to by Little Bill!"

The widow blushed one of her crimson blushes, so compatible with her red hair and florid face, and held down her head for a minute. Then she raised her eyes and they met those of the man they were talking of, and she answered:

"Oh, I see it all now! If Little Bill be guilty, then Root is not guilty! Plain enough! Sure it is that!"

Still Mrs. Buxton did not, nor did many of the citizens of Raceford, see the deep pit of villainy which lawyer Little, groceryman Jones, and lying Little Bill had digged for themselves, and in which they were about to find themselves inextricably entombed.

CHAPTER X.

Tables Turned.

WHEN the three prisoners were brought from jail into Simmons's little court-room, at precisely ten o'clock in the forenoon of the day selected for their preliminary trial, they presented a curious picture—pitiable as well as curious. None of the number appeared really to have enjoyed their brief captivity. Upon the countenances of two had settled an absolute look of restlessness. This was particularly noticeable in Little, the famous criminal lawyer, now himself turned criminal, who was haggard, perceptibly thinner of face, and his dark eyes continually wandered from point to point, as though in search of some wished-for object. If it was his wife that he expected to see, he was fated to disappointment. She had improved the first opportunity presenting itself in several years to glide from beneath Little's heavy and relentless hand. His tyrannical grasp was at last relaxed by the force of inexorable law, and, taking their three children with her, she was even then *en route* for her father's comfortable home in a far eastern State. So the caged lawyer saw not the form of the true woman, whose life he had for years made a daily misery, looking love and encouragement upon him. Indeed, there were very few in the assemblage from whom he could expect

[515]

expressions of sympathy. His whole aspect was that of a chained tiger. His hands moved about nervously, and were deprived of even the poor consolation of a knife and piece of pine shingle, all sharp implements being kept out of their reach, as, from his insane appearance and violent character, even when in his gentler moods, it was feared by those who waited upon him that he might take his own life or that of some other person. Little knew he was driven to a corner.

The groceryman, Jones, was also pale and agitated. His eyes, naturally wanting in expression, wore that sickly green color notably accompanying an attack of jaundice. His nerves were all unstrung, and he held down his head, gazing on vacancy, seeming to recognize no one. His clothing was uncleanly and shabbily constructed. On the whole, he formed no very pleasing sight to look upon. He said nothing, but clasped his hands over one knee and sat quite still, awaiting the beginning of a scene, the result of which he feared would be far from satisfactory. Indeed, he knew evil was in store for him.

Little Bill was, at first, as serene as a summer's morning. The slight flurry there was in his system entirely ceased when he saw that his relatives, Big Bill and Jo Groom, were in the crowd, and had seats near him. He cast his ancient and well-ventilated chip hat upon the table with a dash, as of impatience, ran his fingers through his long, tangled locks, seated himself in an easy attitude, assumed a look as if to say, "Go on with your show! I am ready!" and then proceeded deliberately to stare the audience out of countenance. His sun-bronzed face seemed a shade lighter, because it was cleaner than usual, but his feelings were under good control. In this respect the boy taught his more mature accomplices a lesson that they had not the fortitude to profit by. He acted precisely as he felt. The others were giving color and form to their fears for the future. However his companions might exhibit the white feather, there was no cowardice shown in Little Bill's brazenly impudent visage. As Jo had remarked, while describing his cousin to the agent, Root, he feared nothing human, good, bad, or indifferent. There was one little animal that he did dread. "Who cares!" was in the very swing of the lad's long-skirted coat, and an air of defiance in the dig he made at the brim of his old hat, which he doffed when entering, as he had been instructed by the deputy-sheriff. Little Bill's demeanor might have been founded upon that of Oliver Twist's unsought friend, and the proficient pupil of Fagin, the Artful Dodger, for whom he had formed great respect in a casual perusal of a cheap edition of Dickens. At any rate, it was a fair imitation of that thieving fellow's appearance under somewhat similar circumstances, though he did not threaten the court, as his prototype is said to have done nor ask "Where were his privileges?" He was simply a bit of unadulterated impudence personified.

Deputy Sheriff Babb opened court in his usual style, which was far from ceremonial or orderly.

"Let the people keep quiet! This ere court is about to get to business!"

A lady, with her baby crying vexatiously, said "hush!" "hush!" But it did not obey.

The tall official rapped sharply three times with his calloused knuckles on the plastered wall, then abruptly sank into a seat on the end of a convenient bench. The buzz of conver sation ceased, and the assemblage gave earnest attention to the proceedings which followed.

Such a densely-packed crowd of men, women, and boys had not convened in Raceford to witness a trial since the date of the examination of Bates, for robbery, some months before, in the same apartment. Bates was serving out a three years' sentence at Waupun, and the man who defended him before the court, and before the jury, was now a prisoner, with a prospect of soon keeping his former client company. There was the greatest demand for seats, and the supply did not keep pace with the requirements of the people. The ladies had preference. The boys were compelled to stand, as well as most of the men, the small place being uncomfortably crowded. Skoob, of the East Side *Bugle of Liberty*, was present, spectacles on nose, pencil ready sharpened, and note-book in hand, prepared to take advantage of whatever might be said or done. Jobson, of the West Side *Bird of Freedom*, entered rather late, and had not been fortunate enough to find a seat to fall asleep in, therefore stood, with his two hands stuck in his deep pockets, gazing vacantly at the defendants, while he braced his shoulder heavily against the wall to make his position more endurable. If he proposed taking notes of the trial, he displayed neither pencil nor tablet, and was as much interested as he might have felt, had the proceeding before him been a dog-fight or a trial for the pettiest of petit larceny. But Jobson's memory still holding good, it was easier to refrain from writing, and he was proverbial for preferring that which cost him the least muscular or mental exertion. A joker waited until Jobson was almost asleep, and swaying backward and forward as he stood, when he approached, shouted "copy," in a satanic voice, in his ear, and the editor roused up, opened his eyes, looked around, appreciated the joke, smiled, and relapsed into somnolency. Forty winks, taken as he waited for a proof, late at night, was as good to the brain-weary scribbler as an hour to another man reclining comfortably in bed.

Big Bill and Jo Groom were naturally interested in the trial, but, not knowing anything of the testimony upon which Billy had been implicated, they supposed there was little probability that he would suffer, and had made no effect toward securing immunity. It was not their fight. Both had the greatest confidence in their kinsman's ability, young and inexperienced in the intricacies of the law as he was, to take his own part and manage affairs for himself. When asked what they thought about the arrest, they expressed the belief that it was a superlatively silly farce, or an attempt to frighten Jones on the part of the insurance companies, which would not succeed. The brothers greeted Root and Gross warmly, as they took a seat not far removed from their corner. Both talked and laughed, but still were concerned for Little Bill—and became more so as the trial proceeded. Neither had taken the trouble to inquire as to the contents of Gross's affidavit, and Jo informed Root that if Little Bill had been foolish enough to have set fire to the store, which he did not believe, he was too smart to be caught, and would surely come out all right. Little knew something of the trouble before him; so did Jones Little Bill neither knew or cared. It looked as if his cousins were of a similar way of thinking.

Tillman blew a bugle blast, smothering it in his big pocket-handkerchief, followed by a note by Simmons; Skoob turned over a new leaf of his note-book; Jobson opened his eyes again; Babb rapped with his knuckles on the bench, crying, in a doleful voice, "Order in this 'ere court!" and the two magistrates walked to their table and occupied seats behind it; Tillman announcing, in his hoarse voice, that the examination into the matter of the State *versus* Phineas Little, Nehemiah Jones and Wm. Byrd Groom *alias* "Little Bill Groom," charged, upon affidavit of Willis Gross, with conspiracy to defraud, and, secondly, with the crime of incendiarism, would at once commence.

Justice Simmons, from his painful impediment in speech, usually left such proclamations to his fluent and smooth-tongued associate.

The woman with the crying baby was, by unanimous consent, allowed to go out, and the court business proceeded.

Little's attorney, especially imported from Trafton to defend him, was one Ashmead. He was aldermanic in figure—in fact, puffy; bald as to head, brazen as to face, and in language after the style commonly denominated verbose and windy. As a consumer of good brandy and a scheming politician of the stump-orator sort, he might have amounted to something; but as an attorney the least said about him the better for the fraternity. Among lawyers, even, his reputation was not good. Why Little had retained such a legal nonentity to act for him nobody could tell. But there he was, armed and equipped with a wheel-barrow load of borrowed books and a package of useless papers and documents correspondingly large and bulky before him on the narrow table. Wiping his rubicund face with a soiled linen handkerchief, he threw himself back in his chair, spread out his nether extremities, and awaited the opening of the cause for the prosecution by Mr. Jacobs, the district attorney, who, from the considerable importance attached to the trial, was present to examine the evidence and superintend the investigation in person.

The tall female and the bawling babe entered again, but were hissed out immediately.

Justin Roberts, counsel for Root, and assistant of Jacobs in the prosecution of the present case, was a man of many attractive qualities, was personally known throughout the State for his skill and for being the very opposite of Little and Ashmead in moral and mental caliber, as he was in prominent physical attributes.

Jacobs, from the known prejudice he held against Little, waived his right to make the opening speech in favor of Roberts, who addressed the court for some ten minutes, setting forth in general terms what the State expected to prove. He was followed by Ashmead, who had been industriously prompted by his client, Little, while Roberts was speaking. The Trafton lawyer talked in a shambling, pettifogging, blustering way for half an hour, apparently placing great reliance upon the alleged immaculate character of his party defendant, and the openness of the villainous fraud which he said had been hatched in the fertile brain of the prosecuting attorney, to ruin men, who, unlike that official, were and always had been above reproach. And he gave out more of the same sort of trash, then vigorously wiped his face again, and sat down. The people wondered why he ever got up, as he had done Little no credit, and covered or contravened not a single point in the other lawyer's speech. It was then apparent, if Little was saved the State prison, which, if guilty, he richly deserved, it would not be through the exertions of Mr. Ashmead.

Without attempting to furnish a true copy of the proceedings of the court, as reported to me by my agents, I shall condense those portions having the strongest bearing upon the incendiary case.

How that persevering woman got back again was among the mysteries unexplainable. But there she stood, as large as life, and the infant yelling and kicking in her arms like a young panther in a trap. Simmons looked aghast, blushed a deep scarlet, and said :—

" M-mistress P-p-etersham, it is t-the w-wish of the m-majority t-that t-that ch-child b-be r-removed f-from c-c-court !"

Babb knocked a loud knock. The mother and child were objects of interest. And the youngster screamed, as though in protest, while poor Mrs. Petersham had to take her departure again. Silence once more reigned in court.

The testimony of Willis Gross, after detailing the laughable adventure in getting into and out of the magistrate's dusty closet, was to the effect that he and Simmons had seen the defendant, Little Bill Groom, in company with Little, the latter sitting at his writing table and taking notes of the answers Billy was making to his questions. When roundly abused by the lawyer for his cowardice during the night of the fire, Little Bill answered that he had been promised a reward of one hundred dollars, by Jones, half down and the remainder when his work was done, to set fire to the store and then make oath before a notary public that he had been an accidental witness while Root performed this incendiary act ; in truth, he was to swear that he had seen the sailor in the burnt building, applying the match, and then going to and entering his boarding-house. He was to say he had tried to put out the fire, and being afraid he would be charged with the crime of setting it, ran away, after giving an alarm. This was what he had agreed to do. He had performed part of it, but not a cent of the expected sum had he yet seen. He wanted it before he did any more.

The firing of the store, he more than hinted, he was not guilty of—as for that, neither was Root—but Jones had appeared when he himself got scared at a big black cat that threatened to pitch into him. Jones, as fast as he, Little Bill, retreated, ordered him back, and called him a coward—which he was not—but he could not get over that monstrous and ferocious cat, and he finally succeeded in avoiding Jones and leaping out of the window by which both had entered.

This part of the evidence of Gross was a revelation to most of those who heard it. They knew Billy's hostility to cats, and his penchant for killing them, but it was new to them that he feared to look on them while their eyes gleamed in the darkness of night.

When the lad was safely outside he said he paused a mo ment to see what Jones would do, and that worthy himself lighted a match, by striking it on the sole of his boot, stuck it, while blazing, in a pile of papers, rags, and other combustibles, which had been previously made ready for the purpose. This was near a barrel of rosin, and not far from the kegs of oil, the floor having been saturated with kerosene, and the faucet of the big tin can left wide open. Then Jones clambered out, banged shut the heavy blind, and they left the place, Jones entering Mrs. Buxton's house by a rear way, just as he had probably come out. Billy at last consented that, as he had failed to perform the most particular portion of his contract,

and as Little was anxious for the abatement, he should only
have fifty dollars. That sum they would give him as soon as
the insurance money was collected. Billy and Little wrangled
over this point for some minutes, the two men behind the partition listening all the while. Finally Billy agreed to finish
the arrangement by going upon the witness-stand, and testify-
ing that Root was the incendiary. Then some money was paid
over to the little villain by the attorney. After this, Little
proceeded to instruct the perjured boy concerning the responses to be made by him upon the examination. The hour
when he was supposed to have seen Root come out of the rear
window of the store, which Jones " remembered he had
left unfastened," was shrewdly fixed upon as about half-past
eleven, or after Root had separated from Big Bill and Jo
Groom, and previous to his meeting with Mr. Slayton.

When Gross left the witness chair, the faces of the defendants were observed to be remarkably changed. Little had
warning of what was coming, so had Jones; but Little Bill
was taken completely unaware. Yet the lawyer turned almost
black in the face, and then white again, and Jones was covered
with a cold, clammy perspiration, the color of his skin seeming
to shift to a greenish yellow, while the countenance of the un-
prepared boy expressed only contempt, of the most positive
character, for the childish weaknesses of his partners in guilt.
Jones's head fell forward on his chest, and he did not again look
up until the case was closed, and the handcuffs were upon his
wrists.

Little Bill, while he did not show it, was considerably ex
cited by the unexpected turn affairs had taken. Still his mind
soon recovered its balance, and, while Ashmead was attempting

to argue the inadmissible nature of some of Gross's most telling testimony, he turned to Jo Groom, and beckoned him forward to a seat by his side. Little Bill was fully equal to the occasion. Jo spoke with his cousin, was seen nodding assent to some proposition Billy made, and then resumed his former place. Little Bill, paying no attention to the labored effort of Little's attorney, made known by a simple gesture, that he wanted to confer with the district attorney. That gentleman moved his chair along to the lad's side. Little looked daggers at Billy, but he heeded him not, and went on with his talk to Jacobs. Little's hands trembled. Had they clutched any sort of deadly weapon, it was believed he would have attempted the taking of the boy's life.

Billy was once more as serene as a veteran attorney. He quickly saw what an absurd mess had been made of the whole matter by his accomplices, and was ready to grasp the first support presenting itself, by the use of which his own precious hide might be saved. One result of the talk was that Mr. Jacobs called Little Bill Groom as a witness for the prosecution. That young scamp's testimony need not be repeated. He not only fully corroborated all that Gross had previously given, but unblushingly related time, place and circumstance of the whole conspiracy, from beginning to end, saying that Jones had hired him to paint his building merely as a blind.

Billy was as firm and immovable upon the stand as though the hero of forty trials, and all that Ashmead could do, when it came to cross-examination, was to ridicule the witness for his cowardice in the presence of the feline apparition, and throw a shadow of doubt upon his veracity by showing that if he could be bribed to lie in one instance, he probably would voluntarily falsify in another. In this the Trafton attorney was unsuccessful, as Billy returned such cutting responses that, after a few trials, the matter was ended. Ashmead was forced to accept the inevitable. The case did not rest with Billy alone. He was fully corroborated.

When Billy Groom was through, Justice Simmons stated, from his seat, that, as concerned the scene in the closet, he knew Gross and Little Bill swore to the truth, as he personally saw and heard all that Gross had seen and heard. It had been truthfully represented in the testimony. This definitely fixed the fate of the prisoners in that court.

There was a sensation in the assemblage, in the afternoon, at the conclusion of the speeches of counsel; the magistrates blew their trumpets in nasal accord, and entered upon a whispered consultation, which lasted only a few minutes. Tillman said but little, Simmons having most of the burden of talk to sustain. They arrived at the only conclusion possible to reach under the circumstances. This was that the evidence compelled them to commit the three defendants until bail for ten thousand dollars each could be found for their appearance at the next term of the Circuit Court.

Mrs. Petersham and her pet *would* enter to hear the conclusion. They remained, and the child forgot to scream while Justice Tillman spoke.

No more evidence was needed. The agents of the insurance companies were not examined, but returned to their homes, satisfied that a projected fraud upon their respective institutions had forcibly recoiled upon its inventors. Jones had set fire to his store, hoping to have the crime irrevocably fastened upon his enemy, Root, and in order to secure the full

amount of the insurance, which was at least twenty-five per
cent. above the total value of his building and its entire contents. In the end he not only had to bear alone the loss
of property, failing to receive the money from the insurance
companies, but the tables were turned upon him, and he saw,
in perspective, a long term of imprisonment in the penitentiary, and recognized the galling fact that his supposed rival for
the hand of the Widow Buxton was safe, and fully at liberty
to woo the lady, and win her if he might. His chances of success, judging from appearances, were remarkably good. The
popular verdict was, " Poor Jones !"

None of the prisoners succeeded in finding acceptable bonds-
men in sufficient amounts, and all were therefore transferred,
for safe keeping, to the county jail, the lock-up at Raceford
not being strong enough for the detention of such shrewd
rogues. They were removed the day succeeding their final
committal.

To close up this part of the relation while freshly recalled
to memory, I may say that, at the next spring's term of the
Circuit Court, Jones and Little were duly indicted upon the
two charges of conspiracy and incendiarism, fairly tried, convicted and sentenced to serve the State at Waupun ten years
each. Little Bill, in consideration of his youth and the value
of his evidence in confirming the greater scoundrels' crime,
was let off easy, his sentence being only two years, which he
faithfully worked out and was discharged. He now lives in
the western country, a reformed and better man than he was
boy and youth. Jones died in prison, from nervous prostra-
tion, four years later. Little, after working faithfully at the
shoemaker's bench for five years, and securing the confidence

of the officials, scaled a high wall, one night, in the dark, jumped to the soft ground beyond, made his escape, and has never been seen or heard of since. His fatherless children and husbandless wife still reside in one of the New England States, perhaps all the happier for his prolonged absence.

Root's examination never came off. It was made evident to the most prejudiced citizen that he was entirely innocent. Remaining in the place long enough to settle up his affairs, the operative made preparations to leave, in accordance with orders, Gross having started the second day after the ending of the trial

Root was still in high favor with Jo and Big Bill Groom, and made sure, before leaving for Trafton, that he would be entirely welcome at the camps as a companion. After taking leave of the boys and of Mrs. Buxton, he departed, ostensibly to dispose of his schooner, preparatory to the next spring's business, but really to report at the Agency, in obedience to orders received previous to the fire, his arrest and incidents immediately following.

Mrs. Buxton waved a many-colored bandana handkerchief and her red head very vigorously, as the sleigh disappeared in the distance.

CHAPTER XI.

Bursting a Safe.

MORE than a month elapsed before I thought necessary for Root once more to seek the piny wood region. He found the overland passage more unpleasant than the last one from Raceford. Navigation of lake and river was still closed with an icy barrier, which would only be removed by the opening of spring. But the journey was made. Mrs. Buxton smiled all over her broad countenance when the sailor's comely shadow fell upon her threshold. After greeting the owner of the shadow with much warmth, she said:

"An' why not stop here now, an' settle in Raceford, in some dacent an' respictable business, give over your wanderin's and scrapes, lavin' those Grooms to take care of themselves? Sure, an' its meself that's thinkin' ye are too good a man to be cavortin' about wid the likes of them scapegraces!"

Root could not then explain why, but he had to refuse the tempting proposition.

"Well, well! I can say no more," returned the widow. "I see you're as perverse an' set in your way as ever! Some day you'll regret ye hadn't taken me wholesome advice!"

In a few days he found himself in the logging camp, with Jo Groom, where he remained for several weeks. But Jo was

a smarter rogue than was before believed, and, despite the
most strenuous exertions of the detective, nothing was elicited
from him regarding any recent log-stealing operations. Root
left, after reporting to his prospective partner that he believed he would be able to sell his schooner and find exactly
the steamer suited to their purpose.   Returning to the
Agency, he said he had had all the winter life in the lumber
regions that he desired.

The succeeding season the mills had no sooner commenced
running, than it was discovered that stealing of logs was once
more inaugurated, and the managers of the Booming Company
were desirous that I should resume active operations in their
behalf. I consented, and, early in the month of May, detective Root was dispatched to Raceford with orders to renew his
intimacy with the Groom brothers and their rough-and-ready
companions.   Another capable agent, named Grover, was subsequently started for the same region, to obtain employment,
if possible, in one of the suspected mills at or near Raceford,
and while there to keep correct tally of such illicit logs as
might be cut, with a record of their marks and to whom rightfully belonging.

A third detective went there a little later, found that it
was an eligible locality in which to set up a saloon, and I supplied the necessary fixtures and stock of liquors, cigars, &c.,
for the purpose. This man passed by the name of Westcott.
The idea was, that a small room in the rear of the bar could be
so constructed that any private conversations taking place in it
between representatives of the thieving gentry, could be heard
by the impromptu bar-tender, who had a sharp ear and excel-

lent memory, and anything of importance to the case might be reduced to writing and forwarded to me.

It was nigh the middle of May that the three men were all on the spot, and their business in successful operation.

Westcott's shop soon became a favorite place of resort for the two Grooms, Root, Grover, Slayton, and many of the mill-owners, superintendents, sawyers and laborers. Even Ludwig, who, for a long time had tasted nothing stronger than ale, occasionally refreshed himself at the bar. Westcott was voted by everybody a very clever fellow, and he succeeded in pleasing the residents of both sides of the river equally well. The newspapers, the editors of which had been well sweetened by donations of sundry steaming pitchers of savory and palatable Tom and Jerry, and that class of beverages, were unanimous in giving the saloon commendatory notices. Westcott's accordingly prospered. In the rear apartment much time, after usual working hours, was devoted to the game of poker, in which all the raftsmen and woodsmen were adepts. The sums played for were small, and the amiable liquor-seller turned a blind eye and held a deaf ear to those transactions, which he was supposed to know were infringements of the strict letter of the law. But, after all, very little which could be counted as of definite value was wormed out of the boys.

I finally hit upon a plan which I was sanguine might succeed. The hint, to give credit where credit is due, first came to me from remarks of Jo Groom. This gentle spirit, with his equally gentle brother, Big Bill, had recently been discharged from the Company's works, for sufficient cause—Bill for protracted drunkenness, unfitting him for all labor, and Jo from the reason that he was too frequently seen in company of

Mrs. Slayton at the superintendent's residence. Root was himself, as he reported, in a terrible plight. During his absence
he had been robbed of his money, first by garroters, in Trafton, and then through his partners in business, who had sold
the schooner, with his assent, received the money during his
temporary absence without his consent, and ran off to Canada,
carrying every dollar of the proceeds, leaving him holden for
indebtedness to their seamen, the ship-chandler and sail-maker.
Thus he had to depart from Trafton, and, for safety, again hide
himself in the pineries. Jo was disconsolate. Big Bill was
blue, got very drunk, kept in that state, had the delirium
tremens—" delirium tremendous " as he called it—and ended
by attempting to cut his own throat, his life only being saved
by Root, who seized the long, sharp butcher-knife he was
about to use, and threw it into the river. Here was a trio
desperate enough for almost any emergency. In this strait
they continued for several succeeding days. Finally Jo suggested the robbery of the Company's office. He said Slayton
was preparing to pay off the winter's laborers, and by the first
of June would have stowed away in the big iron safe, beside
jewels and valuables, some seven or eight thousand dollars in
currency. This news he had accidentally obtained from Mrs.
Slayton, with the other fact that the clerk who usually slept in
the rear of the building was soon to absent himself for several
days in the country.

' It'll be an easy job!" said Jo

" I'll not take a hand," answered Root. " You had better
let your mind run on other matters !"

This suggested a plot to catch the thieves, and I at once instructed the operative to gradually fall in with the idea, but by

no means to *lead* Jo on to the committal of a crime. Superintendent Warner visited the region, carrying the orders spoken of, and also for the purpose of admitting Mr. Slayton into the secret, and securing his active co-operation in what was to follow. Shortly succeeding Mr. Warner's return, Jo met Root again.

" Have you been to look at the safe ?" inquired Groom.

" No. Why do you ask ?"

" I tell you, Dave, there's already a heap of cash in it! In a few days the watchman is to take his annual leave of absence, and, to save money, no one is to fill his place! Why don't you join me, and just make a big haul ?"

" I don't care to live at Waupun !"

" Nor I, either! If you go in, we'll both of us be able to ' live in clover' the rest of our lives !"

" Really, I believe we had better die poor, and let it alone !"

To please Jo, the detective did subsequently visit the office on an errand ; Jo was watching, and when the agent left and walked toward the river, he followed.

" I believe it might be done, with the right sort of tools !"

" What make of safe is it ?"

" A Lilly, I think, with cast-iron hinges, double doors, and a combination lock. But how would you go to work, Jo ?"

" Well, I'd first get gunpowder, pulverize it fine, blow it through the crevices with a quill, put a slow fuse to it, fire the fuse and throw the doors off their hinges."

" Then you'd be sure to fail and get caught. In so small a house, built of wood, the explosion would startle all the neighbors. It's plain to be seen that you're no safe-blower. Now come, just let it alone."

"I won't give it up. I mean to do the job, and you've got to help me. I tell you, Dave, there's ten thousand dollars in bills in that safe, if there's a red cent. You know how such things are done. You're no friend of mine, if you refuse me your assistance."

"I'll have to consider the thing, if you put it in that serious light."

Then the two men separated again.

In a few days Jo hunted Root up, as he was working on the dock piling lumber, and they sat down for a moment, under the shade of a huge pile of boards, and Groom again urged the robbery.

"I've been thinking over all the points," said Root, "and decided that it won't pay to touch such a thing with a ten-foot pole."

"That's your final decision, is it? Now I have made up *my* mind quite differently. I'll get through that safe alone, before two months are gone, so help me God!"

Again the detective did all he could to discourage the undertaking. But it was entirely useless. Jo was determined to burst the safe; so, with a show of great reluctance, Root consented to aid him. A trip to Long Pine Bridge was taken, in order that the details of the proposed business could all be explained and rehearsed. They rowed to the rendezvous in a small skiff, having their guns along and shooting a few ducks, to cover the real object of the trip, and, under the protecting branches of the same spreading oak which had sheltered Big Bill and the detective, more than a year earlier, **they** entered upon an earnest discussion of their plans.

" I have found out," said Jo, " that the safe is really a Lilly, as you supposed ; the hinges of the doors are of cast-iron, and if they are once fairly broken off—the bottom ones, at least— the big doors will tumble down, and the entrance will be easy."

" But the breaking of the hinges will necessitate too great a noise. The neighbors will be awakened by the blows."

" I've thought of all that." And Jo put on a wise face, reminding Root of that worn by a knowing physician, about to prescribe an infallible remedy for a sick man. " I can fix the racket. Get one of those wooden-head iron malls—cast iron—wooden filling—all sound deadened. Don't you see ?"

" Yes. But how about a light ?"

" Have a lantern with a slide—bull's-eye—light it—shut it up—cover the office windows with quilts off the clerk's bed— open the lantern—can see as well as in the day time. We'll have half the night to work in. If we can't burst those doors in in four hours, we deserve to be hanged."

" Guess the thing'll hang fire, anyhow, and possibly we'll be hanged too, before we get through with it ! We're sure to be interrupted by some fool or other !"

" I guess not! But if we are—you've got a shooter, haven't you ? I have one ! We can fight "!

It was finally settled that Root should go to Trafton, in which place, he could give out before he left he would be away during several days. He was to procure the dark lantern, return to Raceford by a certain night, meet Jo on the appointed spot, exactly at eleven o'clock, and the two men, in company, would at once proceed to make the attack upon the iron safe. If successful, Root could go back to Trafton, with his share of the booty, or hide himself for a few days, and subsequently make his re-appearance in Raceford. Thus would suspicion be entirely thrown off his shoulders. Jo was to secure all the necessary implements for the task, and secrete them in a fence-corner, near the office, where either person could find them, in a thick clump of bushes and weeds. When they first met, Root was to inquire, in a low voice : "Is that you, Ely ?" If it chanced to be Jo, he was to reply : " Where are you going ?" Root would next say : " To Long Pine Bridge !" This would complete their recognition, and they could at once proceed to business. It was also fixed that they should first meet at Methodist church corner, a well-known, and, late at night, a deserted portion of the town. The conspirators rowed again to Raceford. The next day, true to his promise, Root spread far and wide the report that he was about to depart for Trafton, where he would visit some relatives, and then seek a berth for the season on some lumber-carrying craft. He saw and conferred with Slayton, before leaving, and it was decided that immediately upon his return the detective should, without being seen by any one else, go direct to his, Slayton's, residence, a light in a certain casement being the signal that the coast was clear. Then the detective boarded the evening steamer and started on his journey.

CHAPTER XII.

Trouble Ended.

THE detective arrived safely in Trafton, having enjoyed a delightful trip down the crooked stream, over its sometimes turgid waters, to the city of his destination. He had no object in view, excepting to pass away the hours until the Thursday appointed for the job with Jo Groom, and to procure the lantern, therefore remained a greater portion of the time the guest of his old friend, Captain Perkins, of the *Orient,* which steamer would start for Raceford just in time to deposit him where he wanted to stop. The captain entertained him most kindly, and gave him the best berth in the cabin, next to his own. After purchasing the needed article, which he took aboard the steamer, carefully concealed in his satchel, Root kept closely to the craft, and was jubilant when the lines were cast off, and she put out from the dock for the return voyage. A large town he found to be the worst place in the world in which to be idle. If he had nothing to do, he much preferred being elsewhere. Captain Perkins suggested, in this connection, " in Mrs. Buxton's hotel, for instance ;" and the young man made no reply, which was indicative of his having none to make. That is, the captain had unwittingly spoken the truth, which Root was not bound to confess and would **not** deny.

The return cruise, over the old course, was as pleasant as it well could be in the sweetest season of the whole year on ship or on shore, and it was still early in the evening of the second of June that the *Orient* landed the agent at a small place a few miles below Raceford, where, he informed the captain, he had some particular business to transact, and therefore would remain over night. In compliance with his earnest request, Perkins promised not to reveal the fact that Root had recently been a passenger on his boat, the detective truthfully explaining that a contrary course would be injurious to his business prospects. The captain was too true a friend to do or say anything calculated to interfere with the peculiar trade in which he believed his passenger to be heavily engaged, and from which, indirectly, he, through his steamer, annually realized a handsome profit in the line of freights paying an extra percentage for transportation.

"I'll not say anything to Mrs. Buxton, either," said Perkins, pleasantly.

"That is right. I'll reach that harbor in a few days, and be abundantly able to tell her the news in person. By the way, I may meet you here in time for the trip back to Trafton. I will if I can. Good-by."

And the operative crossed the narrow gang-plank and stood on the wharf. It was a very dark and cloudy night, and the young man confessed to himself a feeling of dejection and loneliness when he had received Perkins's hearty farewell and the steamer was once fairly out of sight.

Quickly repressing such thoughts he looked about him,

seeking bearings which might lead to the road by which he
should reach Mr. Slayton's house. Little was there that
could actually be seen in the gloom that surrounded him, but
he soon managed to pick his way unobserved among lumber
and lath piles, heaps of shingle-bolts and timber, to the winding path, by following which he knew he would come to the
vicinity of Raceford. He must not be recognized by chance
travelers. Several times, in the course of two hours' rapid
walking, was he forced to step aside, into the undergrowth, to
avoid approaching foot-passengers, and men on horseback returning from the village to their homes. Happily he escaped
the eyes of all these persons, and it was with a sensation of
positive relief that he beheld a welcome light shining from
one of the windows of Slayton's house, a sure signal that the
way was open, Mrs. Slayton and her daughter in the country,
and the owner of the residence sitting up impatiently awaiting
his arrival. In a few moments the voyager was gladly greeted
by the willing superintendent, and conducted to the back
sitting-room. A little later he was seated at the dining-table,
enjoying a palatable supper which Slayton had prepared for
him with his own hands, no servants having remained about
the premises.

It was ten o'clock when the detective concluded his meal,
and the instructions he had to give Mr. Slayton concerning the
proposed operation. They decided that the Superintendent,
with Glover and Westcott, the latter party then having employed an assistant in his saloon, enabling him to leave occasionally, should meet at half past ten, in a certain place, proceed to
the vicinity of the office, and there secrete themselves, while Jo
and Root were employed upon the safe. The Agent was not

to enter the office, but would remain outside, to warn Jo should persons approach the scene of their labors. The two operatives, with Slayton, were to move from their concealment as soon as they heard heavy blows upon the safe. Slayton started forward at the hour fixed for him to do so, met his men, and all hid themselves in a convenient outhouse.

Thus far all things worked well. Root, punctual to the moment, ensconced himself in the dark shade of the church-wall. He was, in fact, a few minutes earlier than necessary. The heavens portended rain, and he had been but a little while in his position when it really began to pour down, and finally came in torrents upon him. Soon he was drenched to the skin. But he did not think of deserting his post. Waiting there was a very tedious ordeal, yet he had passed through worse in his lifetime, and kept as still as a mouse until he was sure that the time had come and gone by which Jo should have put in an appearance. A number of belated citizens went past the hiding-place without noticing him in the least, but none bore the shape of the man he expected. Turning the slide of his lighted dark-lantern to the building, and partly opening it, he noted the time by his watch. It was nearly midnight, and Jo had not come.

"It would be too bad," thought the detective, "if he should fail at this moment, after taking so much trouble to meet him."

Jo did disappoint him—did not reach the rendezvous. After remaining until one o'clock, all dripping wet, the agent strode impatiently away and visited the spot appointed for the deposit of the implements, where, after scaling the inclosure and groping about with his hands, he found an ax, an iron bar and some other necessary articles. These proved that Jo had certainly intended keeping his word. What could have happened to prevent the arrival of that important personage? There was no time for speculation, no alternative. He must proceed to the office and inform his associates of the mischance. He did so, when Slayton and Root returned, wet, despondent, disappointed, to the superintendent's house, where they procured a supply of dry clothing, and, after putting it on, sat in the kitchen, smoking, until three o'clock, watching for the return of Westcott, who had been dispatched to the town to find out what had stopped Jo Groom. One tired and sleepy man was not so greatly surprised when informed by the equally worn-out saloon-keeper that Jo was reported to have remained at his drinking place, in the little back room, playing cards, but too drunk to walk straight, until something past midnight. Then Big Bill entered, in about as beastly a condition, and together they started for their respective homes. It was extremely provoking. Jo, instead of keeping sober, as requested, had worked himself into an advanced state of intoxication and probably forgotten the appointment and everything connected with the safe-breaking arrangement.

There was yet one practicable pathway out of the difficulty. Root had fortunately instructed Jo that, should anything occur to prevent his reaching Raceford in season to go into the proposed job, on the night he was expected, he would give him a signal which should signify, "On hand sure to-morrow night at the same hour," and to consist in chalk-marks forming a diamond ◇ and a cross †; and to be made on the outside lower window-frame of the pulpit casement of the church, near which their meeting had been ordered to occur. This could be tried. Perhaps Jo would see it, take the hint and be on hand. Westcott, while *en route* for his boarding-house, made the hieroglyphics in the proper place. As soon as it was sunrise Glover was put on the watch of the window, to see if Jo remarked and understood what the signs meant.

When the hour for business came, Glover, his outer clothing having been nearly dried by exposure to the night air, searched for a good cover. A small drug store stood facing the portion of the church edifice having the window described, and the operative entered it, held a long talk with its needy proprietor, and finally broached the subject of purchasing the stock, fixtures and good-will, sitting meanwhile in a portion of the room commanding a good view of the church. The proposed trade progressed swimmingly, and Glover was ostensibly thinking and figuring how he could divide the deferred payments on the property, when he saw Jo Groom saunter past the church, having paused to carefully examine the mysterious figures, and afterward pass briskly down the street toward Westcott's. In a little while the agent informed the by this time very enthusiastic apothecary, that he could not make the calculation exactly to suit himself, but would take pencil and paper, at the hotel, fix it as it should be, and possibly call on him again in a few days. Expressing his satisfaction, and the hope that the barter might soon be satisfactorily completed, the polite stranger suddenly departed from the drug store, leaving the druggist in doubt whether he ought to be thankful that he had called or not. Glover bore the important information to Root, who was found keeping close to his apartment at Slayton's, passing away the time as best he could.

"Then we may make sure he will keep sober to-day, and be on hand promptly to-night," said Root. "You had better see the sheriff and be equally early at your hiding-place! I will hold myself responsible that Slayton is with you!"

Glover agreed to the proposition and retired to his boarding-place to get rid of his still damp clothes and obtain a little sleep.

Slayton carried the keys of the residence in his own pocket all that day, and only returned to the house to cook and eat his meals, until night, and the operative, carefully lowering the heavy window curtains of his apartment, managed to sleep through the forenoon. In the afternoon he sat and read such books as the superintendent treasured in his library. They were mostly of a dry and uninteresting character, and he soon wearied of their contents. At night, the dwelling seemed to be deserted, but it was not, its owner and the detective being within, enjoying themselves over games at euchre and other similar pastimes until nigh the hour for both to be off and away attending to more serious matters.

On this occasion the weather was more favorable. While the night was dark enough for the purposes of the operation, the air was warm and comfortable, and no clouds above promised tempestuous weather.

Slayton departed, bound for his rendezvous near the Company's office, and Root almost immediately followed. At precisely eleven o'clock the latter found himself at the side of the church; and he had not been more than five minutes standing in his old position when rapid footsteps were heard, and in a few seconds a man, in outline greatly resembling Jo Groom, came around the corner.

"Is that you, Ely?" inquired the agent, moving out upon the sidewalk, feeling well satisfied that he had made no mis take.

"Where are you going?" answered a voice which Root knew to belong to Jo.

"To Long Pine Bridge!"

The two men heartily joined hands, apparently very glad to meet again, and repaired to the hiding-place of their safe-bursting instruments. When fairly in a good locality, where they were unlikely to be overheard, Jo was the first to break silence regarding the previous night's discomfiture.

"The truth is," said the woodsman, "I took too much liquor aboard and could not do as I had agreed! I forgot everything! But I remembered it this morning, when I saw the marks at the church window, and here I am as sober as a judge, and we'll soon be handling the Company's cash from the safe! Forgive me! I'll do my part now! Have you got the lantern lighted?"

Root put as good a face on the matter as he could, said accidents would happen, and continued:

"Yes! The lantern is all right!"

He slightly turned the shade, allowing a small light to illumine the darkness, to prove his good faith, then closed it again.

Jo clambered over the low board fence, and handed out the iron bar, some ropes, and an old and much-battered ax.

"Where's the mall?" whispered Root.

"Couldn't get one! Tried it several times! Too closely watched! So I stole the ax from the blacksmith's wood-pile! It'll do just as well!"

"No, it will not do at all! You'd make noise enough to waken the seven sleepers, with such a bungling affair!"

"I'll use it, anyhow!"

"But I won't go with you, trying to do work with that kind of tools! You promised me you'd have an iron mall with a wooden-head filling. That would be half-way sensible. I guess you're trying to back down from the business!"

"By Heaven! I intend no such thing! And if you won't enter with me, I'll go it alone! D—n the odds! What do I care for a little noise? Everybody within half a mile of the office is fast asleep long before this!"

"Well, I'm glad to see that, after going so far, you are not about to abandon the trick! I admire your pluck, but you are too reckless! However, I'll stick by you, and perform my promise! If any one comes to interrupt, you won't find me running away! Have you a strong piece of cord with you?"

"Yes. But why do you ask?"

"I'll tell you when we gain an entrance to the room."

The men moved noiselessly up to the silent and seemingly-deserted building. No light issued from any of its tightly shuttered windows, and no sound betokened the presence of a living creature in the vicinity.

"Inform me when the way is clear," whispered the detective.

"I will," was Jo's response.

Soon there was heard a grating noise, then another, and Jo said:

"Now all's right!"

The detective called for the cord. Having received it, he

fastened one end to Jo's waist, the other he held in his hand, saying:

"Now, Jo, if I hear or see anything suspicious, I'll jerk quickly three times on the line, like this, when you must immediately stop your hammering. If the danger is over, I'll pull once, this way, and you can go to work again!"

"I understand!" said the woodsman, and in a few seconds he crawled through the window and disappeared, having previously put the lantern and tools within. Root waited, in a sheltered situation outside, in breathless silence, saw a flitting light for a second or more, then the casements were curtained as agreed upon, and only one little ray, left gleaming from a corner of a loose shutter, told that the inside of the building was illuminated. It seemed to the detective that Jo was again about to back water, as there was no immediate evidence of his being engaged. Presently a muffled, crunching sound fell upon his ear, then followed an interim of silence, followed by several quick-falling, loud-sounding and heavy blows. "He's at it with the ax!" was the idea in the listener's mind, when Glover, Deputy-Sheriff Babb (the latter person had taken Westcott's place), and Slayton issued from their cover, ran softly to the doors and windows, nervously turned the already inserted key in the well-oiled lock, and in a moment stood before the astounded burglar, while he still hammered harm-lessly away upon the massive hinges of the safe. In another second his hands were pinioned.

"You're my prisoner!" said Babb.

"Yes," added Glover, "you are caught in the act! State prison opens for you! That's the ticket!"

"I can hardly believe this of you, Jo Groom," exclaimed

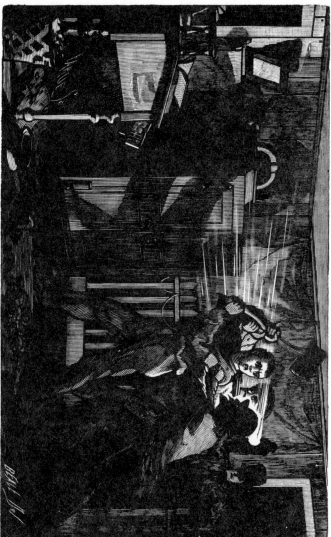

BOOMING LOGS. "*In a second his hands were pinioned.*"

Page 546.

Mr. Slayton, holding the bull's-eye before the prisoner's scowl-ing face, while the rest were searching his person and securing him with his own ropes. The cayenne pepper and billy which they found were utterly useless. He had no time in which to use either. He had paused in the more important work to break open the daily cash drawer, in the office desk, in which about fifty dollars of change and small bills had been carelessly left over night, and the money was deposited in his pocket. The short iron jimmy, employed in breaking the lock, was resting on the floor. How Jo silently cursed himself that he had not acted more cautiously.

"We've got your accomplice, Root, outside," continued Slayton, " and he's on his way to jail! He was nabbed before he had a chance to say a word !"

Jo broke the linen telegraph line from his waist impatiently, glared fiercely upon the men about him, for a moment, and without uttering a syllable, allowed himself to be led away to prison.

But Root had not been captured, nor was it intended that he should be. On the contrary, making his escape to Mr. Slay-ton's house, he secured his satchel, containing a few clothes, walked to the settlement he had left the preceding night, was in time for the *Orient*, which usually touched there, and three hours later was far down the river, bound for Trafton, along with his good friend, Captain Perkins.

" I guess you got through that little business all right ?" queried the Captain.

"Yes ! Everything came out as I expected," returned the operative. But it was not thought necessary to further en lighten his companion as to the precise meaning of the words used.

"I saw Mrs. Buxton, while at Raceford, this trip, and she made particular inquiries about you! Wanted to know if I had seen you in Trafton; how you was gettin' along; if you was well, and heaps of other questions. I said truly I had seen you, and that you had never looked better in your life!"

The operative's face changed color slightly. He said that he was very thankful for his landlady's good opinion, hoped she was well, and then proposed a game of euchre, which he knew from experience would please his tormentor and close his lips, for a time at least.

*　　*　　*　　*　　*　　*　　*　　*　　*　　*

Assisted by Roberts, Jo fairly and completely broke down when interrogated in jail, the following day, before the hour fixed for his examination on the charge of burglary, with the certainty that, in any event, a cell in the State penitentiary was to be his fate, and voluntarily tried to make his case easier by giving up the names of all of the men who, for a series of years, had been engaged with him in depredations upon the Manufacturing Company. Some of the most respectable mill-owners in the locality were inculpated with the Grooms and their nigh accomplices in transactions involving tens of thousands of dollars annually. All were arrested, and the testimony of Jo Groom, Glover, Westcott, Mr. Slayton, and others having knowledge of the subject, was sufficient, under the existing statutes, to send six persons to the State prison at Waupun, to keep the company of Bates, Little, Jones, and Little Bill. Big Bill was made a party defendant, but proffered State's evidence and saved himself; while Jo escaped with a sentence to the penitentiary for one year. It was subsequently reduced to six months, as he had suffered confinement, previous to sentence, for half a year in the county jail. The burglary case was never tried, having received a *nolle prosequi* by the district attorney. It had served its purpose, and was therefore dropped by the prosecution.

The system of log-stealing, thus broken up, was complete in itself, and the thieves, as long as they worked in concert, could hardly have incurred danger of discovery. Perhaps the business never would have been ended and its perpetrators punished, as they were punished, had not Jo Groom, unluckily for himself and his confederates, conceived the desire to burst open the Company's safe. Jo was a very bad man. But he met his fate only a short year succeeding his release from the State institution. Returning to his old haunts in Raceford, after some months' honest work in the pinery, he went to Slayton's residence, proposed an elopement, and the mistress of the house was in the act of departing with him, when her husband returned from a business visit and put a sudden stop to the proceeding. Jo showed fight, drew a revolver and aimed it at Slayton's head. It failed to discharge, from a defective cartridge, and before Groom had time to try another, Slayton seized his rifle and shot his opponent dead in his tracks. The just verdict of the coroner's jury was that the deceased had lost his life by Slayton's hand, but that the superintendent was acting purely in self-defense. What subsequently became of the woman I never learned. Her husband, a white-haired, prematurely-old man, lives in Raceford, making his home with his only daughter, who is happily married to an honorable and wealthy merchant of the place

Westcott's saloon is known no more in the town, the operative having returned to the Agency after disposing of his stock.

Skoo and Jobson still live and fight each other fiercely with their pens as of old. Their newspapers are well patronized and the proprietors fatten upon the feud that one side of the river yet has against the other.

Simmons having been buried with his fathers, Tillman, his brother magistrate, has withdrawn from the bench, and, in a little academy, " teaches the young idea how to shoot."

The success accomplished, Root returned to the Agency, and, after a few months' active service in the South, sent in his resignation, which was reluctantly accepted. I saw him but once afterward, and that was at the conclusion of a voyage on the lake, when he handed me the photograph of a not unhandsome, broad-faced, genial-appearing lady, who, he said, was Mrs. Jasper Root, formerly Mrs. Buxton, of Raceford. And if he is not in that town at the present time, it may be because he is still a sailor, devoted to his calling, and loves a roving life, with a dash of danger in it, on shipboard, better than always sitting around his comfortable hearth-stone.

CRIMINAL REMINISCENCES.

CHAPTER I.

Trapping a Detective.

THE " smart boy " of the period is sometimes very smart indeed. There seems to be a period in the life of every boy when he naturally becomes this " smart boy of the period," and takes to tricks of a brilliant character as naturally as a young miss takes to beaux. Philadelphia had one of these smart boys recently, and he showed, under the pressing neces sity of the occasion, an ingenuity and shrewdness which would have much more become the Philadelphia city detective whom he outwitted.

A Brook street grocer lost fifty dollars from his till, and a lad named Falvey was suspected of the theft. His father very commendably took him to the police-station, and put him in charge of an officer pending an investigation of the matter. After young Falvey was placed in a cell, Detective Swan, of the city force, was ordered to enter and " break him down," which is the detective parlance for securing a confession from a supposed criminal.

[551]

The boy did finally confess to the theft, with loud protestations of grief and repentance, and finally told the officer a regular "Tom Sawyer" story of having hidden it in a certain coal-yard along the docks, and promised to go with the detective and show him where he had secreted the bills.

The two sallied forth in quest of the treasure, the detective triumphant in his reflections of his ability to get at such things speedily, and the boy humble and demure as the picture of the typical good boy in the Sunday-school books. At last they reached the docks and the particular coal-yard where the stolen money had been hidden.

Now these docks or yards are all provided with great numbers of elevated "shutes" used in discharging coal. To one of these the guileful youth led the satisfied detective, where they found a hole just large enough for one person to crawl into. He said the money was hidden in this hole; and the officer, not suspecting the youth was playing any game upon him to escape, directed him to "go along in."

The boy did go in; but that same boy came out at the large instead of the small end of the horn—and that end, it is certain, was not in the immediate vicinity of the detective.

The detective soon began to think that it required a long time for the boy to get out of so small a place. He accordingly put his head into the dark orifice and shouted lustily.

There was no response but the sepulchral echo of his own voice, and besides, it seemed to him that he had drawn a bucketful of cinders into his lungs, while his entire features were eclipsed with the richest possible quality of coal-smut.

Again he hallooed, and threatened to shoot into the hole should the boy not make his appearance immediately at the

The deluded "detective" being rescued.

expiration of one minute. The detective held his watch and cursed his luck; but this threat was of no avail. Finally he did shoot into the dark hole, and trembled a little at the risk he was taking; but it brought no boy and no sound to indicate his whereabouts.

While standing there cogitating what should be the next move, he suddenly heard the sound of some heavy object dropping below. He directly inferred that the keen youngster had outwitted him, and had jumped into the bins below; and he accordingly made all haste to follow, making quite a daring swinging leap over the side of the "shute," landing in the bottom of a huge bin, and where he would rather have given a ten-dollar bill than to have been.

He found to his chagrin that he and the deceitful youth had gone to very different places. The detective was in the bottom of a coal-bin, and nobody within hearing to help him out.

In this miserable position the detective remained several hours, with the sun blazing down upon him. He would yell for assistance for a time, and then he would vary this amusement by cursing, and it is thought that some of the choicest swearing ever done in the Quaker City was executed on this momentous occasion.

At last some laborers came that way, and pulled up the unfortunate officer with a rope, setting him at liberty; but he was wholly unrecognizable, and returned to headquarters without his boy or money, to receive the derisive shouts of his companions, and to be known among them to this day as the " coal heaver detective."

24

CHAPTER II.

The Ghost of the Old Catholic Cemetery.

IT would be a surprise to the general public if the records of all my offices could be thrown open for inspection, so that it might be observed what a *wide range* has been covered by investigations which I have been called upon to undertake —the mysteries to unravel, or crimes to prevent or unearth. It must not be supposed that the services of my Agencies are wholly devoted to criminal matters. Some of the most important legal contests of the times have been decided in accordance with the irresistible array of evidence which a small army of my men have quietly, keenly, and patiently secured; while the operation of immense business interests, like banking, insurance, and railway matters, has often been interrupted by seemingly inextricable confusion and complexity, which threatened great loss, until my services were asked; and by my thorough and complete system, through which almost general and instant communication and information can be secured, I have been enabled to bring order out of chaos, and prevent what might have otherwise resulted in commercial ruin to my patrons. As the individual detective's notice must be brought to everything great and small upon any investigation he may be conducting, so is it true that the principal of a large system of detective agencies must be so situated that he may consider and receive every possible variety of business—always excepting that which is disreputable—and then have means at his command to carry each case, may it be great or insignificant, to a successful issue.

In the pursuit of these cases there is frequently both tragedy and pathos; they are always full of deep and fascinating interest to myself and my operatives, and quite frequently they bring to the surface all phases of ridiculous humor, which I frequently enjoy to the greatest possible degree.

In the summer of 1857, there was located, along the shore of Lake Michigan, within the limits of the city of Chicago, a high, narrow, sandy strip of land, then occupied as a cemetery, known as the "Old Catholic Burying-Ground," or the "Old French Cemetery," from the fact that within it reposed the remains of hundreds who had died in the Catholic faith, as well as large numbers of the early French settlers and their half-breed progeny.

Quaint inscriptions and devices were there seen, and everywhere, upon the great cenotaph or monument, or upon the most modest of graves, the cross, in every manner of design, somber with black paint, or bright with fanciful colors, or still white in chiseled marble, could be found.

The old cemetery has since been removed; and where once stood, in silence and mournfulness, the city of the dead, now are seen splendid mansions of the rich, with magnificent gardens and conservatories, or, in that portion which has been absorbed by Chicago's beautiful Lincoln Park, handsome drives, fine fountains, exquisite lawn or copse; and over all the old-time somberness has come an air of opulence, beauty,

and healthful diversion.   Scarcely could a greater change anywhere be noted than from the former solemnity and desolation
to the present elegance and artistic winsomeness.

In the time of which I write Chicago was much younger
than now.   Twenty years have made the then little city the
present great metropolis.   All the great enterprises which
now distinguish the city were then in their infancy.   Particularly were all institutions of learning having a hard struggle to
creep along; and the medical schools, then just started, were
put to every possible shift for the funds necessary to an existence; and there being often no legal provision for securing
"subjects" for dissection, the few students pursuing their
course of study were compelled to secure these essential aids
to their work by grave-robbery, that greatest and most horrible
desecration imaginable.

The Old French Cemetery being situated less than a mile
and a half from the river—which then, as now, was called
nearly the geographical center of the city—the temptation to
steal newly-buried bodies from so convenient a locality proved
irresistible, and the city was soon startled by a succession of
grave-robberies which excited general indignation and alarm.
Coupled with this indignity to the dead and the friends of
the dead, some malicious persons had entered the cemetery and
wantonly desecrated graves from which subjects had not been
taken.

Some held that this had been caused through religious
ill-feeling, others that it was the result of pure mischief on
the part of such persons as had been concerned in other
impudent and graceless grave-robberies; but the result of it
all was that so much public wrangling and excitement occurred

that a committee of prominent gentlemen, including some of the city officials, called upon me, and desired me to take such measures as would cause a cessation of the outrages, and bring to punishment whoever might be found to have been the perpetrators of the same.

While such was the result of the operation, it is only my purpose here to relate a single incident of the many interesting ones which transpired, and one which, while it illustrates the ridiculous length of absurdity to which an inherent superstition and a hearty fear will lead their possessor, I can never recall without almost uncontrollable laughter.

My plan of operations was as follows:

I detailed eight men from my force, under the charge of Timothy Webster, one of the most faithful men ever in my service—who, it will be remembered, was executed at Richmond as a Federal spy during the late civil war. These were so stationed that every entrance to the cemetery should be guarded, as well as all the new-made graves thoroughly watched. As no word could be spoken lest it might frighten away any culprit before he could be captured, I found it absolutely necessary to devise some simple, though silent and effective means of communication. To effect this I decided upon using several sets of heavy chalk-lines, such as are generally used by carpenters in laying out work. The ends of each line were attached to small stakes driven in the ground about three feet apart. The operatives' station was between these stakes; and, in order that every man should be forced to not only remain at his post, but remain continually awake and vigilant, I required the line to be gently pulled three times, beginning with a certain post, and extending rapidly, according to a pre-arranged plan, and the same signal repeated after a lapse of about one min-ute, in reverse order. This was the general signal that every-thing was as it should be, and nothing new had transpired. This was repeated every fifteen minutes, so that by no possi-bility could any dereliction of duty pass undetected.

Aside from this, the system of signals comprised means of communicating the presence of any outside party, at whatever point the intruder should make his appearance, and such other necessary information as would lead to a silent, swift, and certain capture of any person who might, for any cause whatever, enter the cemetery.

I had detailed men for this work whom I felt I could rely upon. Simple as it may seem to one who has never had such an experience, remaining all night in a grave-yard, with every nerve and faculty on the constant *qui vive* of expectation is not such pleasant work as it may be supposed; and though the novelty of the affair, coupled with all manner of outlandish jokes upon the situation, kept up an interest which lasted a few nights, I began to notice signs among a few of my men indicating that the solemnity and dread of the situation were taking the place of its original romance.

Coupled with this, there were among these eight, as there always are among any like body of men the world over, a few, who, like myself, began to notice these indications of weakness on the part of the more susceptible among them. These braver fellows immediately commenced, with solemn tones and long faces, to relate hobgoblin tales of ghosts and materialized spirits which came from their silent resting-places for unearthly strolls among them. Although I put a stop to this as much as possible, what had already been done had had its desired effect, and

a few of the watchers showed well-defined evidences of genuine fear, and to such an extent that I was finally compelled to
relieve some men, and fill their places with others.

Among the cemetery detail was one young fellow, named
O'Grady, a genuine son of the Emerald Isle, who had come to
me almost direct from Ireland, and who, though he had been
in my service but a few months, had shown native traits such
as gave promise of improvement and advancement. He was
the very life and soul of the detective rooms, and the wonderful tales he related of himself, his ready wit, his true bravery
in all places wherever he had been previously used, and his
quick generosity toward his fellows, had given him an exalted
place among them.

I saw that O'Grady was weakening.

He tried hard not to show it. He endeavored to look bright
and spirited, but it was all up-hill work. He began to get thin
on this grave-yard duty. It was very reflective work. From
eight to ten hours utterly alone, and surrounded by everything
which could fill one's mind with fear and dread, had its effect.
His natural superstition suddenly developed into an abnormal
and unnatural dread, which to the ignorant fellow seemed to
become almost overwhelming. Had he not been such a hero
in his own eyes, I am certain that I could not but have re-
lented; but, under the circumstances, I confess that I heartily
enjoyed his forlorn appearance as he dejectedly left the Agency
to take up his all-night's vigil, which undoubtedly soon became
a genuine terror to him.

Having carried the matter so far, the spirit of innocent
mischief and practical joking, which has always been strong

within me, as many of my personal friends long ago discovered, prompted me still further.

I determined to play ghost for one night, show O'Grady a genuine goblin, and put his often-told tales of personal bravery to a practical test.

Accordingly, giving out at the Agency that I should be absent at a neighboring town for the night, before sundown I secured a private conveyance which took me to a point along the lake shore, about a mile beyond the old Catholic Cemetery; and then, before the time for the detail to go on duty came, disguised all that was necessary to prevent recognition by any chance stroller, I hastily returned to the cemetery through the heavy copse of scrub-oak and willow that then lined the shore at that point, and, entering the place unobserved just as the twilight began to gather heavily, secreted myself within a heavy clump of *arbor vitœ* ornamenting a family lot, not over twenty feet from the point where I had previously learned that O'Grady was stationed each night.

I had no time to spare, for I had thus hardly become one of the cemetery watchers before, one by one, and all in stealth, the men began coming in from every direction, but so secretly and carefully that they might have been mistaken, by one not informed of their purpose, for ghosts or grave-robbers themselves, while Timothy Webster noiselessly sped from point to point, stretching the line which held the men silently to their work.

1 could have touched the fellow as he passed me. In fact, an almost irresistible desire seized me to play Puck, as he sped by, and trip him among the damp, dark weeds.

Pretty soon O'Grady came to his station, groaning and muttering.

As soon as the dark came down upon the old cemetery I left my hiding place and got in line with the tell-tale string.

O'Grady was busy saying his prayers, and of course did not hear me rustling about in the long grass.

My first impulse was to grab a cross from some old-time grave, and toss it, over the stones, in upon him; but by great effort I suppressed this, and soon found myself sitting in a hollow between two mounds, with my hand upon the line.

"One, two, three!"—jerk, jerk, jerk went the line; the first signal was being given.

My hand touched the line as lightly and yet as knowingly as the telegraph operator's fingers touch his well-known instrument; but I made no sign of my presence.

O'Grady answered the signal loyally; but scarcely was his duty done in this respect before he began a sort of a low, crooning wail, half like a mother's lullaby, half like a "keen" at a wake.

"Why did I lave ye, ye green ould sod? Why did I lave ye, ye dear old bogs? Why did I lave ye, ye blue-eyed swateheart? Feule I am that I came to the divil's ould boy, Phinkerton! Feule I am that I sit here by the blissed crosses av the dead, waitin' for the ghouls to rob! Och, murther! happy I'll be if the whole blissed place is tuk away!"

"One, two, three!"—jerk, jerk, jerk, came the signal again, while O'Grady answered it, as I could feel, with an impatient response.

After this, for a time, the brave Irish guardsman weaved back and forth upon the grave where he was sitting; when

suddenly, to my horror, he lighted his pipe and began smok·
ing.

I knew the man had become desperate in his loneliness, and
had arrived at a point of feeling where he was utterly regardless of the success of the operation ; and if I had felt sure of
this when he recklessly lighted his dudeen, I could not but
realize it to my sorrow when, in the glow of his roaring pipe,
I could see that he followed his solace of tobacco by a more
substantial quieter of superstition and fear from a black bottle,
which the bold O'Grady had conveniently set, after each passage to his lips, upon the base of the monument above the
grave where he was sitting.

I was indignant, and yet interested. I felt like dragging
the brave O'Grady from his comfortable quarters, to give him
a good drubbing for his utter carelessness of the interests of
the operation, and I am certain that in my then state of mind
I would have done so if my desire to nearly scare the life out
of him had not been uppermost.

Outside of the fussing and wailing of the O'Grady, there
were no other but unpleasant surroundings in the Old Catholic
Cemetery. Now and then the ghostly hoot of the owl sounded
weirdly from the surrounding tree-tops. From the low copses
beyond came the mournful cry of the whip-poor-will. And
down along the silvery beach of the shore, which gleamed and
darkened as the new moon appeared or was obscured for a time
behind the darkening clouds, floated up and over the dreary
place the sad and ghostly beating of the waves upon the
beach.

It *was* a lonesome place, and it began to occur to me that I
would not care to pass many nights in such a manner myself

but, under the circumstances, I saw that Mr. O'Grady had fixed himself about as comfortably as it well could be done. Every time the signal was given, Mr. O'Grady would resp: n.l, when he would immediately recollect that his good bottle stood idle beside him. After a little he seemed to become so lone some and dejected that he began a sort of conversation, in a low tone, with himself, in which he compelled the bottle, by proxy, to join, all after the following fashion:

"An' it's a big feule ye are, O'Grady. If it were not for meself that's takin' pity on yez, ye'd be dead enthirely."

"Ah, faith!" Mr. O'Grady would reply, with a sigh, "thrue for ye, thrue for ye! If I ever get out of this divel's own schrape, ould Phinkerton 'll never get me in the loikes again!"

"So ye say! so ye say, O'Grady; but yer always and foriver resolvin', and ye come to nothin' in the ind!"

"Don't be worryin' and accusin' me, me dear boy. This schrape wid the graves will be me last. By the rock of Cashel! phat's that?"

This last exclamation from Mr. O'Grady, which was in a tone of great alarm, was caused by my displacing a small footstone, which fell from the elevation of the graded mound with a sharp crash upon the graveled walk below.

I had got my sheet well adjusted, and had intended moving upon the scared Irishman at one rush; but his terribly frightened manner and the unfortunate falling of the footstone caused me to change my plan and decide to bring on the climax in a gradual accumulation of horrors. So I gave a well-defined moan, and watched for the results.

Mr. O'Grady listened for a moment, as if hoping that he

had been deceived; but I could see in the faint light, to which my eyes had become accustomed, that he was trembling violently. He applied his bottle to his lips, and its mouth rattled against his teeth as he did so.

Another prolonged and blood-curdling moan came from the cluster of *arbor vitæ*. This caused Mr. O'Grady to industriously begin crossing himself, and at the same time mutter some prayers as rapidly as his half-drunken lips could dole them out.

I saw that this should not be too far prolonged, for the poor coward might give the danger signal, which would at once bring a half-dozen stalwart fellows upon us; and so, while in his abject fear he was pleading with all the saints in the calendar for protection, I suddenly rose in my ghostly attire and in a moment was upon him, waving my arms and gesticulating very savagely for any sort of ghost that was ever manufactured, but never uttering a word.

"Holy mother of Moses!" yelled O'Grady, springing wildly into the air, and turning a complete back somersault over the base of an uncompleted monument, while I sprang after him.

"Murther! Help! Murther!" howled O'Grady, recovering, and bounding like a deer over four graves at a leap; while I could see, as I flew after him, that my operatives were hastening to the rescue.

I could not help but know that grave consequences might follow my unusual action; but a wild, boyish, and uncontrollable desire to pursue the flying O'Grady suddenly possessed me, and for the time overcame all other motives.

And so away we went together!

"I suddenly arose in my ghostly attire and in a moment was upon him."

Page 584.

Mounds, headstones, clumps of evergreens, newly-dug graves, wheelbarrows, and grave-diggers' litters were cleared as though we two were fox-hounds at a chase. Some sort of in-stinct for safety seemed to direct the wild O'Grady toward the western boundary of the cemetery; and away he went, howling and yelling at every jump, but increasing his speed at each terrified glimpse of the relentless ghost behind him.

Over the fence he went at a bound, cursing and praying at every gasp. I was younger then a score of years, hardy and agile, and I now saw a two-fold reason for keeping pretty well upon the heels of O'Grady. My operatives were in full pur-suit, and "Halt, halt, halt!" was heard on every side; and so, making a running jump of it, although my ghostly toggery impeded me somewhat, I managed to get over the fence with quite as much grace and agility as the wild Irishman in ad-vance. It was well that I did so, for at that moment I could see the flash of several pistols lighting the sky behind, and in-stantly after heard the whispering of several bullets within dangerous proximity to my person. Over the fence scrambled my men in hot pursuit, but swift on the wings of terror and fear sped the horrified O'Grady; and, never for an instant re-linquishing what were certainly unusual exertions on my own part, I sped on wildly after him.

We soon outdistanced my operatives so much that I could see, as I ran, that they were compelled to give up the chase and return defeated; but the witless O'Grady and his venge-ful ghost still swept on and on. That part of the city, then containing but a few scattering residences, was soon passed, and O'Grady and the ghost continued the trial of speed out across the open prairie, still to the northwest. This was traversed in

the most remarkable time ever made, O'Grady still yelling
and cursing and praying, but the ghost, ever silent and relentless, not far behind ; when suddenly we came to the north
branch of the Chicago River, then hardly more than a creek,
into which, with a wild cry of despair, the Irishman plunged,
swimming and scrambling to the other side just as I had
reached the shore, where I gave another spurt to his speed by
an unearthly yell, which seemed to send the man on still faster,
if it could be possible; and the last I heard of O'Grady he
was tearing and bounding through the hazel brush like a mad
bull, beyond.

So far as I know, O'Grady is still running.

He has never been heard of by me or any of my many employees. Though I advertised for him repeatedly, no answer
ever came; and if any one of my readers, whose eyes may
chance to fall upon this sketch, can prove that he is the veritable O'Grady, he can have the small amount of salary still
standing to his credit on my books, which has so far been
wholly unclaimed.

After a hearty laugh on the shore of the North Branch, I
cast my ghostly attire upon the prairie, and, utterly tired and
exhausted, plodded back, through the darkness, to the city,
taking lodgings at an out-of-the-way hotel for the balance of
the night, and was ready for business as usual at my office in
the morning.

Never were there seven more perplexed men than those
who reported the mystery of the night previous at the Old
Catholic Cemetery.

O'Grady was gone—that was certain. His cries for help
had been heard. His wild flight, pursued by a veritable ghost,

which could be vouched for by those who had attempted its capture, was related. There, at the mound of the uncompleted monument, were found a nearly empty whisky-bottle and a still smoldering pipe. But this was all that was known by the honest fellows, or will be known, until this sketch is given to the public, of the Ghost of the Old Catholic Cemetery.

CHAPTER III.

Burglars' Tricks Upon Burglars.

CRIMINALS not only are very ingenious in their schemes against the general public, but they frequently show considerable skill and a certain grade of quiet humor in well-laid plans against each other. An instance of the kind happened in this wise: In 1875, Scott and Dunlap—the famous robbers who robbed the Northampton National Bank of nearly a million dollars, and who are now behind the bars of the penitentiary of that State, through the efforts of my Agencies—had laid their plans to rob a certain up-town New York city bank.

George Miles, *alias* Bliss, *alias* White, the notorious Max Shinburne's old partner, and his party, were concocting a like operation for relieving a down-town bank of its capital.

Now it was found by the Miles party that both banks were to be robbed in like manner, by that method of "bank-bursting" which consists of renting a room above that occupied by the bank, and then tunneling through into its vaults or into the bank offices, and breaking into the vaults in the regular manner.

Miles saw that, if the Scott-Dunlap gang should happen to first complete their job, the publicity given the method employed would set every bank officer in New York investigating the possibility of a like misfortune, and thus defeat his own purpose. He accordingly took two of his men, who were

Sham police charge upon the rival Bank burglars.

wholly unknown to the other party, provided them with complete police uniforms and clubs, and, at a suitable time after nightfall, stationed them in hiding behind the up-town bank, and when the members of the Scott-Dunlap party approached the building " to pipe it off," or take observations, they were of course recognized by Miles's policemen, who drove them away.

The Scott-Dunlap party were now in utter consternation. They felt certain that their scheme had been discovered, or at least that the officers of the bank had had their suspicions in *some* manner awakened, and certainly to that extent which would make their project impossible. To put the matter to further test, on the succeeding night other of their men were instructed to " pipe off " the place still more cautiously. But these too were discovered by Miles's vigilant but bogus police, given chase to, and unmercifully clubbed.

This delayed matters with Scott and Dunlap until Miles and his party, the chief of whom were George Miles, " Pete " Curly, and " Sam " Petris, *alias* " Wooster Sam," got everything ready for their attack on the down-town bank, which was within one block of the First District police-station and the same distance from my New York office, at No. 66 Exchange Place.

In the meantime, it is thought, the Scott-Dunlap party had learned of the down-town scheme, and caused information to be given, and before the Miles party had got fairly at work they were pounced upon by the police. A lively fight ensued, and, although considerable shooting was done, the entire party of burglars escaped, so that two great bank burglaries, where very probably hundreds of thousands of dollars in cash and bonds would have been secured, were prevented through nothing more or less than what was hoped to be a very excellent trick by one notorious set of rogues upon another.

CHAPTER IV.

Remarkable Prison Escapes.

I AM certain that my readers will be interested in the recital of a few instances within my recollection where criminals, either convicts or prisoners awaiting trial for general offenses, have escaped their prison confines in a most ingenious and dramatic manner.

On July 8, 1878, the city of Columbus, Ohio, was startled by a report that some forty prisoners, confined at the State penitentiary there, had escaped, and were "making a lively trial for tall timber" in all directions. A visit to the penitentiary proved that the reports were greatly magnified. Only three prisoners had escaped, but these had shown an amount of enterprise in getting outside of the walls that was truly remarkable.

It was found, too, that even the three did not make their escape together, but that one had got out the previous night. He had been recaptured, and was once more a prisoner, although the other two were still at liberty. The one that had been recaptured had occupied a cell in one of the tiers of cell-houses on which the State was then placing a new roof. He managed, in some way, to dig out of his cell and gain access to the roof. A large derrick for elevating stone, used in the

walls, during the day stood against the prison, but at night was pulled back quite a distance from it. The prisoner stood on top of the wall, and calculating the distance in the darkness, made a leap, the like of which has never been attempted by any acrobat on earth, and, after descending at least thirty feet through the air, caught the derrick rope and slid down the remaining distance, making his escape unobserved.

What nerve and actual bravery were required for this! The convict risked his life more surely than if taking his chances in battle. The slightest miscalculation, the merest mischance, the least failure in estimating his power for leaping, would have caused him to have fallen a mangled corpse upon the stones below.

But all this daring brought no reward to the poor fellow, for he was captured on the Pan-Handle Road, near Summit Station, not ten hours subsequent to his marvelous escape.

The other men did not show as much daring in their escape, but even more shrewdness and ingenuity. They were engaged cutting stone just north of the penitentiary. Through the aid of friends they supplied themselves with citizen's clothing, which they secreted in a closet near where they were working, and leaped from this into a sewer leading into the Scioto River. As soon as they reached the bank, they stripped off their prison garb, and, donning their citizen's clothing, strolled leisurely away. For all that is known, they are still leisurely strolling, as they have never been recaptured.

One of the most desperate prison escapes ever known was made from Sing Sing prison on the morning of May 14, 1875, and would have ended disastrously to more than a score of lives had it not been for the presence of mind of Dennis Cassin, a Hudson River Railroad engineer.

Just north of Sing Sing prison, between the extreme northern guard-house and the arched railway bridge, as you go south, is located the prison quarry, on the east side of the railroad track. From it, over the railroad track, on the west side, extends a bridge, over which stone from the quarry is trundled in wheelbarrows by the convicts.

At about eight o'clock on the morning mentioned, an extra freight train, bound south, slowly approached the prison bridge. The train was drawn by "No. 89," Dennis Cassin, engineer. They were slowly following the regular passenger train from Sing Sing to New York, which had left a few moments before. As the engine reached the trestle, or prison bridge, five convicts suddenly dropped upon it, from the bridge above; they were led by the notorious " Steve " Boyle and Charles Woods.

Four of them ran into the engineer's cab, while the other hastened to the coupling which attached the train to the engine. The convicts on the cab, with drawn revolvers, ordered the engineer and fireman to jump off, which they did, when the convicts put on steam, and the engine started down the road at lightning speed.

Their escape was detected almost immediately, and several shots were fired after them by the prison-guard, but without effect. Then began the pursuit. The superintendent of the railroad was notified quickly, when a telegraph alarm was sounded at all points south of Sing Sing. A dispatch was sent to the Tarrytown agent, directing him to turn the switch at that station on the river side, so as to let the engine, with the

"A thrilling escape from Sing Sing."

Page 572

convicts on board, jump the bank and plunge into the river. Danger signals were also ordered to be set on the down track, and prompt measures of every kind were taken to prevent danger from collision with the stolen locomotive. The track-men in the vicinity of Scarborough saw the engine coming like lightning, or rather saw a vast cloud of smoke and steam and water whirl by with a deafening roar, and gazed with terror at the frightful speed the engine had attained. At Tarrytown crowds of people were gathered, expecting to see the engine dash into the station, and off the switch into the river; but it did not arrive.

After waiting a short time, the Tarrytown agent sent an engine cautiously up the road to look for the stolen property; and " No. 89 " was finally found, with both cylinder-heads broken, three miles north and opposite the " Aspinwall Place." The boiler was full of water and the steam down. The convicts had left the disabled engine a half mile further north, and had disappeared into the dense Aspinwall woods, having first stolen all the clothing which could be found in the engineer's and fireman's boxes in the tender.

Engineer Cassin's wonderful presence of mind undoubtedly prevented a large destruction of property and human life. He was surrounded by the four convicts before being conscious of it, and could feel the cold muzzles of their revolvers against his head. Instantly after he realized what had occurred.

" Get off! get off!" the desperate men shouted. They did get off, and that right lively; but Cassin did not turn from his place until he had prevented disaster. Just before the convicts jumped into the cab, he had three gauges of water in the boiler, and had shut off the pumps; but, as he turned to go when ordered, he shoved the pumps full on, the convicts not noticing the movement. The desperadoes undoubtedly pulled the throttle-valve wide open when they started, and for a little time the engine attained a terrific speed; but finally the cylinders got so full that both heads were blown out, or broken, and that necessarily ended the trip.

None of the daring fellows were immediately recaptured, but the eventual return of the leader of the escapade was effected through my office; and how it all came about necessitates a short sketch of "Steve" Boyle, the leading and most desperate spirit in the escape just narrated.

Boyle is a noted "houseworker," or house-burglar, and general thief, and has nearly always been brilliant and successful in whatever he has undertaken. His work was principally done in the East, until 1867, when that part of the country became too warm for him, and, in company with his "gang," consisting of "Bob" Taylor, "Tom" Fitzgerald, *alias* "Big Fitz," and William ———, *alias* "Black Bill," he removed to Chicago.

Their first operation in that city was very unfortunate for Boyle. They were "working" a residence in the West Division, and Boyle was "doing" the rooms and passing the plunder out to his confederates, when, being very weak from a severe attack of the asthma, he made a misstep, stumbled, dropped his revolver, and caused such a noise that in an instant the gentleman of the house was upon him with a cocked revolver in his hand, and effected his capture easily.

As he was then comparatively unknown in the West, on the plea of ill health, first offense, respectable parents, and the

like, he succeeded in escaping with a sentence of but one ye,r's imprisonment at Joliet, Illinois.

His comrades now employed every effort in their power to secure a pardon for Boyle, using large sums of money for this purpose; but this failing, they eventually found a way of conveying money to him within the penitentiary. Whether or not this was more powerful than whatever instruments to effect his escape Boyle may have secured, I cannot say; but, at all events, a plan of escape was determined on, which proved successful; and, on a certain night, Boyle, at the head of eleven other convicts, made their way from the cells up into one of the guard-towers used for the sentry, and thence, in some mysterious manner, which has never since been fully explained, not only made good their escape, but carried away all the arms—quite a number—which were stored in the tower.

Boyle's hard luck seemed about equal to his good fortune and ability to conquer difficulties.

The second day after escaping from the Illinois penitentiary, as he needed money, himself and another of the escaped prisoners were arrested in Chicago while in the act of "tapping" the till of a North Side German grocery. They were locked up for the night together at one of the North Side stations. Boyle's companion was possessed of a terrible fear that he would be recognized and returned to Joliet.

"Oh, I'll fix all that!" said Boyle, jauntily, and forthwith he set to work and gave his ex-convict comrade such a pummeling—disfiguring his face and blacking his eyes—that his own mother would not have recognized him.

The next morning they were put in charge of separate policemen, who started with their prisoners for the police court on the South Side. The officer in charge of Boyle was a huge German, weighing fully two hundred and twenty-five pounds. When the two had arrived at a point on North Wells Street, near the river, Boyle's keen eyes discovered a house of disreputable character, which he had formerly frequented. A negress, a servant at the establishment, was scrubbing the steps in the early morning before the inmates had arisen, and the basement-door stood wide open. As quick as thought, Boyle planted a terrific blow squarely in the big Dutch policeman's belly, doubling him up like a stage harlequin going backward through a trap, and then, leaping over and beyond the horrified black woman at one bound, darted into the house, and shut and bolted the door behind him. Then he sped through the basement to the rear of the house and escaped. His companion, who had been herded in the "bull-pen" along with the regular daily collection of petty offenders, was finally brought before the police justice, and the groceryman whose till had been robbed failing to identify him, he was fined five dollars, as a simple case of "drunk," on general principles. The fine was paid by some of his friends, who had learned of his predicament, and thus he too escaped.

About this time the other portion of Boyle's gang had endeavored to rob a bank at Schoolcraft, Michigan. They had succeeded in getting into the vault, and had already got open the outer door to a large safe standing within it, when a sleigh-riding party, out on a lark, came dashing up to a point near the bank, shouting and hallooing in a boisterous and roystering fashion. The thieves, thinking they had been discovered, fled from the place, leaving their tools and their nearly secured booty behind them.

From here they went to Kalamazoo, Michigan, and securing new tools from Chicago, made an attempt to rob a bank there, but were all arrested, and, being recognized as the parties engaged in the unsuccessful Schoolcraft job, were held without bail.

Through a friend in Kalamazoo, who was then closely allied with rogues of this class, but who is now a respected citizen of that city, word of their misfortune was conveyed to Boyle in Chicago, who, with a New York thief named Harry Darrah, returned the cheering intelligence that they would be over to Kalamazoo on a certain night, and give them "a break," that is, liberate them.

On the night in question, true to their word, Boyle and Darrah got so far toward the liberation of their friends as to have passed pistols and small steel saws in to them in the jail, when Colonel Orcutt, the sheriff, whose apartments were in the jail building, discovered the efforts being made, and, coming upon the scene *en dishabille*, with cocked revolver in hand, endeavored to arrest the jail breakers.

The men instantly fled, Colonel Orcutt pursuing. He ordered them to halt, but they did not comply; and he began firing upon them, succeeding in shooting Darrah's hat from his head. This only had the effect to increase his efforts to escape. Boyle, whose chronic asthma made it impossible for him to run any distance, suddenly dodged behind a tree, unperceived by the sheriff, and, when the latter passed him in hot pursuit of Darrah, the cowardly ruffian Boyle fired upon him, shooting him through the spine, and effecting a wound from which Colonel Orcutt died twelve hours after. Darrah skulked about the place for a few days, and finally disap-

25

peared; while Boyle, on the same night, secreted himself upon an eastern-bound freight-train, went to Detroit, and from thence into Canada, where, after remaining under cover for a few weeks, he proceeded to New York, being soon after re joined by Darrah, who was subsequently arrested for pocket-picking, and, being identified, was returned to Kalamazoo, where he made a full confession, implicating Boyle in the murder of Colonel Orcutt.

He eluded arrest, however, for nearly a year, when, his bad fortune following him, he was captured in New York while attempting to do what is known as the "butcher-cart" job. This is effected in the following manner:

At a time of the year when street doors of jewelry shops are usually closed throughout the day as well as the evening, a common grocer's, or delivery wagon of any sort, but always selected for its easy-running qualities, and to which is always attached a fast horse, will be driven up to the vicinity of some jewelry store, which has already been fixed upon, and which always has a fine display in the window. This wagon will invariably contain one, and sometimes two persons, aside from the driver. In the meantime a confederate of this "butcher-cart gang" slips up to the door of the shop in question, and deftly inserts a wooden peg or wedge beneath the door, between that and the sill, driving it home with his heel or in any other manner possible. The moment this is done another of the gang at one stroke smashes in the entire window, and the two then grab whatever they can lay their hands upon, always, of course, selecting that which is the most valuable, and rush to the covered wagon in waiting, when, with their booty, they are driven rapidly away, nine times out of ten getting wholly beyond pursuit before the astonished and shut-in shopmen are able to get their own door open.

It was while Boyle was conducting an operation of this kind that he was captured, and, rather than be conveyed to Michigan, to answer the charge of murder, he made no defense, but pleaded guilty to everything brought against him, and was finally sentenced to twenty years' imprisonment at Sing Sing.

It was the boast of himself and his friends that no prison had been built strong enough to hold him, and a special guard was for a time placed over him.

Illustrative of the man's cunning is the fact that, one day, while being so watched, he slipped his jacket and hat upon a broom standing near, and then, noiselessly placing it where he had sat, stole away from his guard entirely. It was some minutes before the watchful guard discovered the trick which had been played upon him, and Boyle had made so good a use of his time that eight hours had elapsed before he was found. He had secreted himself in the prison, with the hope of escaping the same night.

The next instance in Boyle's career worthy of note was the planning and execution of the desperate escape from Sing Sing upon the engine " No. 89," as has been related.

In company with Charles Woods, one of the convicts es caping with him on that occasion, Boyle then secured a "kit" of burglar's tools, and the two proceeded to St. Louis, where they began operating upon small safes in real-estate and brokers' offices. They deposited their tools in what they believed to be a deserted carpenters' shop. The proprietors, returning unexpectedly, discovered the tools, and, informing the police, a detail of officers was at once made to lie in wait for the owners of the suspicious goods, who returned, and, before being given time to explain anything, were unmercifully clubbed and taken into custody.

The men, being utter strangers to the St. Louis authorities, were only given six months in the workhouse. Their pictures were taken, however, and, a set coming into my office, that of Boyle was recognized, when, on his being fully identified by my son, William A. Pinkerton, he was returned to Sing Sing, where, fortunately for society in general, he is now serving his unexpired term of twenty years' imprisonment.

In 1870 George White, *alias* George Miles, *alias* George Bliss, made one of the most remarkably brilliant prison escapes on record. He had, in company with one Joe Howard, another burglar, robbed the bank of an interior New York town, and, securing a noted race-horse of the locality in escaping from the place, ran the animal nearly thirty miles at its fullest speed, until it fell to the earth from sheer exhaustion. The men then brutally cut the throat of the horse, leaving it dying. The men were subsequently captured, convicted, and incarcerated in Sing Sing. While here, White made the acquaintance and friendship of a noted character, named Cramer, familiarly called Doctor Dyonissius Cramer, or "the Long Doctor," now a reformed thief, but in his day one of the cleverest known "stalls" of the "bank-sneak gangs." This "Long Doctor" had a peculiarly inventive genius, and I am happy to say that now, as he has become an honest man, it is securing for him considerable wealth.

His familiarity with White resulted in his inventing—more as a curious experiment than anything else—a hollow rubber apparatus, which, when completed, had the exact appearance of a very large decoy duck. This was also provided with rubber tubes for breathing through; and one morning, when a party of convicts were working along the docks by the side of the river, White, who had secreted the contrivance in his clothing, at an opportune moment adjusted it, and, slipping into the water, calmly floated down the Hudson, passing within twenty feet of the guards, thus making his escape.

His recapture would have been certain, but Colonel Whitley, then Chief of the Secret Service, made such strong representations to the Government authorities that his use by the Government in ferreting out several important counterfeiting cases would be valuable, that he eventually secured for him from the Governor of New York a free pardon. The value of his subsequent services may be inferred when it is stated that Colonel Whitley used him as one of the chief actors in the infamous sham robbery of the safe of the district attorney's office in Washington, when it was sought to ruin the Hon. Columbus Alexander, who was nobly fighting the Washington ring and its corruptions.

CHAPTER V.

Sheridan, the Forger.

THERE was born, near Sandusky, Ohio, in the year 1838, an adventurous lad named Walter Eastman Sheridan. His people were plain but intelligent farmers, and, while not possessed of an over-supply of means, had considerable pride in the boy, gave him a liberal education, and destined him, as fond parents usually do, for some very bright career in life.

He remained at home until about fourteen years of age, when its restraints became too irksome, and full of an adventurous spirit, and feeling able to take care of himself in the world, he did what thousands of boys did before him with various results—he "ran away" from home to seek his fortunes in the then brilliant and fascinating city of St. Louis.

Here he secured employment; but, being without a home and its healthful influences, soon fell into bad company. He was a bright, pleasant-faced fellow; but as he was "too independent" to return to his friends or accept their advice, little tricks were soon resorted to, and the boy readily saw that it was an easy matter to win the confidence of those with whom he came in contact, and before he had become eighteen years of age he was an adept in the art of living genteelly from forced public contributions of a varied character.

His first crime, or rather the first crime for which he was tried, was for horse-stealing at St. Louis, in 1858. He was convicted, and, while awaiting sentence, broke jail and escaped to Chicago.

Being a dashing, rosy-cheeked fellow of elegant address, after he had been in that city for a time, he became the pupil of Joe Moran, a noted confidence man and hotel thief, the couple doing a neat and thrifty business from the beginning.

Sheridan proved so pat about everything he did, and exhibited such aptness and delicate judgment in everything he undertook, that the pair continued in partnership nearly three years, working the hotels of Chicago and neighboring cities, but in the early part of 1861, were arrested in the act of robbing the guests' rooms at the old Adams House in that city. They were both convicted, and given three years each at the Illinois Penitentiary, then located at Alton.

The two men, after serving this term, returned to Chicago together, Moran soon dying of some disease brought on by prison exposure, while Sheridan resumed the same class of operation with the then notorious men of the same ilk, Emmett Lytle, Matt Duffy, and John Supple.

But Sheridan, being a young man of good mind, somewhat cultivated tastes, and large ambition, notwithstanding his reprehensible calling, soon tired of the low associations necessary to this standard of villainy, broke with his old companions, and took a step higher in the profession, becoming the "brains" and leader of "bank-sneaks," consisting of the notorious Joe Butts, Tom Parrell, *alias* "Pretty Tom," and others, and for some time the party did a very successful business, the elegant and refined Sheridan acting as "stall."

As many of my readers may not be very familiar with criminals and their modes of procedure, I will explain what a "stall" is in connection with the neat work of "bank-sneak gangs."

To begin with, the "gang" is the party, generally consisting of about three to five persons working together. As a rule, these persons are gentlemen of elegant leisure, secure large plunder, and have plenty of time to devote to becoming acquainted with the workings of a bank, familiar with the faces and habits of its officers, as also of many of the heavier depositors; and when ready for work have quite as much knowledge of the interior arrangements of the bank as many of its employees. Though there are numberless modes of accomplishing the same thing, the following instances will serve as illustrative of them all.

A gentleman who has business stamped in every line of his face and article of his clothing, steps into a bank about noon, when the officers and several of the clerks are generally at lunch, and either presents a forged letter of introduction or in some other manner compels the respectful attention of the cashier, or teller, as the case may be.

He will very probably produce a figuring-block or tablet upon which are various memoranda and figures, and, while asking questions very rapidly and interrupting them quite as abruptly, conveys to the teller, who has already become somewhat distracted, the information that he, as the trustee for something or somebody, has, we will say, twenty thousand dollars in five-twenty bonds to invest in different securities, and desires five thousand dollars in gold, five thousand dollars in seven-forties, five thousand dollars in ten-twenties, and five thousand dollars in some railroad stock or other.

This affords the cashier, or teller, a series of delicate, if not difficult, calculations, and all this time the business-like "trustee"—who is none other than the "stall"—is annoying him with questions, suggestions, and *probably* other orders as to the character of the investment desired, so that the teller's whole attention is absolutely required to follow the customer's whims and his own calculations.

This is exactly what has been striven for by the "stall," and his eminence in his profession is in just the proportion to his ability to accomplish this, whatever be the means he may employ in doing it.

But before this "stall" begins playing the "trustee" or other game, three of his companions, or pals, called "pipers," are on the look-out for the approach of any of the bank officers or employees, and are ready to sound a signal at the approach of the slightest cause for alarm ; and sometimes other "stalls" are stationed in the bank wherever necessary ; while, at a given signal the "sneak," who is generally a nimble little fellow, slips behind the partition through some open door, or sometimes through open windows, and thence into the bank-vault, where he secures his plunder, which is usually large, because the thieves have taken time to make the operation a success.

After the "sneak" is well away, the "stalls" draw off, so as not to excite suspicion, and the "trustee," after thank-fully receiving the teller's calculations and agreeing to return with the bonds to effect the desired exchange before the close of banking hours, takes his departure. The entire job is done

25*

in ten or fifteen minutes, and frequently the loss is not dis covered for days.

Another game of the "bank sneak gang," but one which requires far more nerve, assurance, and personal bravery, though far less tact and skill, is to become cognizant of parties making heavy deposits at a late hour, when everything is rushing about the bank, and the check desks are crowded.

In this instance the sneak, with a bogus bank-book in his hand, and with a business-like air about him, taps some gentleman with a flush deposit in his hand lightly on the shoulder, and politely calls attention to the fact that he has dropped some money. Looking upon the floor, the latter sees a genuine tendollar bill (which the sneak has dexterously dropped there, of course), and bends over to pick it up, leaving his book and deposit upon the check-desk.

In an instant the polite gentleman has the money left upon the desk and is upon the street, while the robbed and astounded depositor recovers himself and gives chase ; he is, apparently accidentally, but very effectually, impeded by other gentlemen (all pals of the sneak), who run into him and beg his pardon in the most natural manner possible, giving the party— who had invested merely a ten-dollar bill and a little polite ness, and who may have secured several thousand dollars— ample time to escape.

I could fill pages with instances of this kind, but will only mention a few of the heavier robberies of late years, which were all committed in this manner, all of which are probably still fresh in the public mind. They are :

The noted Lord bond robbery, where a million and a half dollars were taken ; the Royal Insurance Company robbery, which could be vouched for by those who had attempted its capture, was related. There, at the mound of the uncompleted monument, were found a nearly empty whisky-bottle and a still smoldering pipe. But this was all that was known by the honest fellows, or will be known, until this sketch is given to the public, of the Ghost of the Old Catholic Cemetery.

The Judge was sauntering along the street, and feeling like partaking of some fruit he stopped at a little apple stand, at the corner of Nassau and Liberty Streets, and in a fatherly manner purchased a few apples of the old apple-woman there. Sheridan accosted him, and so interested him for a moment' that, when he turned to take up the wallet, which he had carelessly laid upon the stand, he found that it was gone. A suspicion flashed across his mind that the handsome stranger had had something to do with its disappearance; but he too was gone. The wallet contained seventy-five thousand dollars worth of bonds, and but a small portion of the plunder was recovered.

One of his first exploits, after becoming a professional, was at Springfield, Illinois, where he was not so fortunate. After the Baltimore robbery, he had come West with Charles Hicks, a Baltimore sneak-thief, and Philip Pierson, *alias* " Baltimore Philly," and their initiatory move was upon the First National Bank at Springfield.

Sheridan called at the bank, and, as usual, proposed some complicated business, lucrative to the bank, which completely engaged the cashier's attention; while Hicks "piped," and Pierson sneaked into the bank, securing packages containing thirty-two thousand dollars, passing the money over to Hicks.

As Hicks was leisurely leaving the bank the president entered, and observing the huge package peeping out from under his summer overcoat, which was not large enough to cover them, grabbed him, and demanded where he got so much money. He replied that he had just drawn it out. But the president suggested that they had better step into his apartment until he could see about it. The cashier at once saw what had been nearly accomplished, and on some pretext handed a card into the president's apartment without exciting Sheridan's notice, instructing the president to send two men to the front of the bank to detain the person conversing with him, which was done, and which resulted in Sheridan's capture, though Pierson escaped.

Sheridan and Hicks of course claimed that they had never seen each other before, but they were put in different cells and given separate trials. Hicks pleaded guilty, and was sentenced to eight years' imprisonment in the Illinois penitentiary at Joliet; but Sheridan played the high moral dodge, gave bail to the amount of seven thousand dollars, which sum he deposited and subsequently forfeited, when the District Attorney set this sum aside towards securing his apprehension, and immediately employed me to use *all* the means at my command to effect his recapture.

I soon ascertained that Sheridan was communicating with Hicks at Joliet, through the latter's brother, who visited him with unusual frequency, and I therefore detailed my son, William A. Pinkerton, with an assistant, to follow out this clue and see what it was worth.

In keeping unremitting watch over this Hicks, my son one evening found himself in the pretty city of Hudson, Michigan, having arrived there on the same train with Hicks.

The latter at once proceeded to the best hotel in the city, still followed by William, who was not long in learning to his surprise that Sheridan owned the hotel, which was being conducted by his brother-in-law, as also a fine fruit-farm in the vicinity of St. Joe, and large tracts of pine and farming lands scattered throughout the State.

Hicks directed the hotel clerk to call him at seven o'clock the next morning, and my son accordingly was put down on the call-book for six.

As great care was necessary to be exercised, lest Sheridan or his friends might learn that he was being so closely followed, William could make only sparing inquiries ; but he did succeed in learning enough to convince him that he was not then at Hudson, and, on awakening bright and early in the morning, he decided on making an attempt to accomplish something which might be of the greatest possible assistance in the future.

Although Sheridan had already become famous as a criminal, no picture of him had ever fallen into the hands of the authorities. The public may not be aware of how much service a good picture of a criminal is to the detective. It will do good duty in a hundred places at one time. Accordingly William ascertained the location of the landlord's family rooms, and, while the occupants were at breakfast, committed a small, and, under the circumstances, quite excusable burglary, resulting in securing a capital photograph of Sheridan, which has for several years adorned the rogues' galleries at my different Agencies. This picture undoubtedly effected the eventual recent capture of this great criminal, as it was the only picture extant, and was placed in the hands of my almost numberless correspondents both in this country and in Europe.

On this particular occasion spoken of, however, it was of no great importance save to familiarize its possessor with the handsome features of Sheridan, who returned to Hudson the same day.

William wisely concluded that it would be foolish to attempt his arrest in the midst of so many friends, who, if they could not effect his forcible escape, would undoubtedly use every possible effort to secure his legal rescue upon some trivial technicality; and consequently followed him for several days, finally capturing him at Sandusky, Ohio.

As it was, my son had a difficult time in getting the criminal to Chicago, as the splendidly-appearing fellow strongly protested to the passengers that he was being kidnapped, and appealed for aid and rescue in the most impassioned manner possible. Finding this of no avail, although it came pretty nearly being successful, he then shrewdly pretended complete acquiescence and when for a moment left alone with the operative who had immediate charge of him, offered that person ten thousand dollars in cash merely for the opportunity of being permitted to jump through the window of the car saloon, although well ironed, so that both men were necessarily watched every mile of the remaining distance.

Even after he had been brought to my Chicago Agency, preparatory to being forwarded to Springfield, a little instance occurred illustrative of the daring character of the man.

For convenience he had been given a seat temporarily in my private office—he being perfectly secure there, and it being necessary for my son to step outside the door for a moment. Scarcely had he done so, when Sheridan espied my snuff-box, and, instantly grasping it, placed himself in a position to fling its contents into William's eyes as he re-entered, with the intention of bounding by him in the confusion which would follow and attempting to escape--which, however, would have been utterly impossible, owing to constant safeguards in use at my offices to cover similar cases.

But his intention was just as determined, notwithstanding all this, of which he, of course, was not aware.

My son re-entered the room slowly—feeling that there might be danger, and knowing his man—with the grim muzzle of a splendid English "Trauter" revolver in front of him; and Sheridan, seeing that his captor was as wary as he was daring and inventive, resumed his seat with the manner of a French courtier, took a pinch of snuff, as he replaced the box, and with airy politeness remarked:

"Billy, that snuff of your father's is a d—d fine arti-cle!"

"For the eyes?" asked William quietly.

"Eyes *or* nose," he retorted. "But I'm very sorry to say that the *noes* have it this time!"

I succeeded in having the man safely conveyed to Spring-field; but Sheridan made his money count in another way than upon my detectives. He had the case fought on every legal technicality which could be brought forward, secured a postponement of trial for nearly a year, and finally a change of venue to the city of Decatur, where, after retaining the very best lawyers in the State of Illinois, and—what was quite as useful—a portion of the jury, he was eventually acquitted, ex-pending altogether for this manner of acquiring liberty the snug little sum of twenty thousand dollars, as he subsequently admitted.

After this affair, Sheridan, who was inordinately ambitious to become noted as one of the most successful thieves in

America, went East, and organized a party of " bank-bursters,"
or bank-robbers, consisting of Frank McCoy, *alias* " Big Frank,"
James Brady, James Hope, Ike Marsh, and others, the crowd
becoming a terror to the East, until so closely hunted there
that its members were compelled to disband; when he assisted
at a robbery of a Cleveland bank, where forty thousand dollars
were taken. This was followed by a raid upon the Mechanics'
(Hawley's) Bank, of Scranton, Pennsylvania, where Sheridan
and "Little George" Corson appropriated thirty thousand dollars' worth of negotiable bonds.

His next exploit of note, and one which struck a very tender
chord in the hearts of several citizens of Louisville, Kentucky,
was his planning of and participation in the Falls City Tobacco
Bank robbery at that city in 1873, when upwards of three
hundred thousand dollars was secured.

The robbers rented an office immediately over the vault of
the bank, and carried on a legitimate business therein for some
months before the robbery occurred. My readers will remember the circumstances of the great Ocean Bank robbery, in
New York, where Max Shinburne's party robbed that bank by
renting an insurance office immediately *below* the president's
apartments, and then sawed through the floor into the bank
and blew open the safe. The same kind of tactics were used
here, only the robbers went into the bank from above instead
of from beneath, and tumbled into the vault direct, instead of
blowing open the vault door.

The gang were divided into regular reliefs, and while one
party were digging away through the night, the other were
posted in a front room over the St. Charles restaurant imme-

diately opposite, from which point a fine but strong silk cord
was stretched to the robbers' windows.   Attached to the end
of this cord, next the windows over the bank, was a pendent
bullet, so that the confederates located over the St. Charles restaurant—whose business it was to watch for any signs of approaching danger—could signal the same on their immediate
discovery.   In this manner the thieves had an abundance of
time and leisure, and finally effected an entrance to the vault
early in the night, when they carried away almost everything
of value the vault contained.

It was Sheridan's generalship and even bravery, if one has
the right to apply that term to a person of this character,
utterly devoid of fear, that caused the retirement of this large
amount of capital from Louisville circulation; and these instances, showing his wonderful genius for schemes requiring
skill, patience, and personal courage, could be multiplied almost
beyond number; but those I have already given will serve to
illustrate his marked ability, and also the almost exceptional
instance of a criminal beginning among the lowest of associates, and by the tact, skill, and frugality which would have
made him a millionaire in respectable life, gradually climbing
higher and higher in his grade of crimes with his companions
as stepping-stones, until he arrives at the very pinnacle of his
criminal calling, and has acquired in that profession everything
which men ordinarily seek for—respect, admiration, and hosts
of friends, as well as great wealth; for Sheridan was worth in
1874 fully a quarter of a million of dollars, while during these
later years of his crimes he maintained most respectable social
and business relations.

All of this eminently fitted the man for becoming, as he really was, the author of the gigantic Bank of England forgeries, although the very caution, ability, and skill which first made the scheme possible eventually led to the work being done by other parties; and it is safe to say that if Sheridan had had the management of the affair throughout it would have proved a success instead of a failure.

The members of the original party subscribing to this Bank of England scheme were Sheridan, George Wilkes, Andrew J. Roberts, and Frank Gleason, while McDonnell and Bidwell, now serving life sentences for the crime, were to conduct the English branch of the operation. Sheridan discovered that the two last-named men were lacking in discretion, as afterward proved true, and he consequently withdrew from the scheme altogether. He then organized a party—consisting of Roberts, Gleason, Spence Pettis, and Gottlieb Engels—for a series of the most gigantic forgeries ever known in America, and finally issued bonds, to the extent of five million dollars, on the following institutions and corporations: New York Central, Chicago and Northwestern, New Jersey Central, Union Pacific, and Calfornia and Oregon Railroads, the Erie Water Loan Bonds, the Western Union Telegraph Company, and other similar great corporations. The floating of these forged bonds ruined scores of Wall Street brokers as well as private investers.

Their execution was almost absolutely faultless, and an instance is given where some of these forged bonds of the Buffalo and Erie roads were taken to the president of the company for examination, having been offered suspiciously low, when he not only prononnced them genuine, but purchased thirty thousand dollars' worth for an investment.

At least half the amount issued was disposed of.

Sheridan now assumed a new character. He became Ralston, nephew of the once great San Francisco banker, who committed suicide after his financial downfall. With this name and plenty of money he became a member of the New York Produce Exchange, and at No. 60 Broadway carried on a successful business as agent for the Belgian Stone Company, dealing largely in all manner of fancy marbles.

On the eventual discovery of the forgeries, Sheridan quietly gathered his assets together, and sped to Belgium—that fashionable retreat for Americans having too little honesty and too much brains.

It is not known just how large an amount Sheridan succeeded in disposing of, but it must have equaled all that of the other large operators. "Steve" Raymond sold ninety thousand dollars' worth, and Charles Williams, *alias* Perrin, one hundred and ten thousand, while the American public was mulcted fully two millions in excess of the amount secured from our English cousins in the Bank of England forgeries.

When I sent my son, William A. Pinkerton, to Europe to capture and return Raymond, which he accomplished, he met Sheridan in Brussels, where he was then living like a prince, with the avowed determination of never returning to America. But he did return here; and that mistake eventually led to my capturing him. He could not live without the excitement of scheming, speculating, criminal adventure, and what was to him the genuine pleasure of transacting business on a large scale.

He slipped back to America, and, under the name of Walter A. Stewart, suddenly appeared at Denver, where he established probably the largest and most expensive hot-house in America, did an immense business in supplying that market with vegetables and rare plants, was elected a director of the German National Bank of that city, and soon established a bank of his own at Rosita, in the Colorado mining districts. Here his spirit of speculation took possession of him again, and he began the wildest kind of gambling in mining stocks, which resulted in his losing every dollar he possessed on earth.

About this time I again got upon Sheridan's trail, and, following him from point to point, learned that he contemplated a trip to the East, to discover his old companions and inaugurate some new and brilliant scheme of robbery. In trusting matters at New York to my son, Robert A. Pinkerton, Superintendent of my New York office, I gradually caused the lines to be drawn in about him; and on the night of March 23, 1876, at eleven o'clock, as Sheridan, *alias* Ralston, *alias* Stewart, was landing in New York city from the Pennsylvania ferry-boat, at the foot of Desbrosses Street, my son Robert slipped his arm through that of the criminal, and quietly said :

"Sheridan, I want you to come to the Church Street police-station with me. I have a bench warrant for your arrest."

He made no resistance, but seemed to give up all hope and courage at once.

As he was without money, the legal fight made for his liberty was not so bitter as had been anticipated, and in consideration of this, and the sympathy created on account of his rapidly failing health, and though he came into New York with eighty-two indictments hanging over his head, his trial and conviction only resulted in a sentence for five years in the penitentiary; which, under the circumstances, will serve all the ends of justice, as undoubtedly before the expiration of that term he will pass from an infamous life to an infamous grave in the little cemetery just above Sing Sing.

THE END.